The Inter-War Economy: Britain, 1919–1939

The Inter-War Economy:
Britain, 1919–1939

Derek H. Aldcroft

Senior Lecturer in Economic History, University of Leicester

B. T. Batsford Ltd London

To Valerie and Michael

First published 1970
© Derek H. Aldcroft 1970

Printed in Great Britain by
Willmer Brothers Limited, Birkenhead, and bound by
C. Tinling and Co. Ltd, Prescot
for the publishers B. T. Batsford Ltd
4 Fitzhardinge Street, London W1

7134 1370 0

Contents

Preface

There are two main reasons for writing this book. First, a considerable amount of new statistical data has appeared in recent years and it seemed necessary to incorporate some of it in a revised study of the inter-war years. Students are noticeably reluctant to handle statistical material, yet statistical analysis lies at the heart of economic history. It seemed, therefore, a good way of introducing students to the wealth of material available and it is to be hoped that after reading this volume they will be encouraged to delve into the statistical sources themselves and draw some of their own conclusions. My second main aim is again directed at students. Since teaching recent economic history at the University of Leicester I have constantly been concerned at the way students present or digest large quantities of factual, but often unrelated and fragmented, information, without exploring properly the key issues or offering any really concrete interpretation. Partly I felt this arose from the sources which they consulted which tend to give priority to descriptive detail and insufficient attention to the main areas of debate. I have concentrated therefore on some of the main economic issues of the period and introduced the detail only when necessary to elaborate the argument or point in question.

In effect this volume parts company with the traditional text. It does not try to cover every inch of the ground but explores in some depth the major components of the economy. In particular, it deals with subjects which are not usually very well covered in the conventional texts. These include aggregate growth, regional developments, fluctuations, sources of growth, the management of the economy and the external balance sheet. In addition, chapters on the main industries and services have been included together with one on income changes and welfare.

Within the limits set I have tried to be as comprehensive as possible, but inevitably certain things have had to be cast by the wayside. Hence I say nothing about trade unions and very little about social welfare legislation. In compensation however, I do try to estimate the effects of taxation and social transfer payments on income distribution, and I believe this to be a more important issue on which to devote valuable printed space than a detailed account of say, social legislation or the activities of the trade unions. Again, there is virtually nothing about agriculture. The subject did not fit very well into the theme of the book and I must admit that I shrank from the task of covering a field about which I know very little and which I find incredibly boring. Finally, the text is not designed for the beginner since it requires some prior knowledge of inter-war developments. Also, readers who feel faint-hearted about statistics and economic terms beware. For these shortcomings I make no apology.

I should like to thank my colleague, Mr P. Fearon, for reading the text and offering comments not all of which I have always acted upon. Miss Judith Watts has slaved away at her typewriter during a long hot summer in order to complete the final draft as quickly as possible, and to her I am extremely indebted. I should also like to thank other colleagues in the Department of Economic History at Leicester for their forbearance and patient acquiescence in my heavy demands on secretarial facilities. Dr W. R. Garside kindly assisted in checking the proofs.

1 The growth of the economy in perspective

Introduction

Many people probably regard the inter-war years as a fairly bleak period. Even students familiar with the economic history of these years tend to take a rather pessimistic view of the economy's performance. Their views are influenced, of course, by at least three memorable features: heavy unemployment, stagnation in some of the basic industries and the periodic crises, particularly the slump of 1929–32. Anyone who lived through this period and who experienced a spell of unemployment will have every reason to feel bitter about the workings of the economic system. It is not surprising, therefore, that many general accounts of the inter-war economy tend to focus attention on the black spots and in so doing reinforce the popular impression of this period.

Certainly economic and social conditions could have been much better during this period. We have no wish to understate the grave social distress arising from queues of unemployed men; nor should we forget that the large pool of unemployed manpower represented a gross waste of economic resources. It does not take much imagination to realize that the growth of the economy would have been materially improved had the labour force been fully occupied. The Macmillan Committee estimated[1] that the loss of output from the unemployment of one million men – the average in the good years – over a period of five years was £1,000 million, that is on the assumption that the

[1] *Report of the Committee on Finance and Industry*, Cmd 3897 (1931), p. 7.

net output per worker was around £200 per annum. In other words the national income would have been £200 million higher per annum had the labour force been fully employed in the best years of the period.

On the other hand, we would get a very distorted view of the economy if we confined our attention solely to the depressing features of the economy; and the same thing would happen if we switched our attention to the more dynamic elements. What we need to do first is to obtain a balanced or overall view of the economy. For this purpose it is essential to examine the economy nationally rather than sectorally. Initially what we want to know is not whether the coal industry stagnated, or the building industry flourished, or that unemployment was higher in some industries and regions than in others, but whether the economy as a whole expanded or declined in these years. If asked to state the case one way or another, the man in the street would probably plump for stagnation on the grounds that heavy unemployment and economic expansion could hardly be compatible. Though this may be a fairly logical answer from the layman's point of view it is by no means acceptable to the economist or to the economic historian. Long-term economic growth can take place even though productive resources such as capital and labour are not fully utilized. Structural and cyclical forces may prevent the optimum use of existing resources. As a result the level of economic activity will be lower than would otherwise be the case, but it does not automatically follow that long-term economic stagnation will ensue. As long as the growth of the more dynamic sectors of the economy is sufficiently strong to offset the drag effects imposed by the structurally weak parts, and provided that the cyclical upswings are stronger and more sustained than the downswings, then one would expect that over any reasonable length of time the economy would be growing in absolute terms.

It is not in doubt that the economy expanded over the inter-war period. But we need to go further than this. There is little point in knowing that British income grew by x per cent per annum unless we have some yardstick with which to assess that performance. Inter-war growth performance must be put in some sort of perspective. For this purpose it can be related to the growth of the British economy over time and it can be compared with the experience of other countries over the same time period. Since at this stage the primary concern is with the aggregate long-term growth of the economy little will be said about those aspects of the economy which are more familiar to the general reader. Only passing reference, for instance, will be made to unemployment, declining basic industries and cyclical fluctuations since these subjects will be covered more fully in later chapters.

TABLE I   *Average annual rates of growth of selected economic indicators of* U.K.

	Net national income	Real income per head	Output per man-hour	Industrial production (including building)	Industrial productivity	Exports	Consumers' expenditure per capita
	(1)	(2)	(3)	(4)	(5)	(6)	(7)
1870–80	1·9	0·8	0·9	2·4	1·2	2·8	1·3
1880–90	4·3	3·5	3·8	1·6	0·5	3·0	1·7
1890–1900	2·1	1·2	1·3	2·8	0·2	0·4	1·0
1900–13	1·1	0·4	0·6	1·6	0·2	4·2	±0·1
1870–1913	2·3	1·3	1·5	2·1	0·6	2·7	1·1
1913–29	0·8	0·8	2·1	1·6		−1·3	0·6
1920–29	2·0	1·5		2·8	3·8	1·6	0·9
1929–38	2·1	1·7	2·1	2·7	1·8	−4·0	1·3
1920–38	2·1	1·6		2·8	2·8	−1·2	1·1
1913–38	1·4	1·2	2·1	2·0		−2·3	0·8
1950–60	2·6	2·1	2·0	3·0	2·2	1·8	2·0
1870–1938	1·9	1·3	1·7	2·0		0·8	1·2

SOURCES   Cols. (1) and (2), C. H. Feinstein, 'National Income and Expenditure of the United Kingdom, 1870–1963', *London and Cambridge Economic Bulletin*, 50 (1964); col. (3), A. Maddison, *Economic Growth in the West* (1964); col. (4), K. S. Lomax, 'Production and Productivity Movements in the United Kingdom since 1900', *Journal of Royal Statistical Society*, A122 (1959), and 'Growth and Productivity in the United Kingdom', *Productivity Measurement Review*, 38 (1964); col. (5) E. H. Phelps Brown and S. J. Handfield-Jones, 'The Climacteric of the 1890s . . . ', *Oxford Economic Papers*, 4 (1952), and London and Cambridge Economic Service, *Key Statistics of the British Economy 1900–1966;* col. (6), A. H. Imlah, *Economic Elements in the Pax Britannica* (1958), and *Key Statistics;* col. (7), Feinstein, *loc. cit.*, and R. Stone and D. A. Rowe, *The Measurement of Consumers' Expenditure and Behaviour in the United Kingdom, 1920–1938*, vol. II, (1966).

Statistical basis of measurement

The most convenient starting point is to consider the pattern of British growth in the inter-war period in relation to the long-term trends.

First, however, a few comments must be made about the statistical indicators used in the analysis. Recent work by economists and statisticians has produced an array of valuable new time series and it is essential to point out briefly the main features and shortcomings of the data.

The growth rates presented in Table 1 are derived from seven major indices. The time series on which the calculations are based are the most up-to-date ones though this does not necessarily mean they are perfect in every respect. All the series, moreover, are subject to revision in the light of current research, though the revisions are unlikely to be of such magnitude as to effect the long-term rates of growth appreciably. The first column of the Table relates to net income and therefore provides an overall picture of the nation's economy. It includes all incomes received by residents in the U.K. and, after an allowance has been made for capital consumption, the net product has been deflated by a cost of living index. Column 2 provides a more refined measure of change in economic welfare since it takes account of population growth. Real income per head is derived simply by dividing the net national income series by the total population. The output per man-hour figures (col. 3) provide a measure of productivity for the economy as a whole. The original series is based on gross domestic output data (gross national product minus net income from abroad) and then divided through by the labour force after adjustments have been made for unemployment and changes in hours worked.[1] This series is probably less reliable than those on which the first two columns are based.

The remaining four columns refer to specific sectors of the economy. For industrial production the new index constructed by Lomax has been used. This is an improvement on the index produced by Hoffmann[2] which, because of its weighting and coverage, was somewhat unreliable for the inter-war period. On the other hand, there is no continuous series for industrial productivity (industrial production divided by the labour force) and so we have to make do with a composite index. For the period before 1914 the productivity estimates are based on the Hoffmann production data used in conjunction with estimates of the occupied population. The main problem here is not the inadequacy of the production figures but the fact that the

[1] For full details of the basis of calculation see A. Maddison, *Economic Growth in the West* (1964), pp. 199–200, 230.
[2] W. G. Hoffmann, *British Industry, 1700–1950* (1955 ed.).

estimates for the labour force have to be extrapolated from the Censuses of Population which were only taken once every ten years. For the post-war period the more reliable series produced by the London and Cambridge Economic Service has been used. But because of differences in composition it is impossible to link the two series together. The last two columns are fairly straightforward. Column 6 relates to the volume of exports while column 7 refers to consumers' expenditure per head. The latter is derived from that part of income spent by individuals (as opposed to the Government) divided by the population and deflated by a price index.

The problems involved in making growth comparisons over time are fairly well known and only a brief reference will be made to one or two of the more relevant ones. Perhaps the greatest difficulty is in the choice of the most appropriate indicators. Here we have chosen seven but it is the first two or three that are the most useful for measuring the progress of the economy as a whole, since the other series only refer to segments of the whole. But no single indicator can provide an accurate guide to changes in economic welfare. Even the figures for real income per head, which are probably the most useful for long-term comparisons, do not tell us anything about the distribution of income. If a growing real income per head is accompanied by increasing inequality in the distribution of the national income then one would have to be more circumspect in making general statements about economic progress. However, this problem need not concern us too much at this stage.[1]

The reliability of the data presents another problem. Even the best of series are subject to margins of error or contain omissions. It is important, therefore, not to lay too much stress on marginal changes since these may well arise from discrepancies within the series.[2] The data for the inter-war period are generally more reliable than those for before 1914 since official statistical reporting increased both in quantity and quality in these years. Nevertheless, they are by no means perfect and there are one or two significant omissions.

[1] For a useful commentary on the different ways of measuring economic progress see M. Lipton, *Assessing Economic Performance* (1968).
[2] Readers who regard this warning as superfluous should read O. Morgenstern, *On the Accuracy of Economic Observations* (1959). On the other hand, Morgenstern conveys the impression that statistical measurement is somewhat valueless because of the errors involved.

For example, there is no very reliable estimate for national income in 1920. On the basis of data for consumers' expenditure and industrial production it was possible to make a very rough estimate of income per head for 1920 which came out very close to that of 1913. Multiplying the result by the total population gave a figure for total national income for 1920 slightly below that of 1913 after correction for price changes. If anything this estimate is possibly on the high side and this would tend to depress the rate of growth in the 1920s. There is also no estimate of output per man-hour for 1920. Here it was difficult to fill the gap because of lack of data on man-hours worked and so 1913 has been used as the main base year.

The choice of the right base years is important when making long-term growth comparisons. It would, for instance, distort the analysis if one chose for any particular time span a base year at the bottom of a slump and a terminal year at the peak of a boom. The best approach is to measure growth from peak to peak. The years 1913, 1929 and 1938 are acceptable for this purpose. It is true that capacity utilization was not the same in each case but they have the advantage in that income and consumption were at their peak in these years. Many writers use 1937 rather than 1938 for the terminal year of the period, but there is not a great deal to choose between them. The main difference is that unemployment rose and industrial production fell in 1938; on the other hand, income and consumption continued to rise. The biggest difficulty however, was in selecting the first base year after the war. 1919 was unacceptable for two reasons; the fragmentary nature of the data and the fact that economic activity had still not recovered properly from the war. The fact that some of the estimates for 1920 are rather tentative might also have been a good reason for choosing a later base year. Unfortunately after 1920 there was a sharp fall in economic activity with the result that the years 1921 and 1922 are not particularly suitable for our purposes. The best year would be 1924 but this is so close to 1929 that one could hardly speak legitimately of the 1920s. Moreover, the use of any of these years as a base would tend to exaggerate the rate of growth for the 1920s.[1] All things considered the best solution appeared to be to take 1920 since it now seems that the level of economic activity in that year was very close

[1] An analysis using the 1924–29–37 sequence has been made by J. A. Dowie 'Growth in the Inter-war Period: Some More Arithmetic', *Economic History Review*, 21 (1968).

to that of 1913.[1] By doing so we shall at least avoid inflating the growth performance of the 1920s.

Whatever choices are made there will always be some critic ready to challenge the procedure adopted. The selection of statistical indicators and the base years has been made only after considerable experiment with a view to eliminating gross distortions in the final results.

It is not immediately clear from Table 1 how the war of 1914–18 affected the British economy. In fact altogether six or seven years annual growth were lost since it was not until 1920 that income and production approached the pre-war levels. The sharp slump after 1920 meant that the economy grew little in the early 1920s; thereafter progress was fairly steady up to 1929. Thus for the decade as a whole the rates of growth of income, production and consumers' expenditure were very similar to the long-term averages over the period 1870–1914, though somewhat higher than those recorded in the decade or so prior to the war (1900–13). The effects of the war can be seen if we examine the period 1913–29, though even then performance was slightly better than in the years 1900–13. The main exceptions to these trends were exports and industrial productivity. Export growth in the 1920s was very low compared with before the war and there was a substantial contraction between 1913–1929. This can be largely attributed to the collapse of the export markets of the basic industries. On the other hand, industrial productivity grew very rapidly indeed. It is probable that the growth of industrial productivity is somewhat inflated by using 1920 as a base because of the relatively low absolute level of productivity in some industries in that year. But even taking later base years (1922, 1923) the rate of growth still works out at more than three per cent per annum.[2]

The economic crisis of 1929–32 imposed a further check to the growth of the British economy though income and consumption kept up remarkably well. Recovery, moreover, set in fairly early and was sustained, so that by the end of the 1930s most indices had far surpassed

[1] For international comparisons 1920 is not a very suitable year as we shall see below.

[2] The figures for domestic output per man show a similar break in trend. There was a slight fall between 1900 and 1913 compared with a rate of growth of 2·1 per cent per annum in the 1920s. The level of productivity was the same in 1920 as in 1913. London and Cambridge Economic Service, *Key Statistics of the British Economy 1900–1966*, Table C.

their previous peaks in 1929. Thus over the period 1929–38 growth rates in most cases were very similar to those of the 1920s and compared favourably with the pre-war trends. Income per head, for example, grew by 1·7 per cent a year as against only 0·4 per cent between 1900 and 1913. Productivity growth was somewhat lower than in the 1920s, while exports registered a very sharp contraction indeed.

Taking the inter-war period as a whole (1920–38) we find that rates of growth of income and consumers' expenditure were very similar to the long-term averages before 1914 but that industrial production and productivity grew somewhat faster. Exports, however, contracted by 1·2 per cent per annum compared with a 2·7 per cent increase between 1870 and 1913. But compared with the decade or more before 1914 growth generally was more buoyant in the inter-war years. During the later nineteenth century there was some slowing down in the rate of economic progress and by contrast the post-war years appear to have experienced an acceleration in growth. Income per head, for instance, grew faster than at any time since the 1880s. But industrial productivity showed the most notable break in trend. The annual rate of growth was 2·8 per cent between 1920 and 1938 as against 0·6 per cent, 1870–1913 and only 0·2 per cent in the 1900s. The differences are so large that it would be difficult to ascribe them solely to inaccuracies in the productivity series.[1] Britain's poor export performance provides the only major exception to these general conclusions.

As against a later decade, the 1950s, growth before 1939 was generally lower except in the case of industrial productivity. By contrast inter-war performance was slightly better than the long-term average for the years 1870 to 1938, though, given the rather marginal differences in most cases, it would be unwise to press this point too strongly. On balance, therefore, we may conclude that the British economy was far from being stagnant in this period since the growth record compares well with that of other periods.

International comparisons

How did Britain's performance compare with that of other countries? Here the problems of analysis are somewhat greater. It is impossible to obtain comparative data for all the series listed in Table 1. In fact

[1] Domestic output per man rose by 1·4 per cent per annum between 1920 and 1938 compared with a slight fall in the period 1900–13.

continuous series for several countries are only available for domestic output and industrial production. Moreover, there are no reliable estimates of output for 1920. As it happens this is not a really serious drawback since 1920 is an unsuitable benchmark year. Britain's recovery from the war effort was quite rapid and by 1920 the level of economic activity was very similar to that of 1913. Most European countries, however, recovered more slowly and in most cases it was not until well into the 1920s that the pre-war levels of output were regained. In view of this discrepancy any calculations based on 1920 would give rather misleading results. A fairer comparison may be gained by using 1913 as a base year. This method also has an additional advantage in that it provides a reasonable indication of the gains and losses wrought by war.

TABLE 2 *Average annual rates of growth of gross domestic product and output per man-hour*

	1913–38		1913–29		1929–38	
	G.D.P.	G.D.P. per man-hour	G.D.P.	G.D.P. per man-hour	G.D.P.	G.D.P. per man-hour
Belgium	0·8	1·5	1·6	2·0	−0·5	0·6
Denmark	1·9	1·3	1·8	1·7	2·1	0·4
France	0·3	2·3	1·6	2·8	−2·2	1·6
Germany	1·6	1·3	0·3	0·8	3·9	2·1
Italy	1·7	2·6	1·8	2·3	1·6	3·2
Netherlands	2·1	1·5	3·3	2·6	0·1	−0·3
Norway	2·9	2·7	2·8	3·0	2·9	2·2
Sweden	1·7	1·6	1·3	0·9	2·6	3·0
Switzerland	2·0	2·4	2·8	3·2	0·6	1·1
Canada	1·4	0·8	2·4	1·3	−0·2	0·0
U.S.A.	2·0	3·0	3·1	2·8	0·0	3·3
U.K.	1·9	2·1	1·6	2·1	2·3	2·1
Unweighted average	1·6	1·9	2·0	2·1	1·1	1·9

SOURCE Calculated from A. Maddison, *Economic Growth in the West* (1964), pp. 201–2, 232.

In Table 2 rates of growth of domestic output and output per man-hour are given for 12 countries including Britain. In the period up to 1929 Britain tended to lag behind other countries in terms of output though her rise in productivity was the same as the average for all countries. This result can be attributed to the weak nature of the boom in the later 1920s in this country compared with abroad. The position was almost reversed in the 1930s. Most countries suffered more severely than Britain from the crisis of 1929–32 while in many cases recovery was slow and protracted. This was especially the case in France, Belgium, Canada and the United States, all of which failed to regain their 1929 levels of output. Britain's rapid recovery from the slump put her near the top of the growth league table. Only three countries, Germany, Norway and Sweden, grew faster than Britain over the period 1929–38. This improvement compensated for relatively slower growth in the previous decade with the result that Britain's performance for the entire period (1913–1938) was not too bad at all. The growth of both output and output per man-hour was more rapid than the average and was better than that of at least six countries (Table 2). What is perhaps most significant is that Britain's inter-war growth record was better, relatively speaking, than either before 1914 or after the second world war, for in both cases her position was near or at the bottom of the league tables. In fact the inter-war period is the only one in which Britain's growth rate has been above the general average of the countries listed in Table 2.

If we use industrial production as the basis of comparison the position is a little less favourable to Britain. During the 1930s, of course, Britain did very well. With a growth rate of 3·4 per cent per annum between 1929–37 she was one of the best industrial performers, being surpassed only by Sweden and Denmark. During the 1920s, however, things were very different. She was then bottom of the league table and her growth rate was less than half the average for all O.E.C.D. countries. But the comparison is not altogether fair in this case because of the use of 1920 as the benchmark year. If we shift the basis of comparison to 1913–37 it can be seen from Table 3 that Britain's relative performance turns out somewhat better, though a number of countries recorded higher rates of growth. Nevertheless, over the entire period 1913–37, or the somewhat shorter period 1924–37, Britain's performance was near the general average. On a relative basis it was also appreciably better than before 1914 and in the 1950s.[1]

Britain's relative importance in the world economy declined in the inter-war years, especially in the first half of the period. This was,

[1] For these comparisons see the data in D. H. Aldcroft, 'Economic Growth in Britain in the Inter-War Years. A Reassessment', *Economic History Review*, 20 (1963), pp. 313–4.

TABLE 3   *Average annual rates of growth of industrial production (excluding building) for* U.K. *and other countries*

	1913–37	1913–29	1920–37	1924–37	1920–9	1929–37
U.K.	2·0	1·3	2·8	3·0	2·3	3·4
All O.E.C.D. Countries	}1·6	1·4	3·7	3·1	5·1	2·2
U.S.	2·9	4·2	2·3	2·7	4·0	0·4
Canada	n.a.	n.a.	4·2	4·7	6·5	1·6
Norway	2·3	1·9	2·8	3·4	2·4	3·3
Belgium	1·5	2·1	3·7	2·3	6·6	0·5
Sweden	3·5	2·4	5·2	5·9	5·0	5·4
Denmark	3·9	3·9	3·6	3·5	3·2	4·0
Germany	1·2	0·9	5·4	5·3	7·6	3·0
France	0·8	2·0	3·4	0·9	7·9	−2·8
Italy	2·4	2·8	4·0	2·8	6·0	1·7

SOURCES   Based on O.E.E.C., *Industrial Statistics, 1900–1959* (1960), p. 9, and K. S. Lomax, 'Production and Productivity Movements in the United Kingdom since 1900', *Journal of Royal Statistical Society*, A122 (1959), p. 196.

of course, nothing new; it was merely the continuation of a trend which had set in well before the end of the nineteenth century. By 1913 Britain had lost her former predominant position in manufacturing production, though she was still the world's largest exporter. In that year her share of manufacturing production was 14·0 per cent compared with nearly 36 per cent for the United States and 15·7 per cent for Germany. By the end of the 1930s Britain's share had fallen to nearly nine per cent while the United States, Russia and Germany, in the order, were the three largest producers (Table 4). The check to exports after the war resulted in a similar fall in Britain's share of world exports, though she managed to maintain her position as the world's leading trader of manufactured goods for most of the period (Table 5). This loss of shares was only to be expected as other nations, especially some of the lesser developed countries such as Japan, increased the pace of their development. On the other hand, the sharp drop in Britain's standing before 1929 can be attributed partly to the fact that the boom of the later 1920s was less vigorous in Britain than abroad. Conversely, in the 1930s, when Britain's economic performance improved relative to that of other countries, her relative position in the distribution of world manufacturing production and exports remained fairly stable.

TABLE 4   *Percentage distribution of world manufacturing production*

	1870	1896–1900	1913	1926–29	1936–38
U.K.	31·8	19·5	14·0	9·4	9·2
U.S.	23·3	30·1	35·8	42·2	32·2
Germany	13·2	16·6	15·7	11·6	10·7
France	10·3	7·1	6·4	6·6	4·5
Russia	3·7	5·0	5·5	4·3	18·5

SOURCE   League of Nations, *Industrialization and Foreign Trade* (1945).

TABLE 5   *Percentage distribution of world exports of manufactured goods*

	1880	1899	1913	1929	1937
U.K.	41·4	32·5	29·9	23·6	22·4
U.S.	2·8	11·2	12·6	20·7	19·6
Germany	19·3	22·2	26·4	21·0	22·4
France	22·2	15·8	12·9	11·2	6·4
Japan	—	1·5	2·4	3·9	7·2
Belgium	5·0	5·6	4·9	5·5	5·9

SOURCES   S. B. Saul, 'The Export Economy, 1870–1914', *Yorkshire Bulletin of Economic and Social Research,* 17 (1965), p. 12, and H. Tyszynski, 'World Trade in Manufactured Commodities, 1899–1950', *The Manchester School,* 19 (1951), p. 286.

It is clear from this brief survey of the inter-war years that one could hardly describe the British economy as being in a state of stagnation. Growth might easily have been more rapid had all resources been fully utilized but the achievements were by no means negligible. Industrial production rose by 62 per cent and real income per head by one third between 1920 and 1938, and by any criteria of comparative assessment the rates of growth of most major indices were respectable, if not spectacular. But perhaps the most notable feature of the period is not that growth took place amidst heavy unemployment, but the fact that it was so unevenly distributed over time, between regions and between different sectors of the economy. Fluctuations in economic activity were quite frequent and often sharp, the northern regions of the country were much less prosperous than their counterparts in the south, while some industries expanded rapidly as others declined. The next three chapters will discuss these features in greater detail and examine some of the sources of inter-war growth.

2 Fluctuations in economic activity

The previous chapter discussed the growth trends of the inter-war period. This showed a long-term upward growth trend. The growth path was not a smooth one however. In fact it was punctuated by a series of fluctuations the downswings of which caused temporary interruptions to the rate of progress. It is to these oscillations around the trend which we now turn.

Some preliminary observations

There are at least three problems that ought to be considered before making an analysis of fluctuations. First, there is the question of the relationship between the trend and the cycle. Secondly, there is the problem of relating fact and theory. Finally, there are a number of difficulties connected with the measurement of cycles.

The relationship between the trend and the cycle has been the cause of considerable debate among economists. Some hold that it is impossible to separate the two while others feel that the cycle and the trend are fairly independent of each other. To some extent this division of opinion has arisen as a result of the way in which the two phenomena have been studied. Much of the work on the causes of fluctuations has tended to emphasize the role of demand, whereas discussions on long-term growth (the trend) have concentrated on supply factors, namely capital, labour and technology. In other words, the cycle and the trend have been tackled from opposite poles and the problem remains to find a suitable theory to weld the two together.[1]

While this is not the place to explore the possibilities of new theories it is important to be aware of the problem. It does seem somewhat artificial to make a clear distinction between the cycle and the trend. In any discussion of the cycle it is surely necessary to know what is happening to the trend, that is whether the general level of activity is rising or falling from one cycle to the next. It is not difficult to show how the two are inter-related, though whether they can be regarded as one and the same phenomenon, as some writers have suggested, is more debatable. A vigorous boom, for example, will obviously generate a growth trend and though the latter willl be interrupted by any subsequent downswing in economic activity the upward trend will be continued through the successive phase of the next cycle. Take the case where a strong boom is generated by large-scale investment in new technology. Eventually as the new technology becomes exhausted investment will tail off and probably fall and this may result in a downturn in activity. In this case investment overshoots itself and results in a situation in which capacity exceeds the level of demand so that businessmen cut back until demand rises to meet the new production potential of the economy. But, generally speaking, in each upswing the economy moves to a higher level of activity than in the preceding one partly because of the explosive nature of investment at the top of the boom, but also because of the built-in tendency for consumption to move on to a permanently higher plane in each boom, while in the slump a ratchet effect operates to prevent consumption (and income) from falling as far as in the previous depression. Each boom is part and parcel of the trend and it is only during the downswing that the trend and cycle part company for, as Goodwin points out, 'there is no such thing as a trend factor which continues to rise through the depression'.[2]

Relating the cycle to the trend does not necessarily help a great deal in determining the causes of fluctuations, but it does make the analysis of them more intelligible in terms of long-run dynamic growth. Nor for that matter does the large amount of theoretical and empirical work on cycles help a great deal in interpreting the fluctuations of any particular period. It is true that research has revealed a number of

[1] See R. M. Goodwin, 'The Problem of Trend and Cycle', *Yorkshire Bulletin of Economic and Social Research*, 5 (1953); R. C. O. Matthews, *The Trade Cycle* (1959), ch. 13.

[2] Goodwin, *loc. cit.*, p. 94.

cycles with similar characteristics, but the pattern is by no means uniform and there is a considerable range of conflicting explanations as to their causes. Although cycles have certain features in common most of them exhibit individual characteristics and no general theory can take account of all such peculiarities. Similarly, it may be possible to isolate key variables which produce a causal sequence in many cycles, but again there is no reason to suppose that that they will always operate in exactly the same way in every cycle. However uniform the pattern of their movements is over time, any prediction based on past observations is liable to be upset by the sudden emergence of random shocks such as wars. In any case, many of the theories or general conclusions about cycles are based on observations from the nineteenth century and as such are not necessarily directly applicable to inter-war conditions.[1] For example, the long wave cycle associated with the name of Kuznets (16–22 years) cannot be used as a basis of interpretation, partly because of the shortness of the period but also because it relates to pre-1914 movements in building, migration and capital exports, the patterns of which altered considerably in the inter-war period. Even more so, the very long Kondratieff cycle of some 40 to 50 years obviously has no meaning for our period. On the other hand, the standard business cycle of the nineteenth century, the Juglar of around 8–10 years duration, and the minor Kitchen cycle of some 3–4 years, are probably of greater relevance to this period.

Giving the differing characteristics of each cycle it is virtually impossible to construct a theory of cycles which would be generally applicable at all times. On the other hand, most cycles do have certain common features and it is possible to make some general comments about the movements of certain components of the economy over the course of the cycle. Most of the main indices of economic activity, national income, consumption, investment, production, prices and profits, can be expected to move in the same direction in both the upswing and downswing of the cycle. Some of them are more volatile than others so that the amplitude of the changes will vary considerably. Moreover, they do not always all move in the same direction. For example, in minor recessions employment and investment may fall off while production and income continue in an upward direction. Alternatively, some variables may be determined independently of

[1] Moreover, some of the observations for the pre-war period were based upon price and employment data and these variables are not always a very good guide to fluctuations in economic activity as a whole.

the cycle. Price movements may run contrary to the cycle if they are influenced by strong external forces.

However, during fairly pronounced cyclical movements most of the indicators will tend to move in the same direction. Of the two components of national income, consumption and investment, the latter is by far the more volatile. This is especially true in the down-swing when investment may fall off very sharply while consumption continues to hold up. The reason for this is quite simple. Most consumption is made out of current income and is therefore unlikely to vary very much from one year to the next. During the early phases of a recession, at least, it may not fall absolutely since consumers will try to maintain their previous living standards by drawing on past savings or by raising their average propensities to consume.[1] Thus in recessions the level of consumption will be cushioned by what might be termed built-in stabilizers.[2] Investment is quite a different matter. Most investment is made from accumulated savings (even if borrowed) rather than from current income, though decisions to invest will be based on future profit expectations and the expected level of national income. If it is anticipated that these will fall then new investment projects will be postponed and there may be some cut-back in replacement investment. The total effect of this may be quite severe especially if the downturn is preceded by a sharp burst of new investment.

Investment therefore plays an important part in cyclical fluctuations. It will tend to exert a destabilizing effect over the course of the cycle. It follows from this that those sectors of the economy catering for investment will react more sharply than those producing consumption goods. Those industries producing durable investment goods such as ships, machine tools, iron and steel, etc., will experience more violent fluctuations than those sectors producing consumer goods such as textiles and clothing or providing services which are consumed immediately. Within the latter sector those industries producing durable goods, e.g. houses and luxury articles, will be more prone to severe fluctuations than those industries making necessities and less durable commodities. When incomes fall consumers are likely

---

[1] Or consumer spending may be bolstered up by increased transfer payments by the Government in times of recession. The role of the Government will be dealt with in Chapter 9.

[2] On the stability of the consumption function see S. Bober, *The Economics of Cycles and Growth* (1968), ch. 4.

to cut back first on luxury goods and durable goods in order to maintain expenditure on basic necessities. Conversely, during boom periods when incomes rise, an increasing proportion of the additional income will be spent on products of a more durable nature.

It is more difficult to generalize about the order in which different sectors react at the turning points of the cycle. Generally speaking, one would expect consumer goods industries to lead at the turning points and investment sectors to lag behind. This can be justified on the grounds that production of consumption goods can be increased or cut back fairly readily; in contrast, investment projects are difficult to curtail suddenly when the boom breaks and hence work already in progress may be continued during the downswing,[1] while at the trough of the depression it is difficult to revive investment confidence until recovery is under way.[2] But within the consumer goods sectors a distinction must be made between durable and non-durable goods. Durable goods industries are likely to lead non-durable sectors at the upper turning point but lag behind at the lower one, though both will respond earlier than investment goods sectors. These differences can be attributed to the consumption effects described above. Consumers' first reaction when depression sets in is to curtail expenditure on durables or luxuries, whereas expenditure on everyday necessities will be maintained for as long as possible. At the lower turning point the consumption effect will work in favour of non-durables for obvious reasons.

Finally, there is the export sector to consider. Generally in the past exports have been particularly sensitive to the cycle and have therefore fluctuated more violently than other indicators. Moreover, they usually tended to lead at both the turning points. It is not immediately obvious why exports behave in the way they do though as we shall see in due course it can partly be attributed to the composition of the export trade in terms of products and markets.

Measuring business cycles is not an easy task. The results of any business cycle analysis will depend upon the type of measuring devices used. For instance, if we take into consideration all fluctuations, how-

[1] Thus in the initial stages of recessions investment goods sectors may act as a stabilizing influence. In fact in 1921, investment actually rose by 14·6 per cent and then fell back in the following year. This, however, was something of a special case due partly to the delayed start in local authority housebuilding. See below, pages 59, 71.

[2] Also, at the trough there will be underutilized capacity which will act as a drag on new investment.

ever minor they might be, then the results will reveal cycles of frequent periodicity and low average amplitude compared with those from an analysis based on the more pronounced swings in economic activity. Another problem is the availability of data. Ideally one requires monthly or quarterly data in order to make a precise examination of turning points, but more often than not the main aggregate data are only available on an annual basis. The choice of indicators will also affect the result. Not all economic indicators move exactly in step all the time so that turning points and the amplitude of swings will vary somewhat from one set of data to another. To take an extreme example, analyses based on consumption and investment separately would produce quite different results. The obvious solution here is to use some aggregate indicator such as national income (or the nearest equivalent), or to construct a composite index from a number of different business indicators. The latter procedure was used by Burns and Mitchell in their study of cycles in the United States, Britain, France and Germany.[1] Some of the series were available on a monthly or quarterly basis which made possible a more accurate assessment of the turning points than could be achieved with national income or industrial production series which, for Britain at least, are only available annually.

Using the reference cycle dates of the National Bureau of Economic Research it is possible to identify five cycles in Britain between 1918 and 1938. Measuring from peak to peak they ran from October 1918 to March 1920, March 1920 to November 1924, November 1924 to March 1927, March 1927 to July 1929 and July 1929 to September 1937 (see Table 6). Up to 1932 the cycles were of fairly short duration compared with those before the war. In the 167 months between June 1919 and December 1932 the average duration for roughly four cycles (trough to trough) was 40 months as against 70·5 months between June 1879 and December 1914.[2] Moreover, the average duration of contractions exceeded that of expansions in this period, whereas the reverse was the case before the war. Even if the relatively long upswing of 1932–7 is included the average duration of inter-war cycles still only works out at just over 49 months, though in this case the length of the expansions was greater than that of the contractions.

[1] W. C. Mitchell, *What Happens During Business Cycles* (1951, N.B.E.R.), pp. 23–4, and A. F. Burns and W. C. Mitchell, *Measuring Business Cycles* (1946, N.B.E.R.).
[2] O. Morgenstern, *International Financial Transactions and Business Cycles* (1959, N.B.E.R.), p. 62.

TABLE 6 *Reference dates of British cycles, 1918–1938*

Peak	Trough
Oct. 1918	April 1919
Mar. 1920	June 1921
Nov. 1924	July 1926
Mar. 1927	Sept. 1928
July 1929	Aug. 1932
Sept. 1937	Sept. 1938

A further interesting feature is the change in the degree of correspondence between British cycles and those abroad. Before the war (1879–1914) the four countries of Britain, France, Germany and the United States, were in the same phase of the cycle in 53·5 per cent of all months whereas between 1919 and 1932 the percentage of similar phasing was only 35·7 per cent. This increasing irregularity was most marked among the three European countries, the percentage of similar phasing falling from 83·1 to 45·2 per cent between the two periods. In fact before the war these three countries were in very close association with each other and it was the United States which tended to be out of step. After the war, however, the phasing of European cycles corresponded more with those of the United States. The change was most noticeable in the case of Britain. The high degree of association between British cycles and those of Germany and France was very much weakened after 1918 whereas there was an increasing tendency for the phasing to correspond with the cycles of the United States. Thus, although after the war the overall degree of similar phasing declined there was a stronger association between European and American cycles which gives some credence to the belief that the United States exported depressions.[1]

On the above evidence it would be possible to argue that the cyclical pattern of the pre-war period was broken after 1918. The standard business cycle or Juglar seems to have all but disappeared from the British scene and been replaced by a shorter cycle of some three to four years duration corresponding to the Kitchen cycle. However, it should be noted that some of the fluctuations were very minor indeed and it is doubtful whether these should be regarded as cycles in the real sense of the term. For instance, the downturn of 1927–8 was very weak and scarcely shows up in the annual data; income con-

[1] *ibid.*, pp. 48–51.

tinued to rise and there was only a modest dip in industrial production largely as a result of recession in one or two sectors, notably construction, shipbuilding and textiles. If, moreover, we remove the early post-war years and 1925–6 on the grounds that these were exceptional years conditioned by the aftermath of the war and the General Strike, then the Juglar pattern re-emerges. Peaks would then occur in 1920,[1] 1929[2] and 1937 giving an average duration of nine and eight years respectively, with corresponding troughs in 1921, 1932 and 1938 giving 11- and six-year intervals. The periodicity is then very similar to that observed before the war.[3]

The amplitude of the post-war Juglar cycle was also very similar to the pre-war one if measured in terms of national income. On the other hand, industrial production tended to fluctuate more violently than before the war and it is probably the movements in this sector which have given the impression that inter-war fluctuations were both more frequent and more vigorous than those in the nineteenth century. Downswings of more than five per cent in industrial production were fairly rare before 1914– the main exception being in 1877–8 when it fell by 10·2 per cent – whereas in two of the inter-war recessions it declined by more than 10 per cent, by as much as 18·6 per cent in 1921 and by nearly 11 per cent between 1929–32.

The pattern of cyclical fluctuations will clearly vary, therefore, according to the type of assessment used. There does appear, however, to be some evidence of the reappearance of the Juglar in the inter-war years, though minor cycles occurred more frequently than before the war. But whichever pattern we prefer it is apparent that the characteristics of inter-war cyclical phases varied considerably. For example, the depression of 1929–32 was much more prolonged than that of 1921 but it was also much milder. Similarly, the recovery from the post-war slump was weaker and more drawn out than that following the depression of the early 1930s. Again, there were certain features which were peculiar to each upswing and downswing of the cycle. Thus before analysing the movements of some of the main variables it will be useful to fill in some of the main details of inter-war fluct-

---

[1] It is true that 1920 was also affected by the aftermath of the war but since the previous peak was in 1913 another Juglar peak could have legitimately occurred in 1920.

[2] Though 1930 if national income is used.

[3] See D. H. Aldcroft and H. W. Richardson, *The British Economy 1870–1939* (1969), p. 25.

uations. For this purpose we shall follow, as far as the annual data allows, the reference dates of the National Bureau.

Chronology of fluctuations[1]

At the end of the First World War conditions were tailor-made for a boom in economic activity. There was a large backlog of investment to be made good as a result of neglect during the war; much worn out machinery and plant required replacing especially in those industries which had been devoted to military production. Some industries, the railways and the coal mines for example, had suffered severe disinvestment during the war. There was also a pent-up demand for consumer goods the supply of which had been restricted during the war as a result of shortages of labour and materials. Many industries had reduced their output for the domestic market by more than one half and by the end of the war the number of workers engaged on production for the civilian market was only about one third that of pre-war.[2] There was also a serious shortage of houses; housebuilding had practically ceased during the years of hostilities and by the end of the war the nation was short of some 800–900,000 houses. At the same time there was in existence a large volume of liquid or near liquid assets, which, coupled with the high level of money incomes, helped to make the pent-up demand effective. Because of the restrictions on investment and consumption during the war, businessmen, the banks and the public had accumulated a considerable amount of purchasing power in the form of bank deposits, cash and short-dated Government bonds. The Government's methods of war-time finance, in particular the large scale issue of Treasury Bills, had done much to increase the liquid state of the economy.[3] Finally, it was expected that exports would rise sharply from the low level reached in 1918.

Businessmen's expectations of a boom were thus by no means misplaced though it was considerably shorter than originally anticipated. Consumers' expenditure rose by no less than 21 per cent between

[1] Reference should be made to Tables 7 and 8 for this section.
[2] *Board of Trade Journal*, 6 March 1919, pp. 308–10. Between 1913 and 1918 private consumers' expenditure fell by about 20 per cent. J. R. Stone and D. A. Rowe, *The Measurement of Consumers' Expenditure and Behaviour in the United Kingdom, 1920–1938*, 2 (1966), p. 144.
[3] At the end of 1918 excess demand was probably in the region of 10 per cent. This was considerably less than after the Second World War.

B

TABLE 7   *Annual percentage change in selected economic indicators, 1918–38*

	Real national income (net)	Gross domestic product	Indus-trial produc-tion	Consumers' expendi-ture	Gross domestic invest-ment	Employ-ment	Exports	Net imports	Whole-sale prices	Retail prices	Average real incomes of all wage earners
	(1)	(2)	(3)	(4)	(5)	(6)	(7)	(8)	(9)	(10)	(11)
1918–19	—	—	+10·2	+20·9	—	—	—	—	+10·6	+ 5·9	—
1919–20	—	—	+11·1	− 0·8	—	—	+28·5	− 1·4	+24·4	+15·8	—
1920–1	− 3·2	−12·1	−18·6	− 5·4	+14·6	−14·4	−30·1	−16·7	−35·8	− 9·2	+3·0
1921–2	− 0·2	+ 7·4	+15·6	+ 3·5	− 7·8	+ 0·8	+38·4	+16·7	−19·5	−18·0	−1·0
1922–3	+ 1·7	+ 3·3	+ 5·9	+ 3·1	+ 2·5	+ 2·2	+ 8·4	+10·0	+ 0·1	− 4·9	−2·9
1923–4	+ 2·4	+ 5·3	+11·1	+ 2·4	+16·6	+ 1·4	+ 2·4	+11·7	+ 4·5	+ 0·6	+1·0
1924–5	+ 5·5	+ 2·9	+ 3·9	+ 2·3	+14·2	+ 1·2	− 1·5	+ 3·7	+ 4·3	+ 0·6	0·0
1925–6	− 3·2	− 2·3	− 5·3	− 0·2	− 2·1	− 2·7	−10·0	+ 4·5	− 6·9	− 2·3	0·0
1926–7	+ 8·6	+ 8·7	+15·2	+ 4·0	+11·3	+ 6·3	+14·5	+ 3·2	− 4·4	− 2·6	+5·0
1927–8	+ 1·5	0·0	− 2·8	+ 1·6	− 1·0	+ 0·5	+ 2·2	− 3·1	− 0·9	− 0·9	−1·0

1928–9	+4·8	+2·4	+5·1	+2·0	+5·4	+1·7	+2·9	+6·7	−2·7	−1·2	+1·9
1929–30	+3·8	−1·4	−4·3	+1·5	+0·5	−2·2	−18·4	−3·0	−12·5	−3·7	+2·8
1930–1	−2·8	−3·6	−6·4	+0·8	−1·8	−2·8	−23·5	+3·1	−12·2	−6·6	+4·6
1931–2	−1·6	+0·1	−0·5	−0·6	−12·9	+0·4	0·0	−13·1	−2·5	−2·4	+0·9
1932–3	+5·4	+4·1	+6·7	+2·1	+3·2	+2·5	+1·1	+1·2	+0·1	−2·8	+1·7
1933–4	+6·6	+5·5	+10·3	+3·2	+21·6	+3·4	+6·7	+5·7	+2·8	+0·7	+0·9
1934–5	+2·8	+4·5	+7·6	+2·7	+4·1	+2·1	+7·4	0·0	+1·0	+1·4	0·0
1935–6	+2·2	+5·4	+9·0	+2·9	+9·1	+3·6	+2·0	+7·6	+6·1	+2·8	0·0
1936–7	+0·9	+3·8	+6·0	+1·8	+3·4	+3·9	+6·7	+6·1	+15·1	+4·8	−2·5
1937–8	+3·1	−1·2	−2·7	+0·5	+1·5	+0·2	−11·5	−4·8	−6·7	+1·3	+2·6

SOURCES Col. (1), C. H. Feinstein, 'National Income and Expenditure of the United Kingdom, 1870–1963', *London and Cambridge Economic Bulletin*, 50 (1964), p. xi (net national income deflated by cost of living index.); col. (2), C. H. Feinstein, 'Production and Productivity, 1920–1962', *London and Cambridge Economic Bulletin*, 48 (1963), p. xiii, G.D.P. from output data; col. (3), K. S. Lomax, 'Production and Productivity Movements in the United Kingdom Since 1900', *Journal of Royal Statistical Society*, A122 (1959), p. 192; col. (4), J. R. Stone and D. A. Rowe, *The Measurement of Consumers' Expenditure and Behaviour in the United Kingdom, 1920–1938*, 2 (1966), p. 144; col. (5), C. H. Feinstein, *Domestic Capital Formation in the United Kingdom, 1920–1938* (1965), p. 38; col. (6), A. Chapman and R. Knight, *Wages and Salaries in the United Kingdom, 1920–1938* (1953), p. 32; cols. 7–11, B. R. Mitchell and P. Deane, *Abstract of British Historical Statistics* (1962), pp. 329, 353, 477–8.

TABLE 8   *Percentage swings in selected economic indicators over phases of the cycle*

	1920–1	1921–5	1925–6	1926–9	1929–32	1932–7	1937–8
Real income	− 3·2	+ 9·6	− 3·2	+15·6	− 0·8	+18·8	+ 3·1
Gross domestic product	−12·1	+20·0	− 2·3	+11·3	− 4·8	+25·6	− 1·2
Agriculture, forestry and fishing	+ 1·2	+ 7·1	+ 3·3	+ 6·4	− 2·0	+ 3·1	− 1·0
Manufacturing production	−22·2	+41·9	− 3·2	+14·7	−10·3	+48·2	− 2·8
Industrial production	−18·6	+41·4	− 5·3	+17·6	−10·9	+45·8	− 2·7
Transport and communications	−10·1	+33·9	− 3·6	+10·0	− 8·7	+19·0	0·0
Distributive trades	−12·5	+18·6	− 3·6	+ 8·8	0·0	+18·4	− 2·9
Total distribution and other services	− 8·2	+ 5·1	+ 1·2	+ 4·8	+ 1·2	+13·6	0·0
Gross domestic investment	+14·6	+25·8	− 3·1	+16·1	−14·1	+47·3	+ 1·5
Consumers' expenditure	− 5·4	+11·8	− 0·2	+ 7·7	+ 1·8	+13·5	+ 0·5
Exports	−30·1	+51·2	−10·0	+20·5	−37·5	+28·4	−11·5
Employment	−14·4	+ 5·6	− 2·7	+ 8·6	− 4·7	+16·6	+ 0·2
Wholesale prices	−35·8	−19·4	− 6·9	− 7·8	−25·6	+27·0	− 6·7
Retail prices	− 9·2	−22·1	− 2·3	− 4·7	−12·2	+ 6·9	+ 1·3
Profits	−33·4	+27·3	− 6·9	−13·7	−25·2	+64·6	− 4·5
Real incomes of wage earners	+ 3·0	− 2·9	0·0	+ 6·0	+ 7·8	0·0	+ 2·6

SOURCES   As for Table 7, and P. E. Hart, *Studies in Profit, Business Saving and Investment in the United Kingdom, 1920–1962*, 1 (1965). Profits cover extractive industry, manufacturing, construction, public utilities, transport and distribution but *not* finance and the professions.

1918 and 1919 and was accompanied by a high level of Government spending. This was followed by a large increase (over 28 per cent) in exports in 1920. Unfortunately, productive capacity was insufficient to meet the expansion in effective demand despite the efforts of businessmen to repair the war-time backlog. The result was that prices rose more rapidly than output, and, in turn, increasing money wages pushed up costs. The price-cost spiral was aggravated by the removal of war-time controls in the spring of 1919, shortages of labour and materials, strikes, transport difficulties and inflationary Government policies.

In effect the boom, which lasted roughly a year (March 1919 to April 1920), was somewhat artificial. Though production expanded it could not keep pace with rising demand and hence inflationary conditions dominated the upswing of the cycle. It developed into a speculative ramp. In fact the outstanding feature of the boom was the extent of the speculative buying in commodities, securities and real estate and the very large number of industrial transactions at inflated prices. The financial orgy was made possible by the extremely liquid state of firms as a result of high war-time profits, the relatively easy money conditions and the large scale creation of bank credit. A good deal of the speculative activity was also based on borrowed money. Some idea of the dimensions involved can be gained from the following figures. New capital issues on the London money market rose from £65·3 million in 1918 to £237·5 million in 1919 and to a peak of £384·2 million in 1920. The figure for 1920 was not again reached until well after the Second World War and most of the increase in new issues represented flotations for domestic purposes.[1]

Between January 1919 and April 1920 nearly £400 million of bank credit was made available for industrial and other purposes, while total bank clearings (London and provincial) rose from £23,000 million in 1918 to £42,000 million in 1920.

The worst excesses occurred in some of the older industries such as cotton and shipbuilding. The flotation of new companies, the sale of old ones and the issue of new shares became almost a daily event in 1919. The prospects of high profits attracted speculators and a large number of companies were bought up and refloated at inflated capital values with, in many cases, the assistance of the banks. In the cotton industry, for example, 109 mills with an original share capital

[1] Before the war the bulk of new issues had been on foreign account. E. V. Morgan, *Studies in British Financial Policy, 1914–25* (1952), p. 264.

of £4·5 million were sold for £31·7 million.[1] The rapid rise in
the price of old and new ships, a consequence of a shortage of shipping capacity,[2] gave rise to even greater speculation in the maritime
industries. For these industries such transactions had disastrous consequences. Their war-time profits were dissipated in a frivolous manner
and they were left with a heavy burden of debt as a result of increased
interest liabilities, the issue of bonus shares and the watering of capital
stock. The cost of overcapitalization in the boom was to remain a heavy
burden to some industries throughout the inter-war period. Moreover, in some cases, shipping and shipbuilding particularly, the boom
called into existence sufficient capacity to last a decade or more. The
unfortunate thing was that it was in those industries whose future
growth prospects were weakest that the most severe speculation took
place.

The end of the speculative spree was signalized in April 1920 when
the Bank rate was raised to seven per cent and the Government decided on a policy of retrenchment in public expenditure. But it would
be wrong to blame Government policies for the collapse of the boom
since it had passed its peak before they had begun to bite. In any case,
given the artificial nature of the boom and its magnitude it was almost
inevitable that it would be brought to a sudden and timely death. The
extent of the speculative orgy in the latter half of 1919 began to cast
doubts among even the most optimistic of businessmen. Moreover, as
a result of excessive financial transactions many firms were heavily
in debt and the banks were becoming increasingly illiquid because of
their large credit commitments to industry. Consumers, too, were showing their resistance to higher prices by the beginning of 1920 and it
is significant that in that year private consumption in real terms fell
slightly compared with a rise of 21 per cent the previous year. It is
probable therefore that business confidence was already on the wane
before the Government announced a change in policy though the
deflationary nature of its content can only have aggravated the subsequent downturn.

The turning point came in the spring of 1920 when unemployment was at its lowest and prices at their peak. Production held up
somewhat longer partly because of a delayed response in building

---

[1] F. Uttley, *Lancashire and the Far East* (1931), p. 45.
[2] To a large extent the shortage of shipping capacity was artificially determined.
See D. H. Aldcroft, 'Port Congestion and the Shipping Boom of 1919–20', *Business
History*, 3 (1961).

activity, though it soon reacted to the squeeze in consumption and the falling off in exports in the latter half of the year. By the middle of 1921 Britain was experiencing one of the worst depressions in history. Some 2·4 million workers or 22 per cent of all insured were unemployed. Apart from investment, which was bolstered up by a large scale programme of subsidized housebuilding, all indices of activity fell sharply; industrial production by 18·6 per cent, exports by 30·1 per cent, total output by 12·1 per cent, real income by 3·2 per cent,[1] employment by 14·4 per cent and wholesale prices by over one third. Money wages also fell in 1921 though real wages actually rose because of the more rapid decline in prices. The position was aggravated by strikes in coal, cotton and a number of other industries.

Though the unemployment position improved in the latter half of 1921 it was not until the beginning of the following year that production and output really began to revive. During 1922 production rose strongly despite a decline in investment and real wages, while in one or two important industries, notably building and shipbuilding, output declined quite substantially. However, there was a very strong revival in exports, an increase of no less than 38 per cent on 1921 and domestic consumption rose by 3·5 per cent. It seems likely that the initial upswing was generated by the export revival and by developments in the consumer goods industries. This was supplemented by growth in the newer industries and later by an upturn in building activity. The recovery in fact continued through to 1925 though there is some evidence of a minor peak late in 1924. But the pattern of growth was very uneven. Real income rose more rapidly in the latter part of the recovery when production and exports were tailing off, while the upsurge in investment did not take place until 1924 and 1925.

In terms of employment the recovery was by no means complete. Even at its lowest in June 1924 the number unemployed was still around one million, or 9·2 per cent of the insured population, and it tended to rise thereafter. Nevertheless, the strength of the recovery between 1921 and 1925 was quite marked. The figures speak for themselves. Domestic output rose by 20 per cent, industrial production by 41·4 per cent, exports by over 50 per cent and investment by just over one quarter. Admittedly these calculations are based on the low levels achieved at the bottom of the 1921 slump; even so, by 1925 income and production were well above the levels of 1920 or 1913.

[1] This figure is only approximate since the estimates for income are rather tentative for these years.

The downturn of 1926 requires little explanation. In comparison with 1921 it was relatively mild and to a large extent it was caused by the industrial troubles of that year. The main burden was borne by the heavy trades which were again affected by export losses. But not all industries were depressed. Expansion continued in vehicles, building, paper and printing, gas, water and electricity and agriculture, though at a reduced rate in some cases.

The 1926 recession can be regarded as a temporary interlude in the recovery from the 1921 slump, since it was caused by a random shock rather than by natural economic forces. Had the General Strike not taken place it is very likely that economic activity would have continued on its upward trend through 1926. But after 1926 the strength of the recovery was very much weakened. Compared with America and certain European countries Britain experienced a rather feeble boom in the later 1920s. Output increased more slowly than in the early 1920s while between 1927–8 industrial production and investment actually fell. The dip in production was very modest however being largely confined to one or two sectors such as building, iron and steel and shipbuilding. In one respect the dampened nature of the boom was advantageous in that it meant that the British economy suffered less severely in the subsequent crash. It is important, therefore, to comment briefly on the reasons for the dampened nature of the boom.

The stock explanation is that exports were at the root of the trouble; that export growth was weakened by high and inflexible wage costs and an overvalued currency. There is some truth in the export thesis though its importance should not be overstated. The volume of exports increased more rapidly than industrial production between 1926 and 1929. This is not to suggest that export growth was entirely satisfactory in the later 1920s for we know that the volume of exports failed to recover to the pre-war level. But it is unlikely that the overvalued exchange was a very important factor restraining Britain's export potential, though no doubt a lower rate of exchange would have made things slightly easier.[1] It is far from clear, moreover, whether high wage costs were the real source of the trouble. Although money wages remained relatively stable in the later 1920s at roughly double the pre-war level, wages in the United States followed a similar course. In fact wages in u.s. manufacturing were more than double those

[1] See Chapter 8.

of pre-war and they were tending to rise slowly in the latter part of the decade.

More powerful alternative explanations of the export lag are not difficult to find. In the first place, international competition in manufactures increased sharply in the later 1920s as a result of rapid revival in European countries, including Germany after the stabilization of her currency, and France and Belgium, both of which were assisted by undervalued rates of exchange. The delayed recovery of Europe after the war had lulled Britain into a false sense of security. Secondly, many of Britain's exports consisted of staple products the demand for which was either declining or rising only very slowly. Moreover, many of the staple products were becoming uncompetitive in world markets because of their high cost arising partly from the technical inefficiency of the industries concerned. The structure and composition of Britain's export trade and markets also worked to her disadvantage. Britain specialized in exporting staple products to primary producers. The effect of this was twofold. Britain was hit severely by industrialization in these countries, while the tendency for the incomes of primary producers to sag in the later 1920s as a result of falling commodity prices, reduced the propensity of these countries to import British goods.

Given this set of unfavourable circumstances a vigorous export-led boom was hardly to be expected. But the failure of the economy to generate a strong boom in the later 1920s cannot simply be explained in terms of exports. A reference to American conditions is instructive at this point. During the 1920s and especially in the latter half, there was a vigorous investment and consumption boom in the United States which was based to a great extent on construction, services, transport and the newer industries. But in Britain these primarily domestically based industries were much less buoyant. The rise in investment was very modest, especially after 1927, while many of the potential growth industries exerted only a moderate impact on the economy. Building, for example, collapsed in 1927–8 as a result of the cut-back in the subsidy programme and over the years 1926–9 there was a negative rate of growth in construction. Most of the service industries, including transport and distribution, only recorded modest rates of expansion, while the rate of growth of some of the newer industries, electricity, electrical engineering and vehicles in particular, was no greater than the average for all industry and considerably lower than in the first half of the 1920s.

Whatever the causes of the weak boom in Britain there is little doubt that it helped to soften the impact of the subsequent depression. The economy did not overshoot itself leaving exhausted sectors in its wake as in America, so that the chances of early recovery were greater than in the latter case. It is generally assumed that the downturn itself originated in the United States and was transmitted to other countries via foreign trade. But in the case of Britain there is some doubt as to whether the initial impulse actually came from this direction. There could well have been a recession in Britain irrespective of what was happening in America. The crucial factor was Britain's export vulnerability, and more particularly the dependence on primary producing markets. As we have seen, the incomes of primary producing countries began to fall in the late 1920s and the turning point in the demand for British exports from South America, British India, the British Colonies, the Far East and South Africa, which absorbed some 40 per cent of British exports, occurred in the latter half of 1928. This naturally exerted a deflationary impact on the British economy. The United States also experienced similar forces though not to the same extent as the u.k.[1] Thus signs of impending recession were already evident some six to nine months or more before the collapse of the American economy.

The subsequent American crash greatly aggravated and accelerated the deflationary tendencies in Britain. The detailed causes of the u.s. downturn need not be repeated here.[2] Briefly it was a reaction to the violent boom of the 1920s which resulted in a drying up of investment opportunities. The position was made worse by the excessive speculation of the late 1920s which eventually led to the famous Stock Market crash of October 1929. Since America was such an important element in the world economy other countries were soon affected by its repercussions. American import demand fell off sharply and this served to depress prices and incomes in exporting countries, particularly the primary producers which accounted for around one half of the American import bill. This in turn created balance of payments problems in these countries and reduced their ability to import from industrial nations including Britain. At the same time the flow of American credit was curtailed and this created problems for debtor countries, especially in central and eastern Europe whose post-war

[1] D. C. Corner, 'Exports and the British Trade Cycle', *Manchester School*, 24 (1956), pp. 132–6.
[2] See R. A. Gordon, *Business Fluctuations* (1952), ch. 13.

reconstruction had been financed partly on the basis of short-term capital inflows. This resulted in further balance of payments problems which eventually led to the international liquidity crisis of 1931. Thus the impact of the American crisis internationally was aggravated by the weak financial position of many primary producers and central European countries.[1] In other words, given the widespread ramifications of the American economy coupled with the instability and weak financial position of many countries in the 1920s, it was almost inevitable that a slump of international dimensions and unparalleled severity would occur in the early 1930s.

In comparison with the experience of most other countries the depression in Britain was mild. For instance, the United States suffered declines of 37, 36, and 31 per cent in real income, industrial production and employment respectively, whereas the corresponding figures for Britain were 0·8, 11 and 4·7 per cent. Only in two respects, namely the decline in wholesale prices and the percentage unemployment at the bottom of the depression, did Britain fare as badly as the United States. Few countries suffered as badly as America but then again few could match the relative mildness of the British recession. Real income in Germany fell by 25 per cent, in France by 12 per cent, in Sweden by eight per cent, and in Australia by two per cent. Virtually the only country to emerge unscathed was Japan.

In view of the export-orientated nature of the British economy and the international nature of the slump it was only to be expected that the external account would be the most severely affected. The volume of exports fell by 37·5 per cent between 1929 and 1932, though even this appears moderate compared with the 30-per-cent fall in the single year of 1921. Income from foreign investment and services fell quite sharply whereas imports held up, with the result that the balance of payments deteriorated from an overall surplus of £103 million in 1929 to a deficit of £104 million in 1931. One or two other indicators registered large adverse swings. Domestic investment fell by just over 14 per cent, though most of the decline occurred in the last year of depression. The worst feature of the British depression was the unemployment. This rose from a low of 1,193,000 (9·5 per cent of the insured population) in the second quarter of 1929 to almost three million (22·7 per cent) in the third quarter of

[1] The international financial aspects of the depression are discussed in more detail in Chapter 8.

1932. Prices also fell dramatically, especially wholesale prices which declined by over one quarter.

But these indicators give a rather one-sided picture of the dimensions of the depression. Unemployment was exceptionally high but it appears rather different when set against the modest fall of 4·7 per cent in total employment. Most other indicators reveal quite a different picture. The fall in real incomes and domestic output was less than 5 per cent, while consumers' expenditure fell only in the last year of the depression and actually increased by 1·8 per cent over the period taken as a whole (1929–32). Even industrial production declined by much less than it had done in 1921.

There were, of course, considerable variations in the amplitude and timing of the swings between different sectors. Industrial production and transport and communication declined by 11 per cent and 8·7 per cent respectively, while output of services and distribution increased slightly. Export sensitive industries tended to be first in and last out of depression, whereas consumer goods industries (especially those producing non-durables) lagged at the upper turning point and responded early in the recovery phase. Producer goods industries, on the other hand, lagged at both turning points and experienced larger swings. Thus by far the largest downswings were recorded in non-ferrous and ferrous metals, mechanical engineering and shipbuilding, whereas the movements in chemicals, tobacco and textiles were quite modest. In some industries the depression was very limited indeed, being confined to one year only. Electrical engineering for example, declined in 1931 but over the course of the downswing its output actually increased. Electricity, paper and printing, and food experienced no proper depression and in all cases output rose between 1929–32. In clothing there was only a very small drop in production while the leather industry recorded a significant increase in output partly because there had been a check to production a year before the slump.

Just as the weakness of the boom in the later 1920s helped to insulate the economy from the full impact of the slump, so the relative mildness of the depression paved the way for an early and vigorous recovery. Business confidence was not completely shattered in Britain as was the case in America and Germany, and any loss of confidence was partly restored by the Government measures of 1931–2, including abandonment of gold and the depreciation of the currency, the imposition of tariff protection, the conversion to cheap money and action designed to curtail public expenditure and balance the budget. Secondly, there was no lack of investment opportunities for business-men once revival began. Investment outlets had not been exhausted in the previous decade as they had been in America. The belated de-velopment of the newer industries and the shortage of housing in par-ticular meant that there was plenty of scope for vigorous growth in the 1930s, despite the drying up of opportunities in the basic export-orientated industries. A further factor of some importance was the very high floor to income and consumption at the bottom of depres-sion. In fact consumption only fell in the final year and over the course of the depression it actually rose. The level of consumption was main-tained principally by three forces: a substantial increase in the real incomes of wage earners largely as a result of the improvement in the terms of trade, a shift in the distribution of income in favour of wage earning groups, and an overall increase in the average propensity to consume.

Although the main force of the depression had been spent by the end of 1931 it was not until the latter half of 1932 that recovery really began to take hold. Unemployment reached a peak in the third quarter of that year and most economic indicators continued to de-cline until late in 1932. The lower turning point probably occurred in the third quarter of 1932 since by the last quarter economic activity had definitely begun to improve.[1] During the course of the following year most economic indices except retail prices rose, and there can be little doubt that 1933 was the first full year of recovery. It is true that there were signs of revival in some of the export-sensitive industries such as textiles during 1931, especially after the devaluation of the currency. But this was a very limited affair and in no sense could it be argued that export-led growth was the key to recovery. The volume of exports remained stable in 1932 and increased by only just over one per cent in the following year, while many of the heavy export industries such as mining, shipbuilding and mechanical engineering remained depressed. Rather, the first real thrust to recovery came largely from non-export sectors such as building and related trades, transport, electricity and the newer manufacturing trades such as vehicles. By 1934 sustained growth had extended to most sectors of the economy though it tended to be most vigorous in the new and domestically based industries and least prominent in the old staples.

[1] League of Nations, *World Economic Survey, 1932–3* (1933). The beginnings of recovery were somewhat earlier in Britain than in most other countries.

Nevertheless, exports picked up smartly in 1934 and 1935 and this helped to revive the older industries. Investment also increased sharply in 1934 when the largest increase of the inter-war years was recorded. The recovery in employment was more modest and by the end of 1934 there were still over two million or nearly 16 per cent of the insured population out of work.

During the course of the next three years the pace of recovery continued practically unchecked. Virtually all industries expanded though the boom was primarily a domestic one, the leading sectors being construction, transport (more especially road transport), the newer industries (e.g. vehicles and electricity) and certain capital goods industries. Most non-durable consumer goods industries and services also grew but their rate of expansion was below the general average, while the rate of growth in agriculture was very low indeed. Exports continued to increase though they remained well below the pre-depression level even by 1937. The progress of recovery in the middle of the 1930s was assisted by the revival of the world economy and the beginning of rearmament.

By 1937, therefore, the record of achievement was considerable. Since 1932 real income had increased by 19 per cent, domestic output by over 25 per cent, industrial production by nearly 46 per cent, gross investment by 47 per cent, and even exports by 28·4 per cent. Moreover, in absolute terms the level of economic activity was far higher than it had been in 1929 and 1913. In fact these years witnessed the largest and most sustained period of growth in the whole of the inter-war period. Yet despite the considerable increase in activity employment rose by less than 17 per cent which suggests that the recovery was accompanied by a steady increase in productivity. As a result unemployment did not fall as far as might be expected. Even at the peak of the boom (third quarter of 1937) it was as high as 1·4 million, that is about 9·1 per cent of the insured population. However, it is important to note that the greater part of this consisted of structural unemployment and that most of the cyclical unemployment had been eliminated.

By the middle of 1937 there were signs that the boom was coming to an end. The rate of growth of income and production slowed down during the course of the year and consumption was restricted by the unfavourable trend in real wages.[1] The boom was reflected in rising prices and costs, a trend accentuated by the pressure on inter-

[1] Real wages were stable in 1934–6, and declined in the next year.

national commodity prices. Wholesale prices, for example, rose by no less than 15 per cent in 1937. Moreover, in some areas and trades shortages of labour were becoming apparent despite the high overall level of unemployment. There were indications, too, of a temporary drying up of investment opportunities. These unfavourable signs, coming as they did after nearly five years of uninterrupted growth, were bound to dampen optimism. Thus some check to growth was probably inevitable, though the position was aggravated by a sharp downswing in exports in 1937–8.[1] Even so the recession was relatively mild and short-lived. Industrial production and domestic output declined by only one or two per cent, while real incomes and consumption continued to increase. The favourable shift in the terms of trade in 1938 was mainly responsible for this contrary trend in incomes and consumption. Few industries suffered a sharp decline in activity except for those dependent on exports such as shipbuilding, textiles and ferrous metals.[2] By the beginning of 1939 the economy had resumed its upward trend and was backed by rearmament and later war.

From this brief sketch of inter-war cyclical history[3] a number of general points of interest emerge. Of the two components of the national income, that is consumption and investment, swings in the latter were by far the more pronounced. Movements in consumption were quite small by comparison and quite often acted in a stabilizing manner in depressions. This, of course, is much as one would expect. Secondly, swings in the main branches of activity, agriculture, industry and services, varied a great deal in magnitude. By far the most volatile element was industrial production whereas the amplitude of the swings in services was usually quite moderate. But overall the most volatile element was unquestionably exports.

Several other points might be mentioned. The leading and lagging sectors at the turning points conform to the pattern expected, though a precise delineation of these would require a detailed analysis of monthly or quarterly data. Apart from the fact that this is not avail-

[1] Richardson maintains that the recession (which started in the autumn of 1937) was due as much to internal causes as to the downswing in activity in the United States. H. W. Richardson, 'The Economic Significance of the Depression in Britain', *Journal of Contemporary History*, 4 (1969), pp. 7–8.
[2] The main exception here was leather, which declined by 12·6 per cent between 1937–8.
[3] A more detailed blow by blow account of the 1930s can be found in H. W. Richardson, *Economic Recovery in Britain, 1932–39* (1967).

able for many series the process of analysis would be too lengthy to attempt here. Profits on the whole tended to move fairly closely with the cycle. On the other hand, changes in employment are only of limited value in charting swings in economic activity. This is especially true of the downswings when declines in employment appear quite modest compared with the changes in unemployment and output.[1] But it is also true of the upswings because of productivity improvements. But the least reliable indicator of all is price data. If the analysis was based solely on prices one would be forced to conclude that the economy was in a state of almost permanent depression between 1921 and 1933. Clearly however, the prolonged fall in prices was determined by external events rather than by the level of domestic activity and hence they do not provide a very good guide to swings in activity.

We cannot hope to survey all the interesting aspects of cyclical change in this chapter. In any case some of these are covered in other chapters. Movements in consumption and real wages are treated in the last chapter, while international aspects are discussed more fully in Chapter 8. Similarly, monetary and fiscal policies (together with public investment) over the course of the cycle are more conveniently analysed under economic management. Here we propose to examine the more volatile elements, namely industrial production, exports, and investment, in order to establish the behaviour of their movements and their influence on cyclical fluctuations.

Industrial analysis

The amplitude of swings in industrial production was greater than that of any other component barring exports. Since the industrial production index does not include services and transport which are less sensitive to cyclical fluctuations, one would expect it to be more volatile than total output or income. On the other hand, the index is a composite of a wide range of industries ranging from heavy producer goods to industries whose output is for immediate consumption. One would expect to see, therefore, considerable variation in the amplitude of swings between industries. It should be obvious, for instance, that industries as far apart as food and shipbuilding will behave

[1] It should be noted, of course, that the contrast between the movements in employment and unemployment is magnified by the different bases on which the changes are calculated and the different coverage of the figures.

somewhat differently over the course of the cycle. Some of these differences are worth examining in more detail.

To do this we have taken the output series for individual industries (using the Lomax indices) and calculated their swings over each phase of the cycle. For this purpose we have ignored the very minor and partial recessions of 1919 and 1927–8, but have included the contraction of 1925–6 since this was more severe than that of 1937–8. This then gives us four upswings, 1918–20, 1921–5, 1926–9 and 1932–7, and four downswings, 1920–1, 1925–6, 1929-32, and 1937–8. These reference cycle phases are determined by the movements in the aggregate production index. Since the latter is on an annual basis it is not possible to pinpoint the turning points precisely, but for the purposes of the investigation at hand this is not a serious defect. More problematical is the fact that not all industries peaked and troughed at the same date even on an annual basis. In fact, in the 1920s in particular, there were considerable variations in the timing of the turning points of some industries. For example, the downswing in the middle of the decade lasted two years (1924–6) rather than one (1925–6) in the case of ferrous metals, shipbuilding, mining and quarrying and chemicals. During the subsequent upswing (1926–9) a number of industries behaved erratically; three industries, timber, electrical engineering and tobacco, continued their expansion into 1930; another seven industries, building materials, building and contracting, ferrous metals, shipbuilding, vehicles, textiles and mining, experienced a temporary relapse between 1927–8;[1] while in leather and non-ferrous metals the boom appears to have petered out by 1929. Similar variations also occurred during the long downswing of 1929–32. Some industries lagged behind at the upper turning point, e.g. timber, electrical engineering and tobacco, while others, notably ferrous metals, chemicals and electrical engineering, began to revive before the end of the depression. For the rest of the period however most industries conformed fairly closely to movements in the aggregate index. Finally, one or two industries had their own individual cycles, more particularly in the 1920s. Textiles, for instance, behaved very erratically, output fluctuating in almost every year. The swings in building and contracting were also erratic though more prolonged than those in the textile

[1] The main setback was in construction which was mainly responsible for the decline in the index of industrial production. Manufacturing output, on the other hand, remained stable.

TABLE 9   *Percentage swings in individual industries over phases of the cycle*

	1918–20	1920–1	1921–5	1925–6	1926–9	1929–32	1932–7	1937–8	Number of times swings occurred above (A), below (B) or contrary (x), to the general trend
All industry	+22·4	−18·6	+41·4	−5·3	+17·6	−10·9	+45·8	−2·7	—
1. Industries in which above average swings predominated									
Shipbuilding	− 7·1	−19·3	−43·9	−24·8	+108·5	−89·7	+924·5	−18·1	7A, 1x
Ferrous metals	+ 4·8	−53·2	+96·9	−36·2	+83·0	−28·4	+96·7	−19·5	7A, 1B
Non-ferrous metals	−40·8	−38·8	+121·9	− 6·7	+13·6	−27·2	+116·6	− 6·0	6A, 1B, 1x
Mechanical engineering	−17·1	−34·3	+81·8	−12·5	+21·3	−36·0	+65·4	+ 1·7	6A, 2x
Mining and quarrying	+ 2·1	−28·3	+49·4	−44·6	+94·1	−18·7	+18·4	− 4·9	6A, 2B
Timber	+72·0	− 7·1	+60·5	+ 4·8	+27·0	−15·2	+52·8	− 3·3	6A, 1B, 1x
Vehicles	+75·1	−12·9	+71·6	+ 5·1	+17·8	−20·2	+107·9	+ 1·6	5A, 1B, 2x
Metal goods, n.e.s.		−38·0	+48·9	+ 1·5	+15·0	−12·2	+67·4	− 1·1	4A, 2B, 1x
Building and contracting	+218·3	+38·5	+39·3	−14·0	− 4·2	−17·6	+53·2	− 4·1	4A, 1B, 3x

2. Industries in which below average swings predominated

Clothing	+13·4	+ 7·0	+20·1	+1·4	+ 9·0	− 1·1	+16·1	− 1·1	6B, 2x
Textiles	+14·2	−32·7	+38·8	−3·8	+ 0·4	− 0·2	+27·9	−10·0	6B, 2A
Electrical engineering	+ 2·8	−14·5	+40·8	−8·5	+14·1	+ 4·9	+73·7	− 1·6	5B, 2A, 1x
Drink	+57·4	−11·8	− 2·6	−3·7	+ 2·9	−20·8	+38·2	+ 3·1	4B, 2A, 2x
Tobacco	+30·8	− 8·4	+ 7·3	+3·5	+19·8	− 8·8	+31·2	+ 2·3	4B, 2A, 2x
Food	+28·1	− 4·0	+20·8	+2·6	+11·0	+11·3	+24·8	+ 2·8	4B, 1A, 3x

3. Industries in which below average and contrary swings predominated

Gas, water & electricity	+ 1·3	− 8·5	+27·2	+3·9	+19·6	+ 7·2	+48·6	+ 3·6	3B, 3x, 2A
Leather	−42·0	−16·1	+55·9	−3·4	− 1·4	+ 9·3	+22·1	−12·6	3B, 3x, 2A
Paper and printing	+169·1	−51·8	+91·7	+3·5	+10·3	+ 4·7	+10·9	− 0·8	3B, 2x, 3A
Precision instruments	—	− 9·4	+17·5	+3·7	+18·9	−14·0	+39·1	+ 2·6	3B, 2x, 2A

4. Industries with no clear pattern

Chemicals	+ 8·6	−28·0	+32·4	−7·2	+26·1	− 2·8	+36·3	− 5·2	4A, 4B
Building materials	—	− 3·2	+34·7	+2·1	+10·2	−13·5	+62·3	− 6·2	3A, 3B, 1x

industry. Expansions occurred between 1918–21 and 1923–27 with corresponding contractions in 1921–3 and 1927–9.

To have taken account of all these individual peculiarities would have made the analysis rather complex. To avoid this it was felt advisable to date the cyclical phases of each individual category on the same basis as the swings for the overall index. The main effect of this is to dampen the magnitude of the swings in those industries which do not conform to the general pattern but the differences remain all the same.

In Table 9, 21 industries have been classified into four main groups corresponding to the degree to which above or below-average swings predominated. The grouping is occasionally slightly arbitrary, while the industrial breakdown is not as detailed as one might wish. Nevertheless, the results show quite clearly the different pattern of behaviour between capital and consumer goods industries. Nine of the 21 industries fall into the first category with above-average swings predominating; no less than seven of these industries had five or more above-average swings out of the total of eight phases. Only half the swings were above average in the remaining two industries, metal goods and building, the latter being something of an exception because of its own peculiar phasing in the 1920s. Apart perhaps from timber, all the industries in this group were the type one would expect to fluctuate violently, that is they were capital goods industries and/or export-sensitive, or as in the case of vehicles the output was a consumer durable.

The second group consists of industries in which below-average swings were prominent. Here there were only six industries and in three of these, drink, tobacco and food, swings below the average occurred in only four of the eight phases. The largest number of below-average swings was in clothing and textiles with six each, though the latter category is not altogether representative owing to its rather heterogeneous composition and the fact that it tended to maintain a cyclical phasing of its own during the 1920s. Nevertheless, it should be noted that, with the possible exception of electrical engineering, all these trades produced articles for immediate consumption. The third group of four industries showed no very distinct pattern though there was a predominance of below-average and contrary swings. This was especially the case in electricity and leather where in only two of the eight phases were above-average swings recorded. Again the industries in this group produced mainly consumption goods or services the main exception being precision instruments. Finally, two industries, chemicals and building materials, had no real pattern at all since above- and below-average swings were fairly evenly distributed. It is perhaps significant, however, that both industries produced intermediate goods.

The results of the above analysis confirm the hypothesis that in general capital goods industries experience more pronounced fluctuations than those producing consumer goods. A firm breakdown into durable and non-durable consumer goods industries is not really practicable with the data available though it does appear that non-durable consumption goods industries tended to fluctuate less violently than consumer durable producers such as vehicles. It is noticeable, too, that contrary swings were most prevalent in the consumer goods industries though in no single industry did such swings predominate. Moreover, fluctuations against the general cyclical trend occurred most frequently during downswings, especially in minor recessions. Between 1925–6, 10 of the 21 industries recorded contrary swings, while in 1937–8 there were seven.[1] Most of the industries acting in a stabilizing manner in depression were consumer-orientated. During recovery periods the number of industries with above- and below-average swings were fairly evenly matched and there were few contrary swings. All industries without exception expanded in the recovery of the 1930s, while in the expansions of 1921–5 and 1926–9 only two industries experienced a decline in output. Only between 1918 and 1920 were there as many as four contrary swings in one expansion, though this is something of an exception because of the excessive war-time expansion of the industries concerned.

It does not follow of course that those industries which fluctuated violently also experienced the fastest rates of growth (that is measured from peak to peak), or conversely, that industries with swings of low amplitude grew slowly. If this were the case then shipbuilding with a 942 per cent increase in output during the recovery of the 1930s should have registered a very high rate of growth between 1929 and 1937. In actual fact, it had one of the lowest rates of output expansion while employment in the industry fell by 13 per cent over the full cycle. The explanation is quite simple. The very high rate of expansion during 1932–7 was a reflection of the very low level of output attained in 1932 as a result of the depth of the previous downswing. The same also applies to mechanical engineering and mining both of

[1] But only two in 1921 and five between 1929–32.

which had wide fluctuations but grew very slowly between 1929–37 (in fact output and employment in mining actually declined). On the other hand, some industries with wide fluctuations, such as vehicles and non-ferrous metals, expanded very rapidly from peak to peak of the cycle. Conversely, electrical engineering and food manufacture, both of which experienced swings below average, recorded quite high rates of growth. In other words, the degree of fluctuation offers no precise guide as to the strength of growth over the cycle as a whole. As Richardson has noted,[1] the only general conclusions that can be drawn is that industries with cycles of average amplitude tended to experience average rates of expansion, while those industries which fluctuated sharply or those which remained relatively stable showed no definite growth trends one way or another.

Finally a few contents must be made about the leads and lags at the turning points. An analysis of monthly employment data made by Phelps Brown and Shackle tends to confirm the points made earlier in this chapter. At the turning points of 1929 and 1937 export-sensitive trades led in both cases while producer goods industries were about the last to turn down. However, consumer goods industries behaved somewhat erratically. Consumer durables followed the export industries in 1929 but were later than producer durables in 1937, while non-durable consumer goods lagged in 1929 but turned down early in 1937. The order of the timing at the lower point was roughly what one might expect: consumer non-durables, export-sensitive, consumer durables and producer goods – in that order, though the placing of the export-sensitive industries is open to question because of the temporary and partial nature of the revival in this case.[2]

There is nothing to be gained by repeating the analysis again and these conclusions may be allowed to stand. Doubt, however, should be expressed as to whether employment data provide a really reliable indicator for this purpose. Unfortunately there are no monthly or quarterly statistics of industrial production which would allow us to test the findings in detail. The annual data can be used for a rough check at least for the downswing of 1929–32. The industries in the van of the downturn covered all types and included building and building materials, chemicals, ferrous and non-ferrous metals, mech-

---

[1] Richardson, *op. cit.*, p. 74.
[2] E. H. Phelps Brown and G. L. S. Shackle, 'British Economic Fluctuations, 1924–38', *Oxford Economic Papers*, 2 (1939).

anical engineering, shipbuilding, vehicles, precision instruments, metal goods (n.e.s.), textiles and mining. On the other hand, the output of a good many consumer goods and service industries (including food, tobacco, paper and printing, clothing, drink, leather and electricity) either remained stable or even increased their output in 1930. Most industries turned down in 1931 including the consumer goods industries which had held up in the previous year. The main exceptions were food, electricity and textiles, the latter staging a partial and somewhat premature revival. Although the overall production index declined in 1932 (though very slightly indeed) recovery was under way in many industries but predominantly in consumer goods and new industries viz: – chemicals, electricity, electrical engineering, tobacco, paper and printing, leather, food, textiles, ferrous metal manufacture and metal goods. The chief consumer durable goods industry, vehicles, did not respond until 1933, while some of the heavy producer goods and/or export-sensitive industries, e.g. shipbuilding, mechanical engineering and mining, hardly experienced much recovery before 1934.

The absence of anything but annual data makes it difficult to say anything about other turning points in view of the fairly short duration of downswings. However, it does appear that a number of heavy trades lagged behind in the revival after the 1921 slump, while in the downturn of the late 1930s the pace was set by producer durables and export-sensitive industries. By contrast, many consumer trades, both durable and non-durable, experienced no recession in 1938 (e.g. vehicles, drink, food, tobacco, electricity all continued to expand).

It would be rash to draw very firm conclusions from these comments though some tentative suggestions can be made. Producer goods industries and consumer durables do appear to have lagged at the lower turning points. On the other hand, they did not lag behind at the peak. If anything they may well have led though the range of industries affected at roughly the same time was fairly wide. Consumer non-durable goods (and service industries) generally remained buoyant in the early phase of the downswing. These industries also experienced early recovery but they were by no means alone in this respect. As far as we can tell from the production data, export-sensitive industries led at the upper turning points but it does not appear that exports led out of recessions. It is to this aspect that we now turn.

Exports and the cycle

Many writers have emphasized the importance of exports in economic fluctuations. Attention has been drawn to the fact they are more volatile than other sectors of the economy and that export-sensitive industries tend to lead in and out of depressions.[1] These inferences are based mainly on nineteenth and early twentieth century experience though attempts have been made to extend the analysis into the interwar period.[2] There are obvious reasons why exports were a source of instability before 1914. Exports constituted a large share of the national product – over one fifth of net national income by 1913 – and many of the staple industries such as textiles, shipbuilding and coal, were heavily dependent on export markets. Thus with the increasing international scope of the business cycle and the tendency for British cycles to synchronize closely with those of other countries it was inevitable, given the open nature of the economy, that exports would be particularly vulnerable to changes in the level of economic activity abroad. In addition, the heavy flow of foreign investment and the repercussions of its fluctuations on the demand for British exports also contributed to the instability of the export component.[3] A further relevant fact was the commodity composition and destination of British exports. A considerable proportion of them consisted of capital goods, while the chief markets were the primary producers. Since the demand for capital goods tended to fluctuate more violently than that for consumer goods and the incomes of primary producers fluctuated more wildly than those of industrial countries, it is not surprising that the amplitude of trade fluctuations was correspondingly large.

Although the relative importance of exports varied somewhat from cycle to cycle it is generally true to say that export fluctuations were quite sharp before 1914 and that they often led at the turning points

[1] See, for instance, W. W. Rostow, *British Economy of the Nineteenth Century* (1948); W. H. Beveridge, *Full Employment in a Free Society* (1944). For a more recent analysis see A. G. Ford, 'British Economic Fluctuations, 1870–1914', *The Manchester School,* June 1969.

[2] W. H. Beveridge, 'Unemployment and the Trade Cycle', *Economic Journal* 49 (1939); Phelps Brown and Shackle, *loc. cit.*

[3] The detailed relationships between investment and exports cannot be explored here. Suffice it to say that the turning points in new overseas issues tended to lead export turning points by up to one year or more. See Ford, *loc. cit.*, p. 117.

of the cycle. Several conflicting forces operated to disturb this pattern in the inter-war years. Reasons can be advanced for expecting exports to play a more prominent role in cyclical fluctuations. For one thing the amplitude of export fluctuations tended to increase in the inter-war period especially in the 1920s and early 1930s. The downswings in particular were very severe. Before the war the volume of exports had rarely fallen by more than 10 per cent in any one recession and the average swing was just over seven per cent (1872–1908).[1] After 1918 the mildest downturn was around 10 per cent (1925–6) while the declines recorded in 1921, 1929–32 and 1937–8 were of the order of 30, 37·5 and 11·5 per cent respectively.[2] Moreover, the amplitude of British export fluctuations was greater than that of world trade as a whole.[3] Secondly, and related to the first point, the increasing importance of capital goods exports (partly as a result of industrial development in newer countries leading to import substitution in consumer goods such as textiles) and the continued reliance on the markets of primary producers whose incomes fluctuated more violently than before the war, tended to make British exports more vulnerable to external events. Thirdly, the closer synchronization between British and u.s. cycles than compared with before the war probably increased the cyclical sensitivity of exports given the rather unstable nature of the American economy. This last point is particularly relevant to the downturn of 1929.

On the other hand, the fact that the instability of exports increased in the inter-war years does not necessarily mean that they dominated the cycle either at the turning points or during the phases of recovery and recession. The impact of export fluctuations was weakened in several ways. First, the importance of exports in the economy declined considerably in this period; from a net national income share of over 23 per cent in 1913 they declined to 17·6 per cent in 1929 and 9·8 per cent in 1938. The newer industries in particular were much less dependent on the vagaries of export demand than the old

[1] F. V. Meyer and W. A. Lewis, 'The Effects of an Overseas Slump on the British Economy', *The Manchester School*, 17 (1949), pp. 235, 241.
[2] Even if we take the change in export volumes from trough to peak as a percentage of the previous peak the amplitude of export fluctuations is still greater in the 1920s though somewhat lower in the 1930s than pre-war. See D. H. Aldcroft and H. W. Richardson, *The British Economy, 1870–1939* (1969), p. 30.
[3] For example, between 1929 and 1932 the volume of world trade declined by about 27 per cent compared with a fall of over 37 per cent in British export volumes. League of Nations, *World Economic Survey, 1932–3* (1933), p. 213.

staples. Secondly, the slower growth in world trade and the overall stagnation in British exports would seem to provide limited scope for exports to exercise a crucial role in fluctuations particularly in recovery periods. Thirdly, the former links between foreign investment and exports were weakened in the 1920s and broken altogether in the 1930s when capital exports ceased. In other words, the declining importance of the foreign trade sector and the concomitant increase in the importance of the home market would appear to indicate that domestic forces had a greater part to play in fluctuations than was previously the case. The fact that the amplitude, though not the timing, of British cycles varied considerably from those of world cycles would appear to lend additional support to this conclusion. Compared with most other countries Britain experienced a sharper boom and slump in 1919–20 and 1921, a more limited recovery especially in the later 1920s, a milder depression in 1929–32, a more vigorous recovery in the 1930s and a weaker recession in 1937–8.

On balance, the above arguments seem to favour a modification of the former role of exports in fluctuations. But the facts must speak for themselves. For the following analysis we have compared movements of exports with those of manufacturing output, rather than industrial production or national income, since it was this sector that was most directly affected by export fluctuations. The accompanying graph (Figure 1) seems to suggest a fairly close similarity between movements in manufacturing output and exports. On closer inspection however, it can be seen that the association was stronger in the 1920s than in the following decade. In 1920–1, 1921–5 and to a lesser extent in 1926–9 large swings in exports gave rise to correspondingly large swings in output (see Table 8). After 1929 the association was much less close. Between 1929 and 1932 exports declined by no less than 37.5 per cent compared with a mere 10-per-cent fall in manufacturing output. This may be compared with declines of 30 and 22 per cent respectively in 1921. Clearly in the later depression the export sector had lost much of its force as a determinant of changes in production. Similarly, in the subsequent recovery exports played a modest role. They were late to recover and grew very much more slowly than manufacturing between 1932 and 1937. The contraction in exports in 1938 also had a very small impact on output.

Taking the period as a whole, it appears that export fluctuations were greater than those for manufacturing output in every phase of the cycle apart from the recovery of 1932–7. In general they played

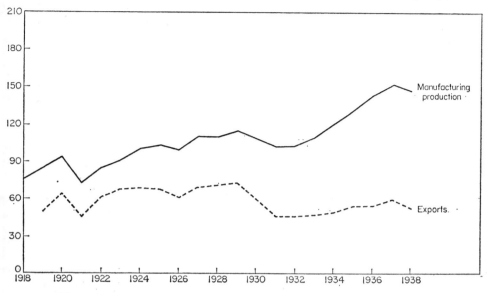

Figure 1   Manufacturing production and the volume of exports, 1918–38

a greater role in depressions than in recoveries from the troughs, though their influence was weaker in 1929–32 and 1937–8 than it had been in 1921 and 1926 (see Table 8). In every recession export swings were larger than those in manufacturing, while they tended to lead other indicators at the upper turning points. The position as regards the recovery phases is less equivocal. They were certainly not crucial in the upswing of the 1930s either at the turning point or through sustained recovery. Exports did not rise appreciably until 1934[1] and the overall increase of 28·4 per cent was quite modest compared with the 48-per-cent increase in manufacturing output. This is consistent with the lessened influence of the old export staples and a domestically based recovery. But for the 1920s the evidence is less clearcut. Between 1921–5 and again in 1926–9 exports rose more rapidly than output, while in the first year of revival in each case (1922 and 1927) there was a steep rise in exports – in fact by as much as 38·4 per cent in 1922 compared with only 14·1 per cent in manufacturing.[2] Yet

[1] The weak and limited revival in exports in 1931 after devaluation was largely abortive in terms of recovery.
[2] In 1927 the increases in exports and manufacturing were fairly similar.

in the first few months of recovery in both cases they lagged behind the upturn in activity while in the later phase of recovery (that is after the first year) export growth flattened out. Thus, although exports did not dominate the recoveries of the 1920s they do appear to have imparted a boost in the first year of the upswings.

The above findings are consistent with the view that the impact of export fluctuations weakened during the course of the period under review. Income and total output were much less affected by export fluctuations than manufacturing output. This of course was only to be expected since these aggregate indicators included large sectors, e.g. transport and services, which were not directly affected by exports and which displayed greater stability through the cycle. Moreover, fluctuations in income were dampened, especially in recessions, by the high floor to consumption and the favourable price trends resulting from improvements in the terms of trade.

The role of investment

As a result of recent work, notably by Dr C. H. Feinstein, it is now possible to analyse in some detail the pattern of investment over the course of the cycle.[1] The discussion in this chapter will be concerned with domestic investment as a whole and the distinction between public and private investment left over until Chapter 9. No account will be taken of foreign investment since this dwindled in importance throughout the period. The share of national income going overseas was quite small after 1923 and by the 1930s there was a net capital inflow into Britain. Even in the peak year of 1920, foreign investment accounted for less than four per cent of GNP as against 9·1 per cent for domestic investment, while in 1930, the last year with a positive outflow, it was a mere 0·6 per cent of GNP. This was in marked contrast to the immediate pre-war period when in many years the share of foreign investment had exceeded domestic investment.[2] Thus for most of this period foreign investment played a negligible role in the generation of fluctuations.

An analysis of investment is justified for at least two reasons. First, fluctuations in investment were greater than those in consump-

[1] C. H. Feinstein, *Domestic Capital Formation in the United Kingdom, 1920–1938* (1965). All the investment figures used in this section are drawn from this source.
[2] Phyllis Deane and W. A. Cole, *British Economic Growth, 1688–1959: Trends and Structure* (1962), p. 333.

tion and total income. Secondly, the timing of investment cycles tended to differ somewhat from that of other aggregate indicators. The unstable nature of investment can be seen from Table 8. In the upswings of 1921–5 and 1932–7 gross domestic investment rose at a much faster rate than income and consumption, while in the depression of 1929–32 it fell by 14·1 per cent but real income only fell very slightly and consumption actually rose. The fact that investment tended to lag at both turning points meant that in some years it moved against the cycle. At the beginning of the period investment peaked in 1921, the year of depression, while in 1922, when recovery had begun, it fell by 7·8 per cent. Even in 1923 there was only a very small increase and the really big upsurge in investment came in 1924 and 1925. During the next four years investment conformed quite closely to the cyclical pattern both in timing and amplitude. After 1929 there was a return to the earlier pattern. In 1930 there was a small increase in investment and only a modest fall in the following year. The really sharp cut-back came in 1932, that is when the rate of decline in most other sectors was either slowing down or in the process of being reversed. The first full year of recovery (1933) was accompanied by only a very small increase in investment, but in 1934 it rose by 21·6 per cent, the largest increase recorded in any one year. Thereafter it continued to rise through to 1938 though at a much reduced rate.

Though the greater volatility of investment undoubtedly increased the overall amplitude of fluctuations in the economy as a whole, there is much less justification for regarding it as a determining force at the turning points. If anything it exercised a stabilizing influence in the early phases of depressions or in short recessions, but because of its lagged reaction it could prolong a recession or delay recovery. This could lead to a situation in which the roles of consumption and investment in income fluctuations were reversed. In 1921, for instance, investment (rising by 14·6 per cent) was clearly a strong stabilizing force and it was the unusually large drop in consumption (5·4 per cent) which was directly responsible for the check to real income.[1] In

---

[1] The experience of 1921 may be considered by some to be exceptional because of the delayed reaction of the building sector following from government intervention in the housing market. But this was not the only sector in which investment increased. Investment in plant and machinery rose very sharply in 1921, while the check to investment in 1922 cannot be attributed primarily to the collapse of house construction.

the following year there was a sharp fall in investment and this prolonged the depression in income despite the recovery of consumption.[1]
Again in 1929–30 and 1937–8 (but not 1925–6) investment held up
at the turning points though in both cases the rate of increase slackened.
In fact in the 1929–32 depression investment did not fall dramatically
until the last year, a fact which no doubt helped to make 1932 a
year of depression rather than one of recovery.

Clearly then, the idea that investment plays a decisive role in fluctuations needs to be modified in the light of the above considerations.
This is not necessarily inconsistent with the view that investment
lags at the turning points are important in determining the nature of
fluctuations or that investment fluctuations accentuate the amplitude of cyclical movements in income. Nor are the lags in investment
especially difficult to explain. Most investment projects have a long
gestation period and so investment started at the top of the boom may
well spill over into the downswing of the cycle. Moreover, businessmen may be reluctant to cut back on investment at the first hint of
recession especially if it is expected to be temporary. Some manufacturers may take advantage of falling capital costs to renew plant in preparation for the subsequent upswing. At the trough the explanation
of the lag is more straightforward. With business confidence at a low
ebb and under-utilized capacity industrialists are hardly likely to be
in much of a hurry to undertake large new capital programmes.

These points apply of course mainly to manufacturing activity
and even then they do not explain the divergencies of investment behaviour between industries. The investment behaviour of new and
rapidly expanding industries over the cycle is likely to differ from
that of, say, old and declining sectors. But the problem is even more
complex when we consider the main components of aggregate investment since not all sectors are affected by the same forces, nor do
they react in the same way to common stimuli. For example, the level
of manufacturing investment will be determined primarily by businessmen's expectations about the future and past profit performance,
while building work, especially residential construction, will depend
on a host of factors including community needs, population movements, the rate of family formation, the level of costs, consumer tastes,
government policy (when relevant), as well as changes in real incomes.
Yet again, investment in certain public and semi-public undertakings

[1] Hence here it could be said that investment reacted to changes in income
which were induced by changes in consumption.

such as electricity or road building may be influenced by the timing of innovations or the desire of the Government to maintain investment in times of recession rather than by purely mundane economic circumstances. In view of the complexity of forces at work there are likely to be a number of investment cross-currents which it is easy to lose sight of in the overall investment total. It is important, therefore, to look more closely at the sectoral patterns of investment.

For this purpose not all sectors need be considered in detail. Agriculture, forestry and fishing, and mining and quarrying can be ignored since investment in these sectors was fairly small, and in the case of the former it varied very little over the course of the cycle. Investment in buildings is also excluded for it is the subject of separate treatment below. This leaves four main sectors for consideration, electricity, gas and water, transport and communication, distribution and other services, and manufacturing. These four groups accounted for nearly 61 per cent of total gross investment in 1929 and just over 58 per cent in 1937.

The smallest of these, at least at the beginning of the period, was electricity, gas and water. Investment in this sector was frequently counter-cyclical. There was a high peak in 1921 and a very slight decline the following year; after this investment rose almost continuously during the rest of the 1920s though it flattened out somewhat in the latter part of the decade (there was a slight dip in 1928). It continued to rise through to 1931, declined in 1932 and 1933, rose slightly in 1934 and then reached a new peak in 1936. This new level was not much higher than in 1931. It then fell in 1937 and rose slightly in the following year (see Figure 2). The dominant influence was of course electricity which was only mildly affected by cyclical forces. The rapid increase in demand for this new source of energy, the large technical and scale economies to be reaped and the previous lag in electricity investment, all combined to produce an upsurge of investment which cut across the cycle. Thus capital expenditure by electricity supply undertakings increased from £9 million in 1920 to £45 million in 1932 (1930 prices) and then tapered off slightly. The counter-cyclical nature of the Central Electricity Board's investment in the Grid system was even more dramatic. This reached a peak in 1932 and then fell off in the recovery of the 1930s to a low of £2 million in 1937.

The largest of the four sectors was transport and communications. Fluctuations in investment were more erratic and much wider than in electricity but in the main they followed a pro-cyclical pattern. A peak and trough in 1920 and 1921 were followed by a rising trend to 1928, though with sharp relapses in 1923 and 1926. Thus the pattern conformed more closely with the general business cycle than with the investment cycle. Between 1928 and 1933 transport investment declined continuously, by no less than 67 per cent. For the rest of the

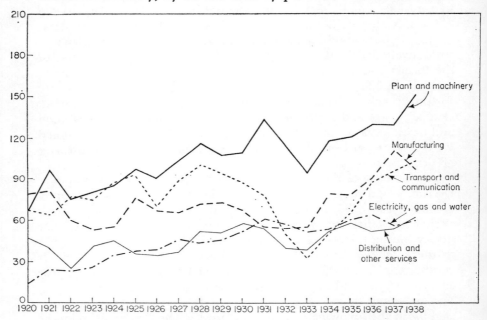

Figure 2   Gross domestic fixed capital formation by sectors, 1920–38
(£mn. at 1930 prices)

1930s there was a strong rise with no recession in 1938. This group consisted of a large number of different branches of transport some of which were declining or stagnating like shipping and railways, while others, road transport in particular, were expanding rapidly. Thus the pattern of fluctuations varied a great deal from sector to sector. The most dramatic swings were in shipping. Two thirds of the decline in gross investment in transport between 1928 and 1933 was due to the collapse of investment in ships. By contrast, investment in railways and other branches of surface transport held up much better especially in the first two years of the slump.

Gross investment in distribution and other services behaved rather erratically in the 1920s and there were some quite large swings. The peak occurred in 1920 to be followed by significant declines in 1921 and 1922; between 1922 and 1924 there was a sharp rise but then investment declined in 1925 and 1926, though very slightly in the latter year. The next two years saw a rise to a new peak in 1928, a very slight fall in 1929 and then a further peak in 1930. Thus up to 1930 this sector had a pattern very much its own. During the 1930s distribution followed a more normal course, that is pro-cyclical. It reached a trough in 1933 and then rose, though with a temporary relapse in 1936, to a new peak in 1938, but one which was not very much higher than that in 1930. Even so, for much of the time it could be regarded as anti-cyclical; a good deal higher in 1930 and 1931 than in most years of the 1930s except 1935 and 1938 (Figure 2). The rather unpredictable nature of investment in this sector is difficult to explain without recourse to a detailed study of the branches that make up this group. Probably the somewhat heterogeneous composition of the group itself gives some clue to the answer; each branch (wholesale and retail distribution, catering, entertainment and sport, professional services, finance and other services and municipal markets), was no doubt influenced by forces peculiar to itself and to some extent independent of the general cycle.

The second largest category was manufacturing investment. Here trends differed somewhat from those in the sectors already considered. In the first place, there was little overall growth in manufacturing investment. The peak of 1929 was lower than the previous one of 1925 which in turn was lower than the one of 1920 or 1921 (there was little difference in these two years). In fact the level of manufacturing investment did not rise above the immediate post-war peak until the late 1930s. Secondly, the decline in the early 1920s was sharper than that of the early 1930s. Thirdly, for much of the time it followed a pro-cyclical course with relatively little lagging at the turning points. The major exception in the latter respect point was in the early 1920s. The post-war peak occurred in 1921 but in the next two years investment declined and it only picked up very slightly in 1924. Thereafter the pro-cyclical course was fairly well maintained. A rise in 1925 was followed by a fall in 1926 and then a revival in the later 1920s. In the subsequent depression the upper turning point coincided with that of the economy as a whole and the trough occurred in 1932. Revival was very weak in 1933 but very marked in 1934; after a slight hitch in the following year there was a strong recovery until the down-

c

turn of 1938. This recovery was based on a group of industries, including the new industries, serving primarily the home market.

It is interesting at this point to examine briefly the movements in plant and machinery investment most of which would be employed in the sectors above, especially manufacturing. The pattern of movements is rather erratic and does not conform at all closely with either the general business cycle or the investment cycle. Peaks occurred in and 1933. There was, as one might expect, a closer correspondence with 1921, 1925, 1928, 1931 and 1938 with troughs in 1922, 1926, 1929 the combined investment in the four sectors discussed above but even here there were divergencies. The most curious feature occurred during the depression of the early 1930s. In both cases the peak occurred in 1928 but whereas investment in the four sectors fell off until 1933, investment in plant and machinery fell slightly in 1929 and then rose to a new and very high peak in 1931 which was not again exceeded until 1938 (Figure 2). The upsurge in electricity investment could account for part of this, while it is possible that manufacturers cut back on new buildings but took the opportunity to renew plant at lower costs.[1] But these explanations are not fully convincing and it may well be that part of the problem is to be attributed to errors in estimation.[2]

Figure 2 and Table 10 bring out clearly the varied pattern of fluctuations between different sectors. The only main sector not included here is dwellings (considered below), while capital formation by type of asset is included in Figure 2 mainly for purposes of comparison (see above.) The cyclical movements were very erratic, especially in the 1920s, with little uniformity in timing and amplitude. Thus only two sectors, electricity and social and public services, both of which were relatively insensitive to cyclical changes, had the same peak year prior to the 1929–32 depression, while the turning points for all sectors ranged from 1928 to 1931. There was a greater degree of uniformity in timing in the 1930s though as can be seen from Table 10, variations in amplitude were very large indeed.[3] This diversity of experience obviously has to be taken into account in any study

[1] Buildings and new works are more sensitive to changes in economic activity than plant and machinery but the lag in the latter is extraordinarily long.
[2] Feinstein, *op. cit.*, p. 229.
[3] At the final peak of 1938 only manufacturing and social and public services had substantially passed their previous peak levels of investment prior to the depression of the early 1930s. In the case of electricity it was slightly below.

of fluctuations but, as Feinstein has observed,[1] it renders difficult the formulation of an adequate model with general applicability. It also makes it difficult to relate investment cycles to the general business cycle in a really meaningful way.

TABLE 10 *Fluctuations in gross domestic investment by sectors*

	Previous peak year	*Trough (1933) as per cent of previous peak*	*Final peak (1938) as per cent of previous trough*
Electricity, gas, water	1931	85	115
Manufacturing	1929	74(a)	207(b)
Transport and communication	1928	33	315
Distribution and other services	1930	67	159
Social and public services	1931	71	193
Total	1930	85(c)	149

NOTES (a) trough year 1932; (b) peak year 1937; (c) trough year 1932.
SOURCE Feinstein, *op. cit.*, p. 40, with slight modifications.

Construction cycles

In view of this rather unpromising conclusion it might seem unnecessary to press the investment analysis further. But so far we have not said anything about one of the most important investment sectors, namely building and construction work. By comparison, the other two types of capital assets, plant and machinery and ships and vehicles, were comparatively small. In most years building and construction work (including civil engineering works) accounted for well over half of the total domestic investment, while in the peak years of 1933 and 1934 the shares of this sector were 68 and 63 per cent respectively. The two most important branches were dwellings and non-residential buildings which accounted for well over 40 per cent of all investment in most years; residential building alone absorbed around one third.

The sheer magnitude of the investment absorbed by construction is not necessarily indicative of the fact that it played a crucial role in fluctuations, though size alone would provide ample justification for analysis. On the other hand, there are grounds for supposing that building exercises an important influence on business fluctuations. However, its relationships with the business cycle are complex and

[1] Feinstein, *op. cit.*, p. 40.

imperfectly understood even though a considerable body of writing has been devoted to analysing these.[1] Most of this work is based mainly on pre-1914 experience, primary attention being focused on movements in residential building. These were found to be longer and of wider amplitude than the standard business cycle and several attempts have been made to explain these characteristics in terms of inverse cycles in home and foreign investment and migration.[2] The independent nature of the building cycle did not mean that it had no impact on fluctuations generally. On the contrary, at times it exerted considerable influence both in a stabilizing and destabilizing capacity. For instance, the domestic boom of the 1890s was aggravated by the upswing in building activity which then became a stabilizing force once the boom had passed its peak. Some in fact have even suggested that the standard business cycle was the product of inverse cycles in building, investment and migration in Britain and the United States.

However, since conditions were considerably different after the war the likelihood of building functioning in the same manner as before 1914 is somewhat remote. For one thing the period is too short for the long swing to show itself clearly. Secondly, foreign investment and migration were much reduced while a new factor, government policy, appeared on the scene. These changes do not mean that building ceased to affect the business cycle; in fact the growing importance of building would suggest the opposite. Rather the implication is that building reacted in a different way and from this it follows that building must be analysed within the context of the time rather than on the basis of some pre-conceived pattern derived from nineteenth century experience.

First then, let us examine the movements of investment in construction as a whole (that is including civil engineering).[3] During the 1920s building investment tended to move in phase with total investment, perhaps not surprisingly since it constituted so large a part of it, but very erratically in relation to the business cycle. Building was relatively low in the boom of 1919–20 but expanded sharply in 1921 when production and income declined, while in the following

---

[1] It is too long to quote here. But see generally J. Parry Lewis, *Building Cycles and Britain's Growth* (1965), and H. W. Richardson and D. H. Aldcroft, *Building in the British Economy Between the Wars* (1968).
[2] Though there has been some reaction against this view; see Richardson and Aldcroft, *op. cit.*, pp. 27–32.
[3] The main references for this section are Table 11 and Figure 3.

TABLE 11 *Gross domestic fixed investment in construction, 1920–38 (£mn at 1930 prices)*

	Dwellings	Non-residential building	Civil engineering works	Total construction	Total investment	Construction as a proportion of total investment
1920	36	80	25	141	267	52·8
1921	74	61	28	163	306	53·3
1922	66	42	41	149	282	53·8
1923	60	49	47	156	289	53·9
1924	85	57	43	185	337	54·9
1925	107	60	54	221	385	57·4
1926	134	56	42	232	373	62·2
1927	147	54	44	245	415	59·0
1928	115	61	38	214	411	52·1
1929	130	72	44	246	433	56·8
1930	122	81	57	260	435	59·5
1931	127	56	61	244	427	57·1
1932	128	49	47	224	372	60·2
1933	168	53	39	260	384	67·6
1934	188	68	39	295	467	63·2
1935	179	77	41	297	486	61·1
1936	178	82	51	311	530	58·7
1937	167	105	57	329	548	60·0
1938	165	98	58	321	556	57·7

SOURCE C. H. Feinstein, *Domestic Capital Formation in the United Kingdom 1920–1938* (1965), p. 38.

year the reverse happened. Then between 1922–27 there was a massive upsurge in construction with no recession in 1926. But there was a sharp relapse in 1928 when most other indicators were rising slowly. The main effect of this set-back was to pull down the industrial production index by a point or two.[1] In 1929 and 1930 building investment rose steadily despite the fact that most other indicators turned down in the latter year. Thereafter there was a greater degree of conformity between building and general economic activity. The

[1] That is including building. The industrial production index excluding building tended to rise slightly while manufacturing remained fairly stable.

former contracted in 1931 and 1932, then expanded until 1937 and declined slightly in the following year. However, the main upsurge in building came in 1933 and 1934 after which it flattened out somewhat.

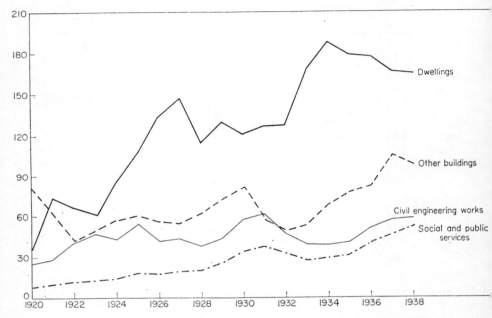

Figure 3   Gross domestic fixed capital formation in construction, 1920–38
(£mn. at 1930 prices)

Though cycles in total investment were determined to a considerable extent by the movements in construction it would be difficult to argue that building played a crucial role in economic fluctuations, at least at the turning points. Usually building lagged behind at the turning points. Thus peaks occurred in 1921 and 1930, that is one year after the downturn in economic activity. A similar lag occurred at the troughs of 1921, 1926 and even 1932, since in the latter year construction fell sharply but most other indicators either fell very slightly or in some cases rose. However, this should not detract from the importance of building as a stabilizer in the depressed years of 1921, 1926 and 1930 and in the boom years of the later 1930s.

So far we have spoken only of the construction sector as a whole. It is important however to distinguish between the three main branches, dwellings, non-residential construction and civil engineering, since each of these was affected by different stimuli (as well as influences common to all three) and hence tended to behave differently. The most important and interesting branch was residential building which deserves treatment at length. But first we must deal briefly with the other two.

On the whole non-residential building might be expected to follow a pro-cyclical course insofar as it consists to a considerable extent of industrial and commercial buildings. But it also includes many other types of buildings, schools, hospitals, churches, which are less sensitive to cyclical change or which are dependent on public policy. Thus the degree of cyclical conformity will depend in part on the strength of the latter elements. In fact, the correspondence was fairly close in the 1930s but less so in the 1920s. Troughs occurred in 1922 and 1927 (though the main fall occurred in 1926), while there was a peak in 1930. But apart from 1930 these were compatible with delayed reaction lags in industrial building. The movements of civil engineering are much more difficult to predict. Insofar as such works as roads, sewers, gas mains, etc., are determined by the construction of new buildings it might be expected that civil engineering would follow the building cycle. But much of this work is also tied up with public policy which is a wholly unpredictable element. Judging from the erratic pattern of this sector it might be guessed that the latter was the prevailing influence. Investment in civil engineering rose strongly between 1920 and 1923 and then fluctuated in every year until 1928. It then rose until 1931, declined until 1933, hardly rose at all over the next two years and then shot ahead to 1938. Thus there were peaks in 1923, 1925, 1927, 1931, 1938 and troughs in 1920(?),[1] 1924, 1926, 1928 and 1934 (or 1933 which was the same as 1934). It is noticeable, however, that civil engineering often moved counter-cyclical especially in recessions, so perhaps Government policy deserves a little more credit than we have accorded it.[2]

Undoubtedly the largest sector of the construction industry was residential building. This branch was subject to a wide range of influences, both economic and non-economic, so that it would not be surprising if its cycles differed somewhat from those of the economy as a whole. Attention was drawn earlier to the long-swing in residential building

[1] It is more than likely that 1920 was a trough year but comparable data is not available for earlier years.
[2] That is by boosting public works in recession.

before 1914, but this pattern did not re-emerge in the inter-war years. In fact it fluctuated as frequently as the economy as a whole with peaks in 1921, 1927, 1929 and 1934 and troughs in 1923, 1928, 1930 and 1938. The breakdown of the former pattern is not difficult to explain. For one thing the international influences relating to the housing cycle were very much weakened in this period. Secondly, new forces emerged on the scene, notably a severe housing shortage arising partly from the absence of building during the war, and the intervention of public authorities in the housing market. Thirdly, many of the economic factors, e.g. real income, building costs, interest rates and the rate of family formation, which affect the rate of building activity, changed more dramatically than was the case before 1914. For instance, building costs fell quite sharply in the late 1920s and early 1930s while interest rates were reduced to a minimum in the 1930s.

These changes not only increased the periodicity of the housing cycle but they also affected the timing of housing fluctuations relative to the general business cycle. During the boom of 1919–20 housing was in a trough, yet in the subsequent year of depression investment in dwellings more than doubled. During 1922 and 1923 housing activity declined but then followed a vigorous and uninterrupted boom until the end of 1927. In 1928 there was a very sharp contraction with an equally large upswing the following year. A modest decline occurred in 1930 but in the remaining two years of depression housing investment rose slightly. In the first two years of recovery there was a massive upswing in housing which petered out by 1935, and for the rest of the decade housing tended to decline. In other words, housing behaved in both a pro-cyclical and counter-cyclical fashion and it would be difficult to point a causal relationship one way or another between housebuilding and fluctuations in general. In the mid 1920s (1923–5) and the early 1930s housing moved with the cycle and thereby facilitated recovery. But in the former case it lagged seriously at the lower turning point, while in the early 1930s it could be claimed that it led since there was a rising trend after 1930 and private enterprise housing had been increasing since 1928. At most other times it moved counter-cyclically. In 1921, 1926 and again between 1930–32, housebuilding rose when economic activity was falling, while between 1935–7 the reverse process took place. Thus if housing was not a crucial determinant of fluctuations at least it acted as an important stabilizing element for much of the time. Its behaviour at the turning points was very erratic, sometimes leading, sometimes lagging and occasionally neither one way or another. Government policy did much to fashion the pattern in the 1920s. The heavy injections of subsidies were partly responsible for the expansions of 1921 and the mid 1920s, while the cut-back in subsidies caused contractions in 1922 and 1928. The low level of building in 1920 could be ascribed to high costs, shortages of labour and materials, and the slowness of local authorities in starting their programmes. On the other hand, the spurt in building in the early 1930s was caused by a variety of economic factors, e.g. falling costs, lower interest rates, rising incomes, which were superimposed on an overall housing shortage.

In general therefore, construction as a whole did not play a crucial role in economic fluctuations during this period. It moved both with and against the cycle and at the turning points it tended to lag behind. Nor would it be possible to reverse the causal sequence. The lagged responses of 1922 and 1928 cannot be attributed to the previous downturn of the business cycle; they were caused largely by relapses in residential building and in both cases changes in Government subsidy policy featured prominently. On the other hand, the lag in all building at the upper turning point of 1929 was not due to residential building since this turned down in 1930, but rather to the buoyancy of the non-residential sector, which behaved pro-cyclical for most of the time, and civil engineering which followed a very erratic course. At the trough of the 1929–32 depression all building tended to lag slightly behind due to the late revival in non-residential building and civil engineering. The modest rise in residential building in 1931 and 1932 was insufficient to counteract contraction elsewhere. However, this sector set the pace in the early years of recovery and when it tailed off in 1935 other construction work surged ahead.

These rather negative conclusions regarding the role of building in fluctuations should not allow us to lose sight of two facts: that building helped to carry the economy forward in the upswings of the mid 1920s (1923–5) and in the early 1930s, and that residential construction often acted as a stabilizing force.

Random or exogenous elements

A comprehensive analysis of fluctuations cannot be written simply in terms of the endogenous elements in the cycle which have been considered above. It is true that some of the variables like exports and

investment were instrumental in determining the amplitude of particular cycles, while at the upper turning points exports usually played an
initiatory role. But these cannot explain everything and there is still
room for the consideration of exogenous factors; these can be classed
under three heads; random shocks, Government policy (mainly monetary) and innovations.

The first of these is perhaps the easiest to deal with. It is not
possible, of course, to explain cycles purely in terms of shocks such as
wars, climatic disasters and political disorders, since we know there
are semi-automatic endogenous factors which operate in a cyclical
manner. Moreover, there has not been over the course of history a
sufficient number of shocks to explain each cyclical phase of activity.
On the other hand, shocks have occurred from time to time which
have affected or upset the pattern of activity. Shocks of course may
simply accentuate the prevailing cyclical tendency, but since they
are random and completely unpredictable they can occur at any point
in time and operate in such a way as to break the normal (if there is
such a thing) sequences of cyclical activity arising from the work-out
of economic forces.

In our period the two main shocks were war and the General Strike.
Clearly the 1926 downturn can be written almost entirely in terms of
the General Strike and the subsequent prolonged stoppage in the coal
trade. The main impact fell on the heavy industries and exports. In
turn, the very sharp upswing in 1927 was a response to the check to
growth in the previous year. The main point to note however, is that
this shock interrupted the upswing from the 1921 trough halfway
through its course, thereby breaking the Juglar or standard business
cycle pattern. The influence of war is more difficult to determine.
In some respects its repercussions were felt long after the event. But
it immediate impact was in the two or three years after 1918. The existence of shortages, pent-up demand, run-down equipment, together
with the removal of war-time controls early in 1919, inevitably gave
rise to a boom of unprecedented proportions, and when it broke,
largely of its own accord, the result was one of the worst slumps in
history. However, contrary to the position in 1926, the shock of war
did not upset the cyclical pattern since on normal expectations a boom
would probably have occurred around this time anyway.[1]

Government policy played a more modified and indirect role. Since

[1] See above, page 30.

this aspect is discussed in much greater detail in a later chapter we need only comment briefly here. In general, Government policy (fiscal and monetary) did not initiate turning points but merely aggravated (on occasions) the inherent cyclical tendencies. This is true even of the 1920s when policy (especially monetary) was determined largely by external considerations and was therefore at odds with the prevailing domestic situation. Perhaps its biggest impact was in the immediate post-war years. But even here the resort to a tighter monetary policy and restriction on public spending to curb the inflationary boom only really began to bite when the boom had already spent itself. Policy therefore had a carry-over effect and served mainly to aggravate the slump of 1921. For the rest of the 1920s Government policy, though not attuned to the needs of the economy, did not exert a very powerful impact and, what is more important, it had a negligible effect on fluctuations. The only other time (apart from the post-war period) that policy (mainly monetary) was employed with the primary aim of influencing the domestic economy was in 1929–30. But in the face of very adverse international conditions the limited attempts to reflate the economy were doomed to failure. During the 1930s policy was generally more favourable, except in the later stages of depression when a restrictive fiscal policy was pursued.[1] During the upswing cheap money prevailed. This certainly facilitated the process of recovery though it was not a crucial factor; nor was the shift to a cheap money policy responsible for the timing of the upturn in 1932.[2] The fact that cheap money and the beginnings of recovery more or less coincided in point of time was largely accidental and should not be construed as implying any strong causal relationship. There is little evidence either that depreciation or the tariff were of any greater moment in this context.[3]

The relevance of innovations to business cycle analysis poses certain problems. For one thing there is the matter of definition. Should innovation (or more widely technical progress) be considered as a systematic variable responding to economic forces and therefore written in as an endogenous element in Schumpeterian style, or does it count as a random element (shock is perhaps too severe a word to use here)? Obviously, this issue is one which could give rise to debate; but there is some justification for regarding it in the latter context

[1] Though see Chapter 9, pp. 304–5.
[2] Chapter 9, pp. 336–44.
[3] Chapter 8, pp. 284–5, 290 et seq.

because of the degree of randomness associated with invention and hence innovation. This is not the most important issue at stake however. It might be questioned whether there is any valid basis for regarding innovation as being of much direct relevance to normal business cycle analysis. True, in recent years we have been made familiar with the importance of innovation (technical progress) in long-term growth, while attention has been drawn, by Schumpeter and later writers, to the tendency for innovational activity to cluster at certain points in time. We could therefore infer that innovation has some part to play in cyclical fluctuations. But its role is limited and imprecise. Though major innovations (and these are the relevant ones here) are prone to clustering, the time span over which they are effected is generally a fairly long one. The application of steam and iron/steel, or electricity and internal combustion, for example, ranged over lengthy periods of time which cut across the standard business cycle. Hence, we might expect to find innovational cycles of somewhat longer duration than those we have been discussing.

These cycles are difficult to locate exactly for obvious reasons. Innovational activity is not easy to measure, possible indicators such as patents or investments providing very imprecise guides. There is also considerable fuzziness or overlapping between one innovation and the next so that it would be difficult to distinguish turning points clearly. Not all industries or sectors of the economy go through an innovational phase at the same time so that booms and slumps may be composed of industries with quite different experiences in this respect. Moreover, it is very unlikely that the upper turning points of the cycle, or for that matter the lower ones, would be determined by innovation. Innovations are not likely to bunch up so closely or dry up very suddenly as to produce a strong enough force to activate the timing of the turning points.

Thus the prospects of explaining inter-war fluctuations on the basis of an innovations theory appear somewhat slender. A quick glance at the evidence confirms this. None of the upper turning points could be remotely connected with the sudden exhaustion of innovational opportunity[1] (temporary saturation of the market or the exhaustion of immediate investment opportunities are somewhat different). Innovation was also of very limited relevance to the upswings of the 1920s. The post-war boom had little to do with innovation;

[1] Perhaps American experience, especially in 1929, offers more support for a causal connection.

it was based very much on the older sectors of the economy in which new technical developments were conspicuous by their absence. Again, in the two upswings of the 1920s (one if we exclude 1926), it would be stretching the evidence to suggest that they were based on the application of new techniques. Certainly the first widespread use of new techniques occurred in some industries, e.g. car production and rayon, together with a minor boom in some smaller but fairly new branches of activity (largely entertainment) in the late 1920s, but taken together these developments were scarcely of sufficient weight to dominate the economy.

The verdict is somewhat more favourable for the recovery of the 1930s. Proportionately the new developments exerted a greater impact than they had previously and they were in the forefront of recovery. On the other hand, there were other factors associated with recovery which did not depend on new innovations, so that one can hardly write recovery simply in terms of new industry innovation. In any case, such developments did not rest on the exploitation of hitherto *untried* techniques. If anything innovational clustering had reached a relatively mature stage of development.[1] Thus, for the most part the inter-war pattern of fluctuations is not explicable in terms of changes in innovational activity.

Conclusion

If the reader has survived this chapter he might be forgiven a feeling of frustration at not having found a convenient and straightforward explanation of the pattern of inter-war fluctuations. Unlike the study of long-term growth where one can say with some precision what the most important variables are, the analysis of fluctuations defies simple and single causal explanations. Each cycle (or each phase of the cycle for that matter) has its own individual features – features which stem from the continued development and adaptation of the economy –

---

[1] This serves to illustrate the difficulties of delineating the phase of innovational activity of most relevance to the cycle. A stage definition of development produces a result favourable to the 1930s. The first stage of new innovation developments occurred in the late nineteenth and early twentieth century but their limited application had negligible effects on the economy. Stage two came with their more widespread application in the 1920s but the overall impact was still weak. Thus their influence was much stronger in stage three, that is the massive application of the 1930s. Presumably the next stage would be saturation of the market after the second world war.

and as such cannot be explained simply in terms of reference to other cycles. Thus the search for a uni-causal explanation or theory of cycles tends to yield disappointing results.

On the other hand, this does not mean that cycles have no common characteristics. We have seen, for instance, that exports and investment usually had swings of wider amplitude compared with those of income and consumption, while some industries were more sensitive to cyclical activity than others. Exports tended to lead at the upper turning points but generally lagged at the troughs.[1] Investment lagged at the upper turning points and often acted as a stabilizing element in the early phases of depression, but lagged in the early months of recovery. Building rarely initiated swings in the economy but often acted as a stabilizing element. And so on. But the incidence of diversity was probably greater than the features of similarity. The amplitude of cycles varied and so did their periodicity, though if we remove the 1926 break the pre-war Juglar can be restored. Even so, the chief causal elements of each boom and of each slump were rarely the same. This was especially the case in the upswings. The boom of 1919–20 was very different from that of the 1930s, the first being a speculative reaction to wartime restriction and based on old staple industries, while the latter represented recovery from a prolonged recession and was dominated far more by new industries, services and building. The upswings of the 1920s were more widely based and had little in common with either. Similarly, the slump of 1921 was an automatic reaction to the post-war boom but was aggravated by restrictive policy measures, that of 1926 was largely the outcome of industrial troubles, the 1929–32 slump was generated mainly by external forces, while in 1938 external forces were again important though temporary exhaustion of investment opportunities at the peak of the boom also played a part. Yet one must again be wary of neat generalizations since in each case a wide variety of influences were at work. Thus the search for a common cyclical pattern or a general explanation of cyclical behaviour is perhaps misplaced; of greater interest is the wide diversity of experience between cycles.

[1] This is more relevant to the 1930s. In the 1920s exports were quite important in the first year of recovery from the 1921 and 1926 recessions though they did not dominate the recovery periods throughout.

3 Regional patterns of development

Regional interdependence

It is important to consider the regional aspects of the economy since the aggregate figures given in the first chapter are likely to mask significant variations between different areas of the country. It is true, of course, that no region or specifically defined area is an isolated unit in itself. The free movement of resources within a national economy gives rise to a considerable degree of interdependence between regions. Inevitably this will mean that regions have certain characteristics in common. For example, cyclical turning points will probably coincide fairly closely in each case. On the other hand, it is unlikely that the dimensions of growth and the amplitude of fluctuations will be exactly the same in each region, because of differences in their structures. A region whose resources are heavily committed to producing capital goods will tend to experience sharper swings in activity in both boom and depression than one which concentrates on consumer goods. Similarly, a region which has a high proportion of its resources devoted to producing staple products the demand for which is declining will presumably experience a slower rate of growth than a region favoured with newer and potential growth industries. Differences in income levels and the distribution of income between regions will also give rise to variation in rates of growth.

The way in which regions affect each other is particularly important. Do fast-growing regions have a beneficial or detrimental impact on those growing less rapidly? In fact either could happen. If regional links are strong fast-growing regions may stimulate activity in less prosperous areas. On the other hand, the latter may lose valuable resources to the more buoyant regions, a situation which could accelerate their relative rate of decline. This is more likely to happen when the growing regions are situated in close proximity to each other and their growth depends on the exploitation of new techniques of an interlocking type which some regions lack. Conversely, of course, slow-growing regions may act as a drag on development elsewhere.

It is impossible to predict exactly what will happen since the outcome will depend upon the interaction of many variables. These include the size and economic strength of regions, their structure, income levels and markets and the types of technology employed. Moreover, the transmission effects between regions will be determined, as with countries, by the degree of economic interdependence between them and the size of the regional multiplier.

These points are worth bearing in mind in any discussion of regional development even though lack of statistical data precludes a rigorous analysis in every respect. There are no figures for inter-regional trade and capital flows for this period and, apart from Scotland, no regional estimates of income and industrial production. In fact the only regional statistics available are those for employment and even these are not fully comprehensive. Nevertheless, employment data can be used to illustrate the main trends in regional development during the inter-war period.

Regional employment trends

As a result of the insurance schemes the Ministry of Labour collected a considerable amount of information on employment both for Britain as a whole and for a number of selected regions. We have used the number insured in employment rather than the figures for the insured population since the latter includes unemployed workers. These figures are not, of course, ideal for purposes of measuring economic activity. For one thing they are not comprehensive; they do not begin until 1923 while not all workers were included in the insurance schemes.[1] Secondly, changes in employment are not necessarily a very good guide to movements in output since no allowance is made for productivity changes. This deficiency is particularly important

[1] Employers, self-employed, most non-manual workers, and certain other workers were not covered by the insurance schemes. By the end of the 1930s about 15·7 million out of a total working population of 22·86 million were insured.

when making regional comparisons. Capital deepening in one region may lead to a low rate of employment growth but a high rate of output growth. In terms of employment the region would be classed as a slow grower whereas in fact the opposite might be the case. These limitations should be borne in mind in the following analysis.

Indices of the insured persons in employment for nine major regions of Britain are presented in Table 12. Over the period 1923 to 1937 employment in the country as a whole rose by nearly one quarter, though there were fluctuations in the level of employment from time

TABLE 12 *Indices of numbers of insured persons (aged 16–64) in employment, 1923–37*

Region	*June 1923*	*June 1929*	*June 1932*	*June 1937*
London	100	120	118	145
South-eastern	100	127	127	159
South-western	100	117	114	140
Midlands	100	111	101	132
North-eastern	100	105	92	114
North-western	100	109	96	112
Northern	100	99	77	102
Scotland	100	105	91	112
Wales	100	85	69	86
Great Britain	100	110	100	124

SOURCE M. P. Fogarty, *Prospects of the Industrial Areas of Great Britain* (1945), p. 15.

to time notably between 1929–32. The rate of unemployment growth varied markedly between regions. In four regions, London, the South-east and South-west and the Midlands, employment grew more rapidly than the national average, while in the remaining regions, covering the northern half of the country, it was well below the general level. One region, the Northern, experienced little growth at all, while employment in Wales fell by 14 per cent.

A similar pattern holds true for shorter periods. During the 1920s it was the southern regions which were growing rapidly whereas the North of the country tended to mark time. The South hardly experienced any decline in employment in the slump of 1929–32, though the number of insured persons rose as a result of an influx of unemployed workers from other areas. On the other hand, most other regions suffered a severe contraction in employment, the main exception being the Midlands which was close to the national average. Recovery from the slump was extremely rapid in the South and Midlands and by 1935–6 the employment levels of 1929 had been surpassed by a substantial margin. Elsewhere employment only just exceeded the previous peak by the end of the 1930s.

The unemployment figures tell a similar story. Throughout the inter-war years unemployment rarely fell below 10 per cent of the insured labour force, though it ranged from a low of 8·7 per cent in May 1927 to a peak of nearly 23 per cent in the third quarter of 1932.[1]

TABLE 13   *Unemployment percentages by divisions (July each year)*

Region	1912–13	1929	1932	1936	Average 1929–36
London	8·7	4·7	13·1	6·5	8·8
South-eastern	4·7	3·8	13·1	5·6	7·8
South-western	4·6	6·8	16·4	7·8	11·1
Midlands	3·1/2·5[1]	9·5	21·6	9·4	15·2
North-eastern	2·5	12·6	30·6	16·6	22·7
North-western	2·7	12·7	26·3	16·2	21·6
Scotland	1·8	11·2	29·0	18·0	21·8
Wales	3·1	18·8	38·1	28·5	30·1
Great Britain	3·9	9·7	22·9	12·6	16·9
South Britain		6·4	16·2	7·4	11·0
North Britain and Wales }		12·9	29·5	18·0	22·8

[1]West and East Midlands.
SOURCES   W. H. Beveridge, *Full Employment in a Free Society* (1944), p. 73, and 'An Analysis of Unemployment, I', *Economica*, 3 (1936).

The real unemployment rates were somewhat lower however since the data refer only to the insured part of the labour force which had a relatively high incidence of unemployment. If adjustments are made to take account of employers, self-employed and other non-insured workers the average unemployment rate for the total labour force works out at 6·8 per cent in the 1920s and 9·8 per cent for 1930–8 as against 12·1 and 16·5 per cent respectively for insured industrial

[1] E. M. Burns, *British Unemployment Programs 1920–1938* (1941), p. 343.

workers.[1] Nevertheless even in the best years unemployment was probably more than double the pre-war average though the limited nature of the data makes precise comparisons impossible.[2] However, despite the deficiencies of the statistics the regional disparities in unemployment are quite clear as a glance at Table 13 will show. Both in boom and depression the southern counties fared better than the northern. Taking an average of the eight years 1929–36, unemploy-

TABLE 14 *Number of factories opened, closed and extended in Greater London and Great Britain between 1932–37*

	Greater London	Great Britain
Factories opened	1,400	3,220
Factories closed	868	2,576
Net increase in number of factories	532	644
Factories extended	307	1,057

SOURCE *Report of the Royal Commission on the Distribution of the Industrial Population,* Cmd 6153 (1940), p. 166.

ment in London and the South-east was roughly half the national level, while in Northern Britain and Wales it was double that of the South (including the Midlands). On the other hand, despite a rapid growth in employment in the South during the 1930s unemployment levels still remained above those of 1929 because of an influx of workers from other areas. It is also important to point out that the disparity between the North and the South was reversed before the war. Then all the southern counties had unemployment rates higher than those further north, while London's unemployment was twice the national average.

The regional trends in activity which are reflected in the employment data are confirmed by information relating to factories established or closed. These were collected by the Board of Trade for the 1930s only. Of the net increase of 644 factories employing 25 persons or more in the six years 1932–7, no less than 532 were located in the Greater London Region. These provided employment for 97,700

[1] E. Lundberg, *Instability and Economic Growth* (1968), pp. 31–2.
[2] See W. H. Beveridge, *Full Employment in a Free Society* (1944), p. 73. For the pre-war period the figures refer only to unemployment in trade unions, while the Ministry's data for the inter-war period do not include unemployed workers who failed to register at the employment exchanges.

workers, equivalent to two fifths of all employment provided by new factories opened in Great Britain. In addition, nearly one third of the extensions to existing factories were located in this region (see Table 14). By contrast Wales, Scotland and parts of Northern England suffered a net loss of factories since the number closed exceeded the number opened during these years.[1]

TABLE 15 *Percentage of total net industrial output in census of production regions*

	1924	1935
Greater London	17·1	24·8
Lancashire and Cheshire	20·8	15·5
West Riding	12·6	10·1
Northumberland and Durham	5·9	4·3
Warwick, Worcs. and Staffs.	11·6	12·3
Midland, South-east, South-west (including part of North) }	15·9	20·2
Wales	5·9	3·9
Scotland	10·2	9·9

SOURCE Political and Economic Planning, *Report on the Location of Industry in Great Britain* (1939), p. 44.

As a result the southern counties increased their share of net industrial output whereas areas further north declined in relative importance. Although the regional divisions in Table 15 do not correspond exactly to those used in previous Tables they are sufficiently close as to make valid comparisons. Clearly the greatest gain was in Greater London whose share of net output rose from 17·1 per cent in 1924 to nearly 25 per cent in 1935. The rest of England, which includes the Midlands, South-East and South-West, also registered a substantial gain. All other regions declined in importance, the biggest losses occurring in Wales, and Northumberland and Durham.

The above regional analysis does, of course, tend to conceal important local characteristics. Both in prosperous and depressed regions there were areas or towns which did not conform to the pattern of the division in which they were located. For example, the prosperous regions of South-east and South-west England contained counties with

[1] *Report of the Royal Commission on the Distribution of the Industrial Population*, Cmd 6153 (1940), pp. 166–7.

high unemployment such as Norfolk, Suffolk, Cornwall, Devon and Gloucester. Similarly, in the North there were areas like Perthshire where the unemployment level was well below the average for the region. Variations in unemployment levels between towns in the same region or county were often very large. Wigan had an unemployment rate of nearly 23 per cent in 1929 whereas in Rochdale it was only 8·3 per cent, although both towns suffered severely in the slump. In 1937 the South-west region had a range from 29·0 per cent in Redruth to 5·4 per cent in Bath; the North-eastern, from 24·3 per cent in Barnsley to 6·0 per cent in Halifax; South Wales, from 16·0 per cent in Llanelly to 41·6 per cent in Merthyr Tydfil. These were by no means the most extreme. Some counties had towns with very wide variations indeed. Chelmsford in the prosperous county of Essex had a rate of 1·6 per cent in 1937 as against 36·4 per cent at Pitsea. Stafford and Kidsgrove in the county of Staffordshire had rates of 3·4 and 44·5 per cent respectively. Finally, in Glamorgan, Resolven had an unemployment rate of only 4·5 per cent whereas at the other extreme Ferndale had 48·1 per cent.[1]

Such local differences were quite common and should occasion no surprise. In general, as with regional variations,[2] they were caused by the particular characteristics of the industrial structure of the localities or towns concerned. Contributory factors may have been differences in the rate of migration or in the age/sex composition of the labour force. Even if data were available it would be impossible, and somewhat tedious, to examine in detail all the local variations. One or two examples will suffice to illustrate the point. The intensity of unemployment in Redruth, for example, was due largely to its dependence on the tin and heavy engineering industries, whereas Bath was much more prosperous because it had a fairly diversified economic structure including a wide range of consumer goods and service industries. Similarly, Barnsley's dependence on coal and heavy engineering gave rise to much persistent unemployment, while Halifax was relatively prosperous because of its machine tool trade. Very often the degree of prosperity of a particular town was determined largely by the fortunes of one industry. The sharp contrast between Bishop Auckland and Consett in County Durham in the later 1930s can be explained largely in terms of the different recovery experiences of the coal and iron and steel industries.

[1] See W. H. Beveridge, *Full Employment in a Free Society* (1944), pp. 324–7.
[2] See below.

Although some of the sub-regional differences were sometimes quite pronounced this does not alter the fact that in general there existed a clear division between the South (London, the South-east and South-west and the Midlands) and the rest of the country. Both in the 1920s and 1930s the Northern half of Britain, including Wales, was less prosperous and had a higher rate of unemployment than the South. Moreover, in the 1930s this disparity between the two halves of the country was greater than it had been in the previous decade.[1]

Types of unemployment

The regional analysis may be carried a little further by examining the incidence of different types of unemployment in various regions. Three main classes of unemployment may be distinguished: (1) short-period unemployment caused by frictions in the labour market and seasonal factors; (2) long-period or persistent unemployment due to structural factors or personal infirmities and (3) cyclical unemployment arising from secular swings in the level of economic activity. Although the inter-war years experienced all three kinds it is difficult to say precisely what volume of unemployment fell into each category at any one time. It is not easy to draw a sharp distinction between short-term and cyclical unemployment, while the volume of persistent unemployment depends very much upon the length of time out of work which is used to define this category. Beveridge attempted an estimate for July 1936 on the assumption that cyclical unemployment had more or less disappeared by that date. He suggested that upwards of 800,000 workers could be classified as short-term unemployed, while the remaining 500,000 or so, who had been out of work for nine months or more, constituted the persistent unemployment.[2] The division is somewhat arbitrary and open to objection. It is far from clear that cyclical unemployment had vanished by the middle of 1936 since the recovery phase of the cycle had not completed its course. Secondly, the above proportions would be altered significantly if we defined persistent unemployment as applying to those out of work for six months or more, or alternatively, 12 months or more, instead of nine. The distinctions between various classes of unemployment

[1] See D. G. Champernowne, 'The Uneven Distribution of Unemployment in the United Kingdom, 1929–36', *Review of Economic Studies*, 5 (1936–7), p. 95.
[2] W. H. Beveridge, 'An Analysis of Unemployment, III', *Economica*, 4 (1937), pp. 180–1.

become even more arbitrary at times of heavy cyclical unemployment since much of the latter can just as easily be classified into either one of the other two groups.

From our point of view these definitional problems need not worry us unduly since, whatever criteria of assessment are used, it is clear that the Northern regions and Wales suffered much more severely from persistent and cyclical unemployment than did the Midlands and South. Of the two the former was by far the worse for it was demoralizing for workers to be out of work for long stretches of time. The problem was particularly acute in the 1930s. Before the depression most of the unemployed had been out of work for six months or less and only five per cent had been out of work for 12 months or more. Long-period unemployment rose rapidly during the downswing of the cycle, and though it declined again after 1933 it remained substantially above that of the previous decade. In the middle of 1936 no less than 24 per cent of the applicants for relief had been unemployed for 12 months or more. The contrast between the regions was quite striking. In London and the South-east this kind of unemployment accounted for only nine per cent of the total unemployed, and in the South-west for 14 per cent. By contrast, in Scotland and Wales it formed 30 and 37 per cent respectively, while in the Midlands, North-east and North-west it ranged from between 25 and 27 per cent. To the total of 325,000 unemployed for 12 months or more in June 1936, London, the Home Counties and South-west England contributed 21,000, the Midlands 30,433, the North-east nearly 90,000 the North-west 64,215, Wales 64,000 and Scotland 55,572. Persistent unemployment in Wales was much higher than it had been at the bottom of the depression.[1]

A somewhat different analysis made by Fogarty illustrates plainly the geographical concentration of cyclical and persistent unemployment. He took London and the South-east as the yard-stick by which to measure the general level of unemployment in each region. Unemployment in any region which was over and above the norm or general level could be termed excess unemployment which would provide a reasonable measure of the relative prosperity of each region. Thus on the basis of the experience of London and the South-east general unemployment for Britain as a whole in 1932 worked out at nearly 1·7 million, as against an actual unemployment level of just

[1] W. H. Beveridge, 'An Analysis of Unemployment, II', *Economica*, 4 (1937), pp. 5–10.

TABLE 16   *General and excess unemployment, 1929–37 (annual average)*

| | | General[1] unemployment 000s | Excess unemployment[2] | | | | |
| | | | Total | Persistent | | Cyclical | |
			Number affected 000s	Number affected 000s	% of insured	Number affected 000s	% of insured
South-east and London	1929	174	—	—	—	—	—
	1932	461	—	—	—	—	—
	1937	244	—	—	—	—	—
South-west	1929	47	21	21	2·5	—	—
	1932	124	31	18	2·0	13	1·4
	1937	64	14	14	1·4	—	—
Midlands	1929	101	66	66	3·7	—	—
	1932	259	121	48	2·5	73	3·9
	1937	133	17	17	0·8	—	—
North, N.E., N.W.	1929	230	324	324	7·9	—	—
	1932	586	574	322	7·5	252	5·9
	1937	277	319	319	7·4	—	—
Wales	1929	33	80	80	13·7	—	—
	1932	85	141	86	13·9	55	8·9
	1937	39	97	97	15·9	—	—
Scotland	1929	77	83	83	6·5	—	—
	1932	184	187	101	7·5	86	6·4
	1937	90	132	132	9·5	—	—
Great Britain	1929	656	573	573	4·9	—	—
	1932	1,699	1,054	576	4·7	478	3·8
	1937	847	580	580	4·4	—	—

NOTES   [1] General unemployment is taken as the level actually experienced in London and the South-east.

[2] Excess unemployment in any area is that in 'excess' of 'general' unemployment.

SOURCE   M. P. Fogarty, *Prospects of the Industrial Areas of Great Britain* (1945), p. 5.

over 2·7 million. Total excess unemployment therefore amounted to about one million.[1]

The results of the analysis are reproduced in Table 16. In the peak years of activity, 1929 and 1937, the excess unemployment for the whole of Great Britain amounted to between 570–580,000 out of a total of about 1·2 and 1·4 million unemployed respectively in each of these years. Practically all of this could be classed as persistent excess unemployment caused by structural factors.[2] The areas most severely affected were Wales, Scotland and Northern England, whereas in the Midlands and South-west the amounts were very small. But within these broad regions there were concentrations around particular areas notably in South Wales, Cumberland, on the North-east coast and in parts of South-west Scotland. These four areas alone, containing 15 per cent of the insured population of the country, accounted for 45 per cent of the persistent excess unemployment. Further heavy concentrations occurred in Lancashire and Cheshire, along the North Wales coast, in Staffordshire and in parts of the West Riding.

During the slump the total excess unemployment rose sharply most of the increase being caused by cyclical factors. The greater severity of the depression outside the South-east can be measured roughly by the difference in each region between the excess unemployment prevailing in 1929 and 1937 and the corresponding excess in 1932. From Table 16 it can be seen that the total excess unemployment in Britain rose from 573,000 to just over one million between 1929 and 1932, and most of this increase was of a cyclical type. The distribution of the cyclical excess was very similar to that of the persistent unemployment, though the Midlands had more cyclical than structural unemployment in 1932. In the South-west and the Midlands less than four per cent of the insured population were affected by cyclical unemployment; but in the North of England and Scotland it was around six per cent, while Wales had nearly nine per cent. Sub-regional concentrations similar to those of persistent excess unemployment were to be found.[3]

---

[1] M. P. Fogarty, *Prospects of the Industrial Areas of Great Britain* (1945), p. 46.

[2] The relative importance of long-period unemployment was much greater in 1937 than in 1929.

[3] Fogarty, *op. cit.*, pp. 7–8.

TABLE 17　Regional changes in numbers insured by industry divisions, 1923–37

	Great Britain		London and Home counties		Midland counties		W. Riding, Notts and Derby		Mid Scotland		Lancs		Northumberland and Durham		Glamorgan and Monmouth	
	1923	1937	1923	1937	1923	1937	1923	1937	1923	1937	1923	1937	1923	1937	1923	1937
Per cent insured in:																
7 'local' industries	24	30	35	38	16	20	14	21	25	33	19	26	16	25	13	22
16 rapidly expanding industries	14	19	21	25	26	30	9	14	10	13	9	16	6	9	4	6
5 rapidly declining 'basic' industries	23	14	1	1	12	7	43	32	24	15	36	24	49	33	59	41
18 other industries	39	37	43	36	46	42	33	33	40	39	36	35	28	32	24	31
All industries*	100	100	100	100	100	100	100	100	100	100	100	100	100	100	100	100
Per cent increase or decrease (−) 1923–37																
7 'local' industries	57		54		67		69		43		47		63		59	

* Do not always sum exactly to 100 because of rounding.

16 rapidly expanding industries	66	69	51	75	46	86	63	49
5 rapidly declining 'basic' industries	−25	−4	−28	−15	−31	−28	−29	−34
18 other industries	14	21	17	15	5	2	18	26
All industries	22	43	28	15	10	8	5	−4

NOTES 1 The '7' local industries are building, distributive trades, gas, water and electricity, road transport, tram and omnibus services, laundries and dry cleaning, bread and confectionery.

2 The rapidly expanding industries include most newer industries.

3 The 5 declining basic industries are coal, cotton, wool, shipbuilding and iron and steel.

4 The 18 other industries are a miscellaneous group covering public works, contracting services, and industries which declined or expanded at less than the national rate.

SOURCE *Report of the Royal Commission on the Distribution of Industrial Population*, Cmd 6153 (1940), p. 276.

Causes of regional disparity

Though employment and unemployment data do not provide the best guide to trends in economic activity the differences between the North and South of the country were sufficiently large to be meaningful. The question is why did the southern counties fare so much better than areas further north.

Basically the discrepancy was due to differences in the composition of industrial structures rather than to differences in the rate at which industries expanded. Most of the northern regions including Wales had a high proportion of their resources in declining industries or heavy capital goods sectors which were particularly vulnerable to the trade cycle. On the other hand, such industries were much less predominant in the South, particularly in London and the South-east, and here the industrial structure was geared towards those industries expanding more rapidly than the national average. This position was not, however, the result of changes in the industrial structure during the inter-war years since it already existed at the beginning of the period. Thus in 1923 well over one third of the insured population of areas such as Lancashire, Northumberland and Durham, South Wales, the West Riding, Notts and Derby were engaged in the five declining industries[1] of coal, cotton, wool, shipbuilding and iron and steel. London and the South-east, however, had only about one per cent of their insured population in such industries, while even in the Midlands the proportion was only 12 per cent. Conversely these areas had more than their fair share of the rapidly expanding and 'local' industries. London and the Home Counties had 56 per cent of their insured population working in these industries, and the Midlands 42 per cent, compared with a national average of 38 per cent. But in areas such as Lancashire, the North-east and South Wales the proportions engaged in these expanding industries were much lower, ranging from 17 to 28 per cent. Mid Scotland was something of an exception with an industrial structure very similar to that of the country as a whole (see Table 17).

Thus to make good their initial deficiency the growth of the expanding industries in the less favoured regions would have had to have been much faster than the national average. In fact, however, this was not the case. But it is important to note that the rate of increase of the expanding and of the local industries in the northern regions was

[1] Declining primarily in the sense of employment opportunities.

not very dissimilar from that elsewhere in Britain, though it was obviously insufficient to offset the decline in the basic industries. Curiously enough the lowest rates of growth in these sectors was in Mid Scotland which started off with a fairly balanced industrial structure. Over the period as a whole the industrial balance of the northern areas improved though by 1937 it was still heavily weighted on the side of declining trades.[1]

Much of the difference in prosperity between the North and the South stemmed from the initial imbalance of the industrial structure. The North had far too many resources tied up in the old basic industries, whereas the South was favoured with a predominance of potential growth industries. Moreover, the existence of a large pool of unemployed labour in the former regions probably exerted a net drag effect on their prosperity, while incomes and effective demand tended to be lower than in the more prosperous regions. Some of the implications of these developments will be examined more fully later.

First it is necessary to examine more closely some of the regions to find out what factors determined their development. Moreover, it is important to emphasize that there were often quite sharp variations in prosperity between different areas of the broad regions discussed so far. Scotland taken as a unit, for example, was far less prosperous than the country as a whole, employment increasing by only half the national rate between 1923 and 1937. But many parts of eastern Scotland, especially Perth, Edinburgh, Aberdeen and parts of the Lothians, were relatively prosperous in comparison with the main industrial belt in the South-west and along the Clyde. Edinburgh, for example, had an unemployment rate well below the average for most of the period and its industrial structure was weighted towards the growing industries. Recovery from the slump was based to a large extent on the rapid expansion of the consumer goods and service trades, including building, vehicles, food and the printing industries, which partly compensated for the decline in the older branches of engineering.

Expansion in the East was not sufficient to offset the contraction experienced in the South-west and the Clyde. This area accounted for over 50 per cent of both output and employment in manufacturing in 1935. A high proportion of the region's output came from the vulnerable, export-orientated sectors. Just over 40 per cent of all workers classified by the Census of Production were employed in mechanical

[1] J. Sykes, 'The Development Areas', *The Manchester School*, 17 (1949), pp. 129–31.

engineering, shipbuilding, coal and iron and steel, as against a national average of 25 per cent. Not all of these industries declined absolutely though they were hit badly by the downswing of the early 1930s. Thus between 1929 and 1937 the output of merchant ships was 58 per cent less than in 1909–13. There were compensations in the growth of certain manufacturing trades such as clothing, footwear, the new light metal industries, and building, though these could not make up for the decline in the basic sectors. Here, as elsewhere in the North, the growth in employment depended upon the composition of the industrial structure at the start of the period and in this respect Scotland was obviously at a severe disadvantage.

Scotland's structural deficiencies were reflected in part in her levels of income and productivity. Over the period her position deteriorated *vis-à-vis* that of Britain as a whole. Industrial productivity rose more slowly than the national average and by 1935 it was some five to nine per cent less than the average, the deficiency being most marked in the newer industries. Similarly, Scottish real income per head rose by only 16 per cent between 1924 and 1938 compared with an increase of over one third in the u.k. with the result that Scotland's share of total income declined slightly. Absolutely real income per head was about 10 per cent lower than the general average, though in the slump of the early 1930s it was up to 20 per cent below. These differences can be attributed mainly to lower levels of income from work, a lower proportion of occupied persons in the population and higher unemployment, all of which were to some extent influenced by Scotland's industrial structure.[1]

The area most severely affected was undoubtedly Wales. It was the only region in which the number of insured in employment fell and there were no really prosperous zones which stood out from the country as a whole. Cardiff with a relatively low unemployment rate for Wales had roughly the same level of unemployment as Dundee, which in Scotland was classed as a severely depressed town. The severity of the situation led to considerable emigration from Wales and as a result the total population of the country declined over the period.

Wales illustrates, par excellence, the dangers of extreme specialization on a narrow band of declining industries. In 1930 blast fur-

[1] See A. K. Cairncross (ed.), *The Scottish Economy* (1954); H. W. Singer and C. E. V. Leser, 'Industrial Productivity in England and Scotland', *Journal of Royal Statistical Society*, 111 (1948); and A. D. Campbell, 'Changes in Scottish Incomes, 1924–49', *Economic Journal*, 65 (1955).

naces, iron and steel smelting and rolling, tinplate, coal and slate mining and quarrying absorbed 70 per cent of the workers enumerated in the Census of Production, and five years later the proportion was still 65 per cent. The other main occupations were tourism and agriculture. The worst hit area was South Wales, particularly the main industrial belt which relied mainly on the heavy industries of coal, iron and steel and tinplate. Local dependence on one or two industries was extremely high; in 1923, for example, 56 per cent of the insured population of the eastern sector were engaged in coal mining, while in some of the valleys such as Rhondda and Pontypridd the proportion was no less than 87 per cent. Further north the range of industries was somewhat wider though the impression of a balanced economy is misleading because of the strong localization of particular industries. Adjustments to changing conditions in Wales were extremely slow compared with the other depressed areas. In fact they merely took the form of shifts of labour out of the contracting industries. There were few rapidly expanding industries and only one new industry, rayon in Flintshire, took root in this period. Thus unemployed workers had little alternative but to emigrate. Those who chose to stay remained unemployed and it is not surprising that at the end of the period prolonged unemployment was higher in Wales than in any other area.

The North-east coast area, including Northumberland, Durham and the Cleveland district of Yorkshire, had the distinction of having the heaviest concentration of unemployment in England. It was also affected very severely by cyclical unemployment. Again the main cause was the heavy overcommitment to industries either in decline or extremely sensitive to the trade cycle. In 1924 a group of six heavy industries, coal mining, shipbuilding and marine engineering, iron and steel, heavy chemicals, shipping and port services and general and constructional engineering, accounted for over 64 per cent of all insured workers. The most severe declines in employment occurred in coal and shipbuilding. In the case of shipbuilding this was mainly due to a rapid fall in output associated with the contraction of the export market. But the fall in coal output was relatively modest and here the chief factor making for reduced employment was the rapid mechanization of mining operations which raised the industry's efficiency. Altogether these two industries lost some 97,000 insured workers between 1924 and 1939.

But the process of adjustment was more rapid in the North-east than in Wales. Between 1924 and 1938 the proportion of insured workers attached to the six basic industries fell from 64.5 to 48 per cent. At the same time the newer and lighter industries began to develop and the rate of growth in the expanding and local industries (see Table 17) compared favourably with the national average. The rapid growth of the chemical industry was one reason for the more prosperous nature of Tees-side compared with the rest of the region. But as with the other depressed areas the problem was not one of slow expansion in the growing sectors but the large proportion of resources devoted to the heavy sectors at the start of the period. In 1923 Northumberland and Durham had nearly 50 per cent of its labour force locked up in rapidly declining industries and only 22 per cent in rapidly expanding and local industries, compared with a national average of 38 per cent. For the level of unemployment to have been the same as that in London and the South-east in 1937 the growing industries of the North-east would have needed to expand at more than twice the national rate.[1]

The last major depressed area to be considered is that of Lancashire. This provides an interesting case study because of the contrast between different parts of the region. There is no doubt that the county taken as a whole suffered severely from both cyclical and structural unemployment, though it fared somewhat better than certain other counties, notably Cumberland and Westmorland in the North-west region. Unemployment was much higher than in the southern counties throughout the period and employment grew at less than half the national rate between 1923 and 1937. Lancashire was also badly affected by short-time working or underemployment. In June 1938 the proportion of cotton workers on short-time was 29.5 per cent, equivalent to total unemployment for about 5.5 per cent of all insured workers in the industry.

Lancashire's main difficulties were centred around districts heavily dependent on cotton, coal and general engineering for employment. This group accounted for about 35 per cent of all insured workers in 1923 and the number of insured workers attached to these trades fell by 200,000 between 1923 and 1937, that is about 11.5 per cent of the total insured population in 1923. The areas worst affected were the Barrow district, dependent on shipbuilding and iron and steel, parts of Merseyside, including Wigan, Warrington and St. Helens (coal)

[1] Fogarty, *op. cit.*, p. 178.

and above all, the chief centres of the cotton industry, including Blackburn, Burnley, the Rossendale Valley, Rochdale, Oldham, Bolton and Preston. The overwhelming importance of the cotton industry in many of these towns resulted in unemployment levels almost as great as those experienced in South Wales. For example, Blackburn, where the cotton industry accounted for 60 per cent of employment, had an unemployment rate of 46·8 per cent in 1931.

On the other hand, one could hardly say that the county suffered perpetual stagnation. Lancashire found little difficulty in attracting new industries and the substantial expansion experienced in building, road transport, clothing, electrical engineering, motor vehicles, rayon, and in a host of smaller trades such as hosiery, furniture and printing, went some way towards offsetting contraction elsewhere. About 21 per cent of the new industrial developments between 1933–8 went to the North-west region (including Cumberland, Westmorland and Cheshire) which contained 14 per cent of the country's population in 1931. Moreover employment in the rapidly expanding trades increased faster in Lancashire than in any other region (see Table 17). The main drawback was not so much the absence of growth industries but the uneven spread of their development. Most of the growth took place in and around the Manchester region, that is outside the districts most in need of new developments. The result was that Lancashire contained areas which were equally as prosperous as the South-east, while there were others which were as bad as almost any in Wales or Scotland. Though considerable progress was made especially in the 1930s, Lancashire still had some way to go to adjust her economy to the collapse of the basic industries. Nevertheless, at the end of the period the county showed remarkable signs of vitality.

A brief review of some of the main developments in the more prosperous regions will serve to illustrate the contrast between North and South. Perhaps the most notable feature of the industrial structure of the South was its diversity together with the virtual absence of declining heavy industries which featured so predominantly in the depressed areas. London, of course, was the classic example. Nearly every main industrial group was represented in the Metropolis and the highest concentration of employment was in building and hotels and clubs (eight and 6·2 per cent respectively of the insured population) both of which expanded rapidly in the inter-war years. There were hardly any declining industries. Out of 40 main occupational groups only four, comprising 3·4 per cent of the insured

D

population in 1937, actually had fewer workers than in 1923. London in fact was an important manufacturing centre with a very wide range of industries, including electrical engineering, food products, light metal trades, vehicles, scientific instruments, chemicals, leather, paper, furniture, clothing, none of which was weighted heavily in the industrial structure. She had, moreover, the additional advantage of being the centre of Britain's financial, commercial and administrative services many of which were affected only marginally by the cycle. In 1934, 47·2 per cent of insured workers were attached to ten service groups compared with a national average of 38 per cent.[1]

It was this diversity together with the high proportion of employment in non-manufacturing industries which was largely responsible for London's prosperity. As Fogarty has remarked, 'London is ... an outstanding example of the advantages to employers and workers alike of the concentration in a single area of a wide range of growing and adaptable manufacturing industries, backed up with highly specialized and efficient technical, commercial, and financial facilities.'[2] It is not surprising, therefore, that London had a very high rate of employment growth and a relatively low level of unemployment. Between 1923 and 1937 the numbers in employment grew at nearly twice the national rate, while unemployment, even at the bottom of the slump, was not more than 13 per cent, that is 9–10 percentage points below the average for the whole country. At the peak of the cycle, 1929 and 1937, unemployment was around 5–6 per cent or about half the national level.

Many of the South-eastern counties were equally prosperous as London itself if not more so. In fact employment in the South-east as a whole rose more rapidly than in the London area between 1923 and 1937. Prosperity was based on extensive residential development, the growth of the newer and lighter industries and the continued expansion of the service sectors. Such developments were facilitated by the general prosperity of the region, good transport links which served a national market, relatively cheap sites and good housing. The South-east also benefited from the influx of labour from other areas. In some towns expansion was very rapid indeed; at Luton the insured population

---

[1] They were distribution, local government, laundries, hotel services, road transport, tram and omnibus services, entertainment and sport, professional services, building and public works contracting. S. R. Dennison, *The Location of Industry and the Depressed Areas* (1939), p. 42.
[2] Fogarty, *op. cit.*, p. 423.

almost doubled and at Slough it quadrupled over the years 1923–37. Generally speaking the South-eastern counties were favoured in at least two respects: they possessed a fairly diversified industrial structure and they had few resources tied up in old staple industries. Hence there was a marked absence of the industrial difficulties which plagued the North. The only really serious problem was the depressed condition of agriculture which affected most of the South-eastern counties, but for this there was adequate compensation in other fields of activity outside agriculture. On the other hand, the industrial structure was not always as diversified as that of London and some towns and districts depended heavily on one or two industries. The prosperity of Oxford and Luton, for example, was very much bound up with the fortunes of the motor car industry. By the later 1930s over 20 per cent of the Luton labour force and 27 per cent of that of Oxford were engaged in the construction and repair of vehicles (including aircraft), an industry which was subject to fairly sharp cyclical fluctuations. But the important point was that this type of concentration was in expanding industries arising very often from the developments in the newer trades, while there were few resources devoted to the declining basic industries. Luton, for example, apart from its vehicle interests, also had a high proportion of workers engaged in trades which were little affected either by structural or cyclical unemployment. Over 25 per cent of the insured population in 1937 was engaged in hat and cap manufacture, while a further 23 per cent gained their livelihood from building, public works, distribution, chemicals, and gas, water and electricity.[1] On the other hand, Slough, another boom town, had a very diversified structure. The most important industry was building which accounted for 11·1 per cent of the insured population in 1937. Other important sectors included electrical engineering, general engineering, non-ferrous metal manufacturing, furniture, chemicals, distribution and the food industries, which along with building accounted for the greater part of Slough's employment expansion.

Finally, passing reference might be made to the East Midlands, covering the six counties of Northampton and Peterborough, Rutland, Lincoln, Leicester, Nottingham and Derby. This was one of the most prosperous areas outside London and the South-east though structurally it was somewhat different. Although the region's industrial structure was reasonably diversified it contained a fair proportion of

Fogarty, *op. cit.*, p. 394.

older trades. It was the main centre for the production of boots and shoes, hosiery and lace which together accounted for 28 per cent of the insured population in 1935.[1] Almost another 20 per cent were attached to the coal and iron and steel industries. But apart from coal, which was concentrated in North Derby and Nottingham, these were not trades which were severely in decline, nor were they affected markedly by cyclical forces. It is true that employment in the footwear and lace industries was tending to fall but this was more than compensated for by the gains in building, hosiery, iron and steel and the service sectors together with the rapid growth of newer industries such as rayon, motor vehicles and electrical engineering. The iron and steel industry is an interesting case since for this region it was virtually a new industry. The main developments occurred in the 1930s when the firm of Stewarts and Lloyds erected a modern iron and steel complex at Corby to utilize the local ores. By 1937 steel output in Northamptonshire had risen to 417,600 tons compared with nothing in 1913, and the two counties of Northampton and Lincolnshire accounted for 13 per cent of British steel output as against only three per cent in 1913.

Population migration and labour mobility

The brief survey of development in various regions has emphasized those features which made for either prosperity or depression. The consequences of the different pace of development in the North and the South remain to be analysed. First, however, we must examine the movements in population and labour and the attempts of the Government to alleviate the problems of the depressed areas.

During the inter-war years there were two distinct geographical shifts in population both of which reversed the dominant trends of the nineteenth century. First, there was a marked shift of population away from the town centres towards the suburbs and second, there was a strong tendency for the South to gain population at the expense of the North. These two movements were only partially related to each other but it is convenient to consider them both at this point.

The movement of population from the city centre to the outskirts was not an entirely new phenomenon. It had, in fact, been taking place well before the end of the nineteenth century. But it was largely confined to the wealthier sections of the middle classes who could afford

[1] The region accounted for between 60 and 75 per cent of the total employment in these trades.

to migrate from congested urban centres. During the early twentieth century this shift was greatly accelerated and in the inter-war period it became the most prominent feature in the distribution of population. For example, of the 131 districts of England and Wales which increased their population by 30 per cent or more between 1921–31, no less than 116 were suburban areas, the remainder being seaside resorts.[1] All the major urban areas, which accounted for roughly one half of the total population, experienced this centrifugal movement. Population at the centre remained constant or even declined while the suburban areas grew rapidly. Thus the central zones of the seven largest urban areas[2] showed a decline in population of 2·5 per cent between 1921 and 1938, whereas population in their suburban areas rose by 32 per cent. Altogether three quarters of Britain's population growth in this period (3·44 million) accrued to the suburbs of the 27 major conurbations.

The process of suburban growth is illustrated clearly by the example of the Greater London Area. After the turn of the century the outer zone expanded rapidly at the expense of the centre. Between 1921 and 1937 population in outer London rose by nearly 1·4 million while the number living in central London fell by almost 400,000. On the other hand, outer London gained far more than inner London lost. This suggests that there was a fairly strong inward movement of population from the rest of the country towards London and that the two movements met or converged on the periphery of the capital.[3]

In this respect the London area was somewhat unique in that two flows of population, one a suburban exodus and the other a regional migration, converged on the outer edge of the region. But the process of suburban migration was not dissimilar to that taking place around most of the large cities such as Manchester, Glasgow, Liverpool, Leeds, etc. Basically the suburban migration was caused by the interaction of a complex set of interdependent push and pull factors. People were encouraged to move to the suburbs because of increasing congestion and the unpleasant surroundings in the city centres. In turn the movement was made possible by rising real incomes, improved

[1] Political and Economic Planning, *Report on the Location of Industry* (1939), pp. 294–8.
[2] London, Manchester, Birmingham, Glasgow, West Yorkshire, Merseyside and Tyneside.
[3] D. L. Foley, *Controlling London's Growth* (1963), pp. 10, 21; *Royal Commission on the Distribution of Industrial Population*, Cmd 6153 (1940), pp. 163, 171.

suburban transport facilities, largely as a result of the development of motor transport, and the extensive provision of relatively cheap accommodation on the outskirts. In addition, the period was characterized by a shift in the socially acceptable standard of housing accommodation with the result that many migrants were motivated as much by changes in tastes as by changes in their incomes. It is impossible to separate cause and effect in this matter but there can be no doubt about the strength of the forces making for a redistribution of population within the major urban areas.[1]

TABLE 18   *Average annual gains (+) or losses (−) through migration, 1923–36*

	1923–31	*1931–36*
London and Home Counties	+ 62,205	+ 71,623
South-east	+ 8,733	+ 18,334
South-west	+ 10,582	+ 11,445
Midlands	− 4,964	+ 5,521
North-west	− 19,275	− 6,942
North-east	− 30,516	− 24,180
Scotland	− 37,559	+ 1,299
Wales	− 31,350	− 22,092
Net inward (+) or outward (−) balance of overseas migration	− 42,144	+ 55,008

SOURCE   Fogarty, *op. cit.*, p. 4.

Suburban growth was not entirely unrelated to the inter-regional movements of population taking place at the same time, for in some cases, notably London, regional and city migrations met in the suburban area. The causes of regional migration were less complex, being determined largely by the absence of availability of jobs. In effect therefore the pattern of regional migration was more or less as one might have expected, namely that the depressed areas lost, and the prosperous areas gained, population. The balance of regional gains and losses through inter-regional migration are shown in Table 18. The chief gains were made by London and the Home Counties, the South-east and the South-west; these three regions attracted over 1·1 million migrants between 1923 and 1936. Rather surprisingly the Midland counties lost on balance over the period, partly because of

[1] These points are discussed more fully in H. W. Richardson and D. H. Aldcroft, *Building in the British Economy Between the Wars* (1968), ch. 14.

difficulties in industrial readjustment in the northern section of the Midlands in the 1920s. By far the worst losses occurred in Wales, Scotland and North-east England. Altogether they lost just over 1·2 million, that is slightly more than the Southern regions gained. Wales was hardest hit of all. Between 1921 and 1939 the Welsh population fell from 2,656,000 to 2,465,000, while the total loss through migration amounted to nearly 450,000. In other words, Wales lost all of its natural increase in population, that is 259,000, plus a further 191,000. Scotland and North-west England also suffered badly in the 1920s, but the position improved in the following decade.[1] During the 1920s overseas migration provided some relief for redundant workers of the depressed regions, but in the following decade this traditional safety-valve was closed and a net inward movement of population occurred (Table 18).

Although most of the migrants moved on their own initiative the process was assisted in part by a special industrial transfer programme inaugurated by the Ministry of Labour in the late 1920s. This scheme was designed to give financial assistance to those people for whom there was little prospect of employment within their areas. The numbers assisted in this way were comparatively small and the scheme proved to be least effective when most needed, that is in the early 1930s. Altogether between 1928 and the middle of 1937 nearly 190,000 men and women benefited from assisted migration, though 56,000 actually returned after transfer.[2] Most of the people aided under the industrial transfer scheme were long distance migrants in that they shifted from the depressed areas to the South.

Though in numerical terms the South gained more or less what the North lost not all migration was of a long distance type. Some districts and towns in the South attracted migrants from neighbouring prosperous areas as well as from the North. Oxford, for example, attracted far more workers from surrounding areas than it did from the depressed regions. In 1936, 43 per cent of all the insured male adults

---

[1] B. Thomas (ed.), *The Welsh Economy* (1962), pp. 7–9.
[2] W. H. Beveridge, *Full Employment in a Free Society* (1944), pp. 63–5. Training centres were also established under the transfer scheme to train unemployed men in new skills. Between 1929 and 1938 over 70,000 men were processed of whom about 63,000 found employment. In addition, industrial transfer centres were set up for rehabilitating men who had lost their physical fitness or industrial moral through prolonged depression. By 1938 these centres had provided courses for over 100,000 of whom less than one third were placed in employment.

in Oxford had come from other parts of the country; of these about
two thirds had come from around Oxford, the Midlands and London
and the South-east, whereas less than one quarter were from Wales
and the North. Though this example is not necessarily typical it does
suggest that there was a considerable amount of short-distance migration and that the migrant workers of the North had to compete for
jobs with workers moving between prosperous regions.

Whatever the exact pattern of migration it is clear that the Southern
regions gained considerably from regional migration. This was undoubtedly an important factor in the uneven distribution of the population increase between the wars. Between 1921 and 1937 the
population of Britain rose by $7\frac{1}{2}$ per cent but in London and the Home
Counties the increase was 18 per cent, while in the Midlands it was
around 11 per cent. All other areas expanded by less than the national
average and Wales and the North-east coast lost absolutely. In other
words, by far the largest part of the increase in population accrued
to the South-east segment of the country. This area accounted for
roughly one third of the population of England and Wales in 1921
yet absorbed just over two thirds of the increase in population. The
Greater London Area alone accounted for over one third of the national
increase which was a greater relative share than in any period since
1801.[1]

Regional policy

Despite the heavy emigration from the depressed regions it was insufficient to prevent the working population from growing faster than
the number of jobs available. The failure of the market to effect readjustment eventually forced the Government to take action. As we
have already seen, in the late 1920s industrial transfer and training
schemes were started. These policies, however, were unable to cope
with the problem. The dimensions of the unemployment in these areas
were so vast and specialized that any scheme of assisted migration
could only act as a temporary palliative. Moreover, the people most
likely to benefit were the young and single workers who were free to
move and had the ability to grasp new skills quickly. In the 1930s,
therefore, the Government resorted to a policy of bringing work to
the workers in what came to be known as the Special Areas.

The Special Areas legislation of 1934–7 established Commissioners

[1] Foley, *op. cit.*, pp. 10–12; *R.C. on Industrial Population*, pp. 36–7.

for Scotland and England and Wales whose task was to promote the economic and social development of four designated areas – Central Scotland, South Wales, West Cumberland and parts of the Northeast coast including Tyneside. They were given powers to attract new industries and firms to these areas and to establish trading estates. They could also contribute towards the rents, income tax and rates of firms for up to five years. Finally, foreign firms were to be encouraged to settle in these areas and the Government was to give the Special Areas priority in the allocation of defence contracts.

Though a novel departure from established practice the new policy could hardly be called a success. The amount of expenditure was very small in relation to the size of the task in hand. By the end of 1938 the Commissioners' financial commitments amounted to about £17 million; only half of this sum had been spent and a good deal of it had gone on land settlement and public health schemes. Just over £2·9 million had been spent on assisting the establishment of new industries, involving 121 firms and the creation of 14,900 jobs. In addition, a further 290 firms had been assisted by capital or other financial inducements, while between June 1936 and the end of 1938 about 190 foreign firms were located in the depressed regions. Finally, a number of Government trading estates were established the chief of which were those at Treforest, Team Valley and Hillington with minor ones at Pallion (Sunderland), St Helen Auckland, Larkhall, and Cyfarthfa. By the end of the period some 12,000 workers were employed in Government-owned factories, mostly on trading estates.[1]

In all, probably less than 50,000 new jobs were created as a result of the implementation of the Special Areas policy. Since in January 1935 nearly 362,000 persons were registered as unemployed in these regions the policy only brought marginal relief. Though the forces of recovery had brought a sharp drop in unemployment by the end of 1937 it still remained about twice the national average. The Commissioners, of course, faced a very difficult task; not only were their powers limited, especially financially, but it was difficult to persuade firms to move since the benefits of the depressed areas were by no means obvious to industrialists. Moreover, the attitude of the Government was hardly one to encourage their work. The areas selected for assistance were few in number and their boundaries were not such as to make possible effective long-range planning. The Government clearly re-

[1] *R.C. on Industrial Population*, pp. 147–8.

garded the policy as a temporary expedient and refused to extend it to other regions. Yet a good case could be made for extending the geographical coverage since a number of depressed areas, e.g. Lancashire, were excluded from its scope.[1] In the main, however, the Government preferred to rely on the provision of maintenance to relieve unemployment. Consequently, as one writer remarked, the efforts to stimulate employment could be regarded as little more than half-hearted concessions to a growing public concern over the persistence of continuous unemployment.[2]

Despite the failure of policy to provide a solution to the unemployment problem in the depressed regions, this does not mean that these areas failed to participate in the recovery of the 1930s, though it tended to occur later than elsewhere. In fact compared with the position at the bottom of the slump the growth of employment in these regions was not very dissimilar to that in the South. This parity of achievement is somewhat misleading however, since unemployment in these areas was much higher in the 1920s and early 1930s than elsewhere. Compared with the peak of 1929 the strength of the revival was very weak. Thus by the end of the period unemployment levels were still well above the national average. Revival was induced by natural rather than policy factors, and though the pattern of recovery differed somewhat from region to region a number of common elements can be discerned. Undoubtedly the unemployment position was eased by virtue of the shift of population to the more prosperous areas, though not all migrant workers managed to find employment. Second, the growth of the newer industries and service trades facilitated recovery though because of the limited importance of these trades, especially the newer sectors, their impact was not very great. The main burden of recovery had to come from the basic staple industries. The revival of these was belated, but it came nonetheless in the later 1930s, assisted by the recovery of trade, the collapse of which had been the root cause of the difficulties, the induced effects of prosperity in the South in the form of demand for certain staple products of the steel and engineering industries, and by the impact of the rearmament boom. This latter factor gave a considerable boost to the depressed regions in the later 1930s since a number of important

---

[2] Though under the Special Areas (Amendment) Act of 1937 the Treasury could give direct assistance to firms settling in the Special Areas or in certain designated distressed districts.

[1] E. M. Burns, *British Unemployment Programs, 1920–1938* (1941), pp. 328–9.

Government defence contracts were farmed out to them. However, the distribution of these contracts was very uneven; most of them went to the West of Scotland and Tyneside whereas some areas, notably South Wales, derived little benefit from them.[1]

Despite the signs of recovery in the later 1930s these regions still remained badly off compared with the South by the end of the period. Long-term structural unemployment remained acute while the industrial base was still narrow and vulnerable. A far too high a proportion of resources was tied to the basic staple trades dependent upon the uncertain growth prospects of the export sector, and sensitive to the vagaries of the trade cycle. Thus in the recession of 1937–8 it was the northern regions and Wales which again fared badly.

Implications of regional disparity

It is useful to consider some of the main implications arising from differential rates of development between the regions. Because of the paucity of data it will not always be possible to make very precise statements. The following points, therefore, should be regarded more in the way of suggestions than positive conclusions.

The large volume of unemployed resources in the depressed regions undoubtedly dampened the growth of the economy as a whole. It goes without saying that had more of these resources been utilized growth would have been faster. Moreover, because of high unemployment and depressed trade conditions real income per head in these regions was lower than on average. This was particularly the case in Scotland where income levels were about 10 per cent below the national average. Income data are not available for other regions but, judging on the basis of industrial earnings information, it is more than likely that most of the depressed regions, especially Wales and the Northeast, had income levels below those of the South and the country as a whole.[2]

---

[1] See H. W. Richardson, *Economic Recovery in Britain, 1932–9* (1967), pp. 283–5, 289–94.

[2] In many of the industries on which the depressed areas chiefly depended earnings were relatively low compared with those in the new and expanding sectors. Thus in October 1938 the average earnings of adult male workers in the textile trade ranged between 50s 9d and 57s 6d whereas workers in vehicles and general engineering earned 83s 3d and 73s 7d respectively. See Fogarty, *op. cit.*, p. 11, and Chapter 10, below.

Yet if this were the case one might have expected the growth of the newer and rapidly expanding industries to have been somewhat slower than in the South. Generally speaking this was not so. In most of the depressed regions these two groups of industries expanded as rapidly as elsewhere and in Lancashire the growth of the 16 rapidly expanding industries was faster than in any other region (Table 17). In part this can be explained by the fact that the growth or newer industries were badly represented in the depressed areas at the start of the period so that their expansion is measured on a very low base. To have made up the leeway these industries would have needed to expand at a much faster rate than elsewhere. The main difficulty was in attracting firms producing new products to these areas and the failure to do so can be attributed to the relatively unattractive surroundings, lower incomes and market forces. It was unfortunate that these areas experienced a lower level of effective demand at the very time when the market was becoming a more powerful determinant of industrial location. During the nineteenth century the North had two great assets: good rail communications and the availability of raw materials, especially fuel. But the strength of these two factors was considerably weakened with the development of road transport and electricity which made industrial location much more flexible. The market therefore became the main influence determining the location of many newer industries and since the South had the advantage of a large and growing population and a higher level of purchasing power it was only natural that the growth industries should tend to concentrate in this area. The process became a cumulative one: new industries were established, incomes grew, population expanded through migration and natural increase, and in turn the market expanded thereby stimulating further development. Moreover, since many of the newer trades were inter-dependent in terms of demand and supply of their products there were obvious economies to be gained from geographical concentration. For example, firms producing components for motor vehicles tended to congregate close to the assembly plants in Oxford and Luton rather than in the North since this reduced transport costs to a minimum.

Thus, given the unfavourably weighted industrial structure at the beginning of the period the depressed areas found it difficult to diversify and adjust their economies, especially as they faced competition from the more firmly established growth industries in the South. The continued growth of this region attracted resources from the depressed areas which prevented any general shortage of labour holding up development in the new sectors. But even in the South unemployment levels remained relatively high and this set a limit to the rate at which unemployed resources moved from the North to the South. This partly explains why in the Northern regions unemployment rates, even in the rapidly expanding industries, were higher than elsewhere, since given the limit to which displaced resources could be absorbed by the South the excess reserves of labour tended to shift from one industry to another within the depressed areas thus causing a levelling up of unemployment percentages between different industries in the same region. Thus in the South in June 1936 only 24 of nearly 100 industries employing more than 1,000 workers had unemployment rates as high as nine per cent, whereas in the North only 25 industries had unemployment rates below 10·8 per cent.[1]

The above comments require some modification however. Despite widespread unemployment shortages of labour did occur from time to time in both depressed and prosperous regions. In the later 1930s there was a scarcity of skilled building workers in Scotland and many housing schemes were delayed for the want of bricklayers and plasterers.[2] Similarly, a study of the engineering labour market in London for the latter half of 1936 revealed the existence of acute shortages and long delays in the recruitment of skilled operatives. Of all the vacancies notified for highly skilled workers only 63 per cent were filled by the labour exchanges and the rearmament boom tended to aggravate the position in later years. That such shortages could exist amid plenty is to be explained by the complex heterogenity of the labour market. No amount of unemployment and labour mobility could solve the basic problem, namely the need to retrain and re-equip redundant workers with new skills. As the authors of the London survey stressed: 'There is no force in the argument that, because engineers are to be found registered as unemployed, there must be a slack to be taken up in this market. The demand for engineering labour is not a simple and straightforward quantity; it is of varied and ever-changing pattern. Unless the quality of supply can be readily adapted, there will be unemployment irrespective of the amount of the supply.'[3] It

[1] D. G. Champernowne, 'The Uneven Distribution of Unemployment in the United Kingdom, 1929–36', *Review of Economic Studies*, 5 (1936–7), p. 104.
[2] *Report of the Committee on Scottish Building Costs*, Cmd 5977 (1938–9), p. 28.
[3] R. G. D. Allen and B. Thomas, 'The Supply of Engineering Labour under Boom Conditions', *Economic Journal*, 49 (1939), pp. 264, 274.

cannot of course be argued that development either in the prosperous or depressed areas was severely handicapped by shortages of skilled labour but it is important to stress that scarcities did occur and that these could not always be relieved simply by transferring workers from one region to another.[1]

In other words, too much emphasis should not be placed on the effects of long-distance migration either as a relief to the depressed areas or as a stimulant to the prosperous regions of the South. It is probable, however, that the migration of labour from the North accentuated the problems of the depressed areas and made them less attractive to industrialists generally. Usually it was the young and the skilled workers who were most willing to move; estimates suggest that one half of the migrants were aged between 15 and 29 and possibly two thirds were under 44.[2] This meant that these regions were robbed of their most able workers and left with the older ones, who were either unskilled or whose skills were unsuited to the needs of the newer industries. It was the older and less skilled workers who constituted the core of the long-term unemployment problem. The four regions of Scotland, Northern, North-West and Wales, which together contained 40 per cent of the total insured population, accounted for 80 per cent of those who had been continuously unemployed for three years or more on 1st May 1939.[3] On the other hand, *ceteris paribus*, the absence of this migration would only have accentuated the unemployment problem in the North. Thus migration provided some partial, short-term relief to the unemployment problem in the North even though from the long-term point of view it meant a loss of the best labour reserves.[4]

But the attractions of the South did not rob the northern regions of all their vitality by any means. With the possible exception of Wales most regions showed signs of adjustment and generally speaking natural increases in population outweighed the losses through migration. Furthermore, the depressed areas stood to gain to some extent

[1] From this it follows that it would be wrong to infer that the uneven distribution of unemployment impaired recovery from the slump in the prosperous regions. *Cf* Champernowne, *loc. cit.*, p. 94.

[2] Richardson, *op cit.*, p. 280. Around 87 per cent of the net outward balance of migrants from South Wales and Northumberland and Durham were under 45 years of age. R. M. Titmuss, *Poverty and Population* (1938), p. 290.

[3] J. Sykes, 'Remedies for Unemployment', *The Manchester School*, 19 (1951), p. 7.

[4] For the effects of regional migration on the age structure of the depressed areas and its ultimate consequences, see Titmuss, *op. cit.*, pp. 285–94.

from the more rapid growth experienced in the South. The absence of adequate regional statistics and data on inter-regional resource flows makes it difficult to say very much about the spill-over effects. Some of the older staple industries, such as shipbuilding and coal, were not affected very much by expansion in the South. On the other hand, steel and non-electrical engineering industries in the North no doubt benefited as a result of the demand from the vehicle and construction industries. But these may well have been more than offset by the North's propensity to import new goods from the South. Taking into account the movement of resources the South probably gained on balance though only marginally.

Conclusion

During the period the pattern of development varied considerably from one region to another. Nevertheless two fairly distinct groups can be discerned. On the one hand, there were the fairly prosperous regions in the South, including most of the Midlands, and on the other, the relatively depressed areas situated in the North, and including Wales. Inevitably the dividing line is somewhat arbitrary. In the Midlands, for example, some areas were as prosperous as the South-east while others were more akin to the depressed areas. Furthermore, sub-regional analysis reveals some marked differences in prosperity between districts and towns within the same broad region.

Although over the period as a whole the South and Midlands grew at a much faster rate than the North, over different phases of the cycle the rate of development varied somewhat. During the 1920s most regions expanded though growth was clearly fastest in London and the South-east. The Midlands, however, fared only marginally better than the North-west. It was in the downswing of 1929–32 that the gap between North and South became really pronounced. All Northern regions including Wales suffered a sharp contraction in employment, whereas in London, the South-east and South-west the depression was very mild. These latter regions were the first to recover after 1932, but further North recovery did not take hold properly until 1935. Yet apart from the North-west the pace of recovery in the depressed regions over the course of the upswing (1932–7) was comparable with that in the South. This, of course, can be partly explained by the fact that the North suffered a much sharper contraction in the downswing. If we measure from peak to peak of the cycle

(1929–37) the North's rate of development was very much weaker than that of the South. Moreover, the North was still very vulnerable to cyclical shocks. The recession of 1937–8 was mainly confined to this half of the country for over much of the South (excluding the Midlands) expansion continued unchecked.

Despite these differences the distinction between the North and the South is by no means artificial. Within each group certain regions stand out as typical. The most prosperous areas in the South were London and the South-east, while South Wales, the North-east coast, South-west Scotland and North Lancashire were the arch examples of depression. The contrast is not difficult to explain. The former group of regions tended to have a fairly diversified industrial base and a high proportion of their resources in new and/or rapidly growing sectors of the economy. Emphasis was on the production of consumer goods for the home market. Conversely, the industrial base of the Northern regions was very narrow; it was tied primarily to the heavy capital goods industries, dependent on exports and vulnerable to fluctuations. Newer industries and local growth industries were poorly represented in these regions. The rate of growth of these latter industries was comparable to that achieved further South but it was insufficient to offset the sharp contraction in the basic industries,[1] which featured so prominently in the industrial structure at the start of the period. It was this initial disadvantage together with the failure to attract a sufficient share of the new and growing industries that was largely responsible for the depressed condition of the North.

The South, therefore, began with an initial advantage in that its industrial base was reasonably well suited to post-war conditions. Moreover, because of higher incomes, a large and diversified market, good housing and communications, the South had greater locational attractions than the North. Growth of the newer sectors tended to feed on itself and faced with this competition the North found it more difficult to attract new industrial developments. Some adjustments were made in the period but by the end of the 1930s the industrial structure of the depressed regions was still maladjusted.

Government policy did little to rectify the imbalance. Though attempts were made to transfer labour and develop a regional policy the programme of action was too little and too late to do more than touch the fringe of the problem. Nor did the Government's fiscal policy

[1] That is insufficient to offset the employment contraction. Output and incomes in all regions, except Wales, expanded over the period.

have much effect in boosting the revival of the depressed areas. This was hardly surprising. Official economic policy was still confined within the strait-jacket of classical economics and positive action to stimulate employment either through macro or regional policies was kept to a minimum.[1] Most action in fact was of the *ad hoc* experimental kind and relief to the unemployed mainly took the form of financial assistance.

[1] Government economic policy is dealt with fully in Chapter 9.

4 Sources of growth

Introduction

In the first three chapters we were mainly concerned with the dimensions of growth and fluctuations in economic activity during the inter-war period. Nothing explicit was said, however, about the determinants of growth. Here, therefore, we propose to take a close look at the main sources of growth. Our main concern will be with economic rather than sociological factors. This is not to imply that the latter have no importance, but concentration on the economic factors can be justified on two grounds. First, it would appear that inter-war growth can be explained fairly readily without reference to social factors. Second, since they defy precise quantification the author would prefer to leave them to writers more competent in the field.

Analysing the sources of growth is not an easy task even under our definition of economic factors. There is a great danger of bordering on two extremes, namely the single causal and multi-causal explanations of growth. The latter is the more complex and unrewarding of the two. It is easy to assemble a whole string of favourable (or unfavourable) factors which have a bearing on economic growth during a particular period, but it is usually much more difficult to attach precise quantitative significance to any one of them. Part of the difficulty arises from the wide range of variables chosen in the first instance and the failure to determine their precise inter-causal relationships.

A neoclassical approach to growth analysis provides the most convenient starting point. Here we measure the contribution made to the growth of output by the three main sources of growth, capital, labour and the residual. The last of these covers everything which contributes to an increase in output per unit of output and includes such things as technical advances, economies of scale, better business organization and improvements in resource allocation. Thus the growth of output can be achieved in one of two ways: either by raising the inputs of capital and labour or by an improvement in the productivity of these factors. For example, if it takes 100 units of capital and 50 units of labour to produce 25 units of output, then to double the latter we should need to add 100 units of capital and 50 units of labour to the existing stock. This assumes, of course, that the capital–labour ratio remains unchanged and that there is no improvement in the residual. Alternatively, the growth of output may be achieved solely by an increase in output per unit of input, while the stocks of capital and labour remain constant. In practice, however, growth is likely to occur as a result of simultaneous changes in all three variables.

Whether or not improvements in the residual are accompanied by increases in capital and labour inputs depends very much on the type of improvement involved. The application of large scale innovations such as electricity, which lead to an increase in productivity, will obviously require additions to the stock of capital and labour. On the other hand, increases in efficiency resulting from a rationalization of plant and work force may be achieved without any additions to the stock of assets or, in fact, by a decline in the capital and labour required. Generally speaking, changes in the residual will be accompanied by changes in the stock of capital and labour, though what applies to the economy as a whole need not be true for individual industries or sectors.

In recent years considerable research has been carried out into the sources of growth. Though there is still disagreement among economists as to the relative importance of the three variables many empirical studies suggest that the residual or technical progress has made the most important contribution to growth.[1] A word of warning is required here. The importance of the residual element may be over-estimated for two reasons. First, some of the studies do not take account of changes in the quality of the labour force with the result that the con-

[1] See R. M. Solow, 'Technical Change and the Aggregate Production Function', *Review of Economics and Statistics*, 39 (1957); O. Aukrust, 'Factors in Economic Development: A Review of Recent Research', *Productivity Measurement Review*, Feb. 1965; E. F. Denison, *Why Growth Rates Differ* (1968).

tribution of the labour factor is under-estimated. Second, some economists have argued that a clear distinction cannot be made between
investment and technical progress. Most technical advances or other
improvements which raise productivity will require capital and
some of these improvements will be embodied in investment which
replaces worn out assets. In other words, the technique of appor-
tioning growth between factor inputs and the residual may well underestimate the contribution of capital if, as is often the case, technical
advances are embodied in investment, especially if part of this investment comprises the replacement of assets. Thus it is gross investment, rather than net additions to the capital stock which are generally
used in analyses of this type, which is of greater significance.[1] We
shall return to this point later, but bearing in mind these qualifications
we can proceed with an analysis of the sources of growth for the
economy as a whole.

TABLE 19   *Annual rates of growth of output and input in the U.K.*

	Output	Output per man	Employ-ment	Capital	Total factor inputs	Residual
1899–1913	1·1	0·1	1·0	1·8	1·3	−0·2
1920–38	1·7	1·2	0·5	1·1	0·7	1·0
1924–38	2·0	0·9	1·1	1·2	1·1	0·9

SOURCE   See text.

Sources of growth

In Table 19 an attempt is made to estimate the growth contribution
of the three variables. A value for total factor inputs is obtained by
weighting capital and labour according to their shares in total output in a particular base year. For the pre-1914 period the base year is
1906 and the respective shares are 0·4 and 0·6, while for the inter-war
years the shares are 0·3 and 0·7 with the base year of 1929. The
difference between the value for total factor inputs and the actual
rate of growth in output can then be attributed to the residual element. This procedure follows that adopted by Matthews in his pre-
liminary study of the long-term growth of the British economy and in

[1] Denison in fact averages the growth rates of the two capital stocks.

fact the first line of Table 19 is taken from his work.[1] The remaining calculations are based on data provided in Feinstein and Chapman and Knight.[2]

Over the period as a whole (1920–38) factor inputs contributed less to the growth of output than the improvement in the residual. In part the low rate of labour input was responsible for this. Employment reached a peak in 1920 which was not regained until well into the 1930s. If we take 1924 as the base year, when the volume of employment was less than in 1920, the rate of growth of labour input to 1938 works out at about 1·1 per cent per annum. Combining this with a capital growth of 1·2 per cent gives an overall factor contribution of just over 1·1 per cent, leaving around 0·9 per cent for the residual. There is something to be said for using 1924 rather than 1920 as the base year since it is easier to find a terminal year with a similar degree of capacity utilization. However, the contrast with the pre-war period is apparent whichever dates one uses as the basis for comparison. Between 1899 and 1913 the growth of output was low compared with the inter-war years despite a steady increase in factor inputs, especially capital. The difference between the two periods seems to have been largely due to the residual element, which changed from a negative quantity before 1914 to about 1·0 per cent in the inter-war years. Over the entire period, 1920–38, total factor inputs increased at only half the pre-war rate, and even between 1924–38 the rate of increase was slightly lower. In fact in the latter period capital employed per head of the occupied labour force remained almost stationary,[3] while the capital–output ratio fell from 2·6 between 1920–24 to 2·3 in 1935–38, reflecting a rise in the productivity of capital.[4]

It would seem, therefore, that the residual element was mainly responsible for the improved growth performance of the inter-war period. The residual, of course, covers a wide range of components. It includes not only the effects of new techniques, shifts in the alloc-

[1] R. C. O. Matthews, 'Some Aspects of Post-War Growth in the British Economy in Relation to Historical Experience', *Trans. of the Manchester Statistical Society* (1964).
[2] C. H. Feinstein, *Domestic Capital Formation in the United Kingdom, 1920–1938* (1965); A. L. Chapman and R. Knight, *Wages and Salaries in the United Kingdom, 1920–38* (1953).
[3] That is measured at first cost values and excluding dwellings. On a depreciated basis there was a slight fall. See Feinstein, *op. cit.*, p. 53.
[4] Ratio of first cost value of all assets excluding dwellings to G.N.P. Feinstein, *op. cit.*, p. 56.

ation of resources, economies of scale and better methods of production, but also a host of what have been termed 'unconventional inputs' including expenditure on health and education, changes in monopoly power and other restrictions on economic activity. Unfortunately, it is not possible to give a detailed breakdown to show how each contributed to the growth of output. It is possible, however, to say something more about the composition of the residual factor. Empirical studies, particularly that of Denison, suggest that the most important items in the residual are advances in techniques, shifts in resource allocation and economies of scale.

On this basis it might be possible to explain the more vigorous growth in the inter-war years (that is compared with before 1914) by the technical advances and economies of scale associated with the structural changes taking place in the economy. The sequence might be described as follows. Before 1914 there were relatively few structural changes in the pattern of activity. By and large the expansion of the economy depended upon the continued development of existing sectors. This was particularly true in the case of the industrial sector which accounted for around 45 per cent of total output. A few large staple industries dominated the field. In 1907 coal, textiles, iron and steel and engineering accounted for 50 per cent of net industrial output, they employed about one quarter of the occupied labour force and supplied 70 per cent of Britain's exports.[1] Resources continued to be poured into these industries despite the fact their rate of expansion (especially productivity) slackened in the couple of decades before the war. Low productivity growth was a function of the slow rate of technical advance, while developments in new, high growth sectors based on inventions such as electricity and the internal combustion engine, were very limited. By 1907 newer industries (electrical engineering, road vehicles, rayon, chemicals and scientific instruments) accounted for only 6·5 per cent of net industrial output and 5·2 per cent of industrial employment.[2] Thus as far as industry was concerned the shift of resources from low to high growth sectors was very limited. The service sectors, transport, finance, distribution etc, expanded quite rapidly at least in terms of employment, and in this respect some of them increased in relative importance. But the rate of output and productivity growth of these sectors was relatively low and could not offset the retardation in the industrial sector.

[1] A. E. Kahn, *Great Britain in the World Economy* (1946), pp. 66–7.
[2] *ibid.*, pp. 106, 109.

In other words, before 1914 Britain's resources tended to be concentrated in slow-growing sectors with a low rate of technical advance, while large-scale innovations, particularly those giving rise to new industries, were slow to mature.[1] Inter-sectoral shifts of resources tended to be between low productivity sectors rather than from low to high growth sectors.[2] The contrast with the post-war situation is quite marked. In the first place, the export-predominant, staple industries (including agriculture) declined in importance and gave way to the new industries, which expanded rapidly by exploiting new techniques and reaping scale economies. In 1935 the new industries accounted for 19 per cent of industrial output compared with 12·5 per cent in 1924 and 6·5 per cent in 1907. This calculation takes no account of electricity supply which expanded very rapidly indeed. Second, the construction and allied trades expanded rapidly compared with pre-war, largely as a result of the massive housebuilding programme. Third, although rail and tram transport stagnated or grew only slowly this was more than compensated for by the vigorous boom in road transport. Finally, the service sectors of the economy continued to expand though their contribution to the growth of the economy was somewhat mixed as we shall see.

A more detailed analysis can now be made to show how each sector contributed to the growth of the economy as a whole. It will then be possible to see what importance can be attached to the new developments listed above.

The industrial versus the service sector

To begin with we may divide the economy into two broad groups: the production and the service sectors. The first group includes agriculture, mining, construction, electricity, gas and water and manufacturing industry, while the second covers all service trades, public administration, professional activities and transport but excludes the Armed Forces. In 1937 these two sectors were roughly equal in terms of output and employment generated, but the service sector accounted for nearly 70 per cent of the total capital stock. Over the

[1] For a recent analysis of this aspect see H. W. Richardson, 'Overcommitment in Britain Before 1930', *Oxford Economic Papers*, 17 (1965).
[2] A more extended discussion of the pre-1914 pattern of activity can be found in D. H. Aldcroft and H. W. Richardson, *The British Economy, 1870–1939* (1969).

inter-war period this sector increased its shares of total employment and the capital stock.[1]

TABLE 20   *Annual rates of growth of output, employment, capital, etc., 1920–38*

	Output	Output per man	Employ-ment	Capital	Total factor inputs	Residual
G.D.P.	1·7	1·2	0·5[1]	1·1[2]	0·7	1·0
Agriculture, forestry and fishing	0·9	3·0	−2·1	0·0	−1·5	2·4
Mining and quarrying	0·2	2·5	−2·3	0·7	−1·4	1·6
Construction	5·4	3·6	1·8	1·8	1·8	3·6
Electricity, gas, water	5·0	2·5	2·5	3·3	2·7	2·3
Manufacturing	2·6	2·7	−0·1	0·7	0·1	2·5
All production	2·8	2·9	−0·1	1·4	0·4	2·4
Transport and communication	2·1	2·0	0·1	0·7	0·3	1·8
Distributive trades	1·3	−0·5	1·8	1·3	1·7	−0·4
All services and transport[3]	0·9	−0·7	1·6	1·6	1·6	−0·7

NOTES   [1] Excludes Armed Forces.

[2] Excludes dwellings.

[3] Includes distributive trades, insurance, banking and finance, public administration, professional and miscellaneous services.

SOURCES   Based on data in K. S. Lomax, 'Production and Productivity Movements in the United Kingdom since 1900', *Journal of Royal Statistical Society*, A122 (1959); C. H. Feinstein, *Domestic Capital Formation in the United Kingdom, 1920–1938* (1965), and 'Production and Productivity in the United Kingdom 1920–1962', *London and Cambridge Economic Bulletin*, 48 (1963); A. L. Chapman and R. Knight, *Wages and Salaries in the United Kingdom, 1920–1938* (1953).

Table 20 produces some interesting results. Despite the importance of the service sector in absorbing resources, its contribution to the growth of the economy was very modest indeed. In fact, output expanded at a rate well below the general average, while a negative residual meant a decline in productivity. Only transport and communication could be classed as buoyant and this was largely due to the influence of motor transport. On the other hand, since the expansion of services was based on factor inputs rather than improvements in

[1] See J. A. Dowie, 'Growth in the Inter-war Period: Some More Arithmetic', *Economy History Review*, 21 (1968), p. 109.

the productivity of resources, it did mean that employment growth was rapid. Barring 1921–2, employment in these trades expanded in every year and the group as a whole accounted for the bulk of the increase in employment during the period. Thus at a time of heavy unemployment and large fluctuations in the level of industrial employment, services acted as a stabilizing force.[1]

Of course there were considerable variations in the rate of employment growth between the main service trades. The biggest absolute gains occurred in distribution (wholesale and retail) where employment rose from 1773·2 thousand in 1920 to 2438·2 thousand in 1938, and in miscellaneous services, from 2025·4 to 2754·8 thousand. This latter group comprised a wide range of activities including entertainment and sport, catering, laundries and dry cleaning, domestic service and hair-dressing. Altogether employment in these two categories rose by nearly 1·4 million. In fact there were few service sectors which failed to register an increase in employment apart from national Government service, though transport and communication only gained slightly. However, this group covered a wide range of transport activities not all of which were expanding. Employment growth was mainly confined to road transport and postal and telegraphic services, while most other branches, railways, tramways, ocean transport and docks experienced contraction.

In contrast most of the main industrial groups experienced low rates of employment growth. In fact employment declined in agriculture, mining and manufacturing, and only construction and electricity registered significant gains. Although the rate of expansion was much higher in electricity, gas and water, the absolute increase in employment was much less than in construction. The latter absorbed over 318,000 additional workers between 1920 and 1938 as against 107,000 in electricity.

Although the rate of capital growth was lower than pre-war it was considerably greater than that of employment and most sectors, apart from agriculture, increased their capital stock. The biggest increases were in construction and electricity, while in most of the service sectors, other than transport, it was well above the average. On the other hand, in mining, manufacturing and transport the rate of growth of the capital stock was quite modest.

It is clear from Table 20 that there was no clearcut association

[1] C. W. McMahon and G. D. N. Worswick, 'The Growth of Services in the Economy. 1. Their Stabilising Influence', *District Bank Review*, 136 (1960), p. 21.

between growth of output and the expansion in factor inputs. It is true that the two sectors with the highest rate of output growth, construction and electricity, also had the highest input growth, though in the case of construction this accounted for only one third of the rise in output. But here the positive association ends for in most other sectors growth and factor inputs tended to be inversely correlated. Thus the service sectors, other than transport, had a high input growth but a relatively modest increase in output, while productivity declined as a result of the weakness of the residual. On the other hand, manufacturing and transport, with low inputs, recorded a creditable performance in output and productivity, largely because of the strength of the residual element. Even mining and agriculture, where inputs declined sharply, did very well in terms of productivity.

The distinction between the two main sectors of the economy is, therefore, quite meaningful with respect to this analysis. Services provided the main source of increased employment but their growth contribution was limited. The reverse was true of the industrial sector. Here input growth was very modest but output and productivity expanded much faster than the economy as a whole. Thus from the point of view of the overall growth of the economy the industrial sector was by far the more important. However, the contribution of each industry within this group varied a great deal as we shall see below.

Industrial analysis

Growth rates of output, employment, capital, etc., have been calculated for 21 industry groups the results of which are tabulated below. They are ranked in order of their rate of output growth. On this basis the division between the new and the old industrial sectors comes out quite clearly. The fastest growers, that is those with a rate of output growth above the average for all industry, included three new industries, vehicles, electricity and electrical engineering, together with building and allied trades, food and non-ferrous metals. Moreover, all these industries had high rates of employment and total input growth. On the other hand, rapid expansion did not necessarily produce high rates of productivity growth. Productivity rose at a rate below the average in four of the eight industries at the top of Table 21 and two of these, electricity and electrical engineering, were new industries.

At the other end of the scale six industries had rates of output

TABLE 21 *Annual rates of growth of output, employment, capital, etc., in selected industries, 1920–38*

	Output	Output per man	Employ- ment	Capital	Total factor inputs	Residual
Vehicles	6·6	3·6	3·0	5·4	3·7	2·9
Building and contracting	5·4	3·6	1·8	1·8	1·8	3·6
Timber and furniture	5·2	5·0	0·2	—	—	—
Electricity, gas, water	5·0	2·5	2·5	3·3	2·7	2·3
Non-ferrous metal manu- facture	4·8	3·6	1·2	1·4	1·3	3·5
Electrical engineering	4·7	1·1	3·6	2·3	3·2	1·5
Building materials	3·7	1·6	2·1	−0·5	1·3	2·4
Food	3·6	2·1	1·5	0·6	1·2	2·4
Clothing	2·7	2·9	−0·2	2·3	0·8	1·9
Precision instruments	2·7	3·0	−0·3	—	—	—
Paper and printing	2·6	1·3	1·3	2·0	1·5	1·1
Metal goods, n.e.s.	2·5	2·1	0·4	—	—	—
Tobacco	2·2	1·7	0·5	2·4	1·1	1·1
Leather	2·1	2·3	−0·2	2·2	0·5	1·8
Chemicals	1·9	1·5	0·4	1·4	0·7	1·2
Mechanical engineering	1·7	3·7	−2·0	0·3	−1·3	3·0
Iron and steel	1·1	3·5	−2·4	0·7	−1·5	2·6
Textiles	0·2	1·6	−1·4	−0·9	−1·3	1·5
Mining and quarrying	0·2	2·5	−2·3	0·7	−1·4	1·6
Drink	−0·2	−1·0	0·8	0·4	0·7	−0·9
Shipbuilding	−2·7	1·9	−4·6	−0·8	−3·4	0·7
Manufacturing	2·6	2·7	−0·1	0·7	0·1	2·5
All industry (excl. agric.)	2·8	2·9	−0·1	1·4	0·4	2·4

SOURCES As for Table 20.

growth well below the general average. These comprised mechanical engineering, iron and steel, textiles, mining, drink and shipbuilding. In textiles and mining there was very little expansion, while drink and shipbuilding actually contracted over the period 1920–38. The textile group, however, covers a number of different branches, some of which expanded. Unfortunately full details are not available for each group but employment data shows that the declining areas were cotton, woollen and worsted, linen, hemp and jute, whereas rayon, silk, and hosiery expanded. In addition, in most of these industries the growth of employment and capital was very modest. There were, too, some sharp variations in productivity growth. Productivity rose rapidly in iron and steel and mechanical engineering, and even in mining, shipbuilding and textiles it was by no means negligible. In fact, of all the industries listed only drink recorded a negative rate of productivity growth.

Finally in the middle range, that is those with a rate of output growth around or below the average (between 1·9 and 2·7 per cent per annum) there were seven industries. These including both old consumer goods industries such as clothing, leather and tobacco and newer trades like chemicals and precision instruments. Most of the industries in this range also had fairly low rates of productivity growth apart from precision instruments. On the other hand, four of the industries, paper and printing, tobacco, metal goods and chemicals had employment growth rates above the average.

Another notable feature was the variations in the residual's contribution. In a majority of industries, but only just, it contributed more to expansion than factor inputs. This is particularly true of the old staple industries such as mechanical engineering, textiles, shipbuilding and iron and steel, which suffered sharp contractions in employment. Presumably the cut-back involved the scrapping of the most inefficient plants, some rationalization and reorganization, with the result that output per man improved. Most of the fast growing industries also had high residuals, though rather surprisingly in the three chief newer industries inputs contributed more to expansion than the residual. The very low productivity and residual rates for electrical engineering are partly to be explained by the nature of the production process – many products and heavy equipment built to individiual specifications – which limited the scope for scale economies and productivity improvements.

What importance should we attach to the newer industries? Recently their role in the inter-war economy has been stressed, particularly with reference to the recovery phase of the 1930s. There is a danger, however, of exaggerating their contribution. As Dowie has pointed out,[1] although all new industries were expanding not all expanding industries were new ones. If we glance again at Table 21 it will be found that nearly all industries could be classed as expanding both in terms of output and productivity, though not necessarily from the

[1] Dowie, *loc. cit.*

employment point of view. The only exceptions were drink and ship-building. In other words, it could be argued that inter-war industrial growth was fairly widely based. On the other hand, it is equally clear that the large staple industries acted as a drag on overall growth though a few achieved reasonable rates of productivity growth. At the top end of the scale it could hardly be said that new industries pre-dominated. Only three of the fastest output growers were new industries, while the performance of chemicals and precision instruments was rather mediocre. Moreover, in terms of productivity growth the comparison is even less favourable to the new industries. Only two, vehicles and precision instruments, were above the average, and the ranking of the first eight was as follows: timber and furniture, mechanical engineering, vehicles, building and contracting, non-ferrous metal manufacture, iron and steel, precision instruments and clothing.

Without stretching the evidence too far we might suggest that industrial development was centred primarily on two inter-related blocks of industries. On the one hand, there were the new industries, especially vehicles, electricity and electrical engineering, but also including rayon, chemicals and precision instruments; on the other, we have the building and allied trades (timber and furniture, building materials and non-ferrous metals). Construction was more important than any of the newer industries taken separately. In terms of output and employment it was twice as large as electricity (plus gas and water), which was the biggest branch of the newer group of trades.

There are at least three good reasons for stressing the importance of these sectors. First, nearly all of them expanded rapidly either in terms of output or productivity and they absorbed an increasing share of the resources devoted to industry. Building and related trades gave employment to some 1364·1 thousand people in 1920 and 1795·2 thousand in 1938, while in the newer industries employment rose from 981·8 to 1582·2 thousand over the same period. Combined these two sectors accounted for 30·5 per cent of the total industrial labour force in 1920, 37·4 per cent in 1929 and 42·2 per cent in 1938.[1] They were also responsible for over 60 per cent of total investment in the u.k. during the inter-war years.[2]

[1] The percentages, though still high, are somewhat reduced if mining is included in the total labour force and a narrower definition of the building trades is used. For alternative calculations see Table 26.
[2] See D. H. Aldcroft, 'Economic Growth in the Inter-War Years: A Reassessment', *Economy History Review*, 20 (1967), p. 321.

Second, their expansion exerted a considerable impact on other industries. From an input – output analysis made by Barna on the basis of data in the 1935 Census of Production, it appears that many of these industries had a relatively high volume of transactions with other industries. This was especially true of vehicles, electricity, electrical engineering and building. To take an obvious example: the development of the motor car industry stimulated or brought into being a wide range of industries, including oil refining, rubber, electrical goods, glass, leather, metallurgy and mechanical engineering. The strongest repercussions came from the building industry. Altogether it bought products from 24 of the 36 main industrial groups listed by Barna, and the total inter-industry transactions on behalf of this industry amounted to nearly £213 million. The main industries from which products were drawn included china and glass, oils and paints, iron and steel manufactures, metal goods, non-ferrous metals, wood manufactures, mechanical engineering and, of course, building materials. Though the total inter-industry transactions of the building industry were small in relation to industrial production as a whole, what is important is that only two other industries, food processing and distribution services, had a greater volume of transactions with other industries.[1] In other words, building had a greater impact on the industrial economy than almost any other industry.

Thus the new industries and the building trades not only generated a demand for each others products but they also exerted a favourable influence on some of the old staple industries, particularly iron and steel, mechanical engineering, metal goods and certain branches of the textile trades. But for these repercussions the growth of the older sectors would have been slower than was actually the case. The third point to note is that the building trades and new industries were by no means independent development blocks. Though the transactions between the two sectors were perhaps not as great as those between different branches within each of the two groups, the indirect repercussions were considerable. The building of over four million new houses in the inter-war period could not fail to exert a significant impact on other sectors of the economy. Not only did this stimulate a demand for a wide variety of community services such as schools, shops, churches and other public utilities, but since most of the new houses were wired for electricity it generated a demand for a wide range of new consumer

[1] T. Barna, 'The Interdependence of the British Economy', *Journal of the Royal Statistical Society*, A115 (1952).

durables based on the new form of power. By 1939 there were already in use in this country some 1·6 million electric cookers, 2·3 million vacuum cleaners, 6·5 million electric irons and nearly 0·5 million electric water heaters. The demand for many other household goods was likewise stimulated by the housebuilding programme. Furthermore, residential building stimulated the development of new transport facilities, while in turn the flexibility, convenience and relative cheapness of motor transport enabled new building to take place in the suburbs of the main industrial cities. The relationships between transport and building were indirect and difficult to define precisely, but there is little doubt that much of the new housing development was dependent on access to new areas provided by motor transport.[1]

Although we may say fairly confidently that the long-term growth of the economy was carried forward by building and the newer industries this does not mean that they were equally important during different phases of the cycle. Given the fact that they were proportionately more important in the 1930s than in the previous decade, one would naturally expect their contribution to be greater in that period. In the first half of the 1930s this was certainly the case since recovery from the depression was determined largely by the early and powerful upswing in these sectors. But in the later phase of revival the growth momentum of both the building trades and the newer industries tended to slacken, while at the same time some of the older staple trades began to make their contribution to recovery.

The position is much less clear cut in the 1920s. In one sense it could be argued that these sectors were of vital importance simply because of the rather sluggish rates of growth experienced in some of the other industries. This is particularly true of the later 1920s when the negative or very low rates of expansion in iron and steel, textiles, mining and shipbuilding, were responsible for the dampened nature of the boom. During these years most of the building trades and new industries registered very high rates of expansion; for example, between 1924–9 the output of vehicles rose by 5·6 per cent per annum, electrical engineering 4·0 per cent, precision instruments 5·2 per cent, construction 7·4 per cent, timber and furniture 7·4 per cent, and electricity 5·8 per cent. On the other hand, in terms of productivity growth the position was more varied. Some of the older industries, like mining and shipbuilding, had quite high rates of productivity

[1] For a more detailed discussion of these points see H. W. Richardson and D. H. Aldcroft, *Building in the British Economy Between the Wars* (1968), Chs. 13, 14.

growth between 1924–9, whereas the reverse was true in the case of certain new industries, particularly chemicals and electrical engineering. When we turn to the early 1920s it is less easy to make out a convincing case for these sectors. The boom of 1919–20 was clearly one based on the old staples and they were instrumental in causing the subsequent slump. In the ensuing recovery both old and new industries expanded rapidly though building, which had acted as a stabilizing influence in 1921, actually contracted till 1923. Moreover, the new industries could hardly have exerted a powerful influence in these years since their relative importance was still quite small. In particular, it is scarcely conceivable that they were mainly responsible for the rapid rise in industrial productivity between 1920–4, which was at the rate of 5·6 per cent per annum. To some extent this rather high rate of growth reflected the rather low level productivity attained at the end of the war, but it was also due to the adoption of more efficient methods of production in some trades, notably engineering. More important however, was the shake-out of labour from many of the older industries which had been grossly overmanned before the war. Thus the output of the mechanical engineering industry rose by six per cent between 1920–4 yet the labour force was reduced by no less than 46 per cent. Similarly, there was a 19 per cent expansion in the output of mining and quarrying despite the fact that employment fell slightly.

But what is important to note is how the growth of individual industries, whether old or new, varied over different periods. This point has been revealed by Dowie in his more detailed temporal analysis of inter-war growth. Taking the two periods 1924–9 and 1929–37 we find that iron and steel shifted from a 0·7 to a 4·4 per cent rate of growth, mechanical engineering from 3·9 to 0·7, textiles −0·9 to 3·1, leather 1·1 to 3·7, tobacco 5·4 to 2·3, electrical engineering 4·0 to 7·8, construction 7·4 to 2·9 and agriculture 3·3 to 0·1. Similar swings are apparent in productivity. Some of the most notable were: chemicals 0·7 to 2·5, iron and steel 0·8 to 3·1, electrical engineering −0·8 to 1·7, textiles −0·7 to 4·3, leather −0·5 to 2·4, mining 4·4 to 1·1 and construction 3·9 to 0·0.[1] Although not all industries showed such diversity of experience these variations obviously make it difficult to generalize about growth patterns in the short-term from a knowledge of long-term trends.

[1] Dowie, *loc. cit.*

The timing of developments in building and the new industries

Given the importance of building and the new industries in the inter-war economy it might be useful to make a few comments regarding the nature of these developments. A more detailed account of industrial changes is given in later chapters. Here we intend to concentrate attention on one important issue, namely why these sectors were more buoyant after, rather than before, the war. The laymen's view of the period would probably lead him to conclude that conditions generally were not particularly favourable to rapid expansion in the new sectors. In fact, however, it can be argued that the opposite was the case.

Let us take building first. Concentration on the housing sector will not be inappropriate since much of the building development consisted of new houses. Throughout the period building activity was at a much higher level than before 1914 and altogether over four million new houses were constructed in the inter-war years. The reasons for this high level of activity are not difficult to find. In the decade before the war building had been relatively depressed since the housing cycle had reached its peak in the early twentieth century. This low level of housebuilding meant that, with increasing population and family formation, the supply of houses was not keeping pace with current demand. By 1914 there was a considerable backlog of demand to make good and, in fact, the time was ripe for another housing boom. Unfortunately the war checked any developments in this direction. The shortage of men and materials and the high price of these factors, especially early after the war, meant that building activity remained at an extremely low level until 1920. Thus by the middle of 1921 there was a serious shortage of houses, amounting to 865,000 at the very minimum. In addition, estimates suggest that over 1·9 million new houses would be needed to satisfy the requirements arising from the growth in the number of families in the first decade, 1921–31.[1] These requirements alone would necessitate the completion of nearly 280,000 houses a year in the 1920s, that is a rate of output almost double the annual rate of output in the peak pre-war boom decade, 1897 to 1906. Moreover, these estimates make no allowance for dealing with the twin problems of urban slum dwellings and over-crowding. During the period many nineteenth century houses were

[1] For the whole period about 3·5 million were required to keep up with family formation.

E

reaching the end of their life cycle. By the mid 1930s over three million houses, or more than one quarter of the total stock, were at least
80 years old. Not all of these houses constituted slum dwellings but
it is fairly certain that the large majority of them failed to satisfy
the minimum requirements of modern accommodation. Needless to
say, the position was worst in large towns and in Scotland where
housing requirements had not been met very adequately before 1914.

Under almost any conditions this large housing deficit would have
been sufficient to ensure a vigorous rate of building. But the process
was assisted by a number of other factors. For one thing the State,
together with the municipal authorities, became an active participant
in the housing market, whereas before 1914 neither central nor local
governments had taken much interest in this field. Basically it was the
severe post-war housing shortage which forced the Government to
intervene. By a series of Acts in 1919, 1923, 1924, the Government
sought to stimulate house construction by advancing subsidies to both
local authorities and private builders. The policy of general subsidization was continued until the early 1930s after which attention was
focussed on slum clearance and the elimination of overcrowding.
The magnitude of the State's contribution can be gathered from the
fact that of the 4·36 million houses built between March 1920 and
March 1939, nearly 1·8 million or roughly 42 per cent of the total,
were constructed with the aid of subsidies, while local authorities
were responsible for something like one third of the new houses coming
onto the market. The State's major contribution was made in the
1920s and at one period, 1919–22, local authorities accounted for
no less than 60 per cent of the new houses built.

Clearly without Treasury subsidies and the intervention of the
local authorities far fewer houses would have been built. On the other
hand, had there been no government policy the supply of houses
would not have been reduced by the number actually subsidized. In
the absence of official intervention private building would have been
higher, and indeed there is reason to believe that the activity of local
authorities in the housing market discouraged both investors and
private builders from expanding the supply of rented accommodation,
especially in the 1920s. In any case, there were strong real forces
favourable to private building development. Costs of construction fell
almost continuously in this period, though the most marked fall,
apart from the sharp decline from the post-war peak, came in the late
1920s and early 1930s. Between 1928 and 1934 the average capital

cost of new houses fell from £432 to £361. This not only stimulated builders to produce more houses but it also meant a fall in the cost of house purchase for the buyer. Moreover, purchasers were also assisted by the fall in interest rates and the liberalization of the borrowing terms of building societies in the 1930s.[1] In addition, the demand for houses was boosted by rising real incomes, especially in the early 1930s, as a result of a favourable shift in the terms of trade. On top of this there was also a non-income influence on demand. It is more than likely that in some sections of the community, more particularly the middle classes, tastes were changing giving rise to the demand for larger and better houses in more pleasant surroundings. All in all the building industry could hardly fail to respond to this powerful group of stimuli.[2]

Having considered the main factors reponsible for expansion in building the vigorous growth in the new industries becomes somewhat easier to understand. Of course not all the factors conducive to housebuilding were relevant to the growth of these industries. For one thing, there was an almost complete absence of Government stimulus, apart from the indirect effects of tariff protection accorded to certain branches of the new industries in the 1920s. Perhaps the most important factor determining the timing of the rapid growth in these industries was the release from technical and commercial contraints. Before 1914, and even for a few years after, these constraints limited their development. All the goods could be produced but for one reason or another the mass production stage of manufacture was still not possible. In rayon, for example, the technical perfection of the processes of manufacture had only just about been completed by 1914, while the manufacture of cheap mass-produced cars and electrical goods was impeded both by technical considerations and the prevailing methods of production. Similarly, the mass production and distribution of electricity was hindered by the multiplicity of electricity undertakings engaged in the industry together with the opposition of vested interests in gas. Thus, although new goods could be produced, they were generally expensive with the result that the mass market could not be tapped. The motor car, for example, was a high-priced, hand-made product which only the upper income groups could afford.

After the war conditions changed rapidly. Technical and commercial perfection of newer products was completed in the 1920s, and

[1] For the influence of cheap money on housebuilding, see Chapter 9.
[2] Most of this section has been drawn from Richardson and Aldcroft, *op. cit.*

in part these changes were accelerated as a result of war-time experience in mass production techniques. The motor industry shifted from a craft to a mass production industry within the space of a few years, and at the same time various technical improvements ensured a better product. Similar changes took place in the rayon and electrical industries, while the generation and distribution of electricity was made much more efficient by the construction of the National Grid system between 1926 and 1934. These improvements in production caused a rapid fall in prices and resulted in an extension of the market. The price of many electrical products fell by about half in the 1920s while between 1923–9 motor car prices fell by 33 per cent. In the case of rayon yarn the price reduction was much greater.[1] The price changes, moreover, coincided with the rise in real incomes and wages and this boosted effective demand even further. On the other hand, before 1914 real wages and incomes had remained fairly stationary and the lack of a market incentive may have helped to retard the development of these industries. Furthermore, one should remember that before the war the export-orientated staple industries were still relatively profitable, whereas after 1920 this was not generally the case. Given the lack of profitable opportunities in the old staple trades it was only to be expected that investment funds would seek new outlets and the most obvious choice was the new industries. Finally, as we have already mentioned, the high level of housebuilding activity tended to stimulate demand for some of the newer products of industry.

The roles of capital and technical progress

It is important at this stage to return to the question of the roles of capital and technical progress in economic growth since there has been considerable controversy about this matter during the past decade or so. Until comparatively recently capital was regarded as the key variable in economic growth, but a number of empirical studies suggest that this emaphsis is misplaced and that the main contribution has come from the residual. In other words, forces which contribute to an increase of output per unit of input have been more important than inputs of capital and labour in promoting the growth of output. The problem is a complex one and requires further examination.

Our analysis of the sources of growth lends support to these con-

[1] For details see D. H. Aldcroft, 'Economic Progress in Britain in the 1920s', *Scottish Journal of Political Economy*, 13 (1966), pp. 306–7.

clusions. From Table 20 it can be seen that the growth in the capital stock contributed less than the increase in employment, while the residual's contribution was more important than that of the two factor inputs combined. Thus, to the 1·7 per cent per annum growth in G.D.P. the residual contributed 1·0 and total factor inputs 0·7 percentage points, while for industrial production the respective shares were 0·4 and 2·4. As we have seen, the high value of the residual, especially in industry, was associated with the shift in resources towards the high growth sectors and the scale economies arising therefrom, and the fairly widespread rate of technical advance which affected old and new industries alike.

On the basis of these calculations it is clear that capital only contributed marginally to the rise in output. Moreover, it certainly was not responsible for the more rapid expansion in output compared with that of pre-war. During the inter-war years the capital stock grew more slowly than before 1914 and in many industries capital per employee declined. In fact, the depreciated value of the stock of assets other than dwellings barely kept pace with the growth in population, while per head of the employed labour force it rose between 1920–5, largely as a result of a fall in employment, remained steady until 1930, after which it declined slowly. Thus by 1938 it was very little higher than it had been in 1920 and somewhat lower than in 1925. The first cost value of the capital stock per employee rose rather more sharply between 1920–5 and continued to rise to 1930 after which it fell, so that by the end of the decade it was about 13 per cent higher than in 1920.[1] In other words, this means that growth due to changes in capital per man was fairly small, probably around 0·1 or 0·2 per cent per annum (on a first cost basis), that is slightly lower than pre-war.

At least two points must be discussed before we draw any final conclusions about the role of capital. The aggregate figures do conceal significant variations between different sectors; this is particularly so in this period since there were rather wide variations in the rate of capital accumulation between different industries. In some of the new industries and in the service sectors capital growth was much more rapid than in the older sectors, some of which were reducing their capital stock. But in few sectors, apart from services, did capital contribute more than the residual. A second and more important problem is that concerning the relationship between capital and tech-

[1] Feinstein, *op. cit.*, p. 53.

nical progress. The distinction between the two is often a fine one and it can be argued that investment provides the vehicle for the introduction of new techniques. Kaldor, for example, maintains that capital is important on the grounds that investment benefits productivity largely because it provides opportunities for learning new methods or enables new technical advances to be introduced.[1] The problem is further complicated by the fact that technical progress may be embodied in replacement investment no allowance for which is made in our calculations which are based on the capital stock figures. Thus it is not the growth of the capital stock (net additions of capital) which is important, but the gross investment figures since these include both net additions to the capital stock and replacement investment. Hence, a low rate of capital stock growth is perfectly compatible with a high rate of economic growth provided that there is a high rate of replacement investment which embodies technical progress.

These points are more easily raised than answered. The task is simplified however if we maintain the distinction between net additions to the capital stock and replacement investment. One would expect capital would be more likely to provide a source for the introduction of technical advances in those industries in which the capital stock was growing rapidly. But in fact this does not seem to have been the case. For this to be so industries with a high rate of capital growth should show a high residual, but Matthews found that the correlation between the two variables for the years 1924–37 was of the order of 0·19 which is very insignificant indeed.[2]

The second and more important problem is that of replacement investment. During the period this accounted for no less than 70 per cent of total gross fixed capital formation, whereas in the couple of decades before 1914 the proportion was only about one third. If embodied technical progress featured prominently in this type of investment then there might well be a case for saying that investment provided a stimulus to technical change. Colin Clark, writing in the 1930s, appeared to hold this view when he observed that 'without new investment the replacement of obsolete capital ... appears to give all the scope necessary for the introduction of technical and organizational improvement and to bring about the rapid increase in productivity under which we are now living.'[3] It is possible to

---

[1] N. Kaldor, 'A Model of Economic Growth', *Economic Journal*, 67 (1957), p. 595.
[2] Matthews, *loc. cit.*, p. 21.
[3] C. Clark, *National Income and Outlay* (1937), p. 272.

point to any number of industries in which this was happening. For example, the use of larger and better blast furnaces in iron and steel, the substitution of the rotary for the fixed kiln in cement-making, or the shift from steam to electric power in industry generally. The effect of these changes was that productivity rose and costs were reduced. Moreover, in each case technical advances were associated with the scrapping of old plant and the substitution of new. But the issue is complicated by a number of factors. We do not know exactly the proportions of replacement and new investment involved in each case. On the basis of the aggregate figures it is probably correct to assume that replacement investment was the more important, though many of the technical changes no doubt led to net additions to the capital stock. Nor do we know what proportion of investment went into static or existing techniques. Finally, it is impossible to separate cause and effect in this matter. Was existing plant scrapped because it was obsolete in the sense that it could not be used any longer, in which case automatic renewal would allow technical progress to creep in by the back door? If this were the case then investment could be regarded as the generator of technical advances. Or did the pressure of new techniques speed up the scrapping of existing plant, not because it was completely worn out but because the new techniques dictated that it should be abandoned?

Obviously it is impossible to give a clear-cut answer here. But it is important to be aware of the problems involved in distinguishing between the respective contributions of capital and technical progress. Although precise estimates cannot be provided we can certainly say that calculations based on capital stock figures do tend to underestimate the growth contribution of the capital variable. Given the high proportion of replacement investment in the inter-war period there is every reason to believe that the share of growth attributable to capital was somewhat greater than our earlier analysis suggested.

Employment growth and the unemployment problem

The thing which stands out in people's minds most about the inter-war period is the unemployment problem. Even in the best years unemployment hovered around the one million mark, that is equivalent to roughly 10 per cent of the insured population,[1] while in the down-

[1] Though the absolute numbers involved would be somewhat greater if all workers were included, the percentage unemployment would be less because of the lower incidence of unemployment among non-insured trades.

swings of the cycle especially 1921, 1930–2, and 1938, it was a good deal worse. The cyclical troughs in unemployment are quite readily explainable and need not concern us here.[1] But it is not immediately apparent why there should have been such a large and persistent core of unemployment. Economic growth was more rapid than before the war, population growth was lower, and for much of the time employment expanded at a similar rate to that before 1914. A student examining the national data for the period 1924–38, the time span most commonly used for the period, might wonder why unemployment remained so high throughout the period.

The origins of the long-term problem really date from the early 1920s. In 1920 employment reached a post-war peak and then fell sharply in the depression of the following year. Thereafter the trend was upwards, though it was until 1936 that the former peak was surpassed. Thus taking the period as a whole (i.e. 1920–38) employment grew at a rate of only 0·5 per cent per annum, which was somewhat lower than the rate of growth of the labour force.[2] Now although the cut-back in employment between 1920–21 was partly due to cyclical factors, it also contained the seeds of the long-term structural problem. For even by 1924 and 1925, when industrial production and total output were at or above the levels of 1920, total employment (excluding the Armed Forces) amounted to only 15·52 and 15·68 million respectively, compared with 16·98 million in 1920. Thus the deficiency in employment in these years can be regarded as the real core of the problem. In large part it was caused by the collapse of employment opportunities in the basic industries as a result of contraction in their markets, a process which began soon after 1920, together with a shake-out of labour from these trades due to excessive overmanning before the war and in 1920. Between 1920 and 1925 employment in mining, mechanical engineering, shipbuilding, iron and steel and textiles (other than rayon and nylon) fell by over one million.[3] It was these large staple export trades which accounted for a large part of the unemployment of the 1920s, and this holds true, though to a lesser extent, for the period as a whole if we exclude unemployment caused by cyclical factors. These five groups accounted

---

[1] See Chapters 2 and 3.
[2] That is the population of working age the growth rate of which was 0·9 per cent per annum. Between 1924–38 employment and the labour force grew at about the same rate.
[3] Data from Chapman and Knight, *op. cit.*

for nearly half of the insured unemployed in Great Britain at July 1929.[1]

There is, however, another angle to the problem. It could be argued that had certain pre-war economic trends continued to prevail in the inter-war years the unemployment difficulties would have been considerably eased. Not all the unemployment can be attributed simply to the contraction in output of the old staples. In fact few industries or sectors experienced an absolute decline in output between 1920 and 1938, though some of the basic industries such as coal, cotton and shipbuilding had reached a peak in 1913. What is important is that most industries, including the old staples, recorded significant productivity gains during the period which was in marked contrast to the position before the war. Thus, a substantial increase in output was secured through a rise in productivity rather than through increased labour inputs.[2] During the years 1899–1913 output per man for the economy as a whole hardly rose at all so that practically all the 1·1 per cent rate of G.D.P. growth came through an increase in employment. On the other hand, between 1920–38 output per man increased at the rate of 1·2 per cent per annum and employment at 0·5 per cent, producing an overall growth of 1·7 per cent. Thus if productivity had maintained the same trend rate as before the war the growth of employment would have risen to 1·6 per cent[3] which would have considerably alleviated the unemployment problem. This is not to imply that the inter-war productivity gains were not welcome from the long-term point of view, but it is perhaps unfortunate that they came at a time when the labour intensive staple industries were finding it necessary to shed labour because of market difficulties. Alternatively, had the basic industries made greater efforts to economize in labour before 1914 resources would have been released earlier for development elsewhere and the inter-war adjustment difficulties might have been modified.

One potential, and more propitious, source of relief to the unemploy-

[1] That is 517,496 out of a total of 1·14 million, *Ministry of Labour Gazette*, Aug. 1929, pp. 294–5.
[2] Though it should be stressed that some of the productivity advances in the basic industries no doubt materialized as a result of the shake-out of labour during contraction phases in the demand for their products.
[3] Assuming, of course, that the same rate of growth of output had been maintained and an elastic supply of labour. The figure for employment growth is unrealistically high however, but the essential point is that employment growth would have been faster.

ment problem failed to materialize. Before 1914 the rate of growth of the labour force was very similar to that of population. During the inter-war years the rate of population growth declined quite sharply to less than half its former rate. If previous trends had held firm one would have expected a similar decline in the expansion of the labour force. This did occur in the 1920s but in the following decade there was a sharp rise in the rate of growth so that for the period as a whole the labour force increased at a substantially faster rate than total population.[1] This divergence between the two rates can be attributed to an increase in the proportion of those of working age (15–64) in the total population and a rise in the proportion of women taking employment, especially in the 1930s. In other words, had the pre-war relationships between the two variables remained the same the growth of the labour force would have been lower and unemployment less severe.

Finally, the unemployment problem was exacerbated by its uneven distribution. The hard core of structural unemployment was centred, as we have seen in Chapter 3, around a number of large staple trades located primarily in the northern half of the country. The difficulties involved in both the retraining and the movement of redundant labour from these regions were immense, while the absence of any proper facilities for dealing with the problem reduced the rate at which resources were reallocated and made the unemployment seem really worse than it actually was. The result was that at times, especially in the later 1930s, some industries suffered acute shortages of labour while large pools of unemployment existed in the North. Even in the depressed areas skilled shortages were not unknown. It would be wrong, of course, to assume that unemployment could have beeen removed by a more efficient system of labour redistribution since it is clear that employment growth in this period was insufficient to cope with the adverse economic trends.

The points made here are not designed to explain away the unemployment problem. However much one looks at the figures it still remains. But the above comments do suggest that there are a number of relevant factors which should be considered when examining the reasons for it, and they also make it easier to appreciate the fact that economic growth and unemployment are not necessarily incompatible.

---

[1] 0·9 as against 0·4 per cent per annum. Between 1901 and 1911 the respective rates were 1·0 and 0·9 per cent. See Matthews, *loc. cit.*, p. 6.

5 The basic industries

In the previous chapters we have been mainly concerned with the more macro aspects of the economy. At some stage it is necessary to disaggregate the economy by considering in more detail the components of which it is composed. Selection, of course, is necesssary since it would be impossible to discuss each industry or sector fully in a book of this sort. The approach adopted here is to divide the economy into three broad groups as follows: (a) the old basic industries the most important of which were coal, cotton, woollen and worsted, shipbuilding and iron and steel; (b) the newer industries, especially electricity, electrical manufacturing, vehicles and rayon, but also including some smaller trades such as aircraft, aluminium and precision instruments and certain branches of the chemical industry such as dyestuffs; we might also include building in this category; finally (c) transport and services, the latter covering a wide range of non-manufacturing activities. In some respects the classification is no doubt arbitrary but it does have the advantage that most of the sectors or trades in any one group have important features in common as we shall see when we come to examine them in detail. Moreover, by no means all industries are covered. The most significant exception is agriculture which does not fit readily into the grouping, but in addition, many smaller trades are either excluded altogether or only receive a passing mention.

The primary aim of the next three chapters, therefore, will be to examine the main trends in some of the more important industries in each group and to focus attention on the forces making for growth and decline as the case may be. First, however, a few comments on the more general aspects of industrial change are necessary.

Trends in industrial structure and business organization

At least two features have already been discussed earlier and require little further elaboration here. These are the broad changes in the structure and location of economic activity. As we have seen, the respective shares of services and industry in total output, employment, etc., did not alter very markedly over the period. On the other hand, there were some important changes within the two main groups. The most notable occurred within the industrial sector and comprised the decline in importance of the basic industries and the concomitant growth of the newer sectors and building. These changes were reflected in the geographical pattern of economic activity. The staple industries tended to be concentrated in the northern regions with the result that as these sectors declined in importance so did the economic importance of the regions in which they were situated. Conversely, the tendency for newer industries or rapidly expanding trades to concentrate in the South and Midlands raised the importance of these regions. Thus between 1924 and 1935 the Northern regions' share of net industrial output fell from 49·6 per cent to 37·6 per cent, whereas the share of the South-east and the Midlands rose from 28·7 to 37·1 per cent.

Changes in the pattern and form of business organization, which affected old and new industries alike, were less spectacular but nonetheless important. These included the widespread use of the corporate form of enterprise, the development of public and semi-public undertakings, the increase in the size of plant and firm and the vast extension in the number of trade associations or cartel-like arrangements for price fixing, information sharing, distributing output, etc. Most of these changes simply represented extensions of developments which had been going on since before 1914. The joint-stock company, for example, had been in widespread use long before the war, though there were still many individually owned firms or partnerships in business. Many of these undertakings converted to corporate form in the inter-war period and by 1938 the majority of industrial firms were joint-stock enterprises. Even so, non-corporate concerns were still to be found quite frequently in retail distribution, in road transport and in many of the small trades. The extension of this form of business organization usually reflected the need to draw in larger amounts of capital from a wider field, though many companies fell short of a stock exchange quotation. In fact the number of public companies declined during the period despite the fact that many private firms became public,[1] while in numerical terms private companies were far more important. The latter were usually small and in aggregate they accounted for less than one third of the total capital of all joint stock enterprises. Nevertheless, the effect of incorporation, whether of a private or public type, led to an increasing divorce between ownership and control in many firms. Certainly most larger companies were managed by executives and directors answerable to a large body of shareholders.

Private enterprise was not alone in the economic field. One of the notable features of the period was the increasing economic participation of the State, which, if we include local authorities, accounted for between 25 and 30 per cent of total national expenditure. Of course, a very large part of this expenditure went on transfer payments, defence and direct government purchases so that the proportion of economic property owned or directly controlled by State organs was very much smaller than these figures would suggest. Nevertheless, direct participation was increasing as both the central and local authorities extended their spheres of influence. Local authorities, for example, had a large stake in gas, water and electricity and in road transport including tramways, together with a host of smaller trading activities. In addition, there were many semi-public utilities such as dock and harbour authorities in which local government participated. The Central Government's interests were less extensive but again increasing. To the Post Office and naval dockyards, which had been controlled by the State for centuries, were added the administration of several new public or semi-public corporations, notably the Forestry Commission (1919), the Central Electricity Board (1926), the British Broadcasting Corporation (1926), the London Passenger Transport Board (1933) and British Overseas Airways Corporation (1939). Indirectly, of course, the State's influence was much wider since in this period it sought to control or regulate the activities of a wide range of

---

[1] The number was reduced by merger and amalgamation.

industries.[1] The role of the State will be discussed fully in Chapter 9 and little more need be said at this stage.

A further feature of the industrial structure was the tendency for firms and plants to increase in size in terms of output and employment. This was caused both by amalgamation and natural growth. Nearly every industry and trade was affected in some way by amalgamation (either horizontal or vertical) and this often resulted in a fairly high degree of concentration and/or complex inter-connections between different industries. Thus over 100 railway companies were absorbed into four large groups in the early 1920s, Imperial Chemical Industries, formed in 1926 from four main firms in the industry, acquired control of more than one third of the British chemical output, while in some of the older industries a complex set of inter-industry holding arrangements were formed in this period. It is difficult to give any precise measure of the changes in size and concentration either at the plant or firm level since comprehensive data on the size-structure of industry is not available before the Census of Production in 1935.[2] There seems little doubt, however, that concentration of economic activity increased. On the basis of the Factory Inspectors' reports Sargent Florence estimated that the mean size of plant in manufacturing rose from 16·5 to 23·5 persons between 1904–38, while by 1935 10 per cent of the largest British plants employed 76 per cent of all persons in factories of 100 or more employees, a proportion similar to that of the United States.[3] In fact over one half of the workers enumerated in the 1935 Census worked in industrial units employing 500 men or more and some of the most highly concentrated plants were to be found in mining, aircraft manufacture, tramways, biscuit-making, iron and steel and the railways. A study made by Leak and Maizels on the basis of the 1935 Census suggests that the concentration of output was very high in some fields, especially

[1] In addition to enterprises controlled by private and State interests there was a third group comprising non-profit-making concerns which included building societies, cooperative societies, and charitable and educational organizations which were registered under special Acts of Parliament.
[2] An additional problem, moreover, is that there are a number of different ways of measuring size, e.g. by employment, capital or output, not all of which produce the same results. On this point see J. Bates, 'Alternative Measures of the Size of Firms', ch. 8 in P. E. Hart, *Studies in Profit, Business Saving and Investment in the United Kingdom 1920–1962*, vol. 1 (1965).
[3] P. Sargent Florence, *The Logic of British and American Industry* (1953), pp. 31–5.

in the newer industries.[1] For example, the percentage of net output accounted for by the three largest units in any one industry was 84 per cent in rayon and dyestuffs, 75 per cent in photographic apparatus, 73 per cent in rubber tyres and tubes, 66 per cent in electrical wires and cables and aluminium, 48 per cent in electrical machinery and 45 per cent in motor car manufacture. In some cases the process of concentration had occurred primarily after the war. By contrast, concentration ratios in many of the staple industries were much lower; in iron and steel blast furnaces 34 per cent, shipbuilding 27 per cent, cotton spinning 26 per cent, iron and steel smelting and rolling 21 per cent, and brewing 18 per cent. At the extreme lower end of the spectrum, a number of industries had percentages of less than 10, including mechanical engineering, woollen and worsted manufacture, furniture, leather, clothing, cotton weaving and building and contracting. On the other hand, there were a number of trades, few of which could be classed as new, where one firm or group controlled 70 per cent or more of capacity. Some of these, as in textile finishing, sewing cotton, wallpaper, Portland cement and flat glass, had originated in the pre-war period, while others came to dominate their markets as a result of mergers and absorptions of competing firms in the inter-war years, the most notable examples being whisky distilling, soap and margarine, matches, glass bottles and seed crushing.

The trend towards concentration and the reduction of competition was reinforced by the widespread adoption of trade associations. These had been common before the war though many new ones were formed in response to government control during the period of hostilities. Most of these were continued afterwards and in the hard market environment of the inter-war period trade associations flourished for the purposes of restricting competition and stabilizing prices. By the late 1930s there were probably over 1,000 in manufacturing alone. Many of these were very loose associations which provided information on prices, sales and other matters to their constituent members. Others, however, had very elaborate restrictive agreements covering prices, output and sales and were more akin to the German cartel-type of organization. The Cable Makers' Association, for example, which covered 90 per cent of total production, controlled the prices and output of the member firms and operated a system of allocating orders on a quota basis. The electrical products and building

[1] H. Leak and A. Maizels, 'The Structure of British Industry', *Journal of the Royal Statistical Society*, 108 (1945).

materials industries were riddled with restrictive agreements some of which were very rigid indeed. But private enterprise was not solely responsible for the growth of associations and agreements. The Government was instrumental in sponsoring many trade associations during the war in order to facilitate the control of industry, while in the 1930s it encouraged the formation of cartel-like arrangements or producer organizations in an effort to curtail competition and bolster up industries in distress. The policy of the Government was an important factor in the acceptance of control in some industries including coal, shipbuilding, iron and steel, agriculture, herring fishing and tramp shipping. In addition, the State sought to eliminate or reduce competition by subsidies, tariffs and restrictive legislation as in the case of civil aviation, iron and steel, beet sugar and road transport.

The reasons for these tends in business organization are not hard to find. Market and technical factors tended to favour the growth in size of units and as the latter increased it naturally affected the type of firm structure. The non-incorporated one-man business or family partnership became increasingly unsuitable as the technical complexity of modern production increased. In some industries, motor car manufacture in particular, large firms or units of production were essential if the benefits of mass production were to be reaped. There were, of course, still many small firms or businesses and although a large number either failed or were absorbed by larger concerns the ranks were continually being filled by new entrants. Numerically small firms predominated but in terms of output and employment they played a minor role. The existence of so many small enterprises was not only due to the tenacity or independence of the individual owner, though this no doubt was an important factor. For some branches of manufacture such as machine tools and boot and shoe manufacture small or medium size firms tended to predominate simply because they were the optimum. In addition to these factors, competition and the uncertain conditions of the period forced firms to co-operate or merge their interests and encouraged the development of restrictive arrangements of one form or another.

It is somewhat more difficult to say exactly what effects these developments had, that is whether they were advantageous in terms of improving efficiency, etc., or whether they simply led to monopolistic arrangements designed to protect the producer. Of course the outcome varied a great deal between one industry and another and it would be very easy to find examples both for and against. Theoretical arguments do not help a great deal in this respect. What is needed is considerably more empirical research into the consequences of these developments. On the whole most writers are dubious about the benefits, particularly those of restrictive trading arrangements. Lucas, in a study made in the 1930s, was rather unhappy about the consequences. He felt that free competition had almost disappeared and that the 'chief function of control has consisted rather of the purely negative task of protecting industry from the most injurious effects of cut-throat competition than of the positive and thorough administration of an industry's affairs'.[1] Up to a point Lucas's conclusions were correct though they cannot pass without qualification and ideally each case needs to be judged on its own merits. Certainly combination and association reduced the degree of competition and probably this was no bad thing in the conditions then obtaining. But it is by no means clear that competition was virtually eliminated. The entry of new firms may have been made more difficult but it was by no means impossible.[2] Moreover, the widespread extension of trade associations to nearly every form of economic activity was not necessarily a sign that competition had ceased to prevail. Though many associations practised some form of price fixing there were still other ways in which competition could assert itself, while the looseness and vulnerability of such arrangements left them open to attack from non-members. Often restrictive trading agreements broke up because of some dispute and fierce price-cutting then ensued, while many producers still feared the threat of foreign competition even after the adoption of general tariff protection in 1932. It is true that the formation of many agreements led to an increase in prices, as in the case of cement-making in 1934. But the raising of prices was often a response to the excessively low level to which they had fallen prior to the formation of agreements rather than a deliberate attempt to exploit the powers of monopolistic control.

The more elaborate control arrangements designed to restrict output, eliminate capacity or encourage the merging of competing interests can be viewed in a more favourable light, at least on the surface. This is not to imply that the methods adopted were the most suitable or that the progress achieved was satisfactory but simply to infer that,

[1] A. F. Lucas, *Industrial Reconstruction and the Control of Competition* (1937), pp. 64, 361.
[2] Though in some cases, e.g. road transport, entry was very difficult after the legislation of the early 1930s.

insofar as some industries suffered from excess capacity, over-production or too many small and inefficient producers, it was an advantage to have some arrangements for dealing with these problems. In some cases, as in cotton, progress was made towards eliminating excess capacity and reducing the number of producers both by voluntary and government sponsored action. However, in general the arrangements for dealing with the problems of the basic industries cannot be regarded as successful. More often than not they were designed to bolster up the industries and tended to protect efficient and inefficient producers alike. They did relatively little to eliminate excess capacity or to improve the overall efficiency of the industries in question.

The effects of the growth in size of undertakings were probably more favourable. It would, for example, be difficult to deny the benefits flowing from the concentration of production in many of the newer trades such as vehicle manufacture, rayon production and electricity supply. Generally one would expect that up to a certain point the larger the firm or plant the greater the scope for scale economies, technical innovation and research, the benefits of which would be reflected in improved efficiency provided that monopolistic exploitation did not offset these. Of course the optimum size of plant or firm varies a great deal from one industry to another and one needs to distinguish between the multi-plant legal entity – the firm, and the individual plant.[1] A firm owning a large number of plants might operate no more efficiently than if the plants were all owned separately by different firms except where substantial interplant economies occur. On the other hand, a large plant producing 100,000 units of product x may operate far more efficiently than 10 separate plants each turning out 10,000 units of the same product. Relevant empirical studies suggest that there is some association between scale and efficiency. Rostas found that efficiency increased with size of unit over a fairly wide field of British industry.[2] However, an attempt to test the hypothesis for 12 industries for the period 1907 to 1948, produced rather low correlation values. The correlation coefficient between the degree of concentration and the increase in productivity per man-hour worked out at 0·57, but the relation between the number of employees

[1] See J. M. Blair, 'Does Large Scale Enterprise Result in Lower Costs?', *American Economic Review, Papers and Proceedings*, 38 (1948).
[2] L. Rostas, *Productivity, Prices and Distribution in Selected British Industries* (1948), pp. 30, 45.

per establishment and the increase in output per man-hour was much lower, at 0·34.[1] Too much should not be written into these low values. Clearly conditions varied a great deal from industry to industry; in some industries increasing returns to scale were very prominent,[2] while in others they were clearly less so. Much depends upon the nature of the product and the production process and the rate of technical advance. Moreover, a low association between scale and efficiency in any particular industry may simply reflect that the economies of scale have not been exploited properly rather than the fact that they do not exist. Insofar as this was the case in certain industries in the inter-war period then there might be greater justification for accepting Lucas's conclusion. Under these circumstances it is probably more fruitful to examine the experience of each industry separately. This task cannot be performed here, though from time to time we shall occasionally refer to the question again.

The basic industries

This chapter is primarily concerned with analysing the fortunes of the large staple industries of coal, cotton, wool textiles, shipbuilding and iron and steel. We have refrained from referring to these industries as stagnating since the term is somewhat misleading unless defined clearly. Not all the staple trades did stagnate in the inter-war period. In fact over the period 1920–38 only shipbuilding experienced a decline in output. Moreover, most of them showed up reasonably well in terms of productivity. However, though most of these industries managed to raise their output and productivity in this period their performance was generally very modest and somewhat below the average for all industry. On the other hand, if we adopt 1913 as the reference year there is greater justification for speaking of decline or stagnation. Generally these industries reached a peak in this year and, apart from iron and steel, output never again returned to pre-war levels.

[1] C. F. Carter and B. R. Williams, *Industry and Technical Progress* (1957), p. 121. *Cf* the study by A. Phillips for the u.s., 'Concentration, Scale and Technological Change in Selected Manufacturing Industries, 1899–1939', *Journal of Industrial Economics,* 4 (1955–6).
[2] For example, Rostas found that output per head in brick manufacturing increased almost continuously with the size of establishment and that plants in the largest size group were nearly twice as productive as those in the smallest. Rostas, *op. cit.,* p. 123.

But what really distinguished these industries from other sectors was their high rates of unemployment and their negative employment growth. As can be seen from Table 22 all of them lost substantial amounts of labour between 1920 (or 1924) and 1938, while in most cases unemployment rates were well above the general average. In fact these five trades together with mechanical engineering accounted for around one half of the total unemployment of insured workers in July 1929.[1]

There were, of course, a number of other industries in which unemployment was high or which experienced a contraction in employment. But it would be difficult to class them as stagnating industries since few of them experienced negative output growth together with high unemployment and a contracting labour force. For example, the level of unemployment was often quite high in building but this was the very opposite of a stagnating industry. Similarly, the clothing, leather, precision instruments and mechanical engineering industries all lost labour during the period but their output and productivity records were quite respectable.[2] There were a few other trades which could be classed as declining since they experienced contractions in both employment and output. These included pottery and earthenware, tinplate manufacture, hand tools and cutlery, saw and file making and the minor textile trades such as jute, linen, hemp and rope manufacture. For the most part these trades were fairly small and in most cases they were related to some larger branch of manufacture. Thus, apart from these minor exceptions, only the main basic industries listed above can be regarded as really declining and from an output point of view this statement is only strictly valid with reference to the base year of 1913. No other major industry group suffered a contraction in output either between the wars or over the years 1913 to 1938.[3]

The five basic industries therefore provide a representative sample of the relatively depressed sector of the economy in this period. Nineteenth century industrial development had been based primarily on these trades and in the immediate pre-war years they reached the peak

---

[1] *Ministry of Labour Gazette*, Aug. 1929, pp. 294–7.

[2] Though mechanical engineering grew steadily in terms of output some of its older sectors such as textile machinery and steam engines and locomotive building declined quite sharply for obvious reasons.

[3] This excludes reference to the transport and service sectors one or two of which, e.g. shipping, were declining.

TABLE 22 *Employment and unemployment in main staple trades, 1920–38*

	1920		1924		1929		1932		1938	
	Employment (000s)	% unemployed	Employment (000s)	% unemployed	Employment (000s)	% unemployed	Employment (000s)	% unemployed	Employment (000s)	% unemployed
Coal	1,083·0		1,056·8	6·8	812·5	18·2	630·0	41·2	674·6	22·0
Cotton	533·7		504·6	15·8	480·2	14·5	364·2	31·1	301·6	27·7
Woollen and worsted	274·5		295·0	7·0	261·1	15·6	234·1	26·6	220·7	21·4
Shipbuilding	282·2		155·1	26·4	139·2	23·2	61·1	59·5	129·1	21·4
Iron and steel	527·2		344·4	19·7	342·2	19·9	231·1	48·5	342·1	24·8
Average percentage unemployment for all industry		⎱ 9·9 ⎰		9·9		9·9		22·9		13·3

NOTES 1 Employment figures refer to man-years in employment.
2 Unemployment percentages are for July each year for unemployed insured workers in Great Britain and N.Ireland.
3 Iron and steel unemployment percentages are those for steel smelting and iron puddling, iron and steel rolling mills and forges.

SOURCES A. L. Chapman and R. Knight, *Wages and Salaries in the United Kingdom, 1900–1938* (1953); and *Ministry of Labour Gazette*.

of their development. At that time they accounted for a large proportion of industrial output and exports. They were all heavily dependent on the export market, in some cases exceptionally so. In 1907 over 80 per cent of the cotton industry's output went abroad, 57 per cent of the woollen and worsted production, 31 per cent of the coal output (including bunkers) and nearly 40 per cent of the output of the iron and steel, shipbuilding and engineering industries. Geographically, these industries were strongly concentrated in the northern regions of the country. Thus in terms of employment over 80 per cent of the cotton industry was located in Lancashire, about the same proportion of the woollen industry was to be found in the West Riding of Yorkshire, more than 50 per cent of the shipbuilding was to be found in Northumberland and Durham and the Clyde area, while in the case of the coal industry 19·2 per cent of the employment was in Northumberland and Durham, 20·1 per cent in South Wales, 17 per cent in the West Riding of Yorkshire and 11·7 per cent in Lancashire, Derby, Northants and Nottinghamshire. Concentration was less marked in iron and steel though the northern areas had more than their fair share of the declining branches. South-west Scotland had 15·3 per cent of the employment in blast furnaces and Cumberland and Westmorland and the Ridings of Yorkshire had 18 per cent. The more buoyant sectors were located in the Midlands.[1]

The decline in output of the staple trades conforms to the theory that industries have an s-shaped long-run growth curve. Most maturing industries reach a stage when diminishing returns set in and rates of growth decline or become negative. Whether diminishing returns are a function of supply or demand contraints is however debatable. Merton suggests that the skewness of innovation in any industry is weighted in its early phase of growth whereas as the industry matures the rate of technical progress tends to slacken and hence leads to a declining rate of growth.[2] Schmookler, on the other hand, believes that retardation in an industry's rate of technical progress is to be explained by the falling off in that industry's rate of expansion which reflects changes in demand rather than supply conditions, though there is obviously some feedback process at work. Thus as an industry matures a given percentage cut in costs does not become more difficult

[1] P.E.P., *Report on the Location of Industry* (1939), Table 1, pp. 262 *et seq.* The figures are for 1931.
[2] R. K. Merton, 'Fluctuations in the Rate of Industrial Innovation', *Quarterly Journal of Economics*, 49 (1934–5).

to achieve but the return from doing so declines as a result of a decline in the income and price elasticity of demand for its products due to market saturation and product substitution.[1]

The latter argument would appear to fit the facts fairly well. Undoubtedly a check to demand, especially from the export side, was the chief factor making for stable or declining growth of these industries. This can be explained by a general slowing-down in the growth of demand for staple products, the competition of substitute products and the substitution of sources of supply. The subsequent contraction in profit margins and the approach of market saturation reduced the incentive to innovate and reduce costs. Hence unit costs rose or were higher than they should have been and this further weakened market demand.

There are, however, certain difficulties in the way of pressing the demand-induced explanation too far. For one thing most of the basic industries experienced a deceleration in the rate of technical progress before the war, especially from the 1890s, even though demand was still fairly buoyant. Second, in some cases, notably mining, technical progress was more rapid than it had been before 1914. In fact most of the basic industries recorded a better productivity performance than before the war though in part this was due to the shake-out of labour from these trades. Third, the experience of these industries since 1950 suggests that rapid technical progress is not incompatible with shrinking demand and declining output. Moreover, the relevance of supply factors cannot be ignored. The fact that the staple industries had a large stock of capital, not all of which was obsolete, no doubt reduced the incentive to innovate. In particular, it was often difficult to innovate partially since the capital stock was geared to a certain pattern of production and it was frequently highly inter-related. Thus it was not easy to adjust it in such a way as to accommodate new techniques in one sector or stage of the production process. And the cost of innovating throughout all stages might be so high as to act as a deterrent. The problem was particularly acute in industries with a decentralized structure such as the cotton industry, where different stages of the productive process, spinning, weaving, and finishing, were under separate ownership. An improvement in spinning machinery, for example, would produce bottlenecks at the later stages of manufacture and would not really be advantageous to the spinners unless the

[1] J. Schmookler, *Innovation and Economic Growth* (1966), p. 204.

other sections were able, or prepared to, adopt new techniques to match those in spinning. Furthermore, technical improvements usually meant greater mechanization and more capital intensive production and in the conditions of abundant labour supply the pressure to move in this direction was not particularly strong. Finally, at a time of reduced profit margins the supply of finance for innovations was limited. This last point can, however, be regarded as part of the feed-back process arising from the demand side.

It would be difficult, therefore, to single out any one particular factor as being the determinant of innovation either over time or between industries. Perhaps the three most important are technological exhaustion, economic and sociological. The slow rate of technical advance in the pig iron industry before 1914 has been attributed to the exhaustion of the technological frontier.[1] Alternatively, the slowing down or contraction in output (and presumably profits) may lead to reduced investment and hence less modern equipment. The cotton industry after 1920 could well be placed in this category. Or again, entrepreneurial weaknesses may result in a reduced rate of technical advance as in shipbuilding. Moreover, in the case of the latter point there are a whole host of relevant factors, including expected trading conditions, past profits, capital bottlenecks, factor prices, etc., which influence entrepreneurs' investment decisions. Clearly too, not every industry is affected in the same way by these forces. The experience of the coal industry in the inter-war years, for example, suggests that technical advance and productivity growth are not incompatible with a decline in output.

With these general considerations in mind we can now proceed to review the main trends of development in the staple industries.

The coal industry

The peak output of the coal industry was in 1913 when 287 million tons were produced, a figure which was never to be attained again. Despite strenuous efforts to maintain production during the war output fell to 231·4 million tons in 1918 partly because of a shortage of manpower. The industry was also affected by a certain loss of export demand. Output was only marginally higher in 1920 and then fell

---

[1] Donald N. McCloskey, 'Productivity Change in British Pig Iron, 1870–1939', *Quarterly Journal of Economics*, 82 (1968), p. 283.

back very sharply in 1921, but the subsequent coal strikes in America and the French occupation of the Ruhr gave a temporary boost to the industry and in 1923–4 output was not very far off that of pre-war. After that the long-term trend was downward the nadir (excluding the year of the General Strike), being reached in 1932 and 1933 when less than 210 million tons were mined. Recovery from the slump was slow and even by 1937 output was still some 7 per cent less than in 1929 and 16 per cent less than 1913, though it was slightly higher than in 1920. The following year saw a further contraction to a level of 50 million tons down on 1913.

The collapse of the export market was responsible for this cut-back. Exports, including ships' bunker coal, had accounted for about one third of all output in 1913, that is 98 million tons. For most of the inter-war period exports remained well below this level (apart from 1923–4) and by 1937–8 they were running at only about 50 million tons per annum. Unfortunately there was no compensation in the domestic market. Home consumption of coal remained practically stable throughout the period and by 1937–8 it was around 185 million tons as against 184 million in 1913.

The stagnation in domestic consumption can be attributed mainly to economies in the use of coal and the application of alternative forms of energy. The household consumption of coal rose only slightly because of the introduction of better grates and the switch to alternative energies, oil, gas but principally electricity, and the extension of fuel economies. For instance, the iron and steel industry's intake of coal fell from 31·4 to 23·3 million tons between 1913 to 1937 even though output in the latter year was well up on 1913. Gas and electricity generating stations increased their demand for coal but this was not commensurate with their expansion in output and did not compensate for the fall in demand from industrial consumers. Thus, a fivefold increase in electricity output was achieved by only a twofold expansion in coal and coke consumption.

The reasons for the coal industry's loss of exports is somewhat more complex. As in the case of the domestic market, foreign demand for coal was affected adversely by the extended use of competitive fuels and by progress made in fuel economy. A further serious loss occurred as a result of the conversion to oil-fired ships. Before the war the bulk of the world's mercantile marine consisted of steamships using coal as a source of energy, but by 1939 over half the world fleet was driven by oil while the navies had changed over almost completely to the new fuel. This change hit Britain particularly hard since she had formerly supplied a large proportion of the world's bunker requirements.

Despite these adverse tendencies Britain's losses cannot be attributed simply to an absolute contraction in world demand for coal. World consumption actually increased though at a much lower rate than before 1914, 0·3 per cent per annum as against 4 per cent before 1914. World production, on the other hand, rose by 0·7 per cent per annum between 1913 and 1937. This meant that there was considerable excess coal producing capacity in existence with the result that the competition for markets increased. Not surprisingly Britain's relative position in the international coal trade declined. In 1913 she had been responsible for 25 per cent of world production and 55 per cent of world exports (including bunkers); by 1937 these proportions had fallen to 19 and 40 per cent respectively. Exports losses were caused by several factors. Some countries which had formerly relied upon British coal supplies were becoming self-sufficient among these being the Netherlands, Spain and the Far East. Second, there was increasing competition from European countries, notably Germany and Poland, in British markets in the Baltic and Mediterranean, and such competition was assisted by various subventions and rebates. Third, many countries in the 1930s placed quantitative restrictions on coal imports and these sometimes discriminated against British coal. Finally, there is the question of whether the industry's competitive efficiency was the cause of export losses.

This latter point is more difficult to establish than most writers imagine. There seems little doubt that the industry was a high cost one, and it is usally argued that the disparity in costs and prices between British and foreign producers was due to high wages, overvaluation of the pound (1925–31) and the structural weakness and technical inefficiency of British mining. The main emphasis is generally placed on the last of these points.[1] In support of this claim it can be shown that output per man-shift rose very modestly between 1913 and 1937 compared with that in other main producing countries (notably Germany, Holland, the United States and Poland) and that by the end of the period output per man-shift abroad was one third or more higher

[1] P.E.P. *Report on the British Coal Industry* (1936), p. 152–5.

than in this country.[1] It is also alleged that the structure of the industry, particularly the large number of small producing units, militated against improved efficiency. While one is prepared to believe that in some countries, especially Germany and the u.s., mining operations were more efficient than in the u.k., it is difficult, in the light of other evidence produced below, to believe that differences in efficiency were the major factor in the situation.

For one thing the international productivity comparisons are based on output per man-shift which is not an ideal measure for this purpose, since it takes no account of non-face workers nor does it allow for variations between countries in hours worked per shift. Second, recent estimates suggest that output per man increased quite rapidly, by as much as 38 per cent between 1924 and 1938, and this seems to be more consistent with what we know about the industry. There was a substantial contraction of the labour force and mechanization proceeded apace. The British coal industry rapidly reduced its earlier backwardness in this latter respect. By 1939, 61 per cent of the coal was cut by machinery and 54 per cent was mechanically conveyed compared with only eight and 1½ per cent respectively in 1913. Technical progress generally was far more evident than it had been before 1914. Similarly, though the industry still remained structurally weak compared with its main competitors, considerable progress was made towards concentrating production in a fewer number of collieries and mines. By 1944 there were 1,630 mines belonging to 740 colliery undertakings, while nearly 80 per cent of total output was produced by less than 129 collieries. Twenty years earlier there had been 2,480 and 1,400 respectively. This is not to suggest that there was no further room for improvement in coal-mining efficiency or that there was no gap between British and Continental practice. The Reid Committee criticized the industry on a number of points including the bad layout of mines, the methods of transport and treatment of coal and the

[1] W. H. B. Court, 'Problems of the British Coal Industry Between the Wars', *Economic History Review*, 15 (1945), p. 20. Indices of output per man-shift in 1936–8 with 1913 = 100 were as follows:

u.k.	114
u.s.	131
Belgium	143
Poland	160
Upper Silesia	166
The Ruhr	172

See Jean Bird, 'Coal', in M. Abrams, *Britain and the Export Trade* (1946), p. 248.

failure to exploit good seams properly.[1] On the other hand, it is doubtful whether the gap was as wide as the output per man-shift figures suggest since, if anything, some of the differences between British and foreign technical practice were narrowing in this period.

But whether a relative high cost industry was the cause of the poor export performance is another matter. Britain was not the only country to suffer a loss of exports. In fact all the leading coal producers, except Poland, had a lower volume of exports in most years compared to 1913.[2] This suggests that the export market as a whole was contracting as a result of increasing self-sufficiency on the part of foreign importers and the substitution effects of new forms of energy. Britain in this respect had more to lose because of her heavy reliance on export markets, added to which she was handicapped by a high cost industry. But the facts do not suggest that export losses were primarily due to inefficiency; had costs been lower it is unlikely that there would have been much improvement in the volume of exports. To a large extent these were caused by exogenous forces outside the industry's immediate control.

Whatever the causes of contraction there is no doubt that the industry was in a bad way. Output, profits and prices were depressed and they fluctuated more sharply than pre-war, while the industry was left with much excess capacity. Before 1914 profits per ton of coal raised averaged 1s 6d or more, but only once, in 1923, was this level exceeded post-war. Between 1924 and 1928 a fall of 10 per cent in the volume of sales and a 33-per-cent reduction in price resulted in an average profit of 1s 2d being converted into a loss of 11d, while during the years 1929–38 profits averaged only half the pre-war level. This instability in prices and profits induced some producers to try to regulate the market in the 1920s, though the attempts were not very successful since many owners refused to co-operate. In the following decade the Government, principally by the Coal Mines Act of 1930, gave its official blessing to control. Compulsory cartelization schemes run by the owners were to allocate output quotas and fix minimum prices for different grades of coal, while a Commission was established to promote amalgamations. The results of the legislation were dis-

[1] *Report of the Technical Advisory Committee on Coal Mining*, Cmd. 6610, 1945. For a commentary on the Report, see A. Beacham, 'Efficiency and Organization of the British Coal Industry', *Economic Journal*, 55 (1945).
[2] See J. H. Jones, G. Cartwright and P. H. Guenault, *The Coal-Mining Industry* (1939), pp. 36, 84.

appointing. It did little to ensure the profitability of the industry or to adjust capacity to the changed demand conditions. In fact the law became a device by which the available business was spread among all concerns regardless of their relative efficiency, and all enjoyed the benefits of fixed prices and restricted output. Since it actually impeded transfer of production quotas to the most efficient units the problem of overcapacity was not tackled seriously. Moreover, the attempts of the Commission to effect amalgamations and concentrate production were frustrated by the determined opposition of the owners. Judged by the number of combinations this section of the Act was almost a dead letter, and the industry achieved much more in the way of voluntary action.[1] Between 1926 and 1936, 56 voluntary mergers, comprising 424 pits and about one quarter of a million workers, were carried through.

Cotton textiles

The industry which registered the most dramatic collapse was undoubtedly that of cotton. The industry was very much geared to the export market and had reached its peak just before the first world war when over 80 per cent of output was shipped overseas. Cotton goods accounted for 25 per cent of British exports by value and Britain's share of international trade in cotton textiles was around 65 per cent. During the war the industry's development was checked because of manpower shortages, curtailment of raw material supplies and restrictions on trade. The resultant backlog of demand led to a violent boom in 1919–20 when large profits were made. Unfortunately these profits were not used to replace obsolete capacity or to improve techniques. Vast sums were paid out to shareholders while speculators, with the aid of bank loans and overdrafts, bought up firms at vastly inflated prices. Many cotton firms became over-capitalized and were left weighted down with a burden of debt to repay at a time when they were least in a position to do so.[2]

The breaking of the post-war boom ushered in a period of almost continuous contraction for the cotton industry. Trends in production can be seen from Table 23. By 1938 cotton textile output (both yarn and piece goods) was less than one half the pre-war level. This de-

[1] See Lucus *op. cit.*, pp. 98–100; Court, *loc. cit.*, p. 18; and Jones, Cartwright and Guenault, *op. cit.*, pp. 151–7.
[2] Freda Uttley, *Lancashire and the Far East* (1931), pp. 44–6.

cline can be attributed almost entirely to the collapse of Britain's main export markets as a result of the development of cotton industries in former markets and competition in third markets by Japan. Although world consumption of raw cotton rose by 36 per cent between 1913 and 1937 the volume of international trade in cottons fell by 38 per cent and Britain's share of the diminished total declined. By 1938 over four fifths of the world's consumption of cotton textiles was supplied by local producers. Britain suffered losses in every market, except South and West Africa, though the greatest decline occurred in the Far East. India, Japan, China and Hong Kong reduced their purchases by no less than 91 per cent over the period. The biggest setback was in India, Britain's best customer. Between 1909–13 India had produced on average 1,141 million square yards of piece goods and imported from Britain 2,741 million. By 1938 Indian domestic production had risen to 4,250 million square yards while imports from Britain were a mere 258 million. Moreover, by the latter date Britain had been ousted by Japan as an exporter of cottons to India. In practically every market the story was the same. Altogether, roughly two thirds of Britain's export losses were attributable to the developments of production by her former competitors while nearly all the remaining third resulted from competition by Japan.

TABLE 23 *Production and exports of cotton textiles, 1912–38 (mn sq. yd.)*

	Yarn (mn lb)		Piece goods	
	Production	Exports	Production	Exports
1912	1,963	244	8,050	6,913
1924	1,395	163	6,046	4,445
1930	1,048	137	3,500	2,472
1937	1,375	159	4,288	1,922
1938	1,070	123	3,126	1,494

SOURCE G. C. Allen, *British Industries and Their Organization* (3rd ed. 1951), pp. 196, 223.

There were very few compensations for Lancashire's premier industry. Though the industry lost much of its trade in cheap goods to native producers of poor countries, high quality lines held up somewhat better. Hence losses in value terms were less than by volume and the incidence of depression varied from one sector of the industry to another. Thus, producers of high quality fine counts suffered less than those making coarse cheap goods, though as time went on competition increased in the better quality trade. A compensatory factor was that home demand increased, albeit slightly, though patterns of demand were changing, partly as a result of the development of rayon. However, the cotton industry was able to adjust itself to some extent to the shifting expenditure patterns in the domestic market. Spinners began to increase the quality of yarn for the expanding luxury trade, while in the 1930s they began to spin staple fibre yarn. Similarly, weavers began to make rayon and mixed fabrics and by the end of the period output of rayon piece goods and mixtures was equivalent to 14 per cent of cotton piece output.

Any cotton industry, however efficient, would not have been able to withstand such inroads into its export markets. Most of the competing countries had certain advantages over Britain, notably lower labour costs, newer equipment, relative absence of transport costs and protective tariffs. On top of this Lancashire had to contend with its own inefficiency. The industry could hardly be called modern and up-to-date and in some respects things got worse in the course of time. Throughout the inter-war years little investment was made in new plant and machinery and in fact from 1928 onwards the industry was, on balance, disinvesting.[1] The result was that the industry's equipment became steadily older and more inefficient. A partial investigation in 1930 showed that for most classes of machinery 65–70 per cent of the plant inspected was more than 20 years old, while the Working Party Report of 1946 drew attention to the fact that a large proportion of the industry's equipment was of pre-1914 vintage and well beyond its efficient working life.[2] Judged by the standards and methods of some of her main competitors, Lancashire's equipment was old-fashioned, it was extensive in relation to turnover, while the structure of the industry was not conducive to efficient operation. The spinning section placed its faith in the old mule spindle instead of the ring spindle which was used widely in other countries. Similarly the weaving branch made little headway with the automatic loom despite the fact that its installation would, in the words of the Platt Report, have 'caused a complete revolution.'[3] In the absence of large scale innovations gains in productivity were fairly modest and were

[1] C. H. Feinstein, *Domestic Capital Formation in the United Kingdom* (1965), p. 107.
[2] See Board of Trade, *Working Party Report on Cotton* (1946), pp. 66–9.
[3] Ministry of Reconstruction, *Report of the Cotton Textile Mission to the United States of America, March-April, 1944* (H.M.S.O., 1944), p. 44.

derived largely from minor technical advances and as a by-product of the contracting labour force.[1] Thus with a large amount of excess capacity and increasingly antiquated equipment the industry became a high cost one and its competitive ability deteriorated.

The failure to progress technically is perhaps understandable given the prevailing economic conditions. Contracting markets were hardly conducive to large scale re-equipment. In any case many firms had little to spend on innovation since profits were low and were often earmarked for paying off debts contracted in the boom of 1919–20. But these are not the only reasons for criticisms were made about the industry's rate of technical progress long before the depressed conditions of the period under review. Possibly the success of the industry in its heyday had rendered it complacent and reluctant to exploit new opportunities. As one official committee observed: '. . . the very success of the Lancashire cotton industry in developing efficient methods in the conditions of the past . . . is today responsible in part for a disinclination to explore new possibilities and try new methods, many of which have already been exploited with success, for example in the southern parts of the United States and in Japan.'[2] Finally, the cost involved in large scale re-equipment was a deterrent in itself. Not only did the introduction of new machines such as ring spindles and automatic looms often necessitate the rebuilding or adaptation of the infrastructure such as buildings, but ideally it required a cooperative effort on the part of the various branches of the industry because of the interrelated nature of the capital stock. The prospects of achieving this however were somewhat remote given the disintegrated nature of the industry, spinning, weaving and finishing being virtually autonomous industries, and the large number of small independent firms involved in each branch.[3]

Nevertheless, despite the disparate structure some attempt was made to regulate the industry's activities and reduce its excess capacity. First reactions of millowners to the onset of depression was to reduce

[1] Output per operative rose by 26 per cent between 1907 and 1937 compared with about 41 per cent for all industry. But productivity in Japan and the u.s. rose much faster. See L. Rostas, *Comparative Productivity in British and American Industry* (1948), pp. 49, 136, and 'Productivity of Labour in the Cotton Industry', *Economic Journal*, 55 (1945).
[2] Economic Advisory Council, *Report of the Committee on the Cotton Industry*, Cmd. 3615, (1930), para. 39.
[3] There were of course some fairly large concerns notably in finishing where a considerable proportion of output was in the hands of large combines.

wages and institute short-time working, but in the later 1920s loose associations were drawn up to prevent weak selling by restricting output, fixing prices and other protective measures. In 1927, for example, the American Cotton Yarn Association was formed for purposes of grading yarns, fixing prices and regulating output. But this and other attempts at regulation failed for several reasons. First, it was difficult to formulate a concerted policy because of the large number of producers involved, many of whom were not keen to co-operate and expressed their doubts by undercutting members of the association. Second, since the industry's difficulties were due to loss of exports, attempts to maintain or even raise prices were hardly likely to strengthen Lancashire's competitive ability. Third, the biggest and most immediate problem was excess capacity but no proper scheme was organized to deal with its elimination partly because the financial circumstances of the industry created a situation which made reorganization difficult to achieve either by agreement among mill-owners or simply through the bankruptcy of weaker units.[1]

Eventually, however, it was realized that a reduction in capacity was the only solution to the permanent shrinkage in demand. This was not before time. By the late 1920s the industry had roughly the same amount of capacity as before the war to meet a very much reduced level of demand. A number of voluntary schemes to rationalize capacity were therefore drawn up. Among the more important were those in the spinning section and one of the biggest ventures was that of the Lancashire Cotton Corporation established in 1929. It acquired over nine million spindles which it eventually reduced to $4\frac{1}{2}$ million. Altogether rationalization schemes of one sort or another brought spindle capacity down to 44 million by the mid 1930s, compared with 56 million in 1929 and 59 million in 1920. Nevertheless, it was estimated that the spinning section still had $13\frac{1}{2}$ million spindles in excess of requirements. In 1936, therefore, tbe Government intervened. The Cotton Industry (Reorganization) Act of that year established a Spindles Board to buy up and scrap 10 million surplus spindles and this scheme was to be financed by a compulsory levy on existing machinery. By the eve of the second world war the Board had managed to sterilize half the specified amount so that the total capacity then stood at 39 million spindles. Reductions in capacity also occurred in other sections of the industry though action was much less organized compared with spinning. By 1938 the number of looms had been re-

[1] G. C. Allen, *British Industries and their Organisation* (3rd ed. 1951), p. 212.

F

duced to 495,000 compared with 700,000 in 1930 and 786,000 in 1912.

Thus by the end of the 1930s the industry was but a shadow of its former self. Output was about half what it had been before the war and cotton goods accounted for 12 per cent of Britain's exports as against the former 25 per cent. Though still the largest cotton industry in the world the British was one among many. In 1937 Britain's consumption of raw cotton was only 9·6 per cent of the world total compared with 19 per cent in 1913, while her share of world spindleage had shrunk from 39 to 26 per cent. Over the same period her share of international trade in cottons fell from 65 to 26 per cent. Moreover, despite the measures of reorganization carried through, much excess capacity remained and the industry taken as a whole was outdated and inefficient compared with its major competitors.

Wool textiles

Though the wool textile industry experienced many of the same difficulties as cotton in this period, its decline was far less severe. The course of production can be seen from Table 24. By 1937 the output of tissues, the main finished product, was only about 16 per cent down on pre-war and this contraction had occurred before 1924. Output of yarn, on the other hand, held up better, except in the early 1930s, and by the end of the period it was very similar to the level of pre-war, while the production of tops was slightly below.

There are several reasons which account for the greater resiliency of wool as opposed to cotton. For one thing the wool industry was much less dependent on the external market; exports accounted for over one half the total value of production before the war (*cf* 80 per cent or more in cotton) and this proportion was reduced to about one quarter by the 1930s. Moreover, in physical terms the difference in export dependence between the two was even greater as a glance at the figures in Tables 23 and 24 show. The contraction in exports was also less than in the case of cotton. The export of tops, for example, held up very well while even in the case of finished goods the decline was less severe than in cotton piece goods. On the other hand, the domestic demand for finished products was declining due to changes in fashion. But for both yarn and finished goods' producers there were some compensations for these setbacks. The substantial recovery of tissue output in the 1930s was partly due to the absence of foreign competition as a result of tariff protection in 1932 which reduced imports of cloth from 50 to 7 million square yards.[1] The worsted yarn trade found salvation in serving the needs of the expanding hosiery industry and by the late 1930s about one half the yarn consumed in Britain was absorbed by the hosiery trade or the hand-knitters. Furthermore, manufacturers attempted to protect themselves by developing specialities and lighter and higher quality fabrics the demand for which was more buoyant as a result of fashion changes. The industry benefited too from the increasing demand for worsted cloth from the multiple clothiers and tailors.

TABLE 24　*Production and exports of wool tops, yarns and tissues, 1912–37*

| | Tops (mn lb.) | | Yarn (mn lb.) | | Tissues (mn sq. yd.) | |
	Production	Exports	Production	Exports	Production	Exports
1912	304·5	41·9[a]	565·1	87·0[a]	572·5	225·9[a]
1924	285·5	41·1	554·5	65·9	440·0	221·5
1930	224·5	28·8	385·0	49·6	324·1	113·7
1935	307·5	55·9	543·0	50·7	412·9	109·9
1937	278·5	40·2	565·8	41·4	445·5	122·8

NOTE　[a] = average 1909–13.
SOURCE　Allen, *op. cit.*, pp. 343–4.

Nevertheless, these compensating factors were insufficient to counteract the industry's export losses. Until the middle of the 1920s however, exports were quite well maintained. Although during and immediately after the war European and colonial markets for British woollens dwindled, compensating markets were found in the Far East, especially in China and Japan, where European dress was rapidly being adopted. Thus by 1924, Japan had become the largest single customer for British tissues. After that date the long-term tendency was for exports to decline in most branches, apart from tops, and by 1937 the volume of exports of yarns and tissues was roughly half what it had been before the war. Losses occurred in most markets except the South African, largely as a result of the development of domestic production behind tariff barriers, though competition from other exporters, especially Japan, became severe.[2] Yet in relative terms Britain

[1] A. N. Shimmin, 'The Wool Textile Industry', in British Association, *Britain in Depression* (1935), p. 364.
[2] *ibid.*, p. 359.

maintained her position quite well. Nearly all countries, apart from Japan, suffered a decline in exports and world trade generally fell more rapidly than the British. Thus, although the volume of trade was smaller Britain secured a larger share of the total by the end of the period and remained the largest exporter of wool products. Her share ranged from 30 per cent in yarns to 48 per cent in tissues in the years 1935–8, though woollen exports as a proportion of total production had in the meantime declined considerably.

Like the cotton industry, the wool textile industry was highly competitive and structurally weak. It consisted of a large number of small firms with few vertically integrated units or large combines except in the combing and finishing branches. This made it difficult to secure combined action to regulate the trade and reduce excess capacity and hence little was accomplished in this respect in the 1930s. On the other hand, the wool industry was probably financially stronger than the cotton industry for two reasons. First, it did not suffer so badly from depressed trade conditions and second, unlike cotton, it did not incur an excessive burden of debt in the post-war boom since little attempt was made to capitalize on the basis of expected future profits. Judging from the industry's investment figures which were positive in every year, the financial position of the industry was not all that bad.[1] However, the higher rate of investment compared with cotton does not appear to have resulted in an efficient and up-to-date industry. Productivity gains were very modest in deed[2] and the criticisms of the Working Party report after the war suggests that most of the industry's machinery was very antiquated and that advantage had not been taken of the latest techniques. In 1940, for example, only 10 per cent of the looms in weaving were automatic as against 66 per cent in the American industry.[3]

Shipbuilding

Shipbuilding was probably the most unstable and severely depressed industry of all during the inter-war years. Apart from the freak year of 1920 output never again reached the 1913 level of 1·93 million gross tons and in most years launchings were well below 1·5 million tons, the average for the years 1909–13. Even in the relatively pros-

[1] Feinstein, *op. cit.*, p. 109.
[2] L. Rostas, 'Comparative Productivity . . . ', *op. cit.*, pp. 144–6.
[3] Board of Trade, *Working Party Report on Wool* (1947), p. 76.

perous years of 1927–30 launchings only reached about 75 per cent of the 1911–13 average. The 1930s were far worse than the previous decade. Between 1931–37 output was well below the million mark in every year, while at the bottom of the slump in 1933 it was but a mere seven per cent of the pre-war level. Because of the nature of the product the industry had always experienced large fluctuations in activity, but the amplitude of the swings was probably greater in this period than ever before. From a peak of just over two million tons in 1920 production slumped to 646,000 tons in 1923 rose again to 1·44 million in the following year and then fell back to 640,000 in 1926. Production then rose to a peak of 1·5 million tons in 1929 after which came the most dramatic collapse on record, to a level of only 133,000 tons in 1933. A slow but steady revival of launchings then took place and by 1938 output just topped the million mark.

The figures for launchings, poor as they were, tend to exaggerate the true position of the industry since capacity in relation to output was very much greater than before the war. Given the fact that between 1913 and 1921 the capacity of British yards increased by about 30 to 40 per cent to meet a demand that was much lower than pre-war, it is not surprising that much of the industry's capacity remained idle. Even in 1920, the best year when tonnage under construction and launchings approached pre-war dimensions, over 50 per cent of the berths were idle, while in the seven years 1923–29 about one third of the industry's capacity would have been sufficient to meet all requirements.[1] The position was even worse in the slump of the early 1930s when launchings fell to negligible proportions; then practically all capacity was idle or underutilized and unemployment averaged well over 50 per cent. Though the proportion of capacity utilized increased somewhat in the later 1930s, as a result of a recovery in orders and the elimination of some capacity, there were still many idle berths at the end of the period.

The position from the British point of view would not have been so bad had the imbalance between capacity and requirements not been repeated on a world-wide scale. Throughout the period world shipbuilding capacity was much greater in relation to demand for new ships than it had been before 1914. The pre-war capacity of the industry would have been more than sufficient to meet all the orders placed during the inter-war years. But in fact world capacity more than doubled between 1913–21 to meet a demand which averaged less than

[1] L. Jones, *Shipbuilding in Britain* (1957), p. 128.

TABLE 25   *World and* U.K. *mercantile shipbuilding output—tonnage launched (000s)*

Annual average	U.K. *Total*	*Export orders*	*Home orders*	*World*	U.K. *percentage of world output*	*percentage of* U.K. *output exported*	*percentage of* U.K. *output to world output for other than British owners*
1909–13	1,522	340	1,182	2,589	58·7	22·4	24·0
1928–30	1,483	401	1,082	2,790	53·1	27·0	23·4
1936–8	936	140	790	2,604	35·8	15·0	7·9

SOURCE   L. Jones, *Shipbuilding in Britain* (1957), p. 64.

previously. That the demand for new ships fell short of available capacity can be explained by a glance at the shipowning side of the equation. Although the world's mercantile marine increased by 46 per cent between 1914 and 1938 the rate of growth was much lower than in the pre-war period. Thus the relative demand for new tonnage was reduced, averaging only 2½ per cent in the 1920s compared with six per cent between 1900–14. The slower rate of growth in shipping was the product of two factors – the partial stagnation in world trade and the increase in efficiency of available shipping capacity. The sharp and somewhat artificial boom in the maritime industries after the war created far more tonnage than was required and by 1923 there was 39 per cent more tonnage available to deal with six per cent less seaborne trade compared with 1913. The position improved somewhat in the 1920s but the sharp fall in seaborne trade in the subsequent slump reversed the position again. In 1932 the tonnage available was 48 per cent greater than in 1913 but the volume of seaborne trade was slightly less. Freight rates fell well below pre-war levels in most trades and 20 per cent or more of the world fleet was laid up. After 1933 there was some improvement with the recovery in trade and stability of tonnage though much excess capacity still remained at the end of the period. The gap between available capacity and requirements was greater than these figures suggest since they take no account of improvements in efficiency. Technical progress, e.g. the adoption of diesel propulsion and better methods of ship construction, greatly improved the speed and carrying capacity of shipping. This means that the carrying capacity of the world's fleet rose much more than the tonnage figures[1] suggest with the result that much of the tonnage in active service was far from being fully utilized.

Given the depressed conditions in the shipping trade it was only to be expected that these would be reflected in orders for new ships, and that given the large volume of excess shipbuilding capacity competition for orders would be acute. However, the disastrous experience of the British shipbuilding industry cannot, as in the case of some other industries, be attributed solely to the collapse of export markets. In fact, more important in absolute terms was the stagnation of the home market. Demand for ships from British owners was much less buoyant than world demand generally. During the best years of the period, 1928–30 and 1936–8, world demand for new ships was slightly greater than the average between 1909–13, whereas the demand from British owners alone was much lower. Over the period as a whole home demand fell by nearly 400,000 tons, that is equivalent to two thirds the reduction in output of British shipyards (see Table 25). The weakness in home demand was due to the decline in the British fleet,[2] the low rate of replacement and, in the 1930s, to the fact that an increasing number of orders were placed abroad.

The position was aggravated by the contraction in warship building, figures for which are not included in Table 25. Before and during the war naval orders provided the industry with a considerable amount of work. Over one half or more of the warship tonnage was built in private yards and at the peak in 1918 they produced more than half a million tons. After the war naval construction was cut back sharply and throughout the 1920s and early 1930s the Admiralty building programme was kept to a minimum. In 1920 less than 20,000 tons were built by private yards and in the next four years these yards built no naval vessels. There was only a slight improvement in the later 1920s but in the depression the warship programme was almost suspended and in 1933 only one small warship was launched from private yards. There was, of course, a revival in warship building following the rearmament boom of the later 1930s so

[1] It is difficult to provide an accurate figure for the composite increase in carrying capacity. One estimate by the League of Nations suggests that the freight carrying capacity of the world fleet doubled between 1914 and 1939. This is probably on the high side but whatever the exact figure it was certainly far greater than the 35- to 40-per-cent increase in world seaborne trade.
[2] See Chapter 7.

that by March 1937 the industry had orders for some 400,000 tons. Taking the period as a whole therefore naval construction was very much lower than before the war. Average annual output between 1911–3 amounted to 132,633 tons whereas only on seven occasions in the inter-war period did the annual output from private yards exceed 50,000 tons and only once did it surpass 100,000.[1]

Proportionally the fall in exports was far greater than that of home orders though in absolute terms the contraction of the lattter was by far more important. Worse still, Britain ceased to be the major supplier to foreign shipowners, while exports as a proportion of total output declined. In the five years before the first world war Britain supplied nearly one quarter of the world's new tonnage requirements (excluding ships for British owners) and exports accounted for over 22 per cent of total production; by the late 1930s these proportions had fallen to under eight and 15 per cent respectively.[2] Furthermore, an increasing number of British orders were being placed abroad. In 1936 and 1938 shipbuilding imports accounted for 14·6 and 16·7 respectively of total tonnage delivered to British owners and in the former year imports actually exceeded exports by 38,000 tons.

These export losses hardly seem surprising given the competitive climate created by the excessive amount of world shipbuilding capacity. But excess capacity apart, nationalistic shipping policies tended to boost foreign shipbuilding at the expense of British. It was only natural that countries which had fostered their maritime industries during war should want to preserve them in peace-time. The result was that subsidization in one form or another became very widespread during this period and there can be little doubt that British shipbuilders suffered as a result. It is true that in the first instance most subsidies went to shipowners, but this affected British shipbuilding in at least two respects. Indirectly British shipowners, faced with competition from subsidized fleets, were less able or less willing to provide sufficient funds for fleet replacement etc. Home orders were therefore lower than they would normally have been. More directly, the orders from foreign owners normally placed in Britain were no longer available since subsidy payments were usually conditional on the vessels being built in national yards. It is difficult to estimate with any precision the impact of nationalistic shipping policies though it is worth noting

[1] Jones, *op. cit.*, pp. 58, 124–7.
[2] Those proportions did vary considerably even from year to year but they were generally much higher in the 1920s.

that British exports were lower both absolutely and proportionately in the 1930s when such policies were being pursued most vigorously.

The second main adverse factor was that British shipbuilding was becoming uncompetitive *vis-à-vis* foreign builders. Here there were several forces at work. To some extent foreign shipbuilders gained a cost advantage through subsidization while labour and material costs were slightly cheaper than in Britain. Currency instability and exchange control – viz the overvaluation of the pound (1925–31) and exchange restrictions in the 1930s – helped to weaken Britain's competitive strength. But probably more important was the fact that British shipyards were becoming obsolete and were not keeping abreast of technical advances. Having built their supremacy on steam British shipbuilders failed to exploit the diesel engine in the twentieth century. Here, of course, part of the blame can perhaps be attributed to shipowners who were reluctant to switch to the new form of propulsion.[1] The lag in basic technology was not the only mistake however. British firms became high cost producers in this period partly because they were slow to undertake the necessary structural, financial and technical reorganization to maintain their former competitive position. Thus by 1939 many of them were badly out-of-date, both as regards equipment and methods of construction. As the historian of the industry has observed: 'In the main, continental and American builders possessed modern and well-equipped yards, whereas in Britian a number of yards dated from the days of wooden ships. Many British yards had not been designed to meet modern requirements, they just grew up from small yards where wooden ships had been built, and were enlarged from time to time as vessels increased in size and complexity. Others were sited on narrow river frontages in circumstances which did not permit of drastic remodelling and reconstruction. The organization of work was carefully considered abroad and so planned that a minimum of work was carried out on the berths'[2]

The state of British shipbuilding in the inter-war years called for drastic action to eliminate excess capacity and improve the technical efficiency of the industry. Yet until the 1930s little was achieved. It is true that shipbuilding benefited from loan guarantees under the Trade Facilities Acts of the 1920s. Altogether 110 ships of 850,000 tons were built with the assistance of these Acts compared with $6\frac{1}{2}$

[1] See Chapter 7, and S. G. Sturmey, *British Shipping and World Competition* (1962), pp. 84–5.
[2] Jones, *op. cit.*, pp. 79–80.

million tons launched from British yards during the period in which the facilities were operative. But the aim was to relieve unemployment rather than promote the reorganization of industries assisted. Thereafter the State did little to assist the industry directly. Shipbuilders did stand to benefit indirectly from the subsidies paid to tramp owners in the 1930s and from the scrap and build provisions of the British Shipping (Assistance) Act of 1935. Unfortunately, the latter provisions were not utilized to any great extent, partly because of opposition from the shipowners, and in all less than 200,000 tons of new vessels were actually built.[1]

The biggest problem, that of eliminating excess capacity, was left to voluntary action. No formal scheme was drawn up until the 1930s however, reliance being placed on the forces of competition and amalgamation to achieve the desired results. Though many yards were in severe financial difficulties few went into liquidation, while most of the mergers, with a few exceptions notably Vickers and Armstrong Whitworths in 1928, took place in the early post-war years. Amalgamation might have provided a partial solution to the problem but it was difficult to find the capital to finance such ventures at a time when many leading companies were being forced to write down the value of their assets. By 1930 it was clear that only an organized scheme for the industry as a whole would be capable of achieving reasonable results. Consequently the industry established the National Shipbuilders Security Ltd., the main task of which was to purchase and scrap redundant or obsolete shipbuilding capacity. This was to be financed by a levy on the sales of participating firms. The company had the backing of practically the whole industry and it secured the support of the Bankers Industrial Development Company.[2] Its work was assisted by the severity of the depression in the maritime trades and in the early years a substantial number of berths was retired. By 1937, 28 yards with a total capacity of more than one million tons had been taken out of commission and this brought the industry's total capacity down to around $2\frac{1}{2}$ million tons or more. Nevertheless, the fact that nearly half the berths were standing idle that year, when tonnage requirements were more buoyant than they had been for some

---

[1] Sturmey, *op. cit.*, p. 109; see also Chapter 7.
[2] This concern was established in 1930 by the Bank of England and the clearing banks and its main task was to be that of reducing and reorganizing the capacity of the staple industries. Its main activities were concentrated on the shipbuilding, cotton and steel industries.

time, suggests that the process of rationalization had still a long way to go. However, as it happened within a year or two the demands of war were to save the industry from a further course of slimming.

Iron and steel

The iron and steel industry is rather a difficult industry to fit into any particular category or group. It could not be classed simply as an old and declining industry, nor could it be considered as a new and rapidly expanding sector. In fact in many ways it stood half way between the two groups. The industry expanded its output even in relation to the base year of 1913, while the production emphasis shifted to the relatively newer branch of steel. On the other hand, it exhibited many characteristics of the basic industries already covered in this chapter. Though output increased it fluctuated quite sharply, exports tended to stagnate, foreign competition in the home market increased, capacity was underutilized and unemployment persistent. Moreover, technically and structurally the industry was rather weak and inefficient. In part these rather contrasting features can be explained by the intermediate nature of the industry's product. Iron and steel is consumed by a wide range of industries producing finished products and as such is subject to the conflicting demands of growing and stagnating sectors. Thus, although depressed sectors like shipbuilding and heavy engineering reduced their demand for steel this was counterbalanced by growing consumption in industries such as vehicles, aircraft, and electrical engineering.

The production figures can be summarized quite readily. During the war the industry's capacity had been increased quite rapidly for obvious reasons. Blast furnace capacity rose from 11 to 12 million tons and that of steel from eight to 12 million. Yet after the post-war boom output was rarely sufficient to meet these capacity levels. The worst hit sector was pig iron. Even in the best year (1937) output barely reached 8·5 million tons compared with 10·26 in 1913, while in the really depressed years of 1921 and 1932 it was but a mere fraction of the pre-war level. Thus for much of the time production was one third to one half less than available capacity, while Britain's share of world pig output fell from 13·2 to 8·3 per cent between 1913 and 1937. The stagnation in the pig iron sector was due to a variety of reasons. For one thing it was affected by a factor common to all iron industries, namely the substitution of steel for wrought and cast iron, though the change had a more serious impact on the British industry which had excelled in these types of products before the war. The increasing use of scrap in steelmaking also curtailed the demand for pig. In Britain the proportion of scrap charged into steel furnaces rose from 30 per cent pre-war to 50 per cent or more during the 1920s and this proportion rose even higher in the following decade.[1] The third main factor was the contraction of the export market as a result of the relative decline in the importance of the iron trade in general and the growth of protected furnaces in former markets. Thus by 1929 exports of pig iron were less than half the pre-war total of 1·12 million tons (1913) and by 1938 they were but a mere 101,000 tons.

The steel sector fared somewhat better though even here the problem of excess capacity was fairly persistent. The first post-war decade was particularly difficult for British steel. Although in common with most countries the industry was affected by the post-war depression of the early 1920s, it shared in the subsequent recovery only to a moderate extent. World output of steel rose from 75·2 to 118·9 million tons between 1913 and 1929, most of the increase occurring after 1924 as a result of rapid expansion in France, the United States, Belgium and Luxemburg. British steel production, though somewhat greater in 1924 compared with 1913 (8·2 as against 7·7 million tons), rose only to 9·6 million tons by the end of the decade. As a proportion of world steel output it fell from 10·2 per cent in 1913 to 8·1 per cent in 1929.

Several forces were responsible for the poor performance of steel. Home demand rose only slowly because of the rather depressed conditions in some of the major consuming industries such as shipbuilding and heavy engineering. More important however were the unfavourable changes on the external side. Exports were lower and imports higher than in 1913; thus whereas in the immediate pre-war years the excess of exports over imports of steel amounted to nearly 2¾ million tons, by 1927–9 the excess was less than one million tons. Exports consisted mainly of finished products the most important of which were steel sheets, tinplate, steel bars, pipes and tubes and rail material though the last of these declined in importance. Much of the imported steel, which came chiefly from France, Belgium and Germany, was semi-manufactured steel used by the finishing trade.

It is difficult to attribute the weakness of the steel industry's transactions to any one particular cause. The growth of steel industries

[1] D. L. Burn, *The Economic History of Steelmaking, 1867–1939* (1940), p. 474.

abroad, foreign tariffs, foreign cartels, subsidized exports and currency difficulties, all of these had an adverse effect on the balance of trade in steel.[1] The position was not helped by the fact that Britain at this time was making a belated technical switch from acid to basic steel in response to changes in world demand, whereas the bulk of the steel produced on the Continent was already of the basic type. But equally important, if not more so, was the fact that British costs were high in relation to those of her competitors due to the relative inefficiency of British production methods, a legacy of the pre-war era, and to the fact that re-equipment, made necessary by war-time losses and partly financed by the State, helped to strengthen Continental superiority in these years.[2]

All producers, whether efficient or otherwise, suffered severely in the slump of 1929–32. Steel production in this country fell by 45 per cent, though this was somewhat less than the decline in world production despite the continued pressure of imports into the home market. By 1933 however, the steel sector was well on the road to recovery and in 1935 production passed the previous peak of 1929. Output continued to rise steadily to nearly 13 million tons in 1937 when for the first time since the war the industry was working at practically full capacity,[3] though a temporary setback was experienced in the following year. During the recovery phase British steel output rose more rapidly than that of most countries so that our share of world output rose again to 9·7 per cent compared with 8·1 per cent in 1929.

Recovery owed nothing to the export trade. From a peak of 4·38 million tons in 1929 iron and steel exports slumped to 1·89 million tons in 1932 and even in the best year of recovery only managed to attain 2·61 million, that is just over one half the pre-war level. In this respect the British steel industry did not stand alone since nearly all producers experienced a similar fate in exports due to increasing national self-sufficiency and restrictions on trade. Thus recovery was domestically based, and was associated with the rapid growth of the newer industries, especially vehicles and electricity, the gradual recovery of the staple industries, and later by the rearmament boom. Between 1935–7 steel output rose by over three million tons and a considerable

---

[1] *ibid.*, p. 402, *passim.*
[2] *ibid.*, p. 408; Allen *op. cit.*, pp. 98–101.
[3] J. C. Carr and W. Taplin, *History of the British Steel Industry* (1962), 587.

part of this can be attributed to the effects of rearmament.[1] Furthermore, from 1932 the home market was protected by a tariff of $33\frac{1}{3}$ per cent which was temporarily raised to 50 per cent in 1935. This had the effect of cutting off the flood of cheap Continental imports which had prevailed up to 1932. In that year imports were only 1·6 million tons as against an average of 2·85 million in the years 1928–31, and for the rest of the decade they remained at a much lower level than in 1929. Although this reduction in imports meant a larger home market for the industry it did tend to raise costs in the finishing sections which had relied on imports of cheap crude and semi-finished steel before 1932.

Though the efficiency of the iron and steel industry increased considerably in the period[2] there seems little evidence to suggest that the gap between British and foreign producers was narrowed to any significant extent. Before the war Britain had been a relatively inefficient high-cost producer compared with her main competitors,[3] and this condition appears to have prevailed post-war. The improvements which took place in steel production were many and varied; they included the shift away from old types of iron and acid steel towards basic steel, the shift in the location of plants to utilize new ore deposits, the replacement of much obsolete plant, the integration and concentration of capacity, the adoption of larger blast furnaces and by-product recovery ovens, attention to fuel economy and a whole host of other improvements. These changes produced an improvement in output per head in all branches of the trade, ranging from 90 per cent (1924–37) in iron ore production to 50 per cent in blast furnaces down to two per cent in tinplate.[4]

But in many respects these developments represented an attempt to catch up on pre-war backwardness. Moreover, the changes were matched by similar, if not better, advances abroad so that the gap between British and foreign producers remained and in some cases may even have widened. A few examples must suffice to illustrate this point. As a result of extensive scrapping and replacement of plant

[1] British Association, *Britain in Recovery* (1938), pp. 370–1.

[2] See Burn, *op. cit.*, p. 483.

[3] Most of the literature points to this conclusion. For a recent synthesis and bibliography see P. L. Payne, 'Iron and Steel Manufactures', ch. 3 in D. H. Aldcroft (ed.), *The Development of British Industry and Foreign Competition 1875–1914* (1968).

[4] L. Rostas, 'Productivity, Prices . . . ', *op. cit.*, p. 117.

the average output of blast furnaces rose from 30,000 tons in 1913 to 83,000 in 1937,[1] but this was still very small compared with an average of 210,000 tons per furnace in the States and 125,000 in Germany. Similar differences existed in the output of steel furnaces. Again in the matter of fuel economy considerable progress was made, especially in the 1920s, but since equally striking improvements were made by our competitors the gap remained more or less as before.[2] Likewise, the concentration of production and integration of works increased in this period but in America and on the Continent the process was carried much further. By 1930, 70 per cent of total British output of iron and steel was produced by 20 firms while about 10 vertical groups controlled 47 per cent of pig-iron capacity and 60 per cent of steel capacity. Yet the 20 British firms had a combined output of steel less than one third that of the U.S. Steel Corporation and about the same as that of the Vereinigte Stahlwerke. In America two firms had 55 per cent of total capacity and in Germany five controlled 70 per cent. Many of the mergers which took place in Britain were initiated by the banks to which many steel firms were indebted, and primary attention was therefore given to reorganizing capital structures rather than to bringing about a more efficient structure, as, for example, by eliminating excess capacity or reallocating plants to ensure that blast furnaces and steel works were placed in close proximity to each other.[3] In many other respects British practice remained inferior to that in the other main producing countries.

Considerable hope was held out for the steel industry in the early 1930s when the Import Duties Advisory Committee recommended stiff tariff protection on condition that reorganization would follow. To assist the process the central organization of the industry was strengthened by the establishment of the British Iron and Steel Federation whose chief duty was to foster schemes of reorganization. In effect, these two bodies became responsible for fixing prices, controlling competition, subsidizing high cost producers and supervising the development plans of the industry. Thus suppression of competition rather than technical reconstruction and rationalization of the industry appears to have been the primary objective of the controlling authorities. The principles of plant specialization and integration of units were

---

[1] Thus between 1929 and 1938 one half the old furnaces were completely eliminated.
[2] Burn, *op. cit.*, p. 434.
[3] See Allen, *op. cit.*, pp. 109–10.

only tentatively applied, while only scant attention was paid to the question of extending best practise techniques. In the words of one contemporary commentator: '. . . the lamentable history of the attempt to reorganize the iron and steel industry on its present basis, in return for protection, seems to indicate that a very wide measure of public control will be necessary if the badly needed work of rationalization is ever to make any real progress.'[1]

Thus by the eve of the second world war the iron and steel industry was larger and more modern than it had been in 1913 and more prosperous than at any time since 1920. There had been many improvements in technique and a considerable advance in productivity. Nevertheless, the gap between British and foreign practice still existed and by the end of the period Britain remained a relatively inefficient and high cost producer.[2]

The basic industries in perspective

This chapter has been concerned with the declining branches of the industrial sector, that is principally the large staple industries of the nineteenth century whose output and employment contracted in the period between 1913 and the 1930s. Apart from iron and steel, which does not fit so readily into this group, all the industries surveyed above continued to decline or mark time after the second world war. Not all declining industries have been surveyed since reasons of space forbid this, while some sectors have been omitted, such as railways and shipping, since it seemed more appropriate to consider them along with services (Chapter 7). Nevertheless, the coverage is sufficiently broad to allow some general comments to be made.

These industries had a number of factors in common. Their decline was primarily caused by the collapse of export markets coupled with a stagnating or slowly growing home demand for their products. A variety of factors were responsible for the weak markets. These included the relatively inelastic nature of demand for their products, the development of competitive substitutes, the growth in foreign competition and national self-sufficiency together with increasing restrictions on trade. The position was aggravated by certain incidental factors such as the overvaluation of the sterling currency, 1925–31, and labour disputes, especially in coal mining.

[1] Lucas, *op. cit.,* p. 121.
[2] Burn, *op. cit.,* pp. 483–4.

Although the collapse of external demand was largely responsible for the plight of these industries internal weaknesses must share some of the blame. The market difficulties came, of course, at the worst possible time. Before the war these industries were relatively high-cost producers due to their inefficiency and slow pace of technical progress. The war and post-war boom left these industries in an awkward position since capacity was greatly extended to a level far in excess of long-term future requirements, while in many cases firms became overcapitalized and burdened with a considerable amount of debt. Thus with the subsequent contraction of their markets these industries found themselves with a large amount of excess capacity and, with falling profit margins and debts to repay, many found it difficult to set aside sufficient money for ordinary depreciation let alone finance comprehensive programmes of scrapping and plant rebuilding. The existence of numerous competing producers made it difficult to rationalize while often attempts at amalgamation merely resulted in further overcapitalization because of the high price of those selling out. Here, as Kahn points out,[1] was 'a vicious circle of competitive weakness, because of their failure to reorganize, bringing financial weakness, and financial weakness in turn making it impossible to attract the capital necessary to effect reorganization'. Eventually the problem became so acute that resort was had to various restrictive measures to control the market, which, though in some cases achieved some reduction in capacity, probably did more to suppress competition than effect a rational reorganization of productive resources.

But we must not give the impression that these industries marked time in every respect. Though conditions were very difficult, considerable technical advances and gains in productivity were achieved and these contrasted sharply with the experience before 1914, when technical progress had been very slow and productivity improvements almost non-existent. Of course, it must be remembered that these advances represented an attempt to eliminate the backlog of past neglect and since similar advances took place in other countries the gap between British and foreign practice remained much the same as before.

The contraction in these trades presented serious problems. The large scale unemployment and consequent social distress were the most serious and vivid to contemporaries. The loss of exports put pressure on the balance of payments (see Chapter 8). Redundant labour

[1] A. E. Kahn, *Great Britain in the World Economy* (1946), p. 76.

was a serious waste of resources and the lost output through unemployment was high.

On the other hand, although the immediate problems were serious there were some compensations. Before 1914 Britain was becoming dangerously overcommited in her structure of production. A large proportion of industrial output was accounted for by a few slow-growing and relatively inefficient staple trades, while the new and potential growth industries were making only very slow progress. The sharp drop in demand for staple products after the war emphasized the need for structural readjustment and led to a large outflow of labour from these industries. Thus employment in the five industries covered in this chapter fell by over one million between 1920–38. If we include all trades in which employment fell then the total contraction amounted to between $1\frac{3}{4}$ and two million workers. The delay in structural readjustment before 1914 and the fact that many of the basic industries had been grossly overmanned undoubtedly accentuated the contraction when it came. But at least it forced, not before time, the basic industries to reassess their position which eventually led to the scrapping of some obsolete capacity. Second, the large outflow of labour tended to result in a rise in productivity since before 1914 the labour force in these industries had been underutilized. Third, the redundant labour provided a reservoir of reserves on which the newer and expanding industries could draw thus easing the pressure on wages. It is true, of course, that much labour remained unemployed but one could argue that had there been no release of labour from the older sectors the growth of the new sectors would have been held up through manpower shortages and the high price of labour. But what might have happened in a different economic setting is anybody's guess.

6 New industries and the building trades

Introduction

The contraction of the basic trades was one aspect of the structural transformation of the industrial economy in the inter-war years. The second main feature was the growth of the new industries and the building and allied trades. Whatever basis of assessment is used, employment, output or capital, there is no doubt that they were expanding sectors, and in most cases rates of expansion were above the national average. Indices of production show that, apart from chemicals and hosiery, all the newer industries[1] expanded faster than the average for all industry over the period 1920 to 1938 or 1913 to 1938.[2] According to Kahn's classification, which is based on Census of Production data, the new industries (including scientific instruments) accounted for 12·5 per cent of net industrial output in 1924, 19·0 per cent in 1935 and possibly getting on for one quarter by the end of the 1930s, compared with only 6·5 per cent in 1907.[3] The employment figures show a similar pattern of expansion. Thus while employ-

[1] That is vehicles and aircraft, electricity supply and electrical manufacturing, chemicals, rayon and hosiery. The last of these has been included in the classification here since it was making increasing use of rayon.

[2] Expansion in chemicals and hosiery was only slightly below the general average. See the indices in K. S. Lomax, 'Production and Productivity Movements in the United Kingdom since 1900', *Journal of the Royal Statistical Society*, A122 (1959), pp. 192–3 and A. E. Kahn, *Great Britain in the World Economy* (1946),p. 106.

[3] Kahn, *op. cit.*, p. 106. His classification is slightly wider than the one used here. If building and contracting is included, the percentage for 1935, for example, is raised to 28·1.

ment in building and the new trades rose rapidly, total industrial employment fell slightly over the years 1920 to 1938 (see Table 26). As a result employment in the new industries as a percentage of the total rose from 11 per cent in 1920 to just over 18 per cent in 1938, while if the building trades are included the relevant proportions are 21·3 and 33·4 per cent.[1] In terms of capital investment the predominance of these industries was even greater; altogether they accounted for well over one half the gross investment of the inter-war period.[2]

It would be difficult to deny the importance of these sectors in the overall growth of the British economy during this period. However, as we have seen, they were not the only industries to experience expansion. Most industries recorded positive rates of growth, at least between 1920 and 1938, and development was quite rapid in many non-manufacturing sectors some of which will be considered in the next chapter. But high rates of growth were not the only factor which distinguished the new from the old. Their expansion was based on the exploitation of new techniques which required a fairly high degree of scientific expertise and technical knowledge. Second, they were structurally different from the old industries. Although initially many small units of production predominated, output was soon concentrated in the hands of a few large producers which enabled mass production techniques to be employed. Third, their dependence on the export market was very much less than in the case of the old staples and their growth was based primarily on the home market. The proportion of exports to total production rarely exceeded more than 25 per cent,[3] and export proportions tended to diminish over time. Moreover, imports of new products tended to be fairly high, especially in the 1920s despite partial tariff protection, and it was not until the following decade that the balance of trade in these goods was favourable.[4] Fourth, in general unemployment rates in the new trades were below the national average and very much lower than those in the old staple

---

[1] It should be noted that these proportions are somewhat lower than thos given in Chapter 4 which are calculated on a slightly different classification.
[2] The proportion is high partly because the product of the building industry is classified as an investment good. But the newer trades also accounted for quite a high proportion of total investment. See the calculations in D. H. Aldcroft, 'Economic Growth in Britain in the Inter-War Years: A Reassessment', *Economic History Review*, 20 (1967), p. 321.
[3] The major exception being motor cycles, a sub-branch of the vehicle industry.
[4] H. W. Richardson, 'The New Industries Between the Wars', *Oxford Economic Papers*, 13 (1961), p. 363.

industries (see Table 26). Finally, for the most part the new industries were located in the South and Midlands rather than on or near the coalfields of the North as was the case with the older industries.

Most of these comments, of course, do not apply specifically to the building trades. But the latter had much more in common with the new group of industries than with the basic trades. Not only did they both achieve high rates of expansion but also the major impetus of that growth came from the home market. Furthermore, developments in one induced changes in the other. The most important links were those between electricity, transport and building. These relationships have already been outlined in Chapter 4 and need not be repeated here.

Motor manufacturing

Before the war Britain was slow to exploit commercially the internal combustion engine which had been developed in the latter part of the nineteenth century. In 1907, 83 per cent of the 65,000 motor cars in use had been imported and the output of all vehicles in that year was around 12,000. Imports of vehicles exceeded exports and accounted for nearly two thirds of total production. Though output rose sharply after 1907 to reach a total of 34,000 vehicles of all kinds in 1913, it was but a mere fraction of the u.s. output and lower than that of France. One of the main reasons for the limited progress before the war was the high price charged for the finished product which meant that few but the wealthier classes of people could afford to own their own vehicles. To a large extent this was due to the character of the production process rather than to a lack of enterprise in the industry. There were far too many small firms producing individual units to prescribed specifications on a one-off basis. Between 1896 and 1914 no less than 393 firms were founded 280 of which had ceased to exist by the latter year, and almost 200 different types of cars were in production during the period.[1] Thus cars were expensive luxury products, and the real stumbling block in the way of a cheap car for the mass market was the methods of production employed rather than the techniques of producing vehicles. A further factor inhibiting growth was the high rate of technical failure of the finished product, especially in commercial vehicles and buses, while operating

[1] S. B. Saul, 'The Motor Industry in Britain to 1914', *Business History*, 5 (1962), p. 23.

TABLE 26 *Employment and unemployment in new industries and building trades, 1920–38*

	1920		1924		1929		1932		1938	
	Employ-ment (000s)	% unem-ployed	Employ-ment (000s)	% unem-ployed	Employ-ment (000s)	% unem-ployed	Employ-ment (000s)	% unem-ployed	Employ-ment (000s)	% unem-ployed
Chemicals	250·7		215·9	8·8	235·6	6·4	214·7	16·2	270·1	7·8
Electrical engineering	171·1		156·2	5·6	197·4	4·1	209·2	16·4	325·5	5·1
Vehicles	227·4		280·3	8·3	362·4	7·5	336·0	22·2	516·2	8·5
Electricity (gas and water)	184·7		193·7	5·7	223·8	5·4	242·4	10·9	291·4	8·1
Silk and rayon	37·7		46·1	4·2	80·3	8·1	69·3	17·7	76·3	17·7
Hosiery	96·2		98·5	5·9	114·5	6·3	110·1	14·8	121·3	11·0
Total	967·8		990·7		1,214·0		1,181·7		1,600·8	
Building and contracting	840·4		775·2	9·9	925·2	8·8	851·6	27·6	1,158·8	13·8
Building materials	84·0		109·1	6·4	133·2	8·1	121·6	20·8	175·3	8·4
Total in building trades	924·4		884·3		1,058·4		973·2		1,334·1	

Total industrial employment (incl. mining)	8,896·9	7,844·9	8,129·2	7,106·4	8,780·9
	9·9	9·9	9·9	22·9	13·3
New industries as % of total employment	10·9	12·6	14·9	16·6	18·2
New industries and building trades as % of total employment	21·3	23·9	27·9	30·3	33·4

NOTES 1 Employment figures are for man-years in employment.

2 Unemployment percentages are for July each year for unemployed insured workers in Great Britain and Northern Ireland.

3 Unemployment percentages in building and contracting are for building only, while those for building materials relate to brick, tile, pipe, etc., making.

SOURCES A. L. Chapman and R. Knight, *Wages and Salaries in the United Kingdom, 1920–1938* (1953), and *Ministry of Labour Gazette*.

costs of the early models were very high. In addition, on the demand side, real incomes remained fairly static in the decade or so before 1914.

The war period brought a further setback. Many firms shifted over to producing armaments or went out of business altogether and the output of vehicles did not alter very much.[1] American production, on the other hand, rose from 485,000 in 1913 to 2·2 million in 1920. By the time the British industry had converted its plants to peacetime production the post-war boom was almost over and it found itself left with much excess capacity. Fortunately, recovery from the 1921 slump was very rapid. In 1922, 73,000 vehicles were manufactured, that is almost twice the output of 1918, and for the rest of the decade there was almost continuous expansion; by 1929 output of all vehicles had reached nearly 239,000, 56,000 of which consisted of commercial vehicles. During roughly the same period (1923–9) motor cycle production rose from 80,000 to 146,000. However, compared with the huge American output of 5·36 million units in 1929 the British performance appears very modest indeed, while both Canada and France had a higher level of production.

However, in the ensuing slump British manufacturers fared very well comparatively speaking. Output in both America and Canada fell by about three quarters between 1929–32 and Continental countries were also badly affected. Even in the worst year, 1931, Britain managed to produce 236,000 vehicles and by 1933 output had already surpassed the 1929 level. Thereafter production expanded more rapidly than elsewhere to reach a peak of 508,000 vehicles in 1937. By then she was the second largest producer and the ratio of British to u.s. production rose from under 5 per cent in 1929 to over 10 per cent in 1937, and to nearly 18 per cent in the following year. The experience of the motor cycle trade was very much less fortunate. Output fell by nearly two thirds between 1929 and 1933 and the subsequent recovery was very slow indeed. Even in 1937 production was only about one half that of the previous peak of 1929. The competition of the small car and the collapse of the export trade largely explain this poor record.

The performance of the industry during this period was certainly impressive and by the end of the 1930s it was in a very much stronger position than it had been just after the war. This success was largely

[1] Emphasis was switched to producing trucks and commercial vehicles for military use.

due to the buoyancy of the home market which on average accounted for 80 per cent of annual production. From 1915 onwards manufacturers received tariff protection in the form of a $33\frac{1}{3}$-per-cent *ad valorem* tariff on imported cars and motor cycles and, apart from a short break in 1924–5, this duty was in force throughout the period and it was later extended to cover commercial vehicles and chassis. Thus, except in the early 1920s when the domestic market was invaded by cheap American cars,[1] British manufacturers had little to fear from imports, and by the late 1930s they were supplying 97 per cent of the domestic market.

It would be wrong to assume, however, that protection afforded an easy life to inefficient producers to exploit the home market. Given the fact that the demand for cars and other vehicles was income and price elastic it was necessary to effect a considerable reduction in the price of the product in order to tap the mass market. But under the production methods prevailing before and just after the war – that is a large number of firms producing expensive products in short runs – this was impossible. In fact, up to 1921 no British maker had attempted to produce for the mass market and the only cheap model on the market was the American Ford. Clearly there was great scope for the exploitation of scale economies.

The great change in the structure and production methods of the industry came after 1922. The small mass-produced car was introduced by Morris and Austin and by the end of the 1920s these two firms accounted for 60 per cent of car production. Altogether the number of firms was reduced from 90 in 1920 to 41 in 1929. Further concentration occurred in the 1930s so that by 1939 there were only 33 producers, six of which accounted for nearly 90 per cent of the market[2] and three (Nuffield, Austin and Ford) for about two thirds. Along with this concentration of production there was a rise in the output of each firm and a reduction in the number of models produced. Similar trends were evident in the commerical vehicle and motor cycle sectors though they were less pronounced. However, concentration had gone even further in the United States. The three leading American producers accounted for nearly 90 per cent of total output and their range of models was lower and production runs much larger than was the case in this country. For example, in 1937 the six leading British producers turned out roughly 350,000 private

[1] When imports exceeded exports.
[2] And for about 80 per cent or over of commercial vehicle production.

cars with over 40 different engine types and an even greater number of chassis and body models; the number of designs was more than that provided by the three top American firms producing 3·5 million cars. The three leading British models accounted for only 27 per cent (81,000 cars) of sales as against 54 per cent of sales for the same number of U.S. models, giving production runs ranging from 350–600,000 per annum. Thus there was still considerable scope for cost reduction through more concentrated and standardized production methods. For a model produced in 1939 at the rate of 20,000 per annum it was estimated that a doubling of this output would produce a reduction of 20 per cent in manufacturing costs.[1] In the light of the above figures it is clear that British manufacturers had some way to go before they exhausted the economies of scale production.

Nevertheless, the rapid shift to mass production techniques after the early 1920s and the economies derived from so doing were instrumental in bringing down the price of cars. The average factory value of private cars in Britain fell from £308 in 1912 to £259 in 1924, £206 in 1930 and £130 in 1935–6; the average retail price of cars dropped by about 50 per cent between 1924 and the middle of the 1930s. Similar, though less decisive, reductions took place in the price of commercial vehicles.[2] These reductions alone would have been sufficient to widen the market considerably but there were at least two other favourable factors on the supply side. Running costs tended to fall steeply due to the technical improvements in the performance of vehicles and the fall in the price of petrol, which by the end of the 1930s was 2d per gallon cheaper than in 1914. Thus between 1928 and 1938 the total costs of motoring (excluding depreciation) per 100 miles by private car fell from 31s 4d to 22s.[3] The second factor was that the reliability of vehicles improved considerably as a result of numerous improvements including such things as pneumatic tyres, better braking, windscreen wipers, self-starters, improved bodywork etc. Higher technical performance was most important with respect to commercial vehicles, especially buses, where reliability, above all, was required.

[1] G. C. Allen, *British Industries and Their Organization* (1951 ed.), p. 169.
[2] A. Plummer, *New British Industries in the Twentieth Century* (1937), p. 87; Society of Motor Manufacturers and Traders, *The Motor Industry of Great Britain, 1939* (1940), pp. 47–8.
[3] If depreciation is included the relevant costs are 44s 4d and 27s 7d respectively. See J. Harrop, *New Growth Industries in an Era of Stagnation and Depression, 1919 to 1939* (Liverpool Univ. M.A. thesis 1966), Table A.38.

It is important also not to ignore the demand side when seeking to explain the growth of the industry. The improvement in real income per head especially in the late 1920s and 1930s, was an important factor in sustaining the demand for new cars particularly in the slump. The comparison with the depressed state of the motor industry in America in the 1930s, when income levels recovered only slowly, is instructive, though it may well be that the American market had been temporarily saturated in the previous decade. Shifts in consumer preferences also probably favoured the growth of car ownership. The desire to own a car became a force in itself irrespective, to a certain extent, of cost. It is significant, for instance, that in 1938 the number of private incomes above £500 a year was only 800,000 whereas total private car registrations were nearly two million. This suggests that the majority of car owners had incomes less than £500 and though many no doubt had to make do with a second-hand car the burden of upkeep was still considerable and must have entailed sacrifices in other directions.[1] Finally, the rapid spread of suburban residential development away from the existing public transport facilities, together with the increasing mobility of the population, encouraged the growth in demand for both private cars and improved systems of street transport. This was associated with a shift away from rail transport which will be considered in the next chapter.

Numerous forces were therefore responsible for the expansion in motor manufacturing. There were, however, one or two factors that had a dampening effect on the market. As far as motor vehicles were concerned Britain was probably one of the most highly taxed countries, the main burdens being the fuel tax and the heavy licence and insurance charges. The trade complained frequently about these impositions, especially in the 1930s when the total revenue raised in fuel and vehicle taxes was greater than the amount spent upon the roads. It is difficult to say exactly what effect taxes had on demand. In the case of the private car market it probably diverted demand towards the smaller, cheaper car with lower running costs since the tax was based on horse-power strength.[2] It is significant that by 1935 about 42 per cent of all cars in use in Britain were of 10 horse-power or less and over 60 per cent of the new cars sold were in this class. As far as commercial vehicles were concerned, taxation, which was based

---

[1] Allen, *op. cit.*, p. 174.
[2] On the other hand, it could be argued that by diverting demand towards the smaller and cheaper car taxation assisted in the extension of the market.

on weight and seating capacity, probably had a more powerful effect in choking off demand. This is especially true in the 1930s when duties on certain classes of vehicles were raised in line with the Government's policy of restricting total demand. This was backed up by legislation restricting entry into both the road haulage and road passenger transport business. These factors account for the rather slow growth of commercial vehicle production compared with that of private cars in the 1930s.

So far we have concentrated attention on the domestic side but the export market for vehicles should not be neglected. It was a steadily growing one throughout most of the period and accounted for around 16–18 per cent of total production in most years. Moreover, over time Britain's strength in the export market tended to improve. For most of the 1920s her competitive power was relatively weak; although exports rose from 11,000 vehicles in 1913 to 42,000 in 1929 they accounted for only 5·5 per cent of the world market in the latter year and in many years imports into the home market exceeded exports. The main exception was the motor cycle trade which supplied the bulk of world exports and in the late 1920s nearly two fifths of the industry's output went abroad. In the following decade the position was reversed. Although vehicle exports fell off in the depression, by 1932 they had almost recovered to their pre-depression level and by 1937 they had more than doubled in volume, amounting to 98,500 units as against 40,200 in 1932. At the later date they accounted for 14·4 per cent of the world market, making Britain the second largest exporter. Most of the exports went to Empire countries. Imports, on the other hand, remained at the same level as in 1924 and were only about one quarter of exports. Only motor cycle exports, which remained well below the 1929 level, failed to experience any sustained recovery in this period.

They improved external performance, especially in the 1930s, cannot be explained simply by increased competitiveness of the British industry, though this was undoubtedly an important factor. To some extent exports were aided by fortuitous factors. The depreciation of the pound sterling in 1931 stimulated early recovery, while Empire preference also helped to boost exports. But perhaps more important was the fact that the exports of the major foreign competitors, America, Canada and France, failed to regain their pre-depression levels even by 1937. In part this could be explained by a loss of competitiveness in these countries due to rather weak home markets. This resulted in under-utilization of capacity and higher unit costs, whereas in Britain a buoyant home market kept down the burden of overhead costs. One further favourable factor was the increasing taxation imposed on vehicles by foreign governments which favoured a shift in demand towards the smaller less powerful car on which Britain specialized.

The motor manufacturing industry was without doubt one of the key sectors in the modernization of British industry during this period. It was one of the largest of the newer trades and its growth depended very much on the exploitation of mass production techniques. In 1938 some half a million workers were engaged in the construction of motor and other vehicles[1] and sales of the industry amounted to over £200 million, while the contribution to Government revenue was around £90 million or one eleventh of the total. Essentially it developed into a gigantic assembly industry which manufactured a finished product from innumerable parts and components drawn from other industries, and in this respect it differed markedly from the older staple industries. The range of products absorbed by the industry was considerable, including iron and steel and steel alloys, machine tools, aluminium, copper, brass, lead, tin, zinc alloys, leather, felt, rubber, timber, paint and glass, together with a large number of finished components such as lamps, batteries and other accessories. Thus the inter-industry demand for products was very considerable and in some cases it accounted for a large proportion of a particular industry's output. For instance, something like one half of the plate glass produced in Britain went to car assembly plants while the demand for rubber accounted for nearly two thirds of British consumption.[2] In addition, it created new technical problems, stimulated road construction and gave rise to a new service trade. In Landes' words, 'no other product yielded so rich a harvest of forward and backward linkages'.[3]

The rayon industry

In contrast to most other branches of the textile group rayon, a man-made fibre derived from wood pulp and cotton linters, expanded

[1] If, of course, we include the transport operating side of the industry then the importance of this sector is much enhanced. Altogether over 1·3 million workers were engaged in the manufacture, operation and servicing of vehicles.
[2] Plummer, *op. cit.*, p. 82.
[3] D. S. Landes, *The Unbound Prometheus: Technological Change and Industrial Development in Western Europe from 1750 to the Present* (1969), p. 443.

very rapidly. Largely as a result of the enterprise of an old-established silk firm, Courtaulds, Britain initially gained the lead in this new field, though before 1914 there were still certain technical constraints (e.g. liability of fibre to damage and breakage) which had to be over-come before production for the mass market was feasible.[1] By the early 1920s most of the technical difficulties had been eliminated and expansion was well under way. At the end of the decade Britain was producing 52·7 million lbs of rayon yarn compared with only around six million lb in 1913 and 1920. The industry was scarcely affected by the depression; only in 1930 did output fall and then very slightly and by 1932 production was well above the 1929 level. Expansion during the 1930s was almost continuous, apart from a slight set-back in 1938, and in 1939 total output amounted to almost 170 million lb over one third of which consisted of staple fibre, the output of which had been negligible before 1932.[2]

Changes in fashion and technical improvements leading to price reductions were largely responsible for the industry's success. In the inter-war years demand shifted away to some extent from heavy cotton and woollen clothing towards lighter fabrics for which rayon was well suited. With continual improvements in the process of production rayon steadily became a more attractive substitute for natural fibres and the production of mixed fabrics gained ground rapidly. Thus to a large extent rayon was complementary to other textiles rather than purely competitive. Many cotton mills, for example, would have been idle but for the new possibilities opened up for weaving high grade mixed fabrics. In the late 1930s over one half the output of con-tinuous filament yarn was woven into cloth (either pure rayon or mixed cloth) by cotton weavers, while nearly 20 per cent of the looms in the cotton industry were weaving fabrics incorporating rayon or staple fibre. In addition, two thirds of the staple fibre was spun into yarn by the cotton industry. Rayon was also partly complementary in other textile trades such as wool and hosiery, the latter absorbing about 40 per cent of the continuous filament yarn.[3]

The fall in price was probably the chief factor making for the success of rayon. Before 1914 rayon was relatively expensive compared

[1] D. C. Hague, *The Economics of Man-Made Fibres* (1957), p. 38.

[2] H. A. Silverman, 'The Artificial Textile Industry', in H. A. Silverman (ed.), *Studies in Industrial Organization* (1946), p. 318.

[3] J. Harrop, 'The Growth of the Rayon Industry in the Inter War Years', *Yorkshire Bulletin of Economic and Social Research*, 20 (1968), pp. 74–6.

with other textile fibres but the continuous fall in prices after the war increased its competitive power. From a post-war peak of 19*s* 3*d* per 150 denier hank (Viscose A Quality) it fell to 4*s* 6*d* in 1929 and to around 2*s* 6*d* in the later 1930s. By the latter date it was roughly half the price it had been in 1913, whereas most other textile fibres were relatively higher compared with pre-war. Thus for much of the period rayon was competitive with wool and pure silk though it was not until after 1945 that the edge was secured on cotton.[1]

The steep fall in price and improvements in quality were the result of rapid technical progress and improved production methods. These developments were assisted by the fact that for much of the time the industry was dominated by two firms, Courtaulds and British Celanese, though in the later 1920s a number of small firms sprang up. This led to excess capacity, a spate of price cutting and the eventual elimination of the weak firms in the early 1930s. By 1939 there were nine other firms besides the two giants, but they were all very small, accounting for only £5·2 million of the issued capital as against £32 million for Courtaulds and £13·5 million in the case of British Celanese. In terms of market shares Courtaulds were by far the largest. They accounted for over one half of total yarn production and nearly all the staple output, whereas British Celanese controlled less than one fifth of the yarn market.[2] Of course there is no golden rule that a quasi-monopoly of this sort produces the best results. Almost certainly technical progress and economies of scale would have been less significant had the market been shared more evenly among a large number of producers.[3] On the other hand, Courtaulds' performance in the inter-war period is not above reproach[4] and there is evidence that at times the firm was reluctant to take the lead in reducing prices. In the early 1930s in particular they were content to follow the market downward and not until 1934 did they exert their leadership by announcing a big cut in prices to strengthen their position and prevent

---

[1] Allen, *op. cit.*, p. 247.
[2] Though British Celanese was the dominant firm in the production of acetate yarn as opposed to viscose yarn in which Courtaulds specialized.
[3] Harrop, *loc. cit.*, p. 73.
[4] 'If in reality its technical dynamism was poor, its management weaker than it should have been, and its organization inappropriate to its required function, these defects were overshadowed by its practical achievements and its solid financial position'. D. C. Coleman, *Courtaulds: An Economic and Social History*, vol. 2, *Rayon* (1969), p. 243.

the entry of new firms.[1] But there is no indication that the company abused its position or for that matter that it was ever in such a dominant position as to dictate to the market.[2]

Despite the remarkable performance Britain lost ground in comarison with other countries. After the war America became the largest producer of rayon yarn and by 1929 both Italy and Germany surpassed the British output. At that date Britain accounted for 12–13 per cent of world production compared with 20 per cent in 1922 and a slightly higher proportion in 1913. During the 1930s Britain's relative importance continued to decline and by the end of the decade she accounted for about 10 per cent of world output, the leading producers being the United States, Japan, Germany and Italy in that order. These countries also dominated the staple fibre market and Britain's share was only about five per cent in 1939. The rayon industry's trading position was never particularly strong, even in the 1920s when Britain was the chief exporter. The lack of reliable statistics and the rather sharp fluctuations in trade make generalizations difficult. During the 1920s exports of rayon yarn grew quite rapidly and accounted for some 20 per cent or more of total production. In the 1930s however, they remained rather sluggish and the export proportion fell to around 10 per cent. The main export growth point was now in rayon piece goods other than mixtures. Quite often the balance of trade in rayon products was unfavourable. In 1924 and 1925, for example, before protection brought a sharp reduction,[3] yarn imports exceeded exports by about 60 per cent and accounted for 40 per cent of British consumption, while in 1933 imports of pure rayon fabrics were twice as large as the equivalent exports. But for most of the 1930s the balance of trade was favourable. Between 1933–8 average annual exports of rayon yarn and piece goods were 9·5 million lb and 64 million square yards respectively, whereas the respective figures for imports were 1·8 million and 25 million square yards.

---

[1] *ibid,*, pp. 219, 239, 335.

[2] In fact the reluctance to initiate severe price cuts before the mid 1930s, which would probably have driven competitors out of business, suggests that the firm was in no way anxious to secure complete domination of the home market. Thus the failure to act as a price leader may be seen as an effort to prevent a complete monopolistic position developing rather than as an attempt to prevent consumers benefiting from lower prices.

[3] Import duties were imposed on both rayon yarn and rayon fabrics in 1925. These duties were lowered in 1934.

Electricity supply and electrical manufacturing

The electrical trades (including the supply of electricity) and the motor car industry were the two most important symbols of industrial modernization in the twentieth century. They not only created the base for a new industrial structure but they also freed the economy from its former dependence on coal and steam as sources of power and locomotion. But in the early stages of development in the electrical field, as to some extent in motor manufacturing, Britain lagged behind. Before 1914 the lead in electrical manufacturing had been taken by America and Germany and the British industry was for the most part an offshoot of the industries of these two countries. In some branches, notably electrical machinery and electric lamp making, the British position was extremely weak. American and German producers tended to dominate the British market either by establishing branch factories in this country or through imports into the home market. Thus, although Britain generally had a favourable balance of trade in electrical products, the fact that so many foreign producers set up factories in Britain meant that a fairly high proportion of domestic output was provided by non-British firms.[1]

The weak position of the electrical trades was partly due to the slow growth of the home market for electrical products. This in turn, of course, depended very much upon the rate at which electricity was adopted as a source of power. Until the middle of the 1920s the use of electricity in Britain advanced rather slowly in comparison with experience in other countries. In the early 1920s there were less than one million domestic consumers and only about half the power applied in industry was electrically driven compared with 73 per cent in the United States and 67 per cent in Germany (1924–5). Consumption of electricity per head was very low indeed: in 1926 it averaged 118 units compared with 900 in Canada, 700 in Switzerland, 500 in the United States, Sweden and Norway, 230 in Belgium and 140 in France and Germany.[2]

[1] See I. C. R. Byatt, 'Electrical Products', ch. 8 in D. H. Aldcroft (ed.), *The Development of British Industry and Foreign Competition, 1875–1914* (1968). In 1913 German exports of electrical machinery and apparatus were more than twice those of Britain and accounted for over 50 per cent of the total exports of the three leading producers.
[2] M. E. Dimock, *British Public Utilities and National Development* (1933), p. 197. There is a very useful comparative survey of electricity developments in Landes, *op. cit.*, pp. 431–41.

G

Several factors were responsible for the relatively slow extension of electric power in Britain. In part, the spread of electric power was held back by the fact that much of her industrial equipment was adapted to traditional fuels. Britain's industrial and urban development had occurred well before the electrical age so that most of her industrial and transport equipment was based on steam and gas, whereas in those countries which developed somewhat later electricity could be more readily adopted. In some countries lack of coal reserves had hindered industrialization and so it was natural that they should take every opportunity to exploit hydro-electric sources of power when this became possible. Britain, on the other hand, had no such sources and the progress of the new energy depended upon the rapidity with which thermal power stations could yield cheap electricity. In the early years the generation costs of thermal stations were relatively high compared with those of hydro-electric plants and, given the cheapness of traditional fuels in Britain, the pattern of energy costs was distinctly unfavourable to the growth in the use of electric power. The high price of electricity was in large part due to the inefficient nature of the generating units. Power was generated by a large number of small, unconnected plants each supplying its own frequencies and voltages. In 1926 there were no less than 592 public generating stations, 492 of which belonged to authorized undertakings. Most of these were very small and in fact 32 stations were responsible for about half the output. Under these conditions it was impossible to secure the production of cheap energy on a wide scale. Most plants were too small to reap the benefits of scale production and load factors were extremely low.[1] Only about one third of the country was reasonably supplied with electricity, the price of which was extremely high owing to the uneconomical methods of producing it. In 1923, for instance, the price per unit of electricity sold was much higher than in many other countries, averaging $2 \cdot 07d$ as against $1 \cdot 05d$ in the u.s., $0 \cdot 72d$ in Canada, $0 \cdot 6d$ in Switzerland and $0 \cdot 46d$ in Italy. Such high prices inevitably restricted the use of the new form of power and many industrialists were compelled to establish their own generating plants.[2]

An attempt had been made in 1919 to reform the chaotic structure of the industry by the Electricity (Supply) Act of that year, but little was achieved because the Electricity Commissioners responsible for reorganization lacked the compulsory powers necessary to make it

[1] They averaged about 25 per cent.
[2] In 1924 just over 40 per cent of all generating plant was owned privately.

effective. It was not until 1926 that more suitable legislation was passed to deal with the problem. This established the Central Electricity Board with monopoly powers over the production of electric power. Its primary duty was to concentrate production in a number of efficient stations and to erect high tension transmission lines to interconnect these stations and link the existing regional systems into a National Grid. The Board did not own the generating stations nor did it have any control over distribution.

The c.e.b. made remarkable progress in reorganizing the supply side of the industry. Within the space of six or seven years, a National Grid system, involving the construction of over 4,000 miles of transmission lines, had been erected at a cost of roughly £29 million. Further minor extensions of the system eventually brought over 98 per cent of the u.k. population within the Grid's orbit. At the same time the generation of electricity was concentrated in a small number of efficient plants. By 1938 the number of generating stations had been reduced to 137, 13 of which supplied 50 per cent of total output. Spare plant, which had accounted for between 70–80 per cent of maximum demand in the 1920s, had been reduced to a mere 16 per cent by the end of the 1930s.[1] As a result of these changes, together with improvements in the technical and thermal efficiency of generating equipment, the average price of electricity per unit sold was reduced to around 1*d* in 1938, that is roughly one half the price it had been in the early 1920s.[2] Total electricity generated rose from 6·7 billion kwh in 1925 to 26·7 billion in 1939.

Although the Board did much to improve the efficiency of electricity generation there was still great scope for progress in other respects. The Board made much less rapid headway with respect to the standardization of frequencies and voltages. Second, the Board had no control over the distribution of energy the organization and structure of which remained as chaotic as the supply side had been before the setting up of the Grid. In fact, the number of distributing agents actually rose by 126 between 1921 and 1932, to reach a total of 661 authorized concerns by the latter date. Of these, 378 were owned by local authorities and the bulk of the remainder by companies. Many of them were very small and inefficient undertakings. The position as regards frequencies and voltages was chaotic. In the early 1930s there were as many as 45 different declared voltages between

[1] H. H. Ballin, *The Organisation of Electricity Supply in Great Britain* (1946), p. 208.
[2] p.e.p., *Report on the Supply of Electricity in Great Britain* (1936), Appendix.

the range of 100 and 480 volts on which consumers were being supplied in different parts of the country.[1] Thus some of the gains secured from the improved system of generation were offset by the high costs entailed in distribution.

Nevertheless, as the price of electricity fell, due largely to cost-reducing improvements on the supply side, the new source of power steadily penetrated the mass market. At the beginning of the period only the wealthier classes could afford to use electricity. In 1920 the number of consumers was only 730,000 and their average income at 1938 prices was £1,212 a year, while even by 1926 the number was only 1,768,000 with an average income of £726. After that date the number of consumers expanded rapidly and by 1938 there were nearly nine million (average income £401), which meant that roughly three-quarters of the houses in the country were wired for the new power.[2] Similarly, by the end of the period most industrial establishments were using electricity in one form or another though many firms continued to generate their own supply. Only in transport was electricity used on a limited scale, partly because of the reluctance of the railways to adopt it.[3]

The growth in electricity consumption was both rapid and continuous in this period – it was not even checked during recessions – and as a result Britain's expansion was substantially faster than that of many other countries. The fall in price was the main factor behind this growth though it was not the only one. The coming of cheap electricity coincided with new industrial developments away from the coalfields, while many older industries switched to electric power once its benefits were apparent. Not only did the substitution bring a reduction in total power costs but it also often entailed fundamental changes in the lay-out of factory plant and production methods which resulted in greater efficiency.[4] No study has yet been made of the savings derived from the change over to electric power in industry, but if American experience is anything to go by the gains may well have been considerable. Even by the late nineteenth century the substitution of electric for steam power brought reductions of be-

[1] Dimock, *op. cit.*, pp. 254–5.
[2] R. Stone and D. A. Rowe, *The Measurement of Consumers' Expenditure and Behaviour in the United Kingdom, 1920–1938*, vol. 1 (1954), p. 418.
[3] The share of lighting and domestic consumption in electricity sales rose from 16·5 per cent in 1920–1 to 34·8 per cent in 1934–5, whereas that of power fell from 71·4 to 55·8 per cent and traction from 10·7 to 7·4 per cent.
[4] See P.E.P., *Report on the Supply of Electricity . . .*, p. 61.

tween 70–80 per cent in a firm's power costs, taking into account savings in fuel, labour and capital, while it was usually found that the resulting rearrangement of production methods made possible an increase in output of between 20 and 30 per cent with the same factor inputs.[1] The potential gains were no doubt greater in the twentieth century when electricity was cheaper, though how far they were realized by British industrialists awaits detailed investigation.

On the domestic side electricity soon found favour once traditional prejudices had been removed. For lighting, cooking and heating it was generally more convenient and certainly cleaner than traditional forms of energy, coal, oil and gas, though for some purposes, especially space heating, it tended to be rather expensive. Domestic consumption was boosted by the fall in price, rising real incomes, the housing boom (most new houses were wired for electricity) and changes in taste. For many householders it became a symbol of a new and brighter era in living conditions the effect of which was to raise the demand for household appliances and gadgets based on electricity. The 1930s, in particular, saw a rapid growth in the demand for such items as cookers, irons, vacuum cleaners, wash-boilers, washing machines, refrigerators and radios. Between 1930 and 1935 electric coooker sales trebled in number, from 75,000 to 240,000 a year, though in the later 1930s demand slackened off to around 200,000. Sales of vacuum cleaners rose from 200,000 in 1930 to 400,000 in 1938, three quarters of which were sold on hire-purchase terms. The most spectacular development, however, was in the field of radio. The number of licences issued increased from three million in 1929 to around nine million at the end of the 1930s, while sales of radio receivers and radiograms rose from just over half a million in 1930 to nearly two million at their peak in 1937. Altogether, consumer expenditure on radio equipment more than trebled between 1930–38 (£6 million to £20 million), while on domestic electrical appliances outlay rose from £3 million in 1924 to £4 million in 1930 and then trebled to £12 million in 1938.[2] Nevertheless, apart from radios and to a lesser extent electric irons, the market for household electrical equipment was far from being saturated by the end of the period. Despite falling prices and the extension of hire-purchase facilities, the purchase of consumer

[1] R. B. Du Boff, 'The Introduction of Electric Power in American Manufacturing', *Economic History Review*, 20 (1967), pp. 512–3.
[2] T. A. B. Corley, *Domestic Electrical Appliances* (1966), pp. 36, 148.

durables was still confined largely to the wealthier classes.[1] It was not until well after the second world war that the mass market for such appliances was exploited.

The rapid expansion of the electricity supply naturally had a marked effect on electrical manufacturing, though the impact varied somewhat from one branch of the industry to another. As a whole the trade was only slightly affected by recession and between 1924 and 1938 output more than doubled while employment rose from 156,000 to 325,500, a large part of which was concentrated in the Greater London region. Yet though electrical engineering was a vigorously expanding sector its record as regards productivity growth was very poor indeed. This was partly because a considerable proportion of output consisted of heavy equipment, such as generating plant, transformers and machinery, built to individual specifications, and this type of work did not allow much scope for mass production techniques and increasing returns to scale.[2]

The position as regards Britain's trading performance in this field is rather complicated. Before the war imports, especially in some branches, had been fairly substantial and as an exporter she was easily outpaced by Germany. But as a result of the disorganization of the German industry during and early after the war Britain's share of exports of the three main exporting countries (U.S.A., Germany, and Britain) rose from 26·1 to 34·5 between 1913–24, while exports formed a slightly higher proportion of output (27·8 per cent) than pre-war. Imports, on the other hand, were smaller in relation to output and exports than before 1914. However, in the later 1920s Britain's exports rose only relatively slowly (£16 million to £19·4 million, 1924–9) and with the rapid recovery of German activity and continued expansion in America, Britain's share fell back to around 26 per cent in 1929. During the same period imports doubled and they accounted for a much higher proportion of exports and production than had been the case in the early 1920s. Thus although the proportion of output exported remained fairly high, around 27–29 per cent in the later 1920s, the industry was not as competitive as its rivals, and despite protective duties on some key articles (e.g. wireless valves)

[1] In relation to the number of houses wired for electricity the number of electrical appliances in use was very small indeed except for radios and electric irons. See P.E.P., *The Market for Household Appliances* (1945).
[2] K. S. Lomax, 'Growth and Productivity in the United Kingdom', *Productivity Measurement Review*, 38 (1964), p. 21.

imports of electrical goods, especially lamps, valves and domestic appliances, remained very large.

During the 1930s the industry's trading position improved despite the fact that exports accounted for a much smaller proportion of output than previously. Between 1929–33 exports fell from £19·4 to £10·1 million but then recovered to a peak of £21·8 million in 1938 when they accounted for about 15 per cent of output. This fall in the share of output exported was not necessarily a sign of weakness but rather an indication of the buoyancy of the home market.[1] American and German exports recovered less rapidly from the slump so that by the end of the period Britain's share in the three country export total had risen to 29 per cent compared with just over 26 per cent in 1929. Imports of electrical goods dropped very sharply in the depression and rose only slowly thereafter; even by 1936 they were less than half the 1929 level and accounted for only a very small proportion of domestic production.[2]

A growing and protected home market, Imperial preference and less severe competition from America and Germany were important factors contributing to the success of the British industry. The industry was probably also competitively stronger than before 1914 and certainly less subject to German and American influence. It is difficult, however, to speak of the industry as a whole since it consisted of so many different branches the experience of which varied a great deal. The cable making section had always been strong and continued to maintain its position in the inter-war years. The heavy section, covering machinery and generating plant, became more viable after the war partly because of the partial removal of American and German control, though more important was the rapid growth in domestic demand resulting from the construction of the Grid system. British skill and traditional engineering practice were well suited to this type of work which involved the construction of large pieces of equipment to individual specifications and designs.[3] But in the newer and lighter section of the industry, including domestic appliances, lamps, batteries, valves, etc., the British position was weaker, especially in the 1920s.

[1] In fact exports might have recovered more rapidly had it not been for the pressure of home demand. By the late 1930s the industry was finding it difficult to fulfil its orders owing to a shortage of skilled labour and key raw materials. British Association, *Britain in Recovery* (1938), pp. 392–3.

[2] Imports ran as follows: 1924, £4·2mn.; 1929, £8·4mn.; 1933, £2·7mn.; 1936, £4·2mn. Kahn, *op. cit.*, pp. 116–7.

[3] *The Economist*, 30 Nov. 1929, pp. 1010–1.

These products were very adaptable to mass production techniques of manufacture and here American producers were more advanced. Britain made a slow start in this section, partly because of the limited nature of the domestic market, at least initially, and partly because of the profusion of small firms producing a wide variety of products which limited the scope for standardization and mass production techniques. The weakness of this sector is shown by the fact that in the later 1920s imports (mainly from America) of goods like radios, batteries, lamps, valves, vacuum cleaners and refrigerators, flooded into the home market. For example, around 80 per cent of the vacuum cleaners sold in Britain were made abroad. Moreover, in some cases, notably the domestic appliance field, British production was dominated by foreign firms.

In the following decade this branch of the industry gained in strength. The market for its products was growing vigorously and this assisted the move towards mass production techniques and the concentration of output.[1] Imports were checked by the tariff though they still remained more important than in other sectors of the industry.[2] Domestic appliance imports in particular fell sharply; imports of vacuum cleaners, for example, fell from 140,000 to 13,000 between 1930 and 1935 and by the latter date domestic production accounted for 97 per cent of all sales as against only 20 per cent prior to the imposition of the tariff. British firms seized the opportunity to expand in these directions and free themselves from foreign control. English Electric and Pressed Steel added a wide range of electrical household appliances to their production lines and in 1935 the latter firm became independent of the u.s. parent company. In the following year Morphy-Richards began making radiant fires and later extended into other lines of production. From the start this firm adopted mass production techniques and was therefore able to undercut some of its competitors. The improvement in this branch of the trade is reflected in the fact that exports rose fairly rapidly and surpassed the 1929 level.

Other new trades

Because of their sheer size the electrical trades and motor manufactur-

[1] Though output was much less concentrated than in cable or machinery manufacture.
[2] In 1935 the bulk of electrical imports consisted of light goods, though they were a much smaller proportion of production than formerly.

ing tended to dominate the developments in the new industrial sector. But there were, in addition to the industries covered already, many smaller new industries or branches of manufacture which flourished during the period. These included certain chemical products, aircraft, aluminium, rubber, food processing and films. Many of these trades were stimulated by war-time demands and received protection or some form of assistance during the inter-war years. The pattern of development was in many respects similar to that of the major industries so that we need only comment briefly on the salient features of these lesser trades.

Strictly speaking the chemical industry taken as a whole was not a new industry. Britain had long had a flourishing chemical industry though before 1914 its main strength lay in fertilizers, soap and heavy inorganic chemicals. On the other hand, in the newer and finer branches of manufacture, notably dyes, perfumes, photographic chemicals, chemical glassware, drugs and medicinal compounds, the British position was rather weak, especially compared with that of Germany.[1] After the war the industry came to be dominated by one or two large groups, the most important of which were Imperial Chemical Industries, an amalgamation of four companies in 1926, and the massive Lever soap combine. The industry's rate of growth in the inter-war period was not spectacular being slightly below the average for all industry, and there was only a modest increase in exports compared with 1913.[2] The rather unimpressive growth performance was partly due to the weighting of the old heavy sectors which grew only slowly in this period.

By contrast developments in some of the finer, and formerly neglected, branches of the trade were quite promising. Before the war Britain had been heavily dependent on Germany for supplies of these products and production in this country was either very small or non-existent. During the period of hostilities our former source of supply was naturally cut off and it was necessary to stimulate domestic output in order to meet war-time requirements. The Government, therefore, encouraged the development of many key commodities formerly imported, notably chemical glassware, synthetic dyestuffs, drugs and photographic chemicals, and after the war protection was granted to certain branches of the organic chemical trade. This

[1] This was not true of all branches, e.g. explosives and paints.
[2] I. Svennilson, *Growth and Stagnation in the European Economy* (1954), p. 293.

was done to foster home production so as to avoid the former peace-time dependence on imported supplies. Perhaps the most notable example of success was in synthetic dyestuffs. Although these had been manufactured in Britain before the war the industry was a small and struggling one and imports (mainly from Germany) accounted for no less than 80 per cent of domestic consumption. The curtailment of foreign supplies during the war forced the Government to provide financial assistance to encourage home production. In 1915 the Government paid £1·7 million to the industry and promoted a new company, British Dyes Ltd., which took over a number of old established concerns. Further consolidation occurred in 1918 out of which emerged the British Dyestuffs Corporation which controlled 75 per cent of total output. Two years later imports of synthetic dyes and intermediate products were prohibited except under licence of the Board of Trade. Partly as a result of these measures a viable domestic industry was created which satisfied national requirements. Output of synthetic dyes rose from 5,000 tons in 1913 to 19,000 in 1924 and to a peak of 29,000 in 1937. By the end of the 1920s the bulk of British consumption was produced at home and there was already a promising export trade. At the end of the following decade exports were nearly twice imports, the latter having dwindled to very small proportions as a result of the prohibition policy. Thus within the space of a few years a viable and efficient dyestuffs industry had been created, a task which had taken Germany nearly half a century.[1]

Many other branches of manufacture were assisted artificially by war-time demand or some form of assistance. Before the Cinematograph Films Act of 1927, which established a compulsory minimum quota for British pictures, film production in this country had been negligible. Thereafter it grew steadily and by 1936 the total number of films registered numbered 418 and a small export trade had been developed. Similarly, the early development of the aluminium industry in Britain was assisted by a safeguarding duty though production remained small and imports accounted for a considerable share of consumption. Another infant industry, food canning, was assisted by the Board of Agriculture and its successor, the Ministry of Agriculture, during and after the war. By 1934 there were 80 factories canning fruit and vegetables compared with six in 1924. But despite the rapid

[1] *ibid.*, p. 290; H. W. Richardson, 'The Development of the British Dyestuffs Industry Before 1939', *Scottish Journal of Political Economy*, 9 (1962), pp. 115-7, 128.

growth in output imports still accounted for a very large share of total consumption of canned foods.[1]

The aircraft industry, on the other hand, was largely a war-time creation and in the immediate post-war years it languished somewhat because of the collapse of military demand. Moreover, in the early post-war years the market was flooded with war-surplus aircraft. Civil aviation did not provide a great source of demand in the early 1920s since it was on a very small scale and the pioneer companies utilized converted military aircraft. Even after the formation of Imperial Airways in 1924 the civil market was never very strong since the company preferred to buy a limited number of reliable aircraft with a long life-span. The industry was therefore in a relatively weak position for most of the 1920s and was largely kept going by orders for light aircraft which were used for private flying, export orders and the intermittent demand for military aircraft. By the early 1930s the industry was employing around 30,000 people and had an output of £8–9 million about one quarter of which was exported. However, there were far too many small firms in relation to total demand and the Government's policy of sharing out contracts helped to perpetuate the large number of firms and led to a variety of different designs. In 1931 no less than 16 firms were in receipt of Government orders and the R.A.F. was using 44 different types of aircraft. The subsequent growth in demand for civil aircraft and the demands arising from the rearmament boom provided a new lease of life for the aircraft industry in the latter part of the 1930s.[2]

Apart from the new branches of manufacture already considered there were a whole host of technical improvements, new processes and new products which were developed or applied extensively in both old and new fields of activity. It would take too long to list them in full but among the more important developments not mentioned specifically in this chapter, the following might be included: new machinery and processes in the clothing trades, prefabricated methods of packaging, alloy steels such as stainless steel, continuous rolling mills in the steel industry, the rotating cement kiln, electro-chemical processes, new methods of oil refining, synthetic solvents, plastics and

[1] For details of these industries, see Plummer, *op. cit.*, pp. 97, 197–206, 230–50, 319–25.
[2] Mr P. Fearon kindly allowed me to draw information from his work on the aircraft industry before publication. 'The Formative Years of the British Aircraft Industry', *Business History Review*, 43 (1969).

rubber, new welding techniques in shipbuilding and a host of inventions which made possible precise measurement and control of industrial operations. Most of these products and processes provided important possibilities for economic development in the two decades after the war and in some cases they led to the establishment of completely new industries, for example oil refining, rubber and plastics. The timing of these developments varied a great deal, some of the basic inventions had been made before or during the war, while not all were applied extensively in the inter-war period. But whatever the degree of perfection and application there is no doubt that the period as a whole was not lacking in technical improvements and new processes.[1]

The building trades

Though building was not a new industry it clearly warrants consideration in any account of the dynamic sectors of the inter-war economy. Not only was it a rapidly expanding industry but it accounted for a large and increasing proportion of national resources in this period. According to the Lomax index of production building and contracting grew at a compound rate of 5·4 per cent per annum between 1920 and 1938, that is double the average rate for all industry, and in fact its performance was only surpassed by one other industry, notably vehicles. As a result its relative importance in the economy was considerably greater than before the war. Investment in all building as a proportion of total fixed investment rose from 32·0 per cent between 1900–9 to 44·2 per cent in the 1920s and nearly 50 per cent in the 1930s. This was equivalent to about five per cent of the national income in the 1930s compared with 2·5 to three per cent pre-war. Similarly building and related trades accounted for 10·4 per cent of total industrial employment in 1920 and 15·2 per cent by the end of the period. (see Table 26).[2] The greater part of this increased activity was due to the buoyancy of the residential sector. Over four million new houses were constructed in the inter-war period and in the 1930s investment in dwellings averaged £158 million per annum at

[1] See Svennilson, *op. cit.*, pp. 21–2; and R. S. Sayers, 'The Springs of Technical Progress in Britain, 1919–39', *Economic Journal*, 60 (1950).
[2] The indirect employment effects were also considerable. See H. W. Richardson and D. H. Aldcroft, *Building in the British Economy Between the Wars* (1968), pp. 284–6.

1930 prices, or more than double the investment in non-residential building (£74·2 million per annum). The expansion of non-residential construction was less marked but it was by no means insignificant.

The expansion in building output was to be welcomed for several reasons. Since it absorbed large amounts of capital and labour it was a particularly suitable form of activity to expand at a time when there were under-utilized resources. Both capital and labour were readily available and there is no evidence that other sectors of the economy were deprived of resources because of the large demands of the building industry. Second, building acted as something of a stabilizing force in the economy. This was largely due to the influence of the residential sector the activity of which tended to remain relatively high during the downswings of the cycle. The high level of residential building in 1921 and again in 1930–2 certainly helped to offset recession in the economy as a whole. Moreover, the rapid expansion in all types of building, but especially residential, between 1932–6 was an important element in the recovery from the slump though by no means so important as many contemporaries and later writers have tried to make out. Third, because of the fairly wide geographical distribution of building activity the regional impact was very favourable. Most regions experienced a fairly rapid growth in building employment and some of the depressed areas in the North did better than regions further south. In Northumberland and Durham, for example, employment rose faster than in any other region barring the Midland Counties. Furthermore, in most of the northern regions, including Scotland, the difference between the rate of expansion in building employment and that in all industries was greater than that of either London and the Home Counties or the Midland Counties.[1]

But perhaps the most important point about the building industry is the wide repercussions it had on the rest of the economy. Many other industries might well have expanded as rapidly but their effects on the economy as a whole would have been very much less. The sheer size of the building industry and its extensive demand for products of other industries meant that its nation-wide effects were very considerable. Like the vehicle industry, construction is an assembly process which requires a large and varied supply of components or materials from other industries. These include not only the basic

[1] *Royal Commission on the Distribution of Industrial Population*, Cmd 6153 (1940), p. 271.

building materials such as bricks, cement, tiles, timber and glass but also a host of other products including iron and steel, paints, pipes, stoves, heating and ventilating apparatus, electrical wiring and wall-paper. It is significant that employment in all these trades expanded much faster than the average for all industry and that building and related trades accounted for more than one quarter of the total increase in insured employment between 1923 and 1938.[1] The indirect effects are equally important though less easy to measure precisely. The construction of houses and other buildings stimulated the demand for many kinds of furnishings and office equipment, consumer durables and electricity. Finally, the extensive suburban building development also gave rise to the need for improved transport facilities. These points have already been covered in Chapter 4 and need not be elaborated here.[2]

Although the multiplier effects of building were probably greater than those of any other single industry, including the newer industries, in one respect it had a very limited impact. Technically the industry changed very little during the period. Methods of construction remained very much the same as they had been in the nineteenth century, that is a vast assembly operation of a large number of different materials by labour intensive methods and with the aid of only a limited amount of capital. There were, of course, a number of new developments including the introduction of new materials and the use of mechanical aids such as steam shovels, excavators and cranes, though most of these were to be found on large building sites and the vast majority of small firms departed little from traditional practice. But there was no massive application of new technology and processes, as has been the case in recent years, such as to revolutionize the methods of construction and result in the industry becoming a major centre for the transmission of new techniques and ideas to other sectors of the economy. In this respect, therefore, its importance was much less than that of the motor vehicle industry or electricity, both of which had a profound impact on technical developments and methods of production over a fairly wide sector of the economy. Given the rather limited nature of technical progress it is not surprising that productivity growth was relatively low compared with that of other industries.

[1] Richardson and Aldcroft, *op. cit.*, p. 287.
[2] They are discussed at length, *ibid.*, chs. 13 and 14.

Between 1924 and 1937 output per employee rose by 1·5 per cent per annum compared with 2·4 per cent for all industry. The high rate of productivity growth recorded for building over the period 1920–38 (Chapter 4) is partly to be explained by the low level of productivity in building in 1920.

If anything it was in the building materials trades that new technical developments occurred, though construction firms stood to benefit insofar as this resulted in better and cheaper materials as in the case of cement or the Fletton brick. Output of the main materials trades, brick, cement, tiles and glass, increased very rapidly in the period and most of these industries experienced fairly rapid technical progress which raised productivity and reduced prices. For example, between 1912 and 1938 cement output almost trebled and the price of cement fell by nearly one third between 1924–38. A considerable part of this reduction can be attributed to technical change involving the extensive modernization and replacement of old equipment. As a result output per man-hour rose by 110 per cent between 1924 and 1935 while material costs fell by 43 per cent giving an overall reduction of 46 per cent in prime costs.[1] Important cost-reducing innovations also occurred in the glass industry, the main effect of which was to transform glass-making into a fully continuous mass production process. The most notable developments in brick and tile production were the perfection of new products, namely the Fletton brick and the concrete tile, both of which could be produced more cheaply than the traditional products.

It could, of course, be argued that the strong demand for materials produced conditions favourable to innovations in these industries. Certainly they were able to take advantage of scale economies though in some cases, notably brick production, the average size of works remained far below the optimum necessary to permit complete mechanization. Also, the growth of the market for materials was presumably conducive to the development of cost-reducing innovations and new products. On the other hand, it is by no means certain that the introduction of new techniques or methods of production in these trades was simply a response to the high level of demand for their products. For example, the rotary kiln in cement-making had been applied extensively long before the demand for cement reached its peak. Similarly, technical progress advanced rapidly in all branches of the glass industry

[1] L. Rostas, *Productivity and Distribution in Selected British Industries* (1948), p. 81.

some of which, notably bottle-making, had no connection with building. Moreover, since there were no significant changes in the design or methods of constructing buildings it could be argued that the nature of the market for materials was not one to encourage the development of substitute products.

7 Transport and the service sectors

Some general features

In view of the importance of transport and services in the economy some discusssion of these sectors must be included in any survey of the inter-war years. By the end of the period they accounted for 53 per cent of total output, just over 48 per cent of all employment and nearly 70 per cent of the capital stock. The service trades, that is excluding transport and communication, covered a multitude of diverse activities and included such broad groups as public administration, professional services, distributive trades, finance, banking and insurance, as well as a host of miscellaneous items such as entertainment and sport, catering and hotels, various household services (e.g. domestic help, window-cleaning and chimney-sweeping), health services, hairdressing, laundries, cleaning and dyeing, and religious and funeral services. Even if adequate information were available it would be impossible to discuss them all in detail. Of necessity therefore, we shall have to select one or two of the more important sectors for detailed scrutiny. First, however, a few words must be said about general trends and the difficulties regarding the interpretation of the data.

In terms of both employment and output most services and transport were expanding during the period, though there were considerable variations in rates of growth between different sectors. The most notable features, however, were the high rates of employment growth and relatively low levels of unemployment. It can be seen from Table 27 that all the major groups of services, apart from transport, recorded increases in employment between 1920–38 which were well above the average for the whole economy. The very high level of industrial employment in 1920 probably exaggerates the difference, though even between 1923–37 service employment rose at twice the rate of industrial employment.[1] As a result the importance of the service sectors increased from 41·1 per cent of total employment in 1920 to 48·3 per cent in 1938.[2] Moreover, the growth in service employment was remarkably steady from year to year; there were no sharp fluctuations as in the industrial sector;[3] even in the slump of 1929–32 employment continued to rise in most service trades, the major exception being transport. In general unemployment levels were well below the national average. In July 1932, when 22·9 per cent of all insured workers were unemployed, the proportion out of work in finance, banking and insurance was 5·7 per cent, in distribution 12·0 per cent, in professional services 6·1 per cent, in laundries, dry cleaning and dyeing 8·2 per cent, and in catering 14·5 per cent. Only in certain branches of transport, notably shipping and dock, river and canal services, was the level of unemployment considerably above the average.[4]

When we turn to the output data a rather different picture emerges. Transport apart, the output of all the main service groups rose less rapidly than the gross domestic product so that their share of total output declined slightly over the period. Moreover, as can be seen from Table 27, the growth of output in most cases was less than that of employment with the result that productivity declined. These general trends are not altered significantly if we use alternative base years.

One would not, of course, expect employment and output to rise at the same rate but the discrepancies between the two are rather large and call for some comment. It is possible that the data estimates are defective. This is particularly true of the output series some of which are based on employment data or deflated wage and salary bills. It is difficult to measure service output exactly and it may well be that the estimates understate the growth in output. The second point is that the data for employment and output are drawn from different

---

[1] C. W. McMahon and G. D. N. Worswick, 'The Growth of Services in the Economy. 1. Their Stabilising Influence', *District Bank Review*, 136 (1960), p. 7.
[2] A similar trend has been observed in the United States by G. J. Stigler, *Trends in Employment in the Service Industries* (1956), p. 6.
[3] Except for the sharp drop after 1920.
[4] *Ministry of Labour Gazette*, Aug. 1932, p. 301.

TABLE 27 *Employment and output in service sectors, 1920–38*

	Employment (ooos)		% increase in employ-ment 1920–38	% increase in output 1920–38
	1920	*1938*		
Transport and communication	1,482·0	1,513·1	2·1	44·9
Distributive trades	1,773·2	2,438·2	37·5	25·0
Insurance, banking and finance	346·6	459·0	32·4	17·6
National and local government	621·6	789·6	27·1	n.a.
Professional services	720·9	949·9	31·8	22·0
Miscellaneous services	2,025·4	2,754·8	36·0	16·3
All services	6,969·7	8,904·6	27·8	17·7[a]
Total economy (excl. Armed Forces)	16,978·5	18,447·6	8·7	35·5[b]
Services as percentage of total	41·1	48·3		

NOTES   [a] = excludes transport and communication.
     [b] = i.e. G.D.P., measured from output data.

SOURCES A. L. Chapman and R. Knight, *Wages and Salaries in the United Kingdom, 1920–1938* (1953), Table 1; and C. H. Feinstein, 'Production and Productivity 1920–1962', *London and Cambridge Economic Bulletin*, 48 (1963), p. xii.

sources and do not always match precisely for each category. This probably does not account for every much of the difference, but it is important to note that the output series for all services excludes transport which grew rapidly, and includes public administration and defence which declined absolutely between 1920–38. However, the main reason would seem to be the absence of productivity improvements, though it is not entirely clear why productivity actually declined in many of the service sectors. These trades are noted for their labour intensive methods and productivity gains have been generally small compared with those in industry. It is possible too that services became overmanned in this period due partly to the ease with which labour could be acquired at a time of heavy unemployment. Generally speaking, there was an absence of large-scale cost-reducing innovations of a type which would reduce the labour content of output, while capital employed per worker was either stationary or declining. Furthermore, there were many small and relatively inefficient units in services so that scale economies were not exploited. In other words, service sectors were yet to experience a technical and mechanical revolution.

The rising share of total employment accounted for by services would seem to be due mainly to the much faster employment expansion in this sector compared with industry, and this in turn can be attributed to the differential rates of productivity advance between the two sectors. On the other hand, it has been argued, mainly on the basis of American experience, that an increasing share of the labour force devoted to services is a reflection of real income changes. This seems a plausible hypothesis. As incomes rise beyond a certain point an increasing proportion of consumers' expenditure will tend to be spent on services and goods with a high income elasticity, while the proportion spent on basic necessities such as food and clothing will decline.[1] The relative strength of the shift towards services will depend, of course, on the extent to which there are other income elastic goods available competing for the marginal increase in consumers' spending power. However, if this had been the case in Britain one would expect the shift in expenditure patterns to be reflected in the output series for services. As the proportion of expenditure on services rises so should the share of service output in total domestic output increase.

The most recent estimates suggest that private consumers' expenditure on most services increased more rapidly than total expenditure on all commodities. On a group of services accounting for around one fifth of consumer expenditure it rose by 53·8 per cent, compared with 31·5 per cent for all expenditure and 35·5 for the total domestic product. However, a good part of this increase was due to transport and communications whose share in total spending rose from 5·6 per cent in the early 1920s (1920–4) to 7·5 per cent in 1935–8, while the share of services other than transport only rose by just over one percentage point from 13·6 to 14·7 per cent. Moreover, the service sector share in consumer spending was actually lower than it had been before the war when it accounted for 17·2 per cent of total spending.[2] This would seem to imply that that growth of service expenditure was checked to some extent by the existence of other alternative in-

[1] Stigler, *op. cit.*, pp. 26–7.
[2] See R. Stone and D. A. Rowe, *The Measurement of Consumers' Expenditure and Behaviour in the United Kingdom, 1920–1938*, vol. 2 (1966), pp. 110, 125.

come elastic commodities, notably transport and consumer durables, both of which increased their shares.

Unfortunately, this does not really solve the problem as to why output of services grew so much more slowly than private consumers' expenditure. There are several possibilities. One is that the figures for consumer spending are not comprehensive by any means since it is not possible to distinguish all service spending separately. Moreover, they do not correspond to the categories for output which include all service output whether consumed privately, by the Government or for export. It is quite possible that the demand for services from the latter two groups was rising much less rapidly than private consumption. The importance of service exports certainly diminished in this period, while it should be noted that public spending on services was still fairly high in 1920 because of the aftermath of war. On the other hand, it is unlikely that these two reasons explain away the problem entirely and we are forced to assume that the output estimates for services somewhat understate their growth. It is interesting to note in this context that the output estimates for transport, which are much less difficult to derive than those for services, are reasonably consistent with expenditure data.

In sum then, we can safely say that transport and services formed an expanding sector of the economy in terms of employment but that as regards output the position is much less certain. Probably the output estimates understate their real growth so that it may well be that their share remained a stable rather than a declining one. The rapid increase in employment as compared with that in the industrial sector can be attributed largely to the absence of productivity gains. The rising demand for services obviously influenced the rate of employment growth but the shift in expenditure patterns towards services was not sufficiently strong to account fully for the rising share of employment attributable to services.[1]

Whatever the change in the relative size of services and transport there can be no doubt about their importance and in view of this it

[1] Too much should not be read into this shift in employment share from the long-term point of view. It appears to have been peculiar to the inter-war period. The long-term trend is of course distorted by the war which had the effect of reducing the importance of service employment. However, between 1948 and the middle of 1960 industrial employment rose faster than that of services. The productivity performance of services was much better in this period too. See McMahon and Worswick, *loc. cit.*, p. 9.

is surprising the scant treatment they usually receive in the literature. The reasons for their expansion in the inter-war period are many and varied; they include rising real incomes and the reduction in income inequality, the spread of suburban development, the growth of a wide range of welfare services, changes in social and domestic habits, and the development of new services and techniques, especially in transport and entertainment. The effect of these influences can be seen from an examination of some of the individual branches of the transport and service trades.

Transport

Statistics of employment give a very misleading impression of the state of activity in transport during the inter-war period. Total employment reached a peak in 1920 at 1,482 thousand and this figure was only surpassed in the late 1930s when employment crept over the 1·5 million mark. Even in 1929 the number employed was only 1,440 thousand and this total was not again exceeded until 1936. However, the output figures show (Table 27) that transport and communications were growing quite rapidly and the consumer expenditure data confirms this conclusion. Private consumer expenditure (at constant 1938 prices) rose almost continuously from £141 million in 1913 to £183 million in 1920, £256 million in 1929 and £344 million in 1938. On a per capita basis expenditure in 1910–14 was £2·89, £5·33 in 1925–9 and £6·91 by the end of the 1930s. As a percentage of total consumer spending the transport sector rose from 3·8 per cent before the war to 6·5 between 1925–9 and 7·5 per cent in 1935–8. These figures refer only to consumer expenditure on passenger transport and communications and take no account of expenditure on the movement of freight.

Rates of expansion of different branches of transport varied considerably. Broadly speaking the railways, shipping, docks, canal and river services and tramways either stagnated or declined, while the most vigorous growth occurred in road transport, air services and postal and telephone services. Unfortunately, comprehensive comparative data of output for each branch are not available but some idea of the dimensions of growth and relative order of magnitudes can be obtained from the quantity indices of expenditure compiled by Stone and Rowe. The relevant figures, which cover only passenger transport, are given in Table 28. Clearly the most rapid growth took place in private transport covering motor cars and cycles. In 1920 this was only a relatively small branch of total transport but by 1938 total expenditure on the purchase and running of vehicles amounted to £135·2 million compared with £178·9 million spent on public transport. In the latter sector rail expenditure rose slightly; expenditure on road transport however increased by over 52 per cent and total expenditure on this branch was nearly twice that of rail by the end of the period. The most rapid growth occurred in bus and coach services which accounted for the bulk of expenditure on road transport in 1938 (£76·2 million). Most other forms of road transport, that is tramways, taxis and horse-drawn vehicles, declined in importance. The other main branch of public transport, namely shipping, declined rather sharply while air transport, though it increased rapidly, accounted for only £0·5 million of expenditure by 1938. Communications also expanded rapidly, especially telephone services, and expenditure on this group of services more than doubled over the period. The only branch which stagnated was telegraphic services and this was partly due to a relative rise in the price of facilities offered and the competition from telephone and postal services.

TABLE 28   *Quantity indices of consumers' expenditure on transport 1920–38 (£1938mn)*

	1920	*1929*	*1932*	*1938*	*% change 1920–38*
Private transport	25·8	78·6	82·7	135·2	+ 424
Public transport of which:	143·0	157·4	142·6	178·9	+ 25·1
Railways	52·6	53·0	45·8	56·3	+ 7·0
Road transport	71·8	89·1	85·4	109·4	+ 52·4
Sea and air travel	18·6	15·3	11·4	13·2	− 29·0
Communication services of which:	14·1	20·4	21·7	29·5	+109·2
Postal	11·3	14·5	14·9	18·0	+ 59·3
Telephone	1·9	5·2	6·2	10·6	+457·9
Telegraph	0·9	0·7	0·6	0·9	0·0

SOURCE   R. Stone and D. A. Rowe, *The Measurement of Consumers' Expenditure and Behaviour in the United Kingdom, 1920–1938*, vol. 2 (1966), pp. 59, 72, 77.

The major development was undoubtedly the rapid growth of road transport and its impact on the railways. This forms the basis of any discussion on inland transport. Other branches of inland transport, canals, rivers and coastal shipping, were only of fairly marginal importance and were declining. Overseas transport was still dominated by shipping, though the early developments in civil aviation are worth recording.

Inland transport: road versus rail

Before 1914 the railways held a quasi-monopoly of inland transport; road transport acted largely as a feeder service to the railways, motor vehicles were few in number, while tramways were almost non-competitive since they served mainly the internal transportation needs of cities. Thus traffic on the railways increased in almost every year and net receipts in 1913 amounted to £44·1 million (excluding receipts from non-railway activities). After the period of war-time control the railways were amalgamated into four main groups by the Railways Act of 1921 which laid down that charges should be such as to yield an annual net revenue equivalent ot that of 1913. In fact, however, the pre-war standard was attained only in one year, 1923, and in most years net receipts fell well below £44·1 million. Thus although the railways never actually made a loss, profits were substantially lower than before the war. The main factors responsible for this adverse trend were the stagnation in traffic, the competition of road transport and the discrepancy between railway charges and costs.

In contrast to the trend before 1914 the volume of railway traffic stagnated in this period. Freight carried actually declined quite sharply and in no single year did it exceed the pre-war level. All classes of freight – merchandise, coal and minerals – experienced a decline and traffic volumes in the 1930s were generally lower than those of the preceding decade. Even in the best year (1937) the volume of merchandise traffic was only 74 per cent of the 1913 level and that of minerals and coal 83 per cent. In terms of ton-miles hauled the decline was probably less marked since the average length of haul increased during the period, but unfortunately no ton-mile figures are available for 1913. Passenger traffic held up rather better but there was little sign of any marked growth, and in the early 1930s it declined quite sharply. By the end of the period it was slightly higher than it had been in 1913, measured both in passenger journeys and passenger miles.[1]

It is often assumed that the check to railway traffic was primarily due to the effects of road competition. Certainly this was severe but it cannot be held responsible for all the railways' losses since it was mainly confined to passenger and merchandise freight traffic. The railways retained their former monopoly in the conveyance of coal and minerals since road haulage was not very well suited to this type of traffic. Unfortunately, the stagnation in the old basic industries and the decline in exports, especially of coal which fell from 73·4 to 35·9 million tons between 1913 and 1938, inevitably meant a reduced volume of traffic for the railways. The depression in these trades was particularly unfortunate from the railways' point of view since heavy freight was an important source of revenue and profit margins on this type of traffic were relatively high. Revenue from the conveyance of coal, for example, accounted for around 20 per cent of all railway receipts. Moreover, the railway network of the nineteenth century had been developed specifically to serve those industries now in decline. The most severe impact fell on those parts of the railway system serving areas where the concentration of activity on coal, iron and steel and shipbuilding was high as, for example in South Wales, South-west Scotland and the North-east of England. Probably the worst hit area was the North-east; in 1932 mineral traffic carried by the railways in this region was only half that of 1924 and even by the end of the 1930s it was still only 69 per cent, compared with national averages of 73 and 90 per cent respectively.[2] Thus for most of the 1930s the London and North Eastern Railway barely managed to earn 60 per cent of its pre-war revenue. By way of contrast the Southern Railway fared much better since the bulk of its revenue came from passenger traffic.

The fall in heavy freight traffic was not compensated for by growth elsewhere, that is in merchandise freight and passenger traffic. The volume of merchandise traffic fell despite a rapid growth in this traffic generally. Much of the newer traffic originated in the Midlands and South with the development of new lines of manufacturing, and in general the railways were not very well adapted to cater for it. But

[1] The statistical data are given in full in D. H. Aldcroft, *British Railways in Transition* (1968), pp. 50–1.

[2] Based on net ton-mile figures. W. Smith, *An Economic Geography of Great Britain* (2nd ed. 1953), p. 593.

it was the growth of motor transport that was mainly responsible for losses in this field and for the check to the growth in passenger business.

The development of this new form of transport was remarkably rapid in the inter-war years. It was still very much a luxury form of travel just after the first world war when less than 350,000 vehicles of all types were in use. But within the next couple of decades great advances were made in the techniques of producing vehicles with the result that both the capital and running costs of motor vehicles were reduced considerably. This, together with rising real incomes, suburban development and an increasing desire for greater mobility, led to a rapid extension of the market and by September 1938 over three million vehicles were in use on Britain's roads. Included in this total were nearly two million private cars, 53,000 buses and coaches and 495,000 goods' vehicles, while the remainder consisted of motor cycles and taxis. The structural organization of the public side need not concern us here except to say that passenger transport was dominated by large scale operators and the municipal authorities, while in road haulage relatively small firms predominated.

Road transport had two main advantages over the railways. First it was a more flexible and convenient form of transport and it was particularly suitable for short-distance and cross-country journeys and for the conveyance of small consignments of merchandise. The advantages of owning a private car do not, of course, need to be emphasized. Second, in terms of price road operators had a distinct advantage. Not only were their costs falling rapidly relatively to those of rail, but they also based their charges on costs of operation whereas the railways generally did not.[1] Thus on many routes road transport became a severe competitor and robbed the railways of some of their best traffic.

It is difficult to make any exact estimate of the railways' losses to the road since there is little statistical data relating to private motoring or to the volume of freight carried by goods' vehicles. In addition, one must not forget that much of the traffic was new and would not

---

[1] Between 1922 and 1937 operating costs of public service vehicles (both passenger and freight) fell by between one third and one half. The average fare charged on buses and coaches fell from 1·98 to 0·96d per mile (1920–38), while on the railways the average fare fell from 0·96 to 0·67d per mile. The higher average fare for buses and coaches is, of course, due to the inclusion of urban bus services. On competitive long-stage routes bus and coach fares were well below those of rail.

have arisen but for the advent of motor transport which often served areas with no proper rail connections or did work which the railways were not fitted to perform. The growth of road passenger transport relative to rail can be seen from Table 29. At the beginning of the period the total passenger miles travelled by rail exceeded those taken on all other forms of land transport and accounted for roughly 60 per cent of the total. By 1938 passenger miles on buses and coaches were nearly the same as the railways, while the latter's share of the total had fallen to 42 per cent. The railways' losses cannot be equated with the gains of motor transport since many of the journeys made by bus or coach were non-competitive. The railways lost heavily on the short and medium distance routes but more or less held their own over longer distances, that is 100 miles or more. There are no exact estimates of the potential losses through competition. Tentative estimates of the traffic the railways would have gained but for the existence of motor transport can be put at between 250 and 300 million journeys, that is over 100 million on account of public road transport and the rest as a result of the use of private cars. In terms of the total number of railway passenger journeys in 1937 (1,295 million) this loss was quite large.[1]

TABLE 29 *Estimated number of passenger miles travelled by final consumers on public land transport in the u.k., 1920–38 (mn)*

	1920	*1929*	*1938*
Railways	19,214	18,912	20,009
Tramways and trolleys	8,058	9,494	8,148
Buses and coaches	3,457	11,307	19,037
Taxis and hire cars	1,264	929	587
Horse-drawn vehicles	216	63	13
Total	32,569	40,705	47,794

SOURCE Stone and Rowe, *op. cit.,* Table 27, p. 71.

Competition in freight traffic was mainly confined to merchandise and again it was most acute over short and medium distances. An estimate in 1929 for an area served by one main line company suggested that road hauliers took nearly 58 per cent of traffic up to a distance of 40 miles, but only 18·5 per cent above that mileage.[2] The break-even point appears to have been around 75 miles above

[1] See my *British Railways in Transition*, p. 57, for the basis of these estimates.
[2] Smith, *op. cit.*, p. 616.

which conditions tended to favour rail. On the other hand, by the 1930s road transport was becoming more competitive over longer distances as a result of three factors: the rapid improvement in the technical performance of vehicles, the ability of road hauliers to quote very low back-haul rates and the fact that speed of transit was not so essential as in the case of passenger traffic. Unfortunately, the absence of reliable data on freight traffic carried by road makes it almost impossible to estimate rail losses. Walker suggests that in 1936 road hauliers were probably carrying 100 million tons of freight compared with 281 million tons by rail. Less than 50 million tons of rail traffic consisted of merchandise freight, a drop of nearly 20 million on 1913. Most of this was lost because of road competition, while the railways would probably have gained as much again had there been no motor transport. Thus, the total railway loss represented some 40 per cent of the total road hauliers' freight.[1]

These two factors – the decline in heavy traffic and road competition – were reponsible for most of the railways' absolute traffic losses, though the potential losses were greater than those actually sustained. Nevertheless, total traffic units (that is passenger and freight combined) were on average lower than before the war, while fluctuations in volume of traffic were both frequent and more severe than before the 1914.[2] These changes were bound to have an adverse effect on railway finances since, given the high proportion of fixed or unavoidable costs in railway operation, units costs tend to vary inversely with the volume of traffic. Thus the operating ratio (that is railway expenditure as a proportion of gross receipts) tends to fall when traffic is expanding, resulting in an increase in profit margins, while the reverse is the case when traffic declines. In all traffic contractions during the period unit costs rose and net receipts declined, while the overall decline in traffic compared with 1913 meant a higher operating ratio and a lower profit margin than before the war.[3] Moreover, because of the inescapable nature of so many costs it was not possible to reduce expenditure as fast as the decline in receipts, at least in the short run.

The railways' position was aggravated by their pricing policy. This is a complicated subject and only the broad essentials can be dealt

[1] Much road freight was non-competitive with rail, e.g. local delivery work. G. Walker, *Road and Rail* (2nd ed. 1947), pp. 20, 127, 129.
[2] Before the war there had been very few absolute contractions in traffic.
[3] The operating ratio was around 80 per cent in the inter-war period compared with 62·3 per cent before the war.

with here. In the first place, railway pricing policy was rather un-
scientific. Essentially it was based on what the traffic would bear rather
than on what it cost to carry that traffic and this inevitably entailed
a considerable amount of cross-subsidization. Hence railway charges
tended to be higher than they should have been on the low cost routes
and too low on the high cost routes. Therefore, road operators, whose
charges were geared to operating costs, were able to cream traffic off
the dense traffic routes leaving the railways with the less profitable
type of traffic. Moreover, the fact that the railways did not cost and
price their services properly meant that they were never in a position
to determine which were the really unprofitable parts of the system
which should have been abandoned.

A further criticism is that the railways did not adapt their pricing
policy sufficiently to meet the new conditions of the inter-war years.
This was partly because they knew too little about the operating costs
of individual routes and partly because their charging powers were
restricted by the legislative provisions of the 1921 Act. It is true that
road competition forced the railways to reduce their charges and in
so doing they made extensive use of their powers to grant exceptional
rates and charges (that is below the standard). Thus the average fare
per passenger mile fell from 0·96*d* in 1920 to 0·75*d* in 1929 and
0·67 in 1938, while the rates per ton-mile for all classes of freight
were 1·65, 1·44 and 1·35 respectively. By the end of the 1930s, 85
per cent of passenger receipts and 70 per cent of goods receipts were
derived from reduced fares and exceptional rates. This policy had a
number of defects. The rate-making procedure became excessively
complex and undoubtedly had an adverse effect on customer relationships. Second, the rate reductions generally consisted of across-the-
board cuts regardless of the relevant costs and the degree of competition. Pricing policy should have been much more discriminating so
as to take account of these two factors. Thus for example, exceptional
rates were used most extensively for that type of traffic least affected
by road competition; in 1935 the largest proportion of traffic carried
at exceptional rates was to be found in the lowest class of traffic (that
is heavy commodities), while only 63 per cent of the freight in the
general merchandise category was carried at exceptional rates, compared with an overall average of 83 per cent.[1] Similar criticisms can
be made about the pricing of passenger traffic. In the latter half of

[1] Walker, *op. cit.*, pp. 130–1; B. Williams, 'Transport Act 1947: Some Benefits
and Dangers', *Journal of the Institute of Transport*, May 1951, p. 154.

the 1930s the average passenger fare per mile was around 0·64*d* whereas it was estimated that to maximize net revenue the railways should have charged an average of 0·904*d* per passenger mile.[1] In fact, the railways should have concentrated their rate reductions on that type of traffic which was profitable but at the same time susceptible to road competition. Conversely, rates should have been raised on that traffic where competition was limited and for which the elasticity of demand for rail transport was low, and also on the less profitable traffic which the railways could have well done without.

Perhaps the most unfortunate effect of the general reduction in charges was that it created a gap between costs and prices. Though prices generally were falling in this period labour costs, which formed a large part of total running expenses,[2] remained fairly stable at more than double the pre-war level, while other costs did not fall *pari passu* with the fall in charges. Thus by 1938, the cost of many railway inputs was around double that of pre-war, whereas the average level of charges (freight and passenger) was only about 50 per cent greater.[3] These estimates are only approximate but they are sufficient to indicate the magnitude of the discrepancy.

This gap between charges and costs was clearly an additional factor making for a reduced net return compared with pre-war. Indirectly, of course, road competition was partly responsible for this discrepancy. The railways were in the awkward position of having rather inflexible costs at a time when prices were trending downwards. Since their competitors' charges were falling it was not possible to raise railway rates to match the level of costs,[4] though, as we have seen, a more scientific pricing policy might have eased the railways' position and made them more competitive. In the circumstances there was only one course of action open to the railways and that was to secure a substantial reduction in overall operating expenses by more efficient methods of operation. It was a difficult task to reduce expenditure in the short run, but over the period as a whole considerable economies

[1] E. J. Broster, 'Variability of Railway Operating Costs', *Economic Journal*, 48 (1938), and 'Railway Passenger Receipts and Fares Policy', *ibid.*, 47 (1937).
[2] By 1930 they accounted for 55·42 per cent of total revenue compared with 33·25 in 1913.
[3] Average passenger fares were only about 22 per cent above the 1913 level. W. L. Waters, 'Rationalisation of British Railways', a Paper presented to the American Society of Mechanical Engineers, 11 May 1938, New York, p. 3.
[4] The discrepancy between charges and costs had originally arisen during the period of wartime control when the Government froze railway charges.

were achieved. These were derived from three main sources: the savings arising from the amalgamation of the companies after the war which probably amounted to about £15 million, improvements in methods of operation and a sharp reduction in the labour force from 575·4 to 476·6 thousand between 1920 and 1938. It is impossible to make a precise estimate of the economies in expenditure since there are so many variable factors to be taken into account, but it is clear that these were not sufficient to counteract the adverse factors affecting the revenue position. There was, of course, plenty of scope for further economies, in particular by drastically pruning the uneconomic parts of the system and by the rationalization of freight handling operations. But the railways never seriously contemplated these courses of action in the inter-war period.

As in many other fields of economic activity the Government intervened in the 1930s. Regulation of transport was of course nothing new. Numerous Acts of Parliament had been passed before 1914 to control the activities of the railways and the difficulties of the railways in the inter-war years were aggravated by some of the provisions of the 1921 Act which carried over many of the restrictive clauses of nineteenth century legislation. The growing competition of motor transport brought pressure from the railway lobby for regulation and in the early 1930s the Government ceded to their request by passing the Road Traffic Act and the Road and Rail Traffic Act. Briefly, the main aims of this legislation were to restrict entry into the road transport industry and regulate the conditions of service. In effect, it checked the growth of the industry and lessened the force of competition, though by that time road operators had already acquired a considerable amount of traffic from the railways. It has been argued that this legislation was detrimental in that it restricted the growth of the least costly form of transport and by so doing protected the railways and made them less enterprising.[1] There is only limited truth in these statements. In particular, there is little evidence that its growth was restricted simply to protect the railways and where proof could be given that increased facilities were required these were usually granted by the licensing authorities. Road competition still remained severe though it might have been much worse had the industry been left unregulated. Some form of control was necessary since there was much duplication and waste in the provision of road transport services, and in some cases the type of service offered was very unsatisfactory as

[1] J. Hibbs, *Transport for Passengers* (Hobart Paper, 23, 1963), p. 45.

the licensing commissioners testified in their early reports. Moreover, there is little evidence to indicate that the railways were any less enterprising in the 1930s than hitherto. On the other hand, it is possible to argue that had there been no legislation road competition would have increased and this would have eventually forced the railways to abandon the unprofitable parts of their system. It has been estimated that the route mileage could have been reduced by about one third if road operators had taken over their traffic routes.[1] The only snag with this argument is that the parts of the railway system ready for cutting were the thin traffic routes which were of least interest to road operators. In any case, it is highly unlikely that the railways would have embarked on a vast pruning operation in the 1930s had road transport been left unrestricted.

Shipping and airways

The branch of transport which suffered most severely in the interwar period was shipping. Prosperous years were few and far between. Freight rates and profits were either declining or at a low level for most of the period. Tramp ship voyage profits per ton, for example, fell from £3·8 in 1920–1 to £0·7 in 1928–9. The worst phase was in the early 1930s at the time of the slump. At the trough, in 1932–3, nearly one fifth of the word's tonnage and one sixth of the British fleet (three million tons) stood idle. Tramp owners suffered more severely than the liner section of the industry. Many companies were barely able to cover their running costs and as a result large arrears of depreciation accumulated, amounting to nearly £10·6 million for British tramp companies alone in the six years 1930–5. In the later 1930s a slow recovery took place and 1937–8 was the only year in which the prosperity of the industry was at all comparable to that of the immediate pre-war years.

It was in this period that Britain's shipping supremacy really began to be undermined. Although she still remained the word's largest maritime power, British tonnage fell both relatively and absolutely. In 1914 the British fleet totalled 18·9 million tons, equivalent to 42·8 per cent of the world tonnage; by 1938 it had fallen to 17·8 million tons or 26·0 per cent of the world total. Over the same period world tonnage rose from 45·5 to 66·9 million tons, an increase of 46 per cent compared with a fall of 5·8 per cent in the British fleet.

[1] R. Brady, *Crisis in Britain* (1950), pp. 264–5.

The share of world trade (by value) carried in British bottoms dropped from 47·5 per cent in 1912 to 39·5 per cent in 1936.

The basic problem in these years was that the world was over-stocked with tonnage. At least three factors were responsible for this: the rapid increase in the size of foreign fleets, improvements in the technical performance of ships and the fall in the rate of growth of world trade. The post-war boom in shipping brought into existence far more shipping than was required, so that by 1923 there was 39 per cent more tonnage to deal with six per cent less seaborne trade compared with 1913. During the later 1920s this imbalance was reduced somewhat but the sharp contraction in trade during the early 1930s resulted in a great surfeit of capacity. At the bottom of the slump world seaborne trade was about the same as in 1913 while the volume of tonnage was some 48 per cent greater. The recovery in international trade after 1933 eventually brought capacity closer into line with the volume of trade by 1937. However, since there had been a considerable improvement in the efficiency of shipping during these years effective capacity was still greater than requirements by the end of the decade.[1] In other words, for most of the time there was considerable excess capacity either in the form of idle or under-utilized shipping space. The utilization of British ships declined by about 25 per cent between 1913 and 1937.[2]

In some respects British shipping was more vulnerable than other maritime fleets to the unfavourable conditions of the period. For one thing Britain had more to lose from foreign competition simply because before 1914 she had supplied a large part of the world's shipping services. The position was made worse by the fact that many Governments assisted their maritime enterprises by subsidies, whereas British shipping remained virtually unaided until the 1930s. But foreign competition was not the only factor responsible for Britain's difficulties. Because of the stagnation in British trade the opportunities for ship-owners in the home trades were diminished. World trade, though less buoyant than before the war, remained above the 1913 level for most of the time. By contrast, the volume of British trade was well below the pre-war level and in the 1930s it was rarely much more than three quarters of its former peak. Though imports tended to rise they were insufficient to compensate for the sharp contraction in exports with the result that imports as a proportion of total trade increased. This proved

[1] See Chapter 5, pp. 164–5.
[2] S. G. Sturmey, *British Shipping and World Competition* (1962), p. 71.

H

to be a double disadvantage for British shipowners. The decline in exports reduced the opportunities for employment for both liners and tramps. In particular, the collapse of the coal export trade, by about half between 1913 and 1938, was a severe blow to tramp vessels and was one of the chief factors responsible for the decline in importance of the tramp fleet. In fact, this sector of the industry never fully recovered from the partial eclipse it had suffered during the first world war and its difficulties were later intensified by a diversion of cargo to liner trades, the rise of industrial carriers and specialized types of ships, and by the increased competition from foreign tramp fleets. The liner trades suffered from both a decline in merchandise exports and a reduced rate of emigration. Non-coal exports dropped from 16·9 million tons in 1913 to 9·8 in 1933 and rarely exceeded much more than 11 million tons during the rest of the 1930s. Emigrant traffic fell sharply after 1914 and in the 1920s it was only 40 per cent of the pre-war rate, while in the following decade there was a net inward flow of people into Britain.

The increase in the volume of imports did little to compensate shipowners for the severe losses in outward traffic. In fact they probably gained very little from the increase partly because of the increased competition of foreign fleets in the homeward trades. It is significant that foreign entrances into this country increased by 85 per cent between 1913 and 1937 while those of British tonnage only rose by 22 per cent, so that the proportion of national to total entrances declined from 65·8 to 55·8 per cent over the period. Subsidies were no doubt partly to blame for the encroachment of foreign fleets into the homeward trades, but perhaps of greater relevance was the increasing use of c.i.f. terms by foreign shippers and the fact that foreign services were often better and cheaper.[1] Moreover, a large proportion of the increase in imports consisted of oil which provided employment for a type of ship largely neglected by British shipowners. Finally, the increasing imbalance between the volume of imports and exports resulted in a surplus of cargo in the inward direction which adversely affected the employment prospects of British ships.[2]

---

[1] Sturmey, *op. cit.*, pp. 70–1.

[2] Before the war the surplus was in the opposite direction. In 1913 the quantum of imports was 56 million tons and that of exports 93·6 million. By 1938 the relevant tonnages were 67·3 and 49·7. In actual fact therefore, the imbalance was considerably less than before the war but the fact that there was now a surplus in the inward direction meant that the scope for foreign competition was greater.

But it is somewhat debatable whether the decline in the home trades can fully explain the stagnation of British shipping. The growth of shipping fleets abroad suggests that there were plenty of outlets for expansion, particularly in non-British trades, and it is significant also that foreign shipowners were encroaching on many British routes. Yet apart from Germany, Britain was the only country which showed a net decrease in tonnage over the period 1914–38. During that time the tonnage of the u.s. sea fleet more than quadrupled, that of Japan trebled, while the fleets of Norway, Italy and Greece more than doubled. Though world trade conditions were less favourable than before the war foreign shipowners appear to have grasped every opportunity of exploiting any profitable outlets available. Thus they not only secured the lion's share of the new trades but they also encroached severely on the established routes of British shipowners. On nearly every major trade route the share of trade carried in British vessels fell, in some cases significantly. Only on one or two of the direct Empire routes were British nationals able to hold their own.[1]

Though the growth of foreign shipping fleets was in some ways inevitable, there is no doubt that it was materially assisted by nationalistic policies designed to achieve a certain degree of self-sufficiency in the maritime field. Shipping and shipbuilding came to be regarded as key industries during and after the war and great efforts were made by foreign countries to build up or maintain war-expanded fleets. To this end a variety of uneconomic expedients was adopted including subsidies for operating and building vessels, grants or loans for replacing obsolete tonnage and relief from rates and taxes.[2] Aid to shipowners was by no means new but its scale and scope were vastly extended in the inter-war years and in some countries it was accompanied by nationalization, flag discrimination and government control of trade and foreign exchange.

British shipping, particularly the liner section of the industry, undoubtedly suffered from the growth of State-assisted fleets. In particular, the rapid expansion of the Italian and Japanese fleets and the maintenance of the German fleet in the 1930s was largely due to subsidies. In the early 1930s foreign subsidies to maritime industries were running at the rate of £33 million a year. By contrast, British

[1] In particular, the Australian–u.k. trade where by the later 1930s the British fleet was a slightly more important carrier than it had been in the early 1920s. See K. Burley, *British Shipping and Australia, 1920–1939* (1968).
[2] L. Jones, *Shipbuilding in Britain* (1957), p. 63.

shipping and shipbuilding industries received very little assistance. Apart from the guarantees to shipbuilding under the Trade Facilities Acts and the advances made to the Cunard Company for the completion of two crack Atlantic liners, the British maritime industry received very little in the way of direct aid until 1935.[1] In that year the British Shipping (Assistance) Act was passed providing a subsidy of £2 million mainly to assist the revival of the tramp fleet. In addition, a scrap and build scheme was started which was designed to reduce excess or obsolete tonnage and encourage fleet modernization. For every ton of new shipping built owners were required to scrap two tons and one ton for every ton modernized. To assist the process the Treasury advanced money or guaranteed loans up to a maximum of £10 million, which it was estimated would be sufficient to build 600,000 tons of up-to-date cargo vessels. The scheme proved largely a failure. Only a small amount of new tonnage was built, while the scrapping proposals appear to have benefited mainly foreign owners who sold their old ships to British shipowners at inflated prices.[2]

Yet though British shipowners lost traffic to subsidized fleets it is significant that shipowners who received little assistance from their governments, e.g. Denmark, Norway, Greece and Sweden, were equally competitive if not more so. In fact, non-subsidized fleets expanded more rapidly than most subsidized ones and they secured an increasing share of world seaborne trade either by conquering new fields or invading former British preserves. With lower operating costs they were able to offer cheaper and better services than their British counterparts. The Norwegian fleet, for example, succeeded in trebling its share of the American trade between 1920 and 1938 at a time when British participation was declining rapidly.[3]

It has been argued that had British shipowners been more enterprising the decline in the position of the British fleet need never have occurred.[4] While this view probably somewhat underestimates the effects of the difficulties faced by shipowners there is no doubt that their problems would have been alleviated had they been more willing to adapt to changing conditions. Openings in non-British and non-liner trades were available had the trouble been taken to exploit them, while the adoption of faster and more efficient vessels, e.g. oil

---

[1] Though some lines received concealed subsidies in the form of mail payments.
[2] Sturmey, *op. cit.*, p. 109.
[3] *ibid.*, p. 127.
[4] *ibid.*, p. 137.

driven ships, would have reduced costs and enhanced the competitive power of British ships. Yet by 1939 only one quarter of the British fleet used diesel propulsion as against around one half in the case of the Scandinavian and Dutch fleets. Similarly, not a great deal was done to exploit new trades. One would have expected, for example, that British tramp owners, who were badly hit by the contraction in the coal export trade, would have moved rapidly into the growing trade in oil. Yet after the war tankers were largely neglected in this country and by the end of the 1930s Britain owned only about one quarter of the world tanker fleet compared with one half in 1913. Here the pace was set by the enterprising Norwegians. By 1939 Norway's independently[1] owned tanker fleet was twice as large as the British and their tankers carried over one quarter of the petroleum imported into Britain.

If one were to argue that this conservative response was a reaction to the difficult conditions of these years one would need to know why foreign shipowners were not affected in the same way. Or alternatively, one would have to find another explanation as to why British shipowners were reluctant to adapt to changing conditions. Perhaps their main fault was not that they failed to invest but that their investments were made unwisely. After the war reserves were high but these were used either to finance frivolous speculative transactions or in building traditional ships which were often unsuited to new conditions.[2] This latter type of policy was continued for most of the period and in part reflected shipowners' satisfaction with their past performance which in turn made them unwilling to explore new possibilities. 'There was an attitude of complacency, that the British industry was best by definition, had the most suitable ships and generally knew best, together with an introverted concern with servicing British trades which was in marked contrast to the extrovert attitude of younger shipping enterprises in other countries'.[3]

Like motor transport, civil aviation was a rapidly growing industry during this period. Yet it remained a very small sector even by 1938. Moreover, air transport was not a profitable business. Practically all airlines made losses and the major firm in the field, Imperial Airways, was only kept going by generous State bounties.

[1] That is owned mainly by shipping firms as opposed to oil companies.
[2] D. H. Aldcroft, 'Port Congestion and the Shipping Boom of 1919–20', *Business History*, 3 (1961).
[3] Sturmey, *op. cit.*, p. 96.

Although flying had been shown to be technically feasible before 1914 it was not until after the war that regular air services were established. In 1919 and 1920 four companies were set up to fly scheduled services to the Continent, but conditions were so unfavourable that they soon had to abandon their efforts for lack of funds. The Government came to the rescue in 1921 by providing subsidies to airlines prepared to run regular services. As a result two of the former companies, Handley Page and Instone's, were revived and later they were joined by two new firms, Daimler Airway and the British Marine Air Navigation Company Ltd. By 1924 these firms were carrying an increasing amount of traffic to the near Continent.

But despite the increase in business aviation remained very unprofitable and it is clear that services could not have been continued without State subsidies. Part of the trouble was that there was far too much capacity on each route largely as a result of competition from heavily subsidized foreign airlines, while the concerns were far too small to effect any reduction in operating and overhead costs. Fluctuations in the level of traffic, the unreliable nature of the early aircraft and poor navigational aids were other factors which militated against the success of the pioneer companies. A possible solution to some of these difficulties appeared to be the formation of one large company. In 1924 this was realized when the Government's chosen instrument, Imperial Airways, was formed, with a capital of £1 million, to take over the four airlines then operating scheduled flights. This company was granted a monopoly of subsidized air transport over a ten year period and it was to receive annual payments on a descending scale up to a maximum of £1 million over the contract period. In return, Imperial Airways undertook to fly one million miles per annum and develop and maintain a network of efficient air services.

By the end of the contract period Imperial Airways had achieved a fair degree of success. Route milage flown rose from 1,520 in 1924 to 15,529 in 1935, while passenger traffic increased from 10,321 to 66,324. The financial strength of the company had also improved. In 1935, when a profit of £140,705 was made, subsidies as a proportion of total revenue amounted to only 27·7 per cent as against 69 per cent in 1930. However, without the subsidy payments, which amounted to well over half a million pounds in 1935,[1] the company would have made a substantial loss. The company's record was not

[1] The subsidy limit having been raised from the original scale set in 1924.

above criticism moreover. It was alleged that it had paid too much attention to fostering Imperial services, some of which were very unprofitable, at the expense of developments elsewhere. Services to Europe had in fact been reduced to a minimum and Imperial Airways had done little to establish services to South America, Scandinavia and West Africa, while it was not until 1937 that the first commercial survey flights across the Atlantic were made.[1]

The neglect of the European routes was felt to be serious. These were fairly profitable and in the early 1930s a number of independent and unsubsidized companies were beginning to establish cross-channel services. Whereupon the Government saw the chance of repeating the policy of the 1920s. In 1935 a second chosen instrument, British Airways, was set up to take over the main unsubsidized companies. This company was given responsibility for nearly all subsidized European services and the task of developing services on hitherto uncharted routes such as the South American. Imperial Airways was allowed to concentrate its activities on Empire routes. The new company had no sooner established a firm footing in Europe than a further reorganization occurred. In 1939 the two companies were merged into the British Overseas Airways Corporation.

Regular internal air services were not started until the early 1930s. Before that time conditions were not favourable to flying in Britain and the Government was not prepared to subsidize services. By the middle of the decade a network of air services had been established in Great Britain and altogether about a score of companies operated 76 different services. All the main town centres were provided with air facilities and most of the islands had been linked to the mainland. However, the market was much too small to support such a large number of companies. None of them made profits and many of them soon went out of business. Thus, in the later 1930s, some attempt was made to consolidate the industry's structure, the main influence behind which was Railway Air Services, a company promoted by the four main-line railway groups. Eventually, Railway Air Services acquired an interest in, or control of, a substantial part of the internal airline business. The majority of the traffic, as on the external side, consisted of passengers, though a small amount of freight and mail was also carried. By 1937 the number of passengers conveyed reached

[1] H. J. Dyos and D. H. Aldcroft, *British Transport: An Economic Survey from the Seventeenth Century to the Twentieth* (1969), ch. 13.

a peak of 161,500, compared with 121,559 in 1935 and 3,260 in 1932.[1]

Though air traffic expanded fairly steadily civil aviation failed to achieve financial viability. Without the heavy subsidies paid to overseas operators and the backing of the railways in the internal field it is unlikely that regular air services would have been carried on for very long. There are several reasons to explain this lack of prosperity. On many routes traffic was very thin and it often fluctuated quite sharply, depending upon the time of day and the month of the year. Under these conditions it was very difficult to achieve economic load factors. The position was aggravated, moreover, by severe competition from more heavily subsidized foreign companies on external routes, while at home many companies competed with each other and also faced the task of attracting custom away from existing forms of inland transport. A further problem was the technical performance of aircraft. In the early years especially, aircraft were very uneconomic to run; they had a small capacity, they had to make frequent stops for refuelling and they required a considerable amount of maintenance which meant that they were out of commission for lengthy periods of time. Nor were they adapted to carry large loads of freight and mail which might have helped to stabilize their overall load factors. In fact as such, air travel was still very much an expensive luxury which only a privileged minority could afford and in no sense had it begun to tap the mass market as in the case of motor transport.

The distributive trades

In terms of both output and employment the distributive trades were the fastest growing sector of services in the inter-war period. Employment in distribution grew more rapidly than in any other sector and by the end of the period accounted for around 13 per cent of total employment compared with 10 per cent in 1920.[2] Output, on the other hand, expanded less rapidly than employment (see Table 27) so that productivity actually declined. This fall in productivity is perhaps

---

[1] For further details see D. H. Aldcroft, 'Britain's Internal Airways: The Pioneer Stage of the 1930s', *Business History*, 6 (1964), and 'The Railways and Air Transport in Great Britain, 1933–1939', *Scottish Journal of Political Economy*, 12 (1966).

[2] Excluding owner-managers and working proprietors. If these are included the total number engaged in distribution in 1938 would be around three million.

somewhat surprising in view of the shift to larger, and presumably more efficient, units in retailing and wholesaling.

Not all branches of distribution developed at the same rate. Merchant firms trading overseas found little scope for expansion because of the decline in the export trade, the more extensive use of direct selling techniques by manufacturers and the competition of foreign merchants backed by government support. The sharp contraction in international trade in the 1930s hit the overseas merchant severely, and although no figures are available it is fairly certain that merchant business declined taking the period as a whole. Similarly, the functions of the wholesaler were being telescoped in these years as some larger retail stores began to do their own wholesaling, while manufacturers cut out the wholesaler altogether by taking over many of his functions such as the packaging and blending of goods. Tentative estimates for 1938 suggest that 53 per cent of the total value of all retail sales originated direct from the producer or importer to the retailer (including the proportion passing through the Cooperative Wholesale Societies), while 43 per cent passed through one or more wholesaling intermediaries and the remaining four per cent was done by producer-retailers.[1] But though on balance the wholesaler tended to lose ground during the inter-war years, the loss in business was probably not very great. The importance of wholesaling varied a great deal from trade to trade and in some cases, e.g. fruit and vegetables, the functions of the wholesaler increased. There were, too, compensations in other directions. For example, many retailers tended to carry smaller stocks than before the war which gave increased scope for expansion in wholesaling.

By far the largest branch of distribution was retailing and it was here that most of the growth occurred. Estimated retail sales in real terms rose by nearly 38 per cent between 1920 and 1938,[2] and much of this increase in business went to the larger retailers. The growth of large scale retailing was primarily a twentieth-century phenomenon. At the turn of the century small scale retailers accounted for the bulk of retail sales and even by the eve of the first world war large units were responsible for less than 20 per cent of all sales. By 1939, however, the latter accounted for one third or more of total trade and in some cases, such as footwear, women's clothing, groceries and provisions,

[1] J. B. Jefferys, *Retail Trading in Britain, 1850–1950* (1954), p. 48.
[2] *ibid.*, p. 45.

dairy produce and chemists' goods, they accounted for more than 40 per cent of the total sales in each group.

There were three main types of large scale retailers; the cooperative societies, the departmental stores and the multiples. Before the war the cooperatives, with about eight per cent of all retail business, had been the largest of the three groups. They continued to expand in the inter-war years; membership of the movement increased from three million in 1914 to 6·5 million in 1938, though these figures give a somewhat inflated impression of the rate of development since they include many non-purchasing members. The main features of development were the spread of their activities into the Midlands and South, both areas having been neglected before the war, and an increase in the scale of operations both on the production and retailing sides. On balance, the cooperatives increased their share of the market and by 1939 accounted for around 10–11 per cent of all sales, though their rate of progress was far slower than that of the multiples. In view of their relatively strong position before 1914 the progress of the societies in the retail field was rather disappointing. Possibly one of the main reasons for this was the fact that they concentrated on a rather narrow range of staple products and failed to branch out into those lines of activity where demand was expanding most rapidly. By the end of the period their main strength lay in food, household goods and clothing, the first of which accounted for some three quarters of all sales. They were also slow to develop modern and attractive methods of display and the quality of their products did not improve very much.[1] In effect, therefore, they continued to cater for the lower income groups.

Though the importance of the departmental stores increased they were never a significant force in the retail market. In 1939 they were responsible for about five per cent of all sales compared with around three to four per cent at the beginning of the period. The number of stores rose from about 200 in 1914 to 500 or so in 1938. However, financial integration between stores developed rapidly and eventually four groups, Debenhams, United Drapery Stores, Great Northern and Southern Stores and the John Lewis Partnership, controlled 200 or more stores. But this trend towards integration was not accompanied by any marked improvements in methods of trading, such as standard-

[1] These qualitative defects have continued up to the present day and have no doubt been partly, if not largely, responsible for the cooperatives' poor performance in more recent years.

ization in selling and pricing policies, nor was much attempt made to institute central buying arrangements on behalf of all the stores in any one group. This absence of centralized control or direction meant that operating costs were relatively high, while fairly large outlays had to be made on advertising. On the whole departmental stores tended to concentrate heavily on women's and children's wear and drapery, though some expansion was registered in furniture, household goods, hardware, pottery and glass.

By far the most vigorous growth occurred in multiple-shop retailing. As a group they accounted for some six to seven per cent of all sales before the war, that is slightly less than the proportion held by the cooperatives. Between 1910 and 1939 the number of separate branches (that is of firms with 10 or more branches) more than doubled, from 19,852 to 44,487, while the number of firms rose from 395 to 680. By the latter date they were responsible for some 18–19 per cent of the retail trade, that is a larger proportion than that of the cooperatives and departmental stores combined. Several changes took place in the structure and organization of multiple retailing. The size of firms increased either by amalgamation or merger or by the opening of new branches. As a result some trades came to be dominated by one or two large groups as, for example, in footwear by Freeman, Hardy and Willis, in groceries by the Home and Colonial Stores and the International Tea Group, in meat by Union Cold Storage, and in chemists' goods by Timothy White and Taylors and Boots Pure Drug Company. But in most trades competition continued to prevail since rarely was anything approaching a monopoly position gained by any one group. A further important development was the emergence of non-specialist or variety chain stores. These had been started in a very small way at the end of the nineteenth century but it was not until after the war that they became of any significance. The number of variety chain stores quadrupled between 1920 and 1939 (300 to 1200), and by the latter date they accounted for 20 per cent of the total sales by multiples as against only three per cent in 1920. Some of the main groups in this sector included the well known firms of Marks and Spencer, F. W. Woolworth, British Home Stores and Littlewoods.

Considerable changes also took place in the pattern of trading and the type of products sold by the multiples. Before the war most of them had concentrated on selling a relatively narrow range of low-priced goods to a working class market and with a minimum of service. In

1915, for example, just over 72 per cent of all sales was represented by food, a further 15 per cent consisted of clothing and the rest was divided among confectionery, stationery, tobacco and miscellaneous items. By the end of the period the system of trading catered much more for the varied demands, both as regards the goods offered and the range of services provided, of a wide section of the community. Food sales as a proportion of the multiples turnover had declined to 45 per cent, while clothing had increased to 26 per cent and other goods to 29 per cent. The multiples now sold a wide range of products including not only food and clothing, but also chemists' goods, pottery, glassware, hardware, jewellery, toys, sports goods, household equipment, books and furnishings. At the same time, in some of the more standardized commodities such as footwear, milk and chemists' goods, integration of the production and distribution processes had been carried out.

There were several factors responsible for the growth of large-scale units and the expansion in retailing generally. The trend towards large scale operations had been apparent before 1914 and some of the influences at work were the same as then. There were economies to be gained by selling and buying on a large scale and the development of new trading techniques in retailing made it possible to extend the scope of operations. The market also became more favourable to developments along these lines. Various factors, e.g. education and advertising, helped to make the consumer market more homogeneous. As the gap between various classes narrowed people tended to buy similar things and this in turn widened the possibilities of national marketing and made possible the use of similar sales techniques by retailers in different parts of the country. This trend was reinforced by the spread of branded goods, the decline of the preparation of foods in the home,[1] and the concomitant development of pre-packaged goods, but, above all, by the rapid growth in the use of motor transport which not only increased the radius of the retailer's operations but also affected the location of shops and the types of service offered. In addition, the increasing range of new household goods, especially consumer durables, also encouraged large scale retailing since many of these products were too expensive to be handled by small retailers. These new developments in retailing also helped to boost the level of consumer demand, though the main forces at work here were un-

[1] Which in turn was associated with a reduction in family size, smaller dwellings and fewer domestic servants.

doubtedly the rise in real incomes and the indirect influences associated with suburban growth and the development of new forms of transport and power.

Though the output of the distributive trades increased steadily the productivity of labour declined during the period. It is not at first apparent why this should be so at a time when the scale of operations, especially in retailing, was increasing. In fact, however, there are several possible explanations of this paradox though it is not easy to attach quantitative significance to them individually. It may be, of course, that the output estimates understate the rate of expansion, though it is unlikely that this was the principal reason. Productivity probably fell more rapidly in the stagnating sectors of distribution, wholesaling and merchanting, where the scope for economies was somewhat less than in retailing. But even in retailing, where larger units were becoming increasingly important, productivity probably declined. For one thing, the economies of large scale retailing were not exploited properly and, in fact, any economies that were gained were probably more than offset by the shift away from the mass distribution of handing on goods to the customer with a minimum of service, towards more complicated and elaborate forms of distribution involving more services to the customer and a greater variety of products. Furthermore, though some smaller retailers lost business to the larger stores few went out of business, so that the average sales per unit fell, while overall the number of shops increased partly because of the spread in suburban development.[1] In other words, the pattern of selling techniques tended to increase unit labour inputs and one estimate suggests that sales per assistant may have fallen by as much as 20 per cent between 1924 and the end of the 1930s.[2] It was not until after the second world war, when new techniques in distribution brought economies in labour and drove the small and inefficient concerns out of business, that the efficiency of the retail trades increased significantly.

The distributive trades were, of course, fairly labour intensive and given the abundant supplies of labour during this period the need

[1] The increase in the number of shops was much more rapid than the increase in population.

[2] H. Smith, *Retail Distribution* (2nd ed. 1948), p. 145. A decline of similar magnitude is obtained by using the Chapman and Knight employment figures for shop assistants and the Jefferys' estimates of retail sales deflated by the cost of living index. But over the whole period, 1920–38, the decline in productivity is quite moderate.

to economize on labour inputs was not very strong.[1] The result was that employment rose more rapidly than the capital stock. This meant that capital per employee declined thus lessening the scope for raising labour productivity. On the other hand, output rose more rapidly than the capital stock so that the capital–output ratio fell and the productivity of capital rose. However, since many other industries improved their capital–output ratios as well as their labour productivity in this period the performance of the distributive trades still looks very poor by comparison.[2]

Other service sectors

The remaining service sectors include public administration, insurance, banking and finance, professional services and a wide range of miscellaneous activities such as entertainment and sport, catering and hotels, laundry and dry-cleaning, and personal service including domestic help. In virtually every case employment expanded rapidly during the period, but the available estimates suggest that output did not keep pace so that productivity declined. A slower advance in services, as compared with that in the rest of the economy, is generally to be expected, but it is not easy to explain why it actually declined. Many of the points raised with reference to distribution are relevant of course and need not be detailed again. In particular, the fact that it is very difficult to estimate real output in many cases and the absence of any sustained growth in the amount of capital per employee. Moreover, in many service trades there is inevitably much under-utilization of labour on account of the discontinuities in the work load. Finally, it should be noted that, in contrast to later decades, little attention was paid to measuring output or streamlining the efficiency of service sectors, partly because there seemed to be little point in trying to economize on labour at a time of high unemployment.

It is virtually impossible to say anything worthwhile in a short space about the structure and output of these trades. Their structures are so diverse and the nature of their output so varied that a detailed

---

[1] Smith (*ibid.*, pp. 131, 142–3) attributes rising costs and declining efficiency to imperfect competition which was enhanced by falling wholesale prices and heavy unemployment.

[2] See Chapter 4 and J. A. Dowie, 'Growth in the Inter-War Period: Some More Arithmetic', *Economic History Review*, 21 (1968), p. 108.

exposition of each branch would be required. We shall confine our comments, therefore, to some of the factors responsible for the growth of these sectors.

Recruitment to the professional services increased by nearly one third between 1920 and 1938. Most of those employed in this category were salaried workers whose numbers rose from 597·7 thousand in 1920 to 767·5 thousand by the end of the period. The two most important groups were teachers and medical staff including doctors, which accounted for well over half of all professional salaried people. Clergymen formed another distinct though small group, while about 30 per cent of the total was made up of a miscellaneous range of occupations covering accountants, lawyers, consultants of one kind or another, veterinary surgeons etc. Apart from clergymen, most groups increased their numbers considerably in these years. Probably the most important single cause of this increase was the extension in welfare services. To a large extent the rise in social welfare expenditure was a twentieth century phenomenon. Around the turn of the century the total expenditure on public social services (including education) came to £35·4 million, or equivalent to 19s 2d per head of population, while by 1920 it had risen to £201·1 million or £4 4s per head; the real increase was, of course, very much less than this since prices generally rose rapidly over the period. Between 1920 and the middle of the 1930s total expenditure almost doubled to about £400 million or approaching £9 per head. Since prices fell by nearly 50 per cent in this period social service expenditure in real terms increased by a multiple of almost four. Altogether around one third of all governmental expenditure went on social services compared with one seventh in 1900,[1] while some 25 million people benefited from social services each year. Of course, a considerable part of the expenditure went on transfer payments but at the same time spending on direct social services such as education, medicine and other community services was increased and this in turn called for more teachers, doctors, nurses and other welfare workers. The numbers engaged in these occupations rose from 385·9 thousand in 1920 to 478·7 thousand in 1938. As one contemporary remarked: 'One of the numerous social changes affected by our many social services has been the silent growth of new professions and the subtle transformation of old ones . . . all alike have

---

[1] Excludes housing expenditure and war pensions. P.E.P., *Report on the Social Services* (1937), pp. 10, 12, 188.

this one new characteristic: they are becoming salaried servants of the community instead of fee-taking advisers of individuals.'[1]

Most of the remaining professional groups were not affected very much by the growth of public welfare services. Apart from clergymen, these included lawyers, solicitors, consultants, scientific workers, surveyors and many other smaller occupations. Individually each of these categories was fairly small but the numbers engaged in them as a whole amounted to 155·7 thousand in 1920 and 230·4 thousand in 1938. In an increasingly complex and educated society the rise in the importance of the professions was only to be expected. For example, one of the largest expansions was in the number of scientific and research workers. The number of research chemists alone is estimated to have quadrupled between 1920 and 1938.[2] The demand for technological and scientific manpower was stimulated by the increasing amount of research carried out by the government and business firms, and, of course, by the growth of new science-based industries such as electricity.

One of the largest absolute increases in employment occurred in the miscellaneous group of services which comprised entertainment and sport, catering and hotels, laundry and dry cleaning, domestic service and a whole host of minor activities such as hairdressing, funeral direction, photography, museums and charitable and political organizations. Overall employment in this category rose by more than 700,000 during the years 1920–38 and few trades failed to register a substantial increase. Contrary to popular conception, even the numbers in domestic service rose and by the end of the period this still remained by far the largest group, accounting for nearly 1,683 thousand out of a total of 2,754·8 thousand. But probably the most rapid growth took place in those activities mainly associated with leisure. Employment in entertainment and sport rose from 101·7 to 247·9 thousand, in catering and hotels from 415·5 to 494·6 thousand, and in laundry and cleaning from 131·3 to 195·5 thousand. Stone and Rowe suggest that expenditure on entertainment and recreation averaged between £200 and £250 million in the interwar years or about five per cent of total consumer expenditure.[3]

Several factors were responsible for the growth of leisure activities. Rising real incomes, especially of the lower classes, meant people had

[1] W. H. Wickwar, *The Social Services* (1936), p. 132.
[2] K. Prandy, *Professional Employees: A Study of Scientists and Engineers* (1965), p. 22.
[3] Stone and Rowe, *op. cit.,* p. 78.

more money to spend on amusement. They had more time, too, as a result of the shortening of the working week after the first world war. The practice of taking an annual holiday also became fairly widespread in these years. It has been estimated that in 1937 the number of holidaymakers away for a week or more was about 15 million and most of this increase had taken place since 1919. It owed little, however, to the holidays with pay movement since in 1937 only about four million workers out of a total working population of 18½ million had paid annual leave.[1] Nevertheless, the increasing popularity of the annual holdiday, though confined to the wealthier sections of the community, led to the rapid growth of seaside resorts some of which catered for millions. By the 1930s Blackpool was receiving some seven million visitors annually, Southend 5½ million and Hastings three million, though many no doubt were merely day-trippers. Their development was based primarily on entertainment and other service trades, the incidence of which was much greater than in the country as a whole. In 1931, nine out of every 1,000 of the employed population in Britain worked in the entertainments industries and 132 out of every 1,000 in personal services, whereas the corresponding figures for Blackpool were 43 and 270, for Southend, 17 and 198, and in Brighton, 21 and 244. Similarly, the average frequency of employment in the distributive trades was very much higher than the national average. In Yarmouth, for example, 20 per cent of the insured population worked in shops, while in Torquay the proportion was about 25 per cent. As one might expect the growth of service trades, especially entertainment, was much more rapid than in the country as a whole. No precise figures are available but according to the Royal Commission on the Distribution of Industrial Population, 'the growth of the services represented by such (seaside and other holiday) resorts, including the service of transport, has been among the most rapid forms of economic growth since the (1914–18) war, and its effect upon the movement of population has been of the first importance'.[2]

The seaside resorts did not have a monopoly of the entertainment trades. The development of organized entertainment for the working

[1] Partly as a result of the Holidays with Pay Act of 1938 there was a sudden jump in the numbers receiving paid holidays. By the middle of 1939 some 11 million workers were covered by various agreements. J. A. R. Pimlott, *The Englishman's Holiday* (1947), pp. 215, 219–21.
[2] *Royal Commission on the Distribution of Industrial Population*, Cmd 6153 (1940), p. 46, note 48.

man was a notable feature of this period. Before that time there had been few opportunities for healthy amusement apart from football matches, the music hall, boxing and wrestling. The relative importance of some of these activities declined with the development of cinemas, dance halls, greyhound racing, new forms of gambling and other sporting events. The cinema was already firmly established at the beginning of the period but its popularity greatly increased with the introduction of the 'talkies' in 1927. During the years 1927–35 the rate of cinema building averaged 160 a year and even in the later 1930s it was still running at around 100. By the end of the decade there were over 4,300 cinemas in Britain and weekly attendances averaged around 19 million.[1] Attendances at most sporting events – cricket, football and boxing – probably increased but these activities were to some extent overshadowed by the growth of entertainments involving some form of gambling. The total value of all bets staked more than trebled over the period and much of this increase was due to the introduction or extension of relatively new forms of betting which offered opportunities and inducements to a wider section of the community. It was in this period that organized greyhound racing became popular, totalisator betting was introduced on racecourses, and that football pools, and to a lesser extent sweepstakes, developed on a national scale. But despite the introduction of new forms of betting, race-horse betting (especially off-course) remained the most popular. In 1938 turnover on football pools was only one fifth that on horse-racing, while even dog-racing was considerably more important than the pools.[2] The turnover of most other forms of entertainment increased and it is difficult to find any instance of absolute decline. Complete figures are not available but one estimate suggests that the average yearly attendances at cinemas, theatres, other shows and sporting events rose from 1,124 to 1,497 million over the period 1920–38.[3]

Rising incomes, more leisure and new forms of entertainment were the main factors responsible for boosting these trades. Shifts in tastes and habits may also have been important influences. The decline in the importance of the family and home-produced entertainment no doubt stimulated people to look outside the domestic circle for amusement. The growth of the catering trades may have been as much a response to changing social habits as to the direct impact of economic

[1] P.E.P., *The British Film Industry* (1952), p. 83.
[2] Stone and Rowe, *op. cit.*, p. 79.
[3] *ibid.*, p. 78.

factors. Dining out certainly became more popular and socially acceptable among the lower orders and the advent of the motor transport made such luxuries more practicable. The figures for consumers' expenditure give some guide to the changing pattern of tastes. It is significant for instance, that the amount spent on alcohol fell sharply from £426·5 million in 1920 to £306·4 million in 1938 (at 1938 prices),[1] whereas expenditure on entertainment and recreation rose from £195·1 million to £262·5 million over the same period, a good part of which no doubt represented a transfer of expenditure from drink. Although to some extent this probably involved a shift of expenditure from one vice to another – from drink to gambling for instance – at least the latter was somewhat more healthy from the physical point of view. Given the decline in the consumption of drink[2] and the rather bleak prospects for some, especially those in the depressed areas, it is probably not surprising that some form of relief was sought in other directions. The Royal Commission on Lotteries and Betting in the early 1930s felt that the craze for gambling was the outcome of bad social conditions. 'The drab social conditions under which many people live, and the monotony of their work create a demand for some relief by way of excitement which is sought in gambling'.[3]

The remaining services can be dealt with quite briefly. Insurance, banking and finance registered an impressive increase in numbers employed, from 346·6 thousand in 1920 to 459 thousand in 1938. Transactions of most financial institutions increased over the period though the most vigorous expansion undoubtedly occurred in building societies whose share and deposit capital rose from £82 to £717 million between 1920–38.[4] The increasing activity of these institutions merely reflected the needs of a growing economy for financial facilities, the nature of which became ever more complex as new forms of credit and insurance (e.g. hire-purchase and motor insurance) became more

[1] Per head of population this represented a drop from £7·94 in 1920–4 to £6·07 in 1935–8. Before the war per capita consumption had been as high as £11·05 per head. Stone and Rowe, *op. cit.*, pp. 110, 126.
[2] Per capita consumption had been falling since the turn of the century and was further checked by wartime restrictions.
[3] *Royal Commission on Betting and Lotteries*, Cmds 4234, 4341 (1933).
[4] T. Balogh, *Studies in Financial Organisation* (1947), pp. 88, 96. The spectacular growth in building societies was, of course, associated with the housing boom and the growth of home-ownership.

widespread. The overall growth of the financial sector was not spectacular when set against the expansion of the economy as a whole.
Numbers employed in government service also rose though the increase (27 per cent) was generally smaller than in other services. In
view of the increasing role of government in society it may seem
surprising that employment in public service did not expand faster.
But it should be remembered that State employment was still at a
fairly high level in 1920 as a result of the aftermath of the war. Thus,
for most of the 1920s the number of civilian employees at the National
level declined. It increased again in the 1930s, especially later in the
decade when defence preparations necessitated the recruitment of
more staff, though even by 1938 numbers employed were still slightly
less than in 1920. Local government employment, on the other hand,
expanded fairly steadily throughout.

8 The external account

Introduction

So far we have said very little about the external side of Britain's economic balance sheet. No study of the period would be complete, however, without some reference to the international economy and to Britain's role as trader, financier and banker in this context. A discussion of the external features of Britain's economy is particularly important in this period since conditions changed so radically from those of the pre-1914 era, and these changes had important repercussions not only on Britain but also on the international economy as a whole.

The international economic system of the late nineteenth and twentieth centuries contrasts sharply with that of post-war. Though in the two or three decades before 1914 Britain's relative importance in world trade and manufacturing was declining – an inevitable process as industrial development advanced in other countries – she remained by and large the nerve centre of the international economy right down to 1914. As a result of her pattern of economic development, that is a concentration of recources in a few large export-orientated industries and the concomitant contraction of the primary sector, Britain's prosperity was heavily dependent on foreign trade. The ratio of foreign trade to national income formed a much higher proportion than that of almost any other country and down to 1914 Britain remained the world's largest trader in manufactured goods, and the largest importer of food and industrial raw materials, while her ships carried around one half the seaborne trade of the world.

Moreover, she was by far the world's largest investor overseas – in 1913 nearly one half of the total international investments was owned by this country – and at the same time she contributed a steady stream of migrants, many of whom had acquired industrial skills, to the developing economies of other countries. In effect therefore, Britain dominated the international economic system and as a result a large part of the world's trade and financial transactions were cleared on a multilateral basis through London's financial and commercial institutions. London was the pivot of the international gold standard and the key currency, sterling, provided a very close substitute for gold. To a large extent the success of the international economic mechanism depended upon the strength of Britain, the relative absence of barriers to the flow of resources and commodities across national boundaries and to the flexible nature of prices, wages and incomes.

This of course is a somewhat idealistic picture of the working of the pre-war system. It never operated as smoothly and automatically as many contemporaries often imagined and the process by which basic disequilibria in the international system were rectified were complex and necessitated considerable intervention on the part of the authorities. For example, the successful operation of the payments system and the maintenance of the gold standard would not have been possible without the management policies of the central banks.[1]

Nevertheless, compared with the post-war period the international economic system was certainly 'an impressive going concern'.[2] Attempts to restore the old economic framework after 1918 met with only temporary success and by the early 1930s the monetary system, which had worked so well before 1914, had collapsed in ruins. The causes of the collapse are complex and will be considered in some detail later. One of the sources of strength before the war was the dominance of Britain in the international field. It is essential, therefore, to examine first how Britain's external position changed in the inter-war years and the way in which this weakened the operation of the international standard.

[1] For a brief but very useful summary of the development of the sterling system and the complexity of the adjustment process, see D. Williams, 'The Evolution of the Sterling System', in C. R. Whittlesey and J. S. G. Wilson (eds.), *Essays in Money and Banking in Honour of R. S. Sayers* (1968), esp. pp. 266–84.
[2] A. J. Brown, 'Britain in the World Economy, 1870–1914', *Yorkshire Bulletin of Economic and Social Research*, 17 (1965), p. 59.

The volume of trade

The central feature in this period was the declining importance of international trade in the British economy. In 1913 exports (excluding re-exports) formed 23·2 per cent of net national income while imports were somewhat higher at 31·1 per cent. These proportions were drastically reduced during and after the war. By 1929 the relevant proportions were 17·6 and 26·7 per cent and by the end of the 1930s (1938) they had declined even further, to 9·8 and 17·6 per cent respectively.[1] The most disturbing aspect of the British trade position was the stagnation in exports. Before the war (1900–13) the volume of exports rose by 4·2 per cent per annum, whereas in the period 1920–38 they registered a negative rate of 1·2 per cent per annum, and as high as −2·3 per cent over the years 1913–38. The rate of decline was not, of course, evenly distributed over time. The volume of exports slumped sharply during the war and in the trade recessions of 1921, 1929–32 and 1937–8, but in most of the intervening years they maintained a slow upward trend, except for a temporary interruption in 1926 as a result of the General Strike. But as Table 30 shows in no year did exports regain their 1913 level; the highest point reached was in 1929 and even then they were only just over 81 per cent of the 1913 volume. In 1921 and 1931–3 they were only around 50 per cent of the pre-war level, and even by the end of the 1930s they were still less than 60 per cent.

There are a number of reasons for the long-term stagnation in Britain's exports as distinct from the downswings experienced in recessions. During the war Britain lost many markets as a result of her inability to supply goods and as a result countries formerly dependent on British goods either sought alternative sources of supply or began to produce the goods themselves. But the underlying causes of continued stagnation must be sought elsewhere. Recent studies suggest that the two most important influences affecting Britain's export position adversely were changes in the volume of world trade and competition, while losses due to changes in the area and commodity composition of trade were relatively modest.[1] Throughout the period world trade

[1] Measured in current values.
[2] A. Maizels, *Industrial Growth and World Trade* (1963), p. 201; and H. Tyszynski, 'World Trade in Manufactured Commodities, 1899–1950', *The Manchester School*, 19 (1951).

TABLE 30   *Index numbers of the volume of exports and imports, 1919–38*

(*1913* = *100*)

| | Total exports | Coal exports | Total imports | Retained imports | | | | Manu-factures |
				Total	Food	Materials	Fuel	
1919	55·0	48·0	87·7					
1920	70·3	34·0	87·7	88·0	88·0	90·7	162·1	77·0
1921	49·5	33·6	74·1	73·5	90·8	55·2	210·5	50·5
1922	68·1	87·5	85·2	86·5	99·5	73·6	201·6	67·2
1923	74·7	108·3	92·6	96·9	114·7	73·0	218·6	83·3
1924	75·8	84·0	103·7	109·1	126·5	83·8	266·1	96·6
1925	74·7	69·2	107·4	113·1	124·3	90·3	262·9	109·8
1926	67·0	28·2	109·9	118·2	122·9	87·5	604·8	110·3
1927	76·9	69·7	112·3	121·2	127·5	91·5	380·7	123·6
1928	79·1	68·2	108·6	117·2	127·5	86·4	384·7	121·8
1929	81·3	82·1	114·8	124·2	131·8	96·3	391·9	127·6
1930	65·9	74·8	111·1	121·2	131·8	87·7	446·0	123·0
1931	50·5	58·2	113·6	124·2	143·6	82·1	418·6	126·4
1932	50·5	53·0	98·8	109·1	139·3	81·4	424·2	71·3
1933	51·6	53·2	98·8	111·1	135·0	90·7	466·9	69·0
1934	54·9	54·0	103·7	117·2	136·1	100·0	511·3	79·3
1935	59·3	52·7	104·9	118·2	135·0	101·9	529·8	82·8
1936	59·3	47·0	112·3	127·3	138·3	115·0	559·7	93·7
1937	64·8	55·0	118·5	134·3	139·3	126·2	583·9	105·2
1938	57·1	48·9	113·6	127·3	143·6	107·5	603·2	89·7

SOURCES   London and Cambridge Economic Service, *Key Statistics of the British Economy, 1900–1966*; B. R. Mitchell and P. Deane, *Abstract of British Historical Statistics* (1962), pp. 121–2; M. Fg. Scott, *A Study of United Kingdom Imports* (1963), pp. 244–5.

was less buoyant than before the war and it failed to keep pace with world production. Yet this can only explain part of the British lag. Between 1913 and 1929 for example, world trade rose in volume by 27 per cent whereas Britain's exports fell by no less than 19 per cent. On the other hand, in the subsequent period, 1929–37, when world trade declined by just over 11 per cent, Britain's exports went down by 20·3 per cent.[1] Thus although Britain fared relatively better

[1] E. Zupnick, *Britain's Postwar Dollar Problem* (1957), p. 24; P.E.P., *Britain and World Trade* (1947), p. 12.

in the 1930s than in the previous decade, on balance her performance deteriorated throughout the period. Her share of total world exports declined from 13·9 per cent in 1913 to 10·8 per cent in 1929 and 10·2 in 1937, while the relevant shares for manufactured exports were 29·9, 23·6 and 22·4 per cent respectively.[1]

It would be misleading, however, to conclude simply that the failure of British exports to keep pace with changes in world trade was due solely to an inability to compete. This was certainly an important factor but hardly does full justice to the British position. It could be argued that Britain's trade losses were greater than those of other countries because of adverse changes in patterns of demand relative to Britain's capacity to supply. For example, the industrialization of new countries and the raising of tariffs led to import substitution on the part of former customers, while demand for some products, e.g. coal, was declining because of the development of substitutes. Similarly, the concentration of exports on markets of low income primary producers would tend to damp down the growth of exports.

In these respects Britain was more vulnerable than most countries. We know that a large proportion of Britain's exports in 1913 consisted of textiles, coal and basic engineering products such as railway material and ships, all of which were declining sectors in world trade during this period. Furthermore, over two thirds of all our exports went to primary producing countries, markets which were poor both from an income and import substitution point of view. The incomes of primary producing countries were depressed, especially in the 1930s, because of falling prices, while Britain was easily the principal loser from the process of import substitution in the semi-industrial countries. Over the period 1913–37 her losses in these markets were substantially greater than those of continental Western Europe and about four-fifths greater than those of the United States. The major losses through import substitution occurred in India and Latin America and the main product affected was textiles. In 1937 Britain's textile exports to India were only about one-seventh of the 1913 volume. Import substitution losses in industrial countries occurred mainly in the 1930s as a result of tariff barriers and other restrictions

[1] Tyszynski, *loc. cit.*, pp. 277–80; A. Maddison, 'Growth and Fluctuation in the World Economy, 1870–1960', *Banca Nazionale del Lavoro Quarterly Review*, 15 (1962), p. 161.

on trade. Thus exports of manufacturers to Germany and France in 1937 were some two-fifths down on the 1929 level.[1]

Of course, it could be argued that though Britain was more vulnerable in these respects, the losses reflected certain internal weaknesses, for example the failure to adapt her export structure to changing market patterns. The predominance of staple exports obviously posed something of a handicap and rendered Britain a potentially weak exporter, especially in the 1920s. But this point should not be pressed too far. Exports of most of the newer industries rose fairly steadily in both the 1920s and 1930s and in some cases there was an improvement in competitive performance. Moreover, as time went on the structure of the export trade improved and by the end of the period there is little evidence that Britain lagged seriously behind the structural shifts in world trade.[2] In any case an export structure weighted in favour of declining sectors does not necessarily act as a drag on the performance of the expanding industries unless it can be shown that the latter were deprived of resources necessary for expansion. That the newer industries failed to compensate for the decline in staple exports can be attributed to the rather sudden contraction of the latter and the large volumes involved, and to the fact that the newer industries were less export-orientated than the older staples.

But shifts in the pattern of economic relationships of a type unfavourable to Britain were not the only reason for her substantial losses. Evidence suggests that an additional factor was the deterioration in the ability of British industry to compete in world markets. If this were not the case then it would be difficult to explain the following. Why, for example, Britain made few trade gains in the rich and expanding markets of North America and Western Europe in the 1920s. Exports to North America rose only slightly during this period while those to Europe fell by 20 per cent between 1913–29. It would be difficult to explain such losses simply by import substitution because world trade was then expanding and industrial countries were increasing their trade with each other. Why in some of her formerly strong markets Britain was being pushed out by alternative suppliers. For example, in 1913 over one half of Japan's imports were British whereas by 1929 the proportion was down to one quarter,

[1] Maizels, *op. cit.*, pp. 93, 226–31.
[2] A. E. Kahn, *Great Britain in the World Economy* (1946), p. 133; H. W. Richardson, 'The New Industries in Britain Between the Wars', *Oxford Economic Papers*, 13 (1961), p. 379.

suggesting a sharp switch to new suppliers, in this case the United States. Or again, in the three relatively rich Dominions of Australia, New Zealand and South Africa Britain's share of their imports fell from three quarters to three fifths over the period 1913–29. Finally, if Britain had been competitively strong would her share of world trade have fallen so sharply? Share losses in some sectors were only to be expected, especially in the staple industries which were affected more severely by import substitution in developing countries, and this in turn would tend to weaken the competitive strength of these industries. But in nearly every major industrial category, whether expanding, declining or stable from the point of view of world trade, Britain's share in each case declined, especially between 1913–29.

TABLE 31   *Shares of world trade gained or lost in each group by* U.K., *1913–37*

	1913–29	*1929–37*
Expanding groups		
Motor vehicles and aircraft	− 5·4	+ 5·8
Industrial equipment	− 7·2	+ 0·7
Iron and steel	−10·6	− 5·1
Electrical goods	− 1·9	+ 1·3
Stable groups		
Agricultural equipment	−14·4	+ 4·6
Chemicals	− 3·1	− 1·4
Non-ferrous metals	+ 3·5	− 1·2
Non-metalliferous materials	− 0·3	+ 1·9
Miscellaneous materials	− 0·2	+ 2·9
Metal manufactures n.e.s.	− 7·1	− 1·4
Books, films, etc.	+ 6·5	− 2·4
Declining groups		
Textiles	− 8·8	− 0·3
Drink and tobacco	+ 7·9	+ 6·6
Railways, ships	− 2·3	−17·3
Apparel	− 5·5	+ 1·6
Miscellaneous manufactures	+ 1·5	0·0
Total	− 6·3	− 1·2

SOURCE   H. Tyszynski, 'World Trade in Manufactured Commodities, 1899–1950', *The Manchester School*, 19 (1951), p. 283.

From Table 31 it can be seen that in the period before the slump Britain's share of world trade in 12 of the 16 major commodity groups declined. Losses, some of which were substantial, occurred in all the expanding groups, while two out of the four gains were in declining sectors. Price and other, non-quantitative information support the proposition that these trends were partly attributable to a decline in competitiveness. An index of export unit values (all manufactured exports) shows a value of 159 for the U.K. in 1929 (1913 = 100) compared with a weighted average of 134 for 12 major industrial countries. British export prices were higher relative to the pre-war base than those of any other country and the price disadvantage affected all the main commodity groups though it was especially pronounced in machinery, transport equipment, textiles, clothing and other manufactures.[1] British trade methods also came in for criticism during this period but since this was a perennial complaint it is difficult to know what importance to attach to it. But it was certainly an additional factor in reducing the competitive strength of British exports.[2]

Overvaluation of sterling in 1925 did not, of course, help matters on the external side though one must be wary of stressing too much the adverse effects of that policy act. It is generally accepted that the return to the pre-war parity in 1925 (that is at $4·86 to the £) overvalued the pound sterling by approximately 10 per cent. While it is hardly conceivable that a rate of exchange of 10 per cent below the old parity would have solved all Britain's economic problems in the 1920s or for that matter prevented the economic and financial crisis of the early 1930s, it has been argued recently that it 'would have provided a better basis on which to solve those problems which centred around the transition of the industrial structure from the nineteenth to the twentieth century'.[3] In particular, by fixing a lower rate Britain would have encountered any subsequent difficulties after a period of relatively faster growth and with a stronger balance of payments, and it might also have made for greater international stability by obviating the impression that in any attempts to improve her position Britain was trying to shift the balance of adjustment onto other countries. On the assumption that the sterling price elasticity of demand for imports was − 0·5 and the foreign currency price elasticity

---

[1] Maizels, *op. cit.*, pp. 509–10.
[2] P.E.P., *Report on International Trade* (1937), ch. v.
[3] D. E. Moggridge, *The Return to Gold, 1925: The Formulation of Economic Policy and its Critics* (1969), p. 79.

of demand for British exports was −1·5, Moggridge has attempted to estimate the effects on British trade and the balance of payments of an implicit appreciation of sterling of 11 per cent between 1924–5 (that is from $4·40 to $4·86 to the £), and an imaginary devaluation of 10 per cent in 1928 (that is from $4·86 to $4·38 to the £). In the first instance he finds that the balance of payments on current account would have deteriorated by roughly £80 million, while in the second it would have improved by as much as £70 million. In both cases the bulk of the change is assumed to come from the trade balance and in particular from the side of exports which, it is estimated, would have declined by 10·5 and 14·1 per cent in volume and value respectively in 1924–5, and risen by 9·0 and 13·3 in the later 1920s.[1]

While the calculations on which these estimates are based are not in dispute – though the elasticity values might be questioned[2] – it is difficult to believe that in the circumstances of the time exports or the trade balance would have changed to the extent envisaged through a 10 per cent variation in the rate either in 1928 or at the time of the appreciation. The overvaluation of sterling only raised export unit values by about 5·8 per cent and by 1928 most of the effects had worn off.[3] It is true that exports still remained uncompetitive but this was due more to unfavourable cost-price relationships in British industry and possibly to slack trading methods than to the rate of exchange. It is unlikely, for instance, that a lower rate of exchange (that is one 10 per cent lower) would have done much to boost the exports of the old staple trades since these were checked by a series of adverse factors including unfavourable long-run changes in demand. The new industries might well have received some benefit though as yet their contribution to total exports was small. In any case it should be remembered that Britain's trade difficulties were compounded by the undervaluation of the Belgian and French currencies in the later 1920s.[4] Thus any attempt by Britain to counteract the handicap by lowering the rate of exchange (or by adopting a lower

[1] For the detailed calculations, see Moggridge, pp. 91–5.
[2] There have, for instance, been several estimates, all different, of the price elasticity of demand for British exports and the range now extends from 0·5 to over 2. For a review of the work in this field see S. F. Kaliski, 'Some Recent Estimates of "the" Elasticity of Demand for British Exports—An Appraisal and Reconciliation', *The Manchester School*, 29 (1961).
[3] C. P. Kindleberger, *The Terms of Trade* (1956), pp. 97–8.
[4] R. S. Sayers, 'The Return to Gold 1925', in L. S. Pressnell (ed.), *Studies in the Industrial Revolution* (1960), p. 322.

one in the first instance) would probably have occasioned appropriate revisions in other currencies so that any benefits would have been temporary.

Moreover, at first glance the trade and payments situation of Britain in the later 1920s appears to give few grounds for alarm. Exports rose faster than production between 1926–9 and on balance export performance compared favourably with that in the years immediately prior to the return of gold when the exchanges had been free to find their own level. In addition, the current account of the balance of payments was in comfortable surplus (apart from 1926 which was an exceptional year), overseas lending continued on a considerable scale and there was little gold outflow. However, these facts do not necessarily mean that sterling was at the equilibrium rate. It can be argued that the results achieved were only made possible by tolerating a degree of under-employment of resources which damped down the demand for imports below the full employment equilibrium level, while, in addition, the relatively high interest rates attracted short-term capital inflows which helped to conceal the overvaluation.[1] It should be noted however that if this were the case then a devaluation (or a rate of 10 per cent below par) which raised exports and activity in Britain would also have raised the demand for imports. Secondly, that given the size and unusual structural spread of unemployment, the full employment rate for sterling would have had to have been very much lower than 10 per cent below the adopted parity which is generally accepted as the degree of overvaluation.[2]

The above arguments do not constitute a case for accepting the rate fixed in 1925 as the right one. Almost certainly it was not. But to assume that a rate of 10 per cent less (that is $4.38 to the £) would have solved all problems is equally untenable. A revised parity would have eased the British situation but in the circumstances a 10 per cent overvaluation was neither here nor there. It would not have made much difference to the international monetary problem nor would it have cured Britain's internal difficulties. And even if it had allowed of a more relaxed monetary policy this in itself would only have made a marginal contribution to easing the domestic situation

[1] S. E. Harris, *Exchange Depreciation* (1936), pp. 154–5; W. M. Scammell, *International Monetary Policy* (1957), p. 52; P. T. Ellsworth, *The International Economy* (3rd ed. 1964), p. 360.
[2] In fact it is difficult to conceive of a realistic full employment rate in the circumstances of the time.

for reasons which will be made clear in the next chapter. Thus perhaps the most unsatisfactory aspect of the return to gold at the pre-war parity was not the effects it had on the British economy, but the fact that it was adopted without any proper analysis of its implications and without any due consideration of possible alternative rates.

Relatively speaking, Britain's ability to compete improved in the 1930s. Gains in trade shares were made in half the major commodity groups in Table 31, notably in three of the expanding sectors, though iron and steel remained a persistent laggard. Through the years 1929–37 British export prices ran fairly closely with those of other countries, though in the early 1930s the decline was more pronounced in Britain.[1] This improvement can be attributed to a number of factors including the rather faster rate of growth in this country in the 1930s and the initial gains from the depreciation of sterling in 1931. In addition, the system of Empire preference made trading conditions easier for Britain.[2] On balance, however, Britain still remained competitively weak at the end of the period since compared with 1913 export prices were higher than those of other countries.

Overall therefore competition was the main factor responsible for Britain's poor export performance in the inter-war years. This was associated with the emergence of new competitors and new products, import substitution and a decline in Britain's ability to compete. In addition, unfavourable shifts in world demand relative to the composition of Britain's exports and the contraction in the volume of world trade in the 1930s were contributory factors. These causes were not of course mutually exclusive. Changes in the volume of world trade were partly the result of industrial development in the importing countries, while import substitution by the latter may have inflicted a loss of competitive strength on the major supplier of exports. It was inevitable that as new countries industrialized, an important exporting nation such as Britain would lose on balance. But the fact that Britain incurred such severe trade losses, especially in the 1920s when world trade was expanding steadily, suggests that some of the blame must be attributed to her declining capacity to compete.

In contrast to exports, imports remained above the pre-war level for most of the period. They were at their lowest in the recession of 1921, but then rose steadily to a level of some 15 per cent above pre-war by 1929. Imports remained on a plateau in the early years of

[1] Maizels, *op. cit.*, pp. 509–10; and Kindleberger, *op. cit.*, pp. 95, 104, 108.
[2] For external policy in the 1930s, see below.

the slump but then dropped sharply in 1932–3 after which they rose to a peak in 1937, when they exceeded the 1913 volume by 18·5 per cent (see Table 30). Generally speaking imports, as exports, moved with the cycle.

There are several reasons why the volume of imports remained fairly buoyant. A large proportion of imports consisted of food[1] the demand for which was relatively inelastic with respect to price and income changes. Thus recessions and other factors had very little effect on the volume of imports. The import restrictions imposed in the early 1930s, for example, only had a marginal long-term impact. The rising trend of imports was determined largely by the increase in population, though the rather abnormal price decline of imported foods may have led to some substitution between imported and home-produced foods, especially in the 1930s. The second main influence was the rapid rise in imported fuels. These increased in almost every year and reached a peak in 1938 (the abnormal peak of 1926 was due to the coal strike). About two thirds of the fuel imports consisted of motor and aviation spirit which accounted for four-fifths of the increase in retained imports in this category between 1924–38.[2]

As one might expect, raw materials, other than fuel, moved fairly closely with the cycle. Yet though raw materials became relatively cheaper in this period the volume of imports remained below the pre-war level until the mid 1930s after which it rose sharply. Price changes no doubt had some effect on the level of imports but this seems to have been more than offset by savings due to new techniques resulting in greater raw material economy, the substitution of new materials, the increasing use of scrap products and a shift in the pattern of output towards industries with a lower average raw material content or with less reliance on imported supplies. For example, the shift away from textile production and the increasing importance of the engineering industries would tend to reduce the demand for imported materials.

Compared with the other major groups, the demand for imported manufactured goods was much more elastic with respect to price and income changes, while imported products were often fairly close substitutes with those manufactured in Britain. Thus it is not surprising to find that imports rose fairly rapidly in the later 1920s

[1] Around 45 per cent in the 1930s. A. Robinson, 'The Changing Structure of the British Economy', *Economic Journal*, 64 (1954), p. 460.
[2] M. Fg. Scott, *A Study of United Kingdom Imports* (1962), p. 40.

and between 1935–7, when domestic activity and incomes were particularly buoyant. On the other hand, imports of manufactures rose continuously throughout the 1920s which suggests that cheaper foreign goods were being substituted for domestic production. The movements of imports in the early 1930s cannot be readily explained in terms of price and income changes. Manufactured imports remained at a high level in 1930 and 1931, and in the latter year at least this was probably due to stockpiling in order to beat the tariff.[1]

The very sharp drop in the volume of imports between 1931–3, by no less than 45 per cent, can be attributed to the tariff rather than to changes in domestic incomes or the price effects of devaluation. The fall in income was very modest in 1931–2 and it was more than offset by a sharp rise in the following year, while the price of imported manufactures in terms of sterling (excluding the tariff) actually fell.[2] The tariff could not, however, prevent a steady rise in imports of manufactures once recovery got under way, though the volume of imports remained well below that of the previous decade.

Set against the contraction in exports the rising import volume might suggest a further indication of Britain's economic weakness on the external front. She was, moreover, one of the few industrial countries whose share of world imports rose over the period as a whole.[3] But it would be wrong to argue that imports were excessive and that they should have been lower because of the poor export performance. Since imports respond largely to changes in the level of domestic activity it was only to be expected that, with rising real incomes and population, the volume of imports would be greater than in 1913. No doubt at times imports of manufactures might appear unduly large, but the overall import trend was not excessive compared with changes in domestic activity. In fact, in relation to income trends import growth was substantially lower than before the war, especially in the 1930s. Moreover, the ratio of the percentage growth of the import volume to that of G.N.P. was around 0·6 for the period 1924–

[1] T. C. Chang, *Cyclical Movements in the Balance of Payments* (1951), p. 101.
[2] See Scott, *op. cit.*, p. 169.
[3] From 15·8 per cent in 1913 to 16·8 in 1938, though there was a slight decline in the 1920s. To some extent this increase was inevitable given the heavy reliance on foreign supplies of food and raw materials, which accounted for about 80 per cent of the total import bill, and the fact that other countries took stronger measures to curb imports. Maddison, *loc. cit.*, p. 161; R. E. Baldwin, 'The Commodity Composition of World Trade: Selected Industrial Countries, 1900–1954', *Review of Economics and Statistics*, 40 (1958), p. 55.

I

37, compared with an average ratio of 0·5 for Western Europe and
1·5 for the United States and Canada.[1] Thus from the payments
point of view (though here we are speaking without reference to prices
and values) the problem was not the unusually high level of imports
but rather the failure of exports to expand to meet the importing
propensity of a growing economy.

Structure of the balance of payments

However, little can be inferred directly about the strength or weakness
of Britain's external account from the fact that the gross barter terms
of trade[2] deteriorated during the inter-war years. Favourable price
changes either on the import or export side, or both, may be sufficient
to offset adverse movements in the volume of trade. But the balance
of trade transactions will still only provide part of the picture. What
we need is a balance sheet of all the u.k.'s financial transactions
with other countries. This is provided by the balance of payments
which is a composite account of a series of different transactions the
movement in any one of which affords only a limited guide to the
state of the overall balance. The balance of payments account can be
divided into three main sections: the current or income account, the
long-term capital account and the short-term transactions or monetary
flows. The first of these comprises transactions relating to exports and
imports, the difference between the two being the balance of trade,
and invisible items or services. The two sides of the account rarely
balance; the balance of trade usually records a deficit but is more than
offset by a large net income from invisible transactions thus producing
an overall surplus on current account. The capital account records
all long-term capital transactions between Britain and the rest of the
world, including repayments and dealings in existing securities. Capital
movements often arise independently of the current account though
in the long run they will be determined by the state of the current
balance. Generally Britain has always had a surplus on current account which has been used for financing overseas investment. The
sum of the two accounts (current and capital) can be regarded as
the basic balance. This rarely balances exactly and the gap is closed

[1] In fact, in the latter half of the 1920s (1924–9) the British ratio (0·9) was
lower than those of Western Europe (1·3), the United States (2·5) and Canada
(2·1). See E. Lundberg, *Instability and Economic Growth* (1968), p. 54.
[2] That is, the volume of exports relative to the volume of imports.

by the third element, monetary movements. Thus a deficit on the basic balance caused by foreign lending exceeding the surplus earned on current account would have to be financed either by cash balances (gold or reserve outflow) or short-term borrowing (net inflow). Conversely, an overall surplus would induce equilibriating monetary movements in the opposite directions. Finally, there is the notorious balancing item representing errors, omissions and unidentified items under all headings and which serves to close any remaining gap in the balance of payments. Unfortunately, this item is often very large and this means it is difficult to say anything very precise about the role of monetary movements.

The three main components of the balance of payments will be discussed in turn. It must be stressed, however, that the data on many items is fragmentary and not altogether reliable and in some cases it is only possible to make meaningful comments on the basis of a good deal of intuitive guesswork.

The current account

It is difficult to make precise generalizations about movements in the trade balance of the current account since there were a number of relevant influences not all of which were pulling in the same direction. The unfavourable relationship between the volume of exports and imports would tend to lead to a deteriorating balance over the long-term, though this was partly offset by the improvement in the price terms on which goods were exchanged. Over the period 1913–38 the net barter terms of trade improved by 43 per cent (see Table 32) though the improvement was somewhat less for the years 1920–38. It was also very unevenly distributed over time. Much of it occurred in 1921 when the terms were almost as favourable as in the early 1930s. Thereafter they deteriorated almost continuously down to 1929, after which there was sharp improvement through to 1933. Between 1934–7 they deteriorated once more and then improved again in 1938. It will be noticed that the favourable trends in the terms occurred in recessions which implies that the trade balance would improve in the slump and deteriorate at other times. On the other hand, the income elasticities of demand for Britain's imports and exports tended to work in the opposite direction. Because we imported mainly food and raw materials in exchange for manufactured goods the elasticity of demand for exports was higher than that for imports. Thus during the slump imports would tend to fall more slowly than exports and the balance would deteriorate, while in recovery periods exports would rise faster than imports with the reverse effect on the trade balance. Before the war this appears to have been the most powerful influence since the balance of trade generally deteriorated in recessions.[1]

TABLE 32　*Import and export prices and terms of trade, 1920–38 (merchandise unit values, 1913 = 100) dollar relatives*

	Imports	Exports	Terms of trade
1920	214	270	126
1921	151	213	141
1922	138	182	132
1923	140	180	129
1924	141	173	123
1925	154	183	119
1926	142	173	122
1927	136	165	121
1928	137	162	118
1929	134	159	119
1930	117	151	129
1931	88	126	143
1932	64	91	142
1933	74	110	149
1934	93	132	142
1935	93	130	140
1936	98	135	138
1937	111	145	131
1938	103	147	143

SOURCE　R. E. Lipsey, *Price and Quantity Trends in the Foreign Trade of the United States* (N.B.E.R. 1963), p. 415.

However, there were two factors complicating the issue. First, the depreciation and tariff of 1931–2 tended to stabilize exports and reduce imports thus making for an improved balance. Second, in the slump and recovery of the 1930s British incomes fell less and then

[1] F. V. Meyer and W. A. Lewis, 'The Effects of an Overseas Slump on the British Economy', *The Manchester School*, 17 (1949), p. 237. *Cf* I. Mintz, *Trade Balances during Business Cycles: U.S. and Britain since 1880* (N.B.E.R., Occ. Paper 67, 1959), p. 41.

rose more rapidly than those of other countries. This had the effect of boosting imports relative to exports and would thus aggravate the balance.

The turn out of the balance can be seen in Table 33. The first thing to point out is that the adverse balance was much larger in monetary terms than before the war. In the three years 1911–3 the adverse balance on merchandise trade averaged £134·3 million per annum whereas it was frequently £200 million or more in the inter-war period. In other words, the long-term improvement in the terms of trade was not sufficient to offset the adverse trends in exports and imports. The limited effect of the terms can be seen if we compare the years 1925–9 with 1934–8. Despite the fact that the terms of trade improved considerably between the two periods the adverse balance was on average very similar in both cases. This can be explained by the fact that while imports held up fairly well exports dropped sharply. Second, compared with the early 1920s the balance of trade deteriorated over the period. This can hardly be explained by a deterioration in the terms of trade except perhaps in the later 1920s. However, this does not mean that changes in the trade account were wholly unaffected by shifts in the terms of trade. There was some tendency for balances to improve in depression and deteriorate in prosperity, though changes in the terms of trade were not always responsible for these movements. The balance improved in the 1921 recession though the change was fairly marginal compared with the substantial improvement in the terms. Clearly the effects of the latter were offset by the more rapid fall in incomes in Britain compared with abroad. In the following year the adverse balance was reduced substantially despite a deterioration in the terms; presumably income effects were again the dominant element since the rate of recovery was slower in Britain. On the other hand, the sharp rise in the adverse balance in 1924 and the continued large imbalance through to the end of the decade is more difficult to explain. The terms only exercised a limited influence for in this period they remained relatively stable. Moreover, the income effects should have been favourable given the more rapid rate of growth abroad than in Britain. The main problem seems to have been the failure of exports to respond to rising world incomes, while imports rose steadily in volume as a result of the increasing propensity to import manufactures and new fuels.

Three main influences were operative in the subsequent depression. Between 1929–31 the terms of trade improved sharply which would work in favour of an improved balance. Depreciation and the tariff also had a similar effect. Conversely, the slower decline in British compared to world income had an adverse effect. The income effect clearly predominated in the first two years, when the balance deteriorated appreciably. Exports, both in volume and value, fell much more than imports. In fact the volume of imports remained comparatively stable between 1929–31, and though in value they fell by 29 per cent this was quite moderate compared with a decline of 45·6 per cent in the value of exports. The adverse trend in the balance was reversed significantly in 1932. Since the terms remained stable in that year most of the swing could be attributed to the impact of depreciation and the tariff, which checked the fall in exports and caused a sharp reduction in imports. The balance improved in 1933 and again policy factors were largely responsible, though the terms also improved once more. After 1933 the income effects of British recovery and declining terms tended to lead to a worsening of the balance as imports rose faster than exports, though in 1935 there was a temporary improvement due to the rather belated recovery in exports. The position was further aggravated in 1936–7 by worsening trade terms due to the sharp rise in primary product prices. Thus by 1937 the adverse balance was higher than in any previous year barring the exceptional years of 1919 and 1926. The subsequent collapse of primary product prices in 1938 led to a favourable shift in the terms and an improvement in the balance.

An adverse balance of trade was of course nothing new. Throughout the nineteenth century the value of imports had always exceeded the value of exports but the difference between the two was more than offset by net receipts on invisibles, leaving a substantial surplus for investment overseas. There were, however, two basic differences comthan previously. As Table 33 shows, net invisible income was generally more unfavourable while the net income from services was less buoyant than previously. As Table 33 shows, net invisible income was generally lower in the 1930s compared with the previous decade while it fluctuated quite sharply with the cycle. The cyclical behaviour of invisible income is understandable. The two main components were income from shipping and financial services and returns on overseas investments, both of which were affected strongly by changes in world economic activity. Shipping and financial receipts were closely correlated with world trade while income from investments tended to be lower in times of recession, either because of default on fixed interest payments or because of a fall in the yield on equities. The generally lower level of income from services in the 1930s is quite easy to explain. First, during the early 1930s returns were generally low because of the world-wide depression. Second, shipping earnings remained low because of the depressed level of freights and the fact that British owners were losing custom to foreign fleets. Third, cheap money conditions enabled overseas borrowers to convert their loans to lower rates of interest which automatically led to a decline in returns to investors.

TABLE 33 *Balance of payments transactions of the* U.K., *1919–38* (£mn)

A. *Current Account*

	Imports	Exports and re-exports	Trade balance	Net income from invisibles	Current account balance
	(valued f.o.b.)				
	(1)	(2)	(3)	(4)	(5)
1919	1,464	963	−501	372	−128
1920	1,749	1,569	−180	415	235
1921	987	822	−165	284	119
1922	913	836	− 77	250	173
1923	996	898	− 98	267	169
1924	1,164	953	−211	282	71
1925	1,199	940	−259	306	47
1926	1,129	790	−339	324	− 15
1927	1,104	839	−265	347	82
1928	1,086	853	−233	356	123
1929	1,107	848	−259	362	103
1930	948	666	−282	210	28
1931	784	461	−323	218	−105
1932	639	422	−217	166	− 51
1933	618	422	−196	196	0
1934	681	460	−221	214	− 7
1935	721	536	−185	217	32
1936	780	520	−260	243	− 17
1937	945	606	−339	283	− 56
1938	846	562	−284	230	− 54

B. *Capital Account*

	New overseas issues[a] (6)	Repayments (7)	Other long-term movements[b] (8)	Net long-term movements (9)
1920	− 53			− 53
1921	−116			−116
1922	−135			−135
1923	−136			−136
1924	−134			−134
1925	− 88			− 88
1926	−112	27		− 85
1927	−139	34		−105
1928	−143	35		−108
1929	− 96	49		− 47
1930	− 98	39	40	− 19
1931	− 41	27	15	1
1932	− 37	48	10	21
1933	− 83	67	10	− 6
1934	− 63	42	−15	− 36
1935	− 51	81	−70	− 40
1936	− 61	107	−20	26
1937	− 60	61	10	11
1938	− 29	39	30	40

NOTES   [a] = includes refundings but excludes conversions and estimated foreign subscriptions.
[b] = estimated dealings in existing securities, direct investments, etc.

C. *Basic Balance and Monetary Movements*

	Basic balance (10)	Net gold movement (11)	Short-term capital movements (12)	Residual or balancing item (13)
1920	182	43		−225
1921	3	11		− 14
1922	38	13		− 51
1923	33	16		− 49
1924	− 63	12		51
1925	− 41	10		31

1926	− 100	− 12		112
1927	− 23	− 3		26
1928	15	− 7	23	− 31
1929	56	16	− 27	− 45
1930	9	− 5	17	− 21
1931	− 104	33	− 99	170
1932	− 30	− 17	− 100	147
1933	− 6	− 201	179	28
1934	− 43	− 142	26	159
1935	− 8	− 56	− 54	118
1936	9	− 227	129	89
1937	− 45	− 99	− 12	156
1938	− 14	74	− 137	77

SOURCES London and Cambridge Economic Service, *Key Statistics of the British Economy 1900–1966*; B.R. Mitchell and P. Deane, *Abstract of British Historical Statistics* (1962), p. 335; A. E. Kahn, *Great Britain in the World Economy* (1946), p. 126; T. C. Chang, *Cyclical Movements in the Balance of Payments* (1951), Table at p. 144.

Since the balance of trade and net income from invisibles tended to move in opposite directions over the cycle the overall balance of payments depended upon the relative strength of each item. The movement of the current account balance was somewhat varied. Until the early 1930s it deteriorated in recessions and improved in the booms though the conformity was not very marked in this respect. After 1932 there was no real pattern. The current account fluctuated during the course of recovery and deteriorated sharply near the peak of the cycle. Two features are noticeable however. The overall deterioration in the current account surplus between the 1920s and the 1930s, when it was predominantly in deficit, was due largely to the weakening of the invisible component. On the other hand, the year to year fluctuations in the balance corresponded closely to those of the merchandise balance. In every year, except 1921, the merchandise account moved in the same direction as the current account, whereas the conformity in movements between the latter and the invisible account was evident in less than half the number of years (see Table 33).

The capital account

It is more difficult to make a proper analysis of the capital side of the balance of payments because of the incomplete nature of the statistical data. The series for new overseas issues on the London market (col. 6, Table 33) provides only a very rough guide to the net long-term capital movements. Up to 1928 it is based on data compiled by the Midland Bank which excluded conversion issues, refundings and foreign subscriptions to new issues. From 1929 Sir Robert Kindersley adjusted the series to take account of refundings and the portion of issues taken up by foreigners, though no allowance was made for conversions. Moreover, until 1926 there is no reliable information on repayments, while estimates for dealings in existing securities and direct investments only begin in 1930. Thus for most of the 1920s at least the data on long-term capital transactions are very fragmentary with the result that many of the errors and omissions are inevitably included in the residual element of the accounts.

The long-term decline in foreign investment is evident from the figures in Table 33. During the 1920s it held up fairly well though at a lower level than pre-war. New overseas issues averaged £115 million a year between 1920–29[1] compared with £200 million in the years immediately prior to the war. This rate of investment was barely sufficient to maintain the pre-war stock of overseas assets which amounted to about £4,000 million. When allowance is made for repayments and other unidentified items, the loss of overseas assets during the war,[2] and the revaluation of holdings, the total stock of foreign investments by 1929–30 was probably in the region of £3,7–3,800 million.[3] After 1929 new overseas issues dropped to about half their former level averaging about £58 million a year between 1930–8. In 1932 and again between 1935–8 repayments exceeded new issues and there was a net inflow on capital account. In fact, on average, the net flow of capital was inward during the 1930s and by the end of the decade Britain's overseas investments were around £3,700 million.

Alongside this decline in investment there was a marked shift in the geographical distribution of the new investments. Overseas investment became much less important relative to home investment. Of the new issues floated in London between 1911–13 almost 80 per

[1] If data for all items were available the net capital outflow would probably be less.

[2] Estimates of war-time losses vary a great deal, ranging from £400 to £1000 million. Probably about 10–15 per cent of total investments or £400 to £600 million were realized. See Kahn, *op. cit.*, p. 137; and E. V. Morgan, *Studies in British Financial Policy, 1914–25* (1952), p. 331.

[3] Royal Institute of International Affairs, *The Problem of International Investment* (1937), p. 142.

cent were on overseas account and the remainder for u.k. domestic purposes. By 1934–8 the distribution had been completely reversed; just over 82 per cent of the new issues were on account of domestic requirements compared with 18 per cent for overseas borrowers. At the same time there was a sharp swing away from foreign and towards Empire investment. Before the war non-Empire investment accounted for 45·4 per cent of all issues and Empire for 34·7 per cent. By the 1930s issues on foreign account had almost dried up; they formed a mere 2·4 per cent of the total while Empire issues, though much reduced, accounted for 15·3 per cent of all issues.[1]

There are several explanations of the changed volume and pattern of British lending abroad. The primary cause must be the fact that the surplus on current account was insufficient to support a volume of lending of pre-war dimensions. Though for much of the 1920s the current account yielded a substantial surplus it averaged £111 million a year as against £206 million in the years 1911–13. This represented a decline of 46 per cent in monetary terms and considerably more in real terms. Thus throughout the 1920s the overall surplus was slightly less than the amount invested abroad and in the four years 1924–7, when the basic balance was in deficit, the excess investment had to be financed by short-term monetary inflows. For most of the 1930s the current account was in deficit and any new borrowings had to be financed by repayments of capital, the sale of securities and/or by short-term borrowings.

But the weakness of the current account was not the only reason for the reduced volume of lending. The potential strain on the balance of payments might have been greater had other factors not reduced the incentive to invest abroad. For one thing the unofficial embargo on foreign loans in the early 1920s and the more stringent control in the following decade limited the scope for foreign borrowing. Second, international economic conditions were much less favourable for large scale overseas investment than before 1914. Currency disorganization, especially in Europe, hampered lending in the early 1920s, while depression, currency problems, defaulting, and restrictive economic policies served to discourage overseas investors in the 1930s. Third, foreign borrowers were deterred from floating issues in London during the 1920s because of the relatively high interest rates charged compared with those in New York. In every year between 1922–29 it was cheaper by $\frac{1}{2}$ to $1\frac{1}{2}$ per cent for foreign loans to be raised in the

[1] Kahn, *op. cit.*, p. 139.

United States rather than in Britain.[1] Effectively the United States was by far and away the largest foreign lender in this period and her total overseas investments rose from £513 million in 1913 to £3,018 million in 1929. Fourth, home investment became steadily more attractive relative to foreign investment during these years. This was especially so in the 1930s since the collapse of the export trades ensured that recovery was based on industries producing primarily for the domestic market. The difference between the yields on all foreign securities and those on gilt edged declined significantly. The differential of two per cent in favour of foreign securities which had prevailed before the war was rarely attained in the inter-war years, and in the period 1929–33 the differences were 1·6, 1·1, 0·2, 0·6 and 0·9 per cent. Such differential yields were barely sufficient to cover the extra risk involved especially in the uncertain conditions of the 1930s.[2] Finally, the savings of those most likely to invest abroad, that is the rentier class, were being whittled away by increasing taxation, shifts in the distribution of income and lower returns on equity investments and on overseas investments.[3]

The switch towards Empire as opposed to foreign securities is not difficult to understand in the circumstances of the inter-war period. It reflected the increasing interest in Imperial contacts, a movement which in itself was a response to the more difficult trading conditions experienced in foreign countries especially in the 1930s. The links between the Empire and Britain became noticeably stronger with the granting of Imperial preference in 1932. Moreover, Empire countries provided a much safer haven for investors' funds than foreign countries, while the fact their securities were accorded trustee status (under the Colonial Stock Acts, 1877–1934) meant that the Dominions and the Colonies were able to borrow more cheaply in London than would otherwise have been the case.

The basic balance and monetary movements

The basic balance is derived from the sum of the current and capital accounts. One would expect some sort of correspondence between movements in the two sides of the account otherwise the balance of

[1] *The Problem of International Investment*, p. 137.
[2] *ibid.*, pp. 137–8.
[3] Kahn, *op. cit.*, p. 138 and ch. 10.

payments would be permanently in surplus or deficit. Thus when the current account is in surplus it is reasonable to expect an outward movement of capital and vice versa. During the 1920s, for example, there was a sizeable surplus on the income account which was almost sufficient to cover the outward movement of capital. When the surplus dried up in the following decade the rate of new lending dropped sharply and in a number of years the net movement of capital was in the reverse direction. On the other hand, it was unusual for the accounts to balance precisely in any one year or for that matter over a period of years. Sometimes, as in 1926 and 1931, the basic imbalance was very large, while the annual swings were sometimes considerable.

The reason for these discrepancies are fairly obvious. Certain leads and lags are involved on either side which make it difficult to achieve balance at any point in time. Also the imprecise nature of the statistics gives plenty of scope for discrepancy and the large residual or balancing item contains many of the errors and omissions. But these factors apart, it is normal for temporary discrepancies between the income and capital accounts to be closed by movements of gold or short-term capital. Thus when the basic balance moves from surplus to deficit gold or currency reserves would be exported and short-term capital imported (or both may occur simultaneously), while when the balance moves the other way the direction of gold and short-term funds would be reversed.

The question is how far did gold and short-term capital act as equilibriating forces to the basic balance during this period. The inadequate nature of the statistics makes a precise analysis of their roles very difficult indeed. There is no continuous series for short-term capital movements before 1928 and even after that year the data are far from perfect. The residual item does of course include certain unidentified short-term capital movements but since it also contains errors and omissions from other series it is not very useful for identifying capital flows. Fortunately, the figures for net gold movements are reasonably accurate so that it is possible to say something about the forces making for equilibrium.

From the figures in Table 33 it is fairly clear that up to the collapse of the gold standard in 1931, gold movements did not act as an equilibriating device. Gold flows were very small in relation to changes in the basic balance and the direction of the changes was very random. When the balance was positive gold tended to be moving out of Britain and vice versa. Only in five of the 12 years (1924, 1925, 1928, 1930, and 1931) did gold move in an equilibriating fashion and in three of these the magnitude of the changes was too small to be classed as a significant balancing item. It seems safe to assume, therefore, that short-term capital closed the gaps in the balance of payments during these years. It seems fairly certain, for instance, that capital imports were quite large (probably £150 million or more) between 1924–7, that is when the basic balance was in deficit, and that these funds were attracted by the relatively higher short-term rates of interest in Britain compared with elsewhere.[1] Conversely, in the early 1920s and again in 1929 short-term capital probably flowed out in response to a positive basic balance. On the other hand, in 1928 and 1930 a positive balance was accompanied by an inflow of short-term funds while the large outflow in 1931 was actively disequilibriating in view of the large deficit on the basic account. However, the position in 1931, and to a lesser extent in 1930, was complicated by excessive movement of funds as a result of the financial crisis which will be discussed more fully below.

There is little evidence that either gold or capital movements played a significantly equilibriating role in the 1930s. The movements were so large in relation to the balance that it is clear that they were not determined primarily by the need to close the accounts. Gold was imported in large quantities in every year except 1938, while if we add in the residual item there was a continuous inflow of short-term capital over the same period (see Table 33). Since there was fairly close reciprocal agreement between the two series gold and short-term capital movements offset each other and the balance of payments equilibriating mechanism was only of minor importance in influencing such movements. The influx was determined partly by recovery and the return of confidence in Britain and the desire of foreigners to find a safe depository for their funds rather than the attraction of high rates of interest. An additional factor was the steady growth of sterling balances in London held by Empire countries. Of course, this influx of funds did not indicate a strengthening of the balance of payments position, rather the opposite, since the flows could easily be reversed, as in 1938, when the pound came under pressure. Fortunately however, the working of the Exchange Equalization Account prevented these funds from affecting the course of recovery.

[1] Chang, *op. cit.*, pp. 134–6.

The 1931 crisis and the collapse of gold

From the trends in the balance of payments outlined above it is clear that Britain's external position was weakened considerably in this period, especially in the 1930s. On the other hand, though Britain's position was weaker in the 1920s than before 1914 the current account remained in surplus and capital continued to be exported on a considerable scale. It was not until 1931 that the income account registered a substantial deficit, an adverse swing of £200 million having taken place between 1929 and the year of crisis. But this adverse balance was not the main cause of the crisis. Certainly it aggravated the position since it helped to undermine confidence in Britain's economic position, but the immediate cause of the crisis was the problem of short-term liquidity. On the other hand, the collapse of the international monetary system is only really intelligible in the light of the long-term factors which undermined its operation.

The events leading up to the crisis have already been outlined in some detail and only the salient features need be recounted here.[1] The beginning of the pressure on international liquidity really began in the late 1920s when the primary producing countries were faced with falling prices and incomes due to overproduction and stockpiling. As a result these countries ran into balance of payments difficulties. Agricultural prices fell by about 50 per cent between late 1929 and mid 1931 and the primary producers, most of them debtor countries, were faced with large payments deficits and an outflow of funds. Demand for accommodation from the main creditor countries was not forthcoming however. The flow of funds, both on long and short-term account from the two main creditors, the u.s.a. and France, slackened in 1928–9 and by 1930 both these countries had become capital importers, while London was not in a strong enough position to grant accommodation on a sufficient scale. The failure of the creditors to render assistance meant that many primary producers were forced to leave the gold standard and devalue their currencies. By 1930 six Latin America countries, Canada, Australia and New Zealand had abandoned gold.

It is possible that the crisis might have been checked had the creditor

[1] See the excellent articles by D. Williams, 'London and the 1931 Financial Crisis', *Economic History Review*, 15 (1962–3), and 'The 1931 Financial Crisis', *Yorkshire Bulletin of Economic and Social Research*, 15 (1963).

countries been more willing to assist the primary producers at the onset of their difficulties in the late 1920s. But by the spring of 1930 the situation was beyond repair. By then the deflationary process had spread to Europe and America and with falling incomes, unbalanced budgets, balance of payments deficits and internal monetary difficulties, the reaction of governments was to pursue deflationary policies which only aggravated the situation. In these circumstances there was little prospect of the debtor countries finding accommodation. Moreover, the situation was exacerbated by a wave of bank crises in the u.s.a. and Europe. In America alone 1,345 banks collapsed in 1930 and a further 687 folded up in the first half of 1931. During the latter half of 1930 and in 1931 the banking crisis spread to Europe culminating in the failure of the Credit Anstalt and the collapse of the German banking system in the summer of 1931. The crises enormously increased the demand for liquidity and the bulk of the strain fell on London as one of the few places still willing to grant accommodation. Between June 1930 and December 1931 London lost £350 million of foreign funds, and the outflow reached panic proportions in the summer of 1931 when something like £200 million left the country.[1] This rapid rate of withdrawal was largely occasioned by the continental financial crisis, but the position was undoubtedly aggravated by the loss of confidence in Britain's ability to maintain solvency as her payments position deteriorated and in the light of the unfavourable short-term liquidity position. In the circumstances there seemed to be little else to do but release the existing parity of sterling and so on 21 September 1931 Britain officially went off gold.

It has been suggested that the Bank of England's policy was weak and ineffective during the crisis and that this only served to undermine confidence. No attempt, for instance, was made to push up interest rates to attract funds to strengthen Britain's position. It seems very unlikely that Britain could have handled the crisis single-handed and the prospects of her preventing the collapse of the monetary system were remote. Though the liquidity panic was the immediate cause of collapse it must be recognized that there were several long-term forces working to undermine the international gold standard. Given these it was almost inevitable that sooner or later the system would disintegrate.

The reasons for the successful working of the standard before 1914

[1] That is, 13 July to the collapse of sterling. S. V. O. Clarke, *Central Bank Co-operation, 1924-31* (1967), p. 216.

are fairly obvious. To a large extent the strength of the system lay in the fact that it was managed primarily by one strong financial centre, London. Sterling and gold were virtually inter-changeable and as Scammell has pointed out this gave to the Bank of England 'not only the role of regulator of the British monetary system but, in great part, that of regulator of the gold standard and the international payments system'.[1] The main aim of the monetary authorities was to maintain convertibility of the currency and preserve the relationship between gold reserves and the quantity of money. Thus if gold flowed out in response say to a deficit on the balance of payments the Bank would raise its rate and restrict credit and through the price and income adjustment process the outflow would be checked or reversed.[2] Conversely, if gold flowed into Britain the measures were put into reverse. In effect the success of the operation depended upon the flexibility of prices in response to gold movements. Moreover, it was also dependent on support from abroad in that the main gold standard countries observed similar procedures when faced with a gold inflow or efflux.[3] In addition, the operation of the system was facilitated

---

[1] W. M. Scammell, 'The Working of the Gold Standard', *Yorkshire Bulletin of Economic and Social Research*, 17 (1965), p. 33. *Cf* W. A. Morton, *British Finance, 1930–1940*, (1943), p. 18.

[2] Very often a change in the Bank rate was sufficient to check the drain. Moreover, if gold losses occurred as a result of a fall in exports this in itself set in motion equilibrating forces. A fall in exports would reduce domestic incomes and this in turn would reduce the demand for imports and hence check the gold loss. A similar adjustment process would take place if the gold loss occurred through a sudden increase in imports.

It should be pointed out, however, that the classicists regarded the adjustment of demand and supply to price changes as the chief factor making for a restoration of equilibrium to the balance of payments once it had been disturbed. They were not unaware that differential income changes might influence the demand for imports and exports and hence assist in the adjustment process, but they regarded such influences as playing a subsidiary role compared with variations in price. The classical economists also assumed, though wrongly, that the adjustment process had few adverse effects on output and employment.

[3] There is some difference of opinion on this matter. Bloomfield has questioned the degree of co-operation involved between the main monetary authorities and doubts whether the 'rules of the game' were ever explicitly formulated by central banks. 'The success of the classical gold standard seems to have been attributable . . . primarily to a combination of unusually favourable institutional circumstances rather than adherence to any specific code of rules of central banking behaviour'. Of course, much depends on how one defines the rules. If not explicitly stated central bankers certainly implicitly followed certain procedures, the most obvious being that primary consideration was given to maintaining convertibility and

by London's ability to continue lending abroad in times of financial stringency and this in turn depended upon her almost impregnable position as a short-term creditor.[1] Many other factors also contributed to the success of the system. The world economy was generally expansionist, there were few serious financial or banking crises and confidence in the financial strength of London and sterling remained unquestioned.

The differences between the pre-war and post-war monetary system were many and varied and the climate within which it operated were very different. In the first place, it was not a full gold standard that was re-established in the 1920s. Gold coins disappeared from internal use and the new standard was a gold bullion one. But not all countries adopted even this limited form. Many countries, through lack of gold reserves and other factors, were forced on to a gold exchange standard. This meant they held as part of their legal reserves against their note issues, obligations payable at sight in terms of foreign currencies which were legally convertible into gold. The big drawback to this system was that more than one currency was built on the common foundation of a convertible currency and in the event of crisis in one country a whole series of currencies might be affected.

The second main problem was that of short-term liquidity. As the importance of the relation between reserves and internal liabilities diminished that between reserves and external liabilities at short-term became much more vital. Government and other fixed interest bearing international debts had vastly increased and the international pool of short-term funds was much more mobile than before the war.[2] Had attempts been made to ascertain the exact volume of these short-term

---

that when gold moved in or out appropriate action was taken. Moreover, in the passive sense of avoiding offsetting action of gold drains and acquisitions on commercial bank reserves the 'rules' were followed. On the other hand, if a wider interpretation of the rules is taken to include action by the central banks to reinforce the effects of reserve movements on the domestic credit base, then clearly they were not adhered to either before or after 1914. A. I. Bloomfield, *Monetary Policy Under the International Gold Standard* (1959); *'Rules of the Game of International Adjustment'*, in G. R. Whittlesey and J. S. G. Wilson (eds.), *Essays in Money and Banking in Honour of R. S. Sayers* (1968), pp. 27–30.

[1] Williams, *Economic History Review*, p. 515. For the role of short-term funds in the adjustment process see D. Williams, 'The Evolution of the Sterling System', in Whittlesey and Wilson, *op. cit.*, pp. 277–80.

[2] Royal Institute of International Affairs, *The Future of Monetary Policy* (1935), p. 127.

liabilities a clearer idea would have been gained of the strength and weakness of various currencies.

It is now apparent that Britain's short-term creditor position was much weaker than contemporaries realized. Before the war Britain's liquid assets (mainly gold and sterling acceptances on foreign account) had been well in excess of her short-term liabilities. A contraction of £250 to £300 million in her stock of short-term assets left Britain a net debtor on short-term account at the end of the war. During the 1920s liabilities tended to increase as Britain became a depository for foreign balances. Unfortunately, liquid assets were not increased correspondingly, while some of the short-term funds were used for long-term investment and were therefore difficult to realize at short notice. Thus by June 1930 short-term liabilities were more than double our liquid assets.[1] Estimates vary as to the exact position but it appears that gross liabilities were in the region of £760 million while short-term foreign assets stood at £176 and gold reserves at £156 million, giving a net liability of around £430 million.[2] This position was alright so long as confidence in London was maintained and there was no panic withdrawal of funds. But once the demand for liquidity increased and foreign balances were withdrawn as in 1930–31, London was unable to withstand the strain without either depletion of the reserves, the realization of short-term assets or further borrowing abroad. But all three solutions entailed certain difficulties. The depletion of the gold reserves would only have reduced confidence further and would probably have led to an earlier collapse of sterling. In any case, the Bank of England's reserves (mainly gold and foreign exchange) were only sufficient to offset part of the liabilities since part of the gold reserve was earmarked as backing to the domestic note issue, while recourse to special measures to release additional reserves to support the currency were more likely to aggravate than alleviate market fears and uncertainties.[3] The realization of Britain's short-term assets abroad was rendered very difficult owing to the fact that many of them were locked up in European financial centres which

[1] For a more detailed examination of the causes of these developments, see C. P. Kindleberger, *International Short-term Capital Movements* (1937, 1965 reprint), pp. 126–32.
[2] Williams, *Econ. Hist. Review*, p. 528; *Report of the Committee on Finance and Industry*, pp. 112, 302; Morton, *op. cit.*, p. 35; R.I.I.A., *The Problem of International Investment* (1937), pp. 340–1.
[3] Liabilities were some three times the Bank's free reserve in 1928. Clarke, *op. cit.*, pp. 141, 183.

were themselves in an illiquid state. The only other solution was to borrow abroad to cover the outflow of funds. Since most countries were experiencing financial difficulties this was easier said than done, though in the last stage of the crisis (August–September) some £130 million worth of credits were scraped up in New York and Paris.[1] 'It was this inability to either retain previously invested funds in London or to attract further investment by foreigners that was the root cause of London's short-term difficulties'.[2] Williams suggests that had the Bank raised its discount rate early in 1931 the position might have been eased. The assumption here is that higher interest rates would have attracted funds to London and/or prevented existing funds from leaving. It is doubtful, however, whether this would really have solved the problem. The loss of confidence and the severity of the liquidity panic were so great that it is unlikely that much could have been done to retrieve the situation.[3] In any case, raising the Bank rate would probably only have increased the distrust in sterling. On the other hand, it is not altogether clear why the Bank did not resort to the traditional remedy of dealing with a drain of reserves. Possibly the awareness that higher interest would make the domestic situation even worse prevented the Bank from taking a stronger line.[4] During the course of the 1920s the use of the interest rate weapon as a flexible instrument to control the exchanges had been circumscribed in part by domestic considertions and it was becoming clear that the twin goals of domestic and external stability could not be pursued simultaneously. One had to go and in the end it was the gold standard. Devaluation, however distasteful to the authorities, was preferable to further doses of deflation necessary to secure adjustment under the gold standard.[5]

Even had Britain's short-term position been stronger it is doubtful whether she would have been able to hold the international monetary

[1] However, they were insufficient to hold the situation and their effect was weakened by the fact that they were made in two separate tranches instead of one single package, the second of which was not arranged until the first had been exhausted. Clarke, *op. cit.*, p. 204.
[2] Williams, *Economic History Review*, p. 522.
[3] According to Clarke sterling was beyond salvation whatever measures had been adopted. Clarke, *op. cit.*, p. 204.
[4] See Morton, *op. cit.*, p. 44.
[5] It is somewhat ironic that when gold had gone Bank rate was raised to six per cent as a gesture of reassurance and to prevent inflation! See A. Feavearyear, *The Pound Sterling* (1963, rev. ed. by E. V. Morgan), p. 366.

system together for much longer. The restored standard contained the seeds of its own destruction. The conditions in which it operated and the way it was re-established were quite different from those before the war. The new gold standard did not evolve, as before 1914, under conditions favourable to its development but was forced back into play by authorities determined to return to what they regarded as 'normalcy'. The struggle to get back onto gold is evidenced by the time taken to make the necessary adjustments and stabilize the currencies after the early post-war disorders. Thus it was not until the middle of the 1920s, or even after, that most countries could claim to be back on gold in some form or other. Moreover, a number of important countries returned to gold at parities out of line with their existing level of costs and prices. The most notable examples were the overvaluation of sterling and the undervaluation of the Belgian and French currencies. Three important countries with wrong parities were enough to impose a strain on the system apart from other complicating factors.

Nor was the system managed in the same way. No one would deny that the pre-war gold standard required a certain amount of management even though there might be debate as to the precise rules of the game. Moreover, Britain was clearly the leading participant in this respect. The weakening of Britain's financial strength during and after the war and the rise of New York and Paris as important financial centres transformed the situation. These two centres competed with London for the employment of funds the flow of which 'ceased to be under any single, centralized control.'[1]

The dispersal of control was not in itself fatal to the successful operation of the new standard. If the main centres had been more prepared to co-operate and manage the system on pre-war lines things might have worked out more smoothly. But the emergence of new financial centres tended to lead to competition at the very time when conditions could least stand it. A co-ordinated policy would have required that countries losing gold or reserves raise their discount rates to check the outflow and that countries in surplus should reduce theirs or take other measures to check the influx, but there is little evidence that policies were co-ordinated consistently in this way. The Macmillan Committee in their report noted that movements of gold had ceased to have what used to be considered their 'normal' effect on the domestic credit policies of certain countries, notably France

[1] E. Nevin, *The Mechanism of Cheap Money* (1955), p. 15.

and the United States.[1] The system demanded, moreover, that creditor countries should reinject their surpluses into the world economy either by investment or loans, as Britain had done before 1914, so that the payments system was not immobilized through lack of capital. But the two largest creditors, America and France, failed to follow policies conducive to the smooth operation of the payments system. Though American overseas investment was on a considerable scale in the 1920s most of it went to Europe and was used either to finance reparation payments, as in the case of Germany, or was used in a way which did little to increase the foreign exchange earnings of the borrowing countries. High American tariffs also made it difficult for debtor countries to pay off their debts in the form of goods. French investment tended to be dominated by political motives; much of it was of a short-term nature and liable to be recalled and converted into gold at short notice. Moreover, neither country was prepared to continue lending when conditions in the debtor countries became difficult in the late 1920s.

In effect therefore, American and French policies were inconsistent with the gold standard. Their desire for liquidity drained the system of gold at a time when there was increasing need for greater liquidity because of the much larger volume of international short-term indebtedness. In the three or four years before the crash France employed virtually the whole of her international surplus in the purchase of gold and short-term liquid claims and her gold stock more than doubled. The gold reserves of the main creditor countries rose rapidly in the 1920s, especially in the latter half of that decade, and by 1930 eight countries held 82 per cent of the world's stock while nearly 70 per cent of that amount was owned by France and America.[2] France, moreover, was the largest short-term creditor in the world. Thus in view of their strength France and America were in the best position to alleviate the crisis. Yet when it came to the crunch their policies merely accentuated the difficulties. Britain was left to handle the affair almost single-handed and given her weakened position there was little hope of her being able to restore equilibrium.

That France and the United States followed policies which were inconsistent with the maintenance of the gold standard is partly understandable. Neither country had had the experience of Britain

[1] *Report of the Committee on Finance and Industry* (1931), p. 69.
[2] Though for a view which plays down the adverse effects of the maldistribution of gold, see Morton, *op. cit.*, ch. vii.

in managing the payments system and neither was prepared to sacrifice internal stability to shore up a system which they had not created in the first place. Since even Britain was not prepared to concede complete priority to external equilibrium it was hardly to be expected that other countries would be prepared to do so. This conflict between domestic and external equilibrium had only arisen occasionally and in a comparatively mild form before the war, though even then the Bank was not entirely unmindful of the domestic impact of its external policy.[1] But in the post-war period this conflict became chronic and in 1931 it was critical.[2] Thus although in some respects there might have been a greater degree of co-ordination among central bankers in this period, this was insufficient to offset the effects of the growing weight attached by central banks to domestic policy objectives. And in any case these co-operative efforts were 'wholly inadequate to sustain the gold standard in the face of the underlying disequilibria and major institutional changes of the 1920s that were fundamentally responsible for its collapse'.[3] On the other hand, had the authorities been prepared to give pride of place to external equilibrium they would have found it increasingly difficult to effect adjustments through prices and incomes as occurred before 1914. The increasing inflexibility of prices and wages, due largely to the growth of organized labour and price-fixing associations,[4] removed yet another of the favourable factors which facilitated the working of the system before the war. This meant that instead of adjustments being made through prices and incomes they were made more through changes in the level of employment. The authorities were prepared to go only so far in this direction and in the final analysis they preferred to abandon gold altogether.

In sum, therefore, the dice were loaded heavily against the post-war gold standard. The conditions under which it worked and the way in which it was operated were so different from those obtaining before 1914 that its downfall was only a matter of time. That it came when it did can be attributed to the development of the liquidity crisis. But this short-term problem merely exposed the inherent long-term weak-

[1] See Scammell, *loc. cit.*, p. 41.
[2] Feavearyear, *op. cit.*, p. 361.
[3] Bloomfield, 'Rules of the Game', p. 31.
[4] Nevin appears to lay considerable stress on this point. It should not be pressed too far however, since there is some doubt as to how inflexible prices and wages had become. See Chapter 10.

nesses of the international monetary system and exerted pressures which that system was not capable of withstanding.

Aftermath of the crisis

The crisis of 1931 left its mark on the world economy. Most countries eventually abandoned gold and devalued their currencies. Economic policies were no longer geared to external equilibrium; domestic recovery now became the prime objective of economic policy. To shield domestic economies from external influences a battery of restrictions was employed including tariffs, import quotas, exchange controls and special devices to iron out fluctuations in the exchanges. The pre-1914 system of multilateral trade and payments and the free flows of commodities and capital was finally at an end. Instead nationalistic economic policies and managed currencies became the order of the day. The finishing touch to the old system came with the breakdown of the World Economic Conference in 1933 which effectively 'signalized the end of any general attempts at international action in the economic field during the inter-war period'.[1]

Although British policy in the 1930s was not nearly so autarchic as in some countries, e.g. Germany, the pattern of development, especially on the external side, was very similar. Sterling was devalued in 1931, an embargo was placed on foreign lending, fluctuations in the exchanges were taken care of by the Exchange Equalization Account,[2] and tariffs and to a lesser extent quotas, were used to shut out imports. By and large it was natural forces rather than policy factors which were responsible for recovery. Domestic policy was confined largely to cheap money and certain specific measures, e.g. Special Areas legislation and rationalization schemes, the impact of which was fairly marginal.[3] On the external side the changes constituted a marked departure from established practice but again the effects were relatively slight. The two most important policy items were devaluation and the tariff, the results of which are discussed below.

Devaluation of the pound

The freeing of the exchanges was not a policy measure designed specifically to foster domestic recovery but it obviously had important

[1] H. W. Arndt, *The Economic Lessons of the Nineteen-Thirties* (1944), p. 242.
[2] For details, see Chapter 9.
[3] Domestic policy is discussed in Chapter 9.

implications for the economy as a whole. In view of the magnitude of the depreciation – some 30 per cent expressed in terms of gold or non-depreciated currencies – and its potential importance at the time, that is coming after a period when the exchange had been over-valued and at the bottom of an externally generated slump, it is surprising that there has been relatively little systematic study of its repercussions.[1] Given this neglect there seems to be some justification for spending a little space on analysing its implications though we shall not be able to cover the territory fully in this exercise.

It is important first of all to determine the likely effects of devaluation. Stated briefly, a devaluation would normally be expected to improve a country's economic health.[2] A devaluing country should secure a competitive advantage in international trade since export prices fall in terms of foreign currency while import prices rise in terms of domestic currency.[3] These price effects should induce a rise in exports and check imports which will stimulate domestic activity. The second main effect is likely to be an improvement in the trade balance and the balance of payments, principally through greater exports and less imports. Thirdly, in a deflationary setting devaluation should bring some relief from deflationary pressures; prices will fall less or rise relative to those elsewhere and this will produce a more favourable price-cost structure. In particular, the freeing of the exchanges will boost exports and make it easier to follow expansionary policies which will raise domestic activity and strengthen the upward movement in prices.

The successful work-out of a devaluation along these lines will of course depend on certain conditions being fulfilled. Preferably competitive devaluation should not occur abroad. If other major currencies are devalued at a similar point in time and by roughly the same magnitude then the comparative advantage for the country initially devaluing will be severely reduced if not completely wiped out. Secondly, for the volume of exports to be raised significantly the elasticity

[1] The 1931 devaluation is frequently cited example-wise in the literature on international economics but its effects are rarely analysed in depth. Probably still the most extensive and thorough study of the British and other devaluations is S. E. Harris, *Exchange Depreciation* (1936).
[2] I say normally, since certain conditions must hold if devaluation is to be effective (see below).
[3] Export prices in terms of domestic currency remain unchanged as do import prices expressed in foreign currency. This of course assumes a *ceteris paribus* situation.

of demand for exports should be relatively high. The position with regard to the balance of trade and payments is more complex. In order for the balance of trade to improve the price elasticities of demand for exports and imports must be favourable. If the depreciation is to be effective the amount received by the devaluing country for its exports must be raised or held constant and the payment for its imports reduced (in terms of foreign currency). Since depreciation lowers export prices in terms of foreign currency the price elasticity of demand for exports must be equal to or greater than one in order to maintain or increase the former level of exchange earnings. Conversely, since import prices in foreign currency remained unchanged, at least initially, then an elasticity of demand for imports of anything above zero will reduce the demand for imports and lower the foreign currency import bill.[1] It follows therefore that if the sum of the elasticities of demand for exports and imports is greater than unity the balance of payments will improve, while if less than one it will deteriorate. This condition assumes that supply elasticities are fairly high and that the deficit in the balance of payments is not large.[2] The larger the deficit the higher will need to be the elasticities to rectify the imbalance.

Even if these conditions hold the improvement may be offset by other factors. If the devaluing country is an important world trader then other countries may take exception to its action and retaliate, not necessarily by devaluing themselves, but by increasing restrictions on imports which will reduce the scope for the devaluing country to push its exports. Alternatively, exporters may adjust their prices and thereby offset in part the price effects of devaluation. For example, domestic exporters may take advantage of the situation and raise their prices while foreign exporters may absorb part of the unfavourable currency exchange by lowering prices.[3] Furthermore, the income effects must be considered. Assuming that devaluation raises exports relative to those of the rest of the world then incomes will rise faster than elsewhere. Now if the devaluing country has a relatively high marginal propensity to import part of the rise in income will spill over into imports which will offset in part the decline in imports

---

[1] The same results can be obtained by working through in the domestic currency.

[2] If the sum of the elasticities is less than one then appreciation of the currency will improve the balance. It is possible however for the balance to improve even with an elasticity sum of less than unity providing the supply elasticities of exports or imports are very low.

[3] The effects of such action will depend upon the size of the elasticities.

brought about by the price effect. Generally speaking such income changes will dampen the balance of payments effect of exchange rate adjustments but they will not eliminate it altogether.[1] Apart from these secondary income changes, income elasticities of demand for exports and imports may be particularly relevant to the consideration of trade movements at times when incomes are rising or falling rapidly at varying rates in different countries, since they may offset or even wipe out the price effects of exchange rate adjustments.

Clearly the results of devaluation will depend upon the interaction of many factors though in most cases one would expect it to lead to some comparative gain. Apart from the general considerations listed above, which are relevant to most devaluations, an assessment of the British devaluation of 1931 is complicated by the unusual circumstances in which it occurred. It took place near the bottom of a depression when export and import prices, especially the latter, were falling rapidly and when incomes abroad were falling faster than in Britain. It was accompanied soon after by tariff protection and by increasing tariffs and trade restrictions in other countries. These factors obviously complicate the assessment of the impact of devaluation.

Other considerations apart, one would expect some benefits from devaluation given the fact that the pound had previously been over-valued. But the advantages, such as they were, were very soon whittled away by similar action abroad. A number of countries, mainly debtor primary producers, had devalued before Britain and in 1931 most of the British Empire countries and a number of others left the gold standard and pegged their currencies to the pound. Then between September 1931 and August 1932 a further 12 countries abandoned gold while another wave of depreciation was sparked off when the dollar was devalued in 1933. Thus by the end of 1933 most major currencies and many minor ones had depreciated; the chief exceptions were those of France, Italy, Holland, Belgium, Czechoslovakia, Switzerland and Poland which formed the hard core of the gold bloc group, and Germany and many central and south-eastern European countries which practised exchange control. The magnitude of the depreciations varied somewhat – some of them were larger than the British – but effectively the British advantage from devaluation lasted only a short time, probably two years or less.[2]

This does not mean that there were no gains at all for Britain.

[1] See C. P. Kindleberger, *International Economics* (3rd ed.), 1963, p. 213.
[2] Morton, *op. cit.*, p. 151.

Though depreciation failed to produce the expected upsurge in exports Britain did gain a comparative advantage, at least initially. For the record British exports recovered earlier than those of some major countries, particularly compared with the United States, Germany and France and other gold bloc and exchange control countries, and up to 1935 or so exports outstripped the growth in world trade. Over the recovery period as a whole British exports more or less kept pace with the expansion in world trade, a performance distinctly better than that of the 1920s. On the other hand, as we have pointed out earlier, export growth was not dramatic and contributed little to the revival in domestic activity.

Only part of this improvement can be attributed directly to the price effects of depreciation and most of the gains accrued in the first two years or so. The early devaluation helped to check the fall in export volumes compared with elsewhere, with the result that in the period 1931–3 or possibly up to 1934 Britain was able to secure a larger share of world exports despite the fact that export volumes remained rather sluggish. Thus the average level of exports in 1932–4 compared with 1931 was considerably above that of the u.s.a., Germany, Japan, and the gold bloc countries. It is interesting to note however that the greatest export gains were made in countries with depreciated standards rather than with countries still on gold where the potential advantages were greatest. Thus after devaluation the percentage of exports going to countries with no depreciation declined, it rose to those countries with less depreciation than the u.k., while there was an even larger rise to those countries with a greater depreciation than Britain.[1]

This suggests that the income effects of depreciation were more important than the price effects. Countries which left gold were more prosperous or experienced earlier recovery than those still on gold (which continued to deflate) and they were therefore in a better position to increase purchases from each other. In effect the price effects of depreciation were probably very limited indeed despite the fact that initially Britain was able to offer her exports on favourable terms compared with 1931. This can be explained by the low elasticity of demand for British exports due to the sharper decline in income in some of Britain's major markets, extensive depreciation abroad and the continued deflation and increasing restrictions on trade in countries still on gold and in the exchange control countries. In other

[1] See Harris, *op. cit.,* pp. 121, 130, 132, 148, 149.

words, it was the revival in activity and incomes in those countries off gold that helped to make the British devaluation effective, insofar as it was effective.

The importance of the indirect income effects should not be under-rated. The improvement in the British trade position between 1932 and 1935 was associated in part with the early and relatively large improvement in the condition of some agricultural and primary producing countries and exchange depreciation contributed to this improvement. In particular, it brought financial relief to many debtor countries and enabled them to pursue policies favourable to recovery. This of course was not the only influence at work. Imperial preference fostered stronger trade links with the Dominions and Colonies, while trade agreements with foreign countries may have helped to stimulate exports. The early recovery in the new industries was also of some importance.

One thing is certain however: depreciation did not result in an export-led recovery. Exports rose very slowly compared with domestic production and by 1937 they were no higher in volume than in 1930 and very much lower than in 1929. Nor did depreciation contribute very much to the improvement in the balance of payments in the early 1930s.

The balance of payments on current account had deteriorated sharply in 1929–31 and unfavourable movements in the merchandise trade balance were partly responsible for this deterioration (see Table 33). Despite an improvement in the terms of trade (which might have been expected to improve the balance) import values fell very much less than export values with a consequent widening of the deficit. The modest fall in British income compared with abroad together with the low elasticity of demand for British imports meant that imports were maintained at a relatively high level, whereas the sharper fall in world income and the high income elasticity of demand abroad for British exports caused a large decline in exports. Hence income changes were more powerful than price effects in these years. Depreciation had little effect on the trade balance one way or another in 1931. Since it was only operative in the last quarter of the year it affected the average exchange rate for the year as a whole only by seven per cent, whereas export unit values fell by one sixth and import unit values by one quarter (dollar relatives) producing an 11 per cent improvement in trade terms.[1]

[1] C. P. Kindleberger, *The Terms of Trade* (1956), p. 104.

During 1932 and 1933 the balance of payments improved considerably and the deficit of 1931 was wiped out. This improvement was due largely to the reduction in the adverse trade balance from £323 million in 1931 to £196 million in 1933. Since the bulk of the change occurred in 1932 it cannot be attributed to the terms of trade since these deteriorated slightly in that year.[1] Nor does it seem likely that depreciation was particularly favourable in this respect. The demand for imports was inelastic with respect to both price and income changes, while the price elasticity of demand abroad for British exports was fairly low because of the income effects.[2] Thus at best devaluation stabilized the level of exports but it was from the side of imports that the improvement came. Imports were cut back sharply in both volume and value in 1932 and there was a further decline in values in 1933. The price effects of devaluation probably had only a marginal influence on the contraction of imports. The factors mainly responsible were the tariff[3] and to a lesser extent the reaction to the anticipated purchases of 1931 and the continued decline in import prices.[4] The modest improvement in the terms of trade in 1933 also assisted the process. Thus depreciation made little contribution to the change in the balance up to 1933 and thereafter movements in the balance were determined largely by the pace of domestic recovery and the terms of trade.

Overall then depreciation played a rather minor role in the improvement of Britain's external account. The benefits were both temporary and slight. It did not initiate an export-based recovery and the improvement in the trade balance can be attributed largely to other factors. It was not until 1934 that exports began to show signs of proper recovery and by that time the advantages of devaluation had been wiped out by counter-action abroad. On the other hand, depreciation was not entirely a lost cause. For a short time Britain gained a comparative advantage in world markets and this helped to stabilize

---

[1] Though they improved again in the following year.
[2] No exact estimates are available but it is probable that the sum of the elasticities was less than one. Kindleberger (*The Terms of Trade*, p. 106) suggests that the inelasticity of British demand for imports was as great as that abroad for British exports.
[3] For which, see below.
[4] Dollar unit values for exports and imports fell by 28 and 27 per cent respectively in 1932 compared with an average depreciation of 23 per cent. Kindleberger, *The Terms of Trade*, p. 104.

the level of exports,[1] while the spread of depreciation abroad contributed to a rise in activity in other countries and this helped to maintain the demand for Britain's exports as time went on. Moreover, it should be noted that exchange depreciation helped to modify or check the deflationary tendencies in Britain, at first by a relative rise in prices, that is a smaller decline than elsewhere, and later by an absolute rise,[2] since it allowed expansionary policies – cheap money and free spending – to be pursued. This rise made for a more favourable domestic price-cost structure and hence increased business confidence. Perhaps on reflection this was the most important contribution of devaluation for, as Harris observed in the 1930s, 'Exchange depreciation seems to help more by improving the price-cost structure at home, thus contributing towards a more satisfactory business situation, than by capturing foreign trade at the expense of rivals.'[3]

Tariff protection and imperial preference

The adoption of general tariff protection in 1932 represented a radical departure from previous policy. In 1930 some 83 per cent of Britain's imports came in duty free. The remaining 17 per cent were subject to varying degrees of duty. Most of these represented revenue duties and had been imposed in the nineteenth century. But, in addition, a number of duties were levied during the war and in the 1920s on key or strategic products. These included motor cars, synthetic dyestuffs, scientific instruments, wireless valves, magnetos and a number of other products. Most of these duties remained in force after the adoption of general protection. The abandonment of free trade came in a number of stages. Late in 1931 an emergency levy was imposed on manufactured imports and certain horticultural products in order to check the flow of imports. This was replaced in 1932 by a new tariff structure. A general 10-per-cent *ad valorem* tariff was placed on all imports other than food and certain raw materials, but higher duties could be imposed, especially on manufactured products and luxury goods, on the recommendation of the Import Duties Advisory Committee. These duties did not apply to the Empire but were made

[1] Presumably had there been no devaluation or had it come later Britain's external position would have deteriorated further as long as incomes continued to decline abroad.
[2] Particularly compared with countries still on gold.
[3] Harris, *op. cit.*, p. 179.

the basis of an Empire preference scheme negotiated late in 1932 at Ottawa. By these arrangements Britain gained minor tariff concessions and increased preference for British products in Dominion markets, in return for which Britain guaranteed free entry to most Dominion products and increased the margins of preference by imposing additional duties on certain goods imported from foreign countries.[1] Finally, a system of quota restrictions on foreign food imports, together with certain quantitative limitations on Empire imports were imposed to safeguard the British farmer.

Briefly the results of the tariff arrangements were as follows. Most Empire and colonial imports were admitted free or at nominal rates of duty. Conversely, the greater part of foreign imports were subject to tariff protection. The percentage of imports free of duty was about 25·0 per cent after Ottawa compared with 83 per cent in 1930. Tariffs of 10 per cent were levied on 28·3 per cent of foreign imports, of 11–20 per cent on a further 22 per cent, and over 20 per cent on another 7·7 per cent. The remaining 17 per cent of foreign imports still came under the old revenue and safeguarding arrangements.[2] Moreover, some of the commodities on the free list were restricted by other methods. Tariff restrictions tended to be more severe on products from European countries. The highest rates of duty were levied on manufactured and semi-manufactured products and the lowest on food and raw materials, a considerable proportion of which were on the free list.[3] However, the general levels of tariffs on various categories were altered from time to time as a result of the recommendations of the Import Duties Advisory Committee. On balance the trend was in an upward direction and by the end of the period the number of articles subject to duty and the average rate of duty levied were higher than in 1932.[4] A number of the earlier *ad valorem* tariffs were replaced by more onerous specific duties.

The task of analysing the effects of the tariff is not an easy one. The ramifications of the policy were many and varied and often the influence was of an indirect nature. Moreover, the position is complicated by the fact that it is difficult to disentangle the effects of protection

[1] The Imperial preference scheme was extended to the Crown Colonies in 1933.
[2] See J. H. Richardson, *British Economic Foreign Policy* (1936), p. 128; and H. Hutchinson, *Tariff-Making and Industrial Reconstruction* (1965), p. 156.
[3] Some of which were restricted by other methods.
[4] Arndt, *op. cit.*, p. 109. Though tariff levels and other restrictions were less severe than in other countries.

from those caused by other factors such as currency depreciation, cheap money, improved terms of trade and natural recovery forces, all of which occurred at a similar point in time. Only a full-scale econometric study would reveal the precise gains and losses arising from the policy. In the absence of such a study we shall have to confine ourselves to assessing the broad impact of tariffs on Britain's trade, industry and employment and the way in which they affected the structure and pattern of trade.

Normally one would expect the imposition of tariff protection to lead to a fall in imports and an improvement in the balance of trade. But the direction and magnitude of the changes in both cases depends on so many factors that it is difficult to make dogmatic generalizations. Much will depend on the severity of the tariff and its coverage, its timing, the elasticity of demand for imports, the behaviour of exports and the terms of trade and a host of other factors. A low tariff applied on a general basis may be too weak to have much effect on the level of imports, while even a moderate or severe tariff may have little effect if the elasticity of demand for imports is very low. Similarly, if the cost of the tariff is absorbed by foreign exporters, through a reduction in the price of their products, imports may remain unchanged. Even assuming that tariff protection does lead to a drop in imports it does not necessarily follow that the balance of trade will improve. The export position may deteriorate for several reasons. Tariff protection will tend to make the home market more attractive and manufacturers may be induced to switch their resources away from export production. This is more likely to happen in boom conditions than at a time when capacity is under-utilized. Second, the imposition of retaliatory tariffs by foreign countries may reduce the demand for British exports. Third, tariffs will raise the cost of imported materials (assuming these are subject to duty) and hence push up the costs of exports thereby reducing their competitiveness. Thus the adverse repercussions on the export side could conceivably offset the gains accruing from any reduction in imports.

Since the various possibilities are almost endless the best approach is to seek recourse in the facts of the situation. The short-term effects were favourable partly because of the fortuitous timing of tariff protection. Imports were running at a high level in 1931 and the immediate effect of the new duties was to bring about a sharp fall in imports. The volume of imports fell by 13 per cent in 1932 and remained stable in the following year. Food imports only declined

K

288 The external account

moderately (and then only against the peak level of 1931)[1] while imports of materials and fuel actually rose over the period 1931–3. Of course these items were only affected marginally by the tariff since their demand elasticities were fairly low so that the trends are not unexpected. The main burden was borne by manufactured goods on which the incidence of tariffs weighed most heavily. Retained imports in this category fell by over 45 per cent and much of this could be attributed to the tariff.[2] The drop in the total volume of imports was reinforced by declining prices so that the total value of imports fell by more than the volume, from £784 million in 1931 to £618 million in 1933, a decline of 22·2 per cent (see Tables 30 and 33).

The indirect short-term effects of the tariffs on exports are not readily discernable from the trade data. It is possible that any indirect adverse repercussions were compensated for by the initial benefits from depreciation and the beginnings of recovery. In any case exports had reached their trough in 1931 before protection. The volume of exports remained almost stable in 1932 and 1933 and there was a modest fall in values in 1933 as a result of price changes. The significant improvement in the balance of trade between 1931–3 was, however, due largely to changes on the import side (Tables 30 and 33).

Tariffs could not staunch the flow of imports for ever, By 1934 they had begun to rise again and they continued to do so until 1937 when they surpassed in volume terms the previous peak of 1929. This increase was partly to be expected during the recovery phase of the cycle. The question is whether protection damped down the volume of imports to a lower level than they would otherwise have been. The fact that the volume of imports rose less rapidly than exports and industrial production over the course of recovery suggests that the tariff did exert some effect. On the other hand, manufactured imports, on which the tariff bore most heavily, rose more rapidly than total imports, and considerably faster than exports and industrial production. It is true that imports of manufactures started off from a very low level in 1932–3 and did not regain their previous peak by 1937. Nevertheless, their very vigorous revival does seem to indicate that protection was exercising a limited influence in checking imports. In part this can be explained by the relatively low level of British tariffs which was insufficient to offset the competitive advantage of overseas ex-

---

[1] Probably due to the fear of restrictions. Taking 1929 as the base food imports rose through to 1931 and then fell back slightly in 1932–3.
[2] See above, pp. 255, 284.

porters. In a study of 25 commodities for 1937 MacDougall found that our tariffs fully offset the American competitive advantage in the British market in only two commodities, paper and glass containers. On the other hand, in those commodities in which Britain had a price advantage in the U.S. market the level of tariffs was usually sufficiently high to offset it.[1]

Thus British tariffs were probably too low to act as a really effective barrier to imports. Moreover, their effects were partly mitigated by price cutting and dumping in the British market by foreigners with excess capacity. Conversely, British exporters faced higher tariffs abroad and they were in a weaker position competitively. The tariff also had the effect of inducing manufacturers to concentrate on the home market in the recovery of the 1930s. Thus exports rose only modestly in this period and remained far below the peak of 1929. It is true that in volume terms exports rose somewhat more rapidly than imports during the recovery phase, but then it should be noted that they fell much more sharply than imports in the preceding slump. But the more rapid rise in the volume of exports was insufficient to offset adverse price trends, especially the rapid rise in import prices in the later 1930s, so that in terms of value imports outpaced exports and the balance of trade deteriorated (see Table 33).

One of the chief features of the inter-war economy was the decline in the importance of international trade and the concomitant growth in importance of the home market. The climax of this development came with the recovery of the 1930s which was based primarily on the home market. Inevitably these developments have been associated with the tariff protection of 1932 though few, except perhaps contemporaries, would go so far as to argue that protection was the main determinant of the home boom of the 1930s. Generally speaking, protection was a minor factor in the process of recovery.

Nor was the decline in the importance of international trade in the British economy something which began in the early 1930s. Exports and imports as a proportion of national income had in fact reached their peak in 1913 after which they declined in importance. By 1931, that is before protection, imports as a share of national income were 20·8 per cent and exports (plus re-exports) were 12·1, whereas the corresponding proportions for 1913 were 31·1 and 28·0.

[1] G. D. A. MacDougall, 'British and American Exports: a Study Suggested by the Theory of Comparative Costs, Part I', *Economic Journal*, 61 (1951), pp. 699, 704–5.

By comparison the institution of tariff protection only caused a moderate decline in these shares. By 1938 imports accounted for 17·6 per cent of national income and exports for 11·1 per cent and, indeed, after 1933 the shares remained remarkable stable. Thus the trend towards greater self-sufficiency had clearly made its major advance before general protection.

Given this decline in international trade and the contraction of the basic export industries it was more or less inevitable, tariff or no tariff, that the recovery from the slump would be based mainly on the domestic market. This does not mean, of course, that the tariff had no part to play in the recovery process. By curtailing imports the tariff presumably acted as a confidence booster to businessmen and helped to stimulate investment and output in protected industries. A recent writer has in fact suggested that it 'proved on balance of significant and essential value in aiding Britain's recovery, not only by giving an initial stimulus to rise from the slough, but in the longer term also'.[1] How far this was the case depends upon the extent to which newly protected industries were responsible for the recovery and whether their rate of development was in any way associated with tariff protection.

As far as the first point is concerned it is essential to point out that early recovery was far from being based solely on newly protected industries. In fact some of the pace setters in the initial phase of recovery consisted of sectors largely unconnected with foreign trade such as building, distribution and certain other services trades, or industries like motor manufacturing, which had been protected long before 1932. Second, many of the industries which received protection for the first time in 1932 were old staple trades which contributed only marginally to recovery. At best protection probably checked output from falling further in these sectors but in the long-term it may well have helped to bolster up relatively inefficient industries and delayed much needed reorganization. Third, the relationship between output, employment and imports in the newly protected industries does not lend much support to the proposition that tariffs were crucial to recovery. In an analysis of 20 industries, Richardson found that the rate of employment growth between 1930–35 was very modest and no greater than that in manufacturing industry generally. Moreover, there was no clear-cut association between movements in imports and the growth of employment and output of these industries.

[1] Hutchinson, *op. cit.*, p. 165.

In fact in some industries in which imports fell sharply, e.g. machinery, cotton goods, wool manufactures, clothing, leather goods and hats and caps, only moderate increases in output were recorded, while certain rapidly growing industries such as chemicals, glassware, pig-iron, and non-ferrous metals, experienced relatively small contractions in imports. There were of course some notable exceptions. The toy and steel products industries grew rapidly and experienced a fall in imports well above the average.[1]

The above considerations do not suggest that tariff protection was of vital significance. Moreover, in the later 1930s, when imports of manufactures rose sharply, it must have had even less influence. But we should not assume from this that protection was of no importance at all. The fact that most newly protected industries experienced a fall in imports in the early 1930s must obviously have helped to raise business expectations. The relative lack of association between changes in imports and rates of growth of these industries, though suggestive, is no conclusive proof of the complete ineffectiveness of tariffs unless we can assume that all other factors remained equal. If, moreover, we speculate as to what might have happened had there been no protection then the case for protection is strengthened. With excess capacity in many competing industries abroad Britain, as the only free market, might well have been flooded with cheap (artificially priced) imported manufactures on a much greater scale than in the 1920s.[1] This would certainly have depressed confidence, prolonged the depression, especially in some of the old staple industries, and weakened the forces of recovery. The tariff, at the levels set, did not, of course, afford complete protection nor did it rank as a crucial ingredient in recovery, but it did offer some respite to certain industries, especially iron and steel which had been severely hit by imports before 1932. Despite its modest contribution however, in the conditions then prevailing free trade by one country alone was untenable.

The use of the tariff weapon to stimulate domestic activity (assuming heavy imports are responsible for excess capacity) may well turn out to be self-defeating if the policy leads to retaliation abroad since this will result in a diminished demand for exports from the country originally imposing restrictions. This line of reasoning is, however, largely inapplicable to Britain at the time in question. For one thing the pattern of Britain's development after the war made it very un-

[1] H. W. Richardson, *Economic Recovery in Britain, 1932–9* (1967), pp. 247–51, 257.
[2] Imports of manufactures more than doubled between 1921–9.

likely that exports would be the growth booster after the slump. Second, exports had more or less reached their nadir before protection was imposed, though the tariff may have had a marginal drag effect on the subsequent rate of recovery of exports. Third, tariffs were fairly general abroad by the early 1930s so that the adoption of protection in Britain did not spark off a tariff scramble, though some countries did raise the level of their tariffs and resorted to other forms of trade restrictions.[1] In fact, far from arguing that Britain's export prospects were harmed by protection it could be claimed that given the conditions then obtaining Britain needed a tariff to use as a bargaining counter in trade negotiations. Without this weapon she was powerless to compete in a world riddled with trade restrictions. In contrast to the position before the war, the international trade system of the 1930s represented 'a series of exclusive bargains between governments on the basis of strict reciprocity',[2] and the tariff became a vital instrument for exacting concessions.

Though Britain's foreign trade was not controlled as rigidly as that of some European countries the tariff was used in this country as a bargaining device. Bilateral trade negotiations were concluded with some of Britain's main non-Empire trading partners, while the Ottawa agreements established the system of Imperial preference with the tariff being used as a negotiating counter. In addition, specific tariff increases were threatened to extract concessions from foreign producers. The steel tariff for instance, was raised to 50 per cent in 1935 in an effort to force the European Steel Cartel to reduce its exports to Britain.

On balance the measurable effects of the agreements on Britain's trade were slight. The series of bilateral agreements negotiated with foreign countries, the most important of which were with the Scandinavian countries, certain eastern European countries and South America, brought remarkably few reductions in tariffs, and concessions on either side were very slight. The major exceptions to this rule were the agreements with France in 1934 and that with the United States in 1938.[3] One of the chief difficulties from the British point of view was that we could not grant large concessions without breaking our

---

[1] Though even these increased restrictions were a response to trade depression rather than to Britain's shift to protection.

[2] R. C. Snyder, 'Commercial Policy as Reflected in Treaties from 1931 to 1939', *American Economic Review*, 30 (1940), p. 802.

[3] F. Benham, *Great Britain under Protection* (1941), p. 145.

pledge to the Dominions to maintain a minimum margin of Imperial preference. The most Britain could do was to promise that duties would not be increased. In general, trade between the contracting parties rose and in some of the trade agreement countries, especially the Scandinavian and the Argentine, British exports made headway, though in others, notably Finland and Norway, they lost ground. Overall Britain probably gained slightly since exports to these countries rose faster than imports from them.[1] But the total effects were very small and some of the gains were offset by adverse indirect repercussions of the bilateral arrangements. These sometimes resulted in increased competition in third markets from countries excluded from the agreements. The most notable example was that of British coal, the Scandinavian market for which was increased by agreements concluded in 1933 and 1934. As a result Scandinavian countries reduced their purchase of coal from Germany and Poland and so the latter intensified their competition in Mediterranean and other markets not covered by agreements. Thus the gains of Scotland and the Northeast in Scandinavian markets were offset by the losses of South Wales in other markets subject to Polish and German competition, and in fact total coal exports actually declined between 1932–6.[2]

The Ottawa arrangements, though concluded on a bilateral basis, were of a different sort. Since the Empire countries were largely exempted from the original tariff of 1932 Britain was able to extend preference to the Dominions only by raising restrictions (tariffs and in some cases quantitative controls) against foreign imports. In return, British imports into Dominion countries were granted preference, though this largely took the form of an increase in their tariffs against foreign goods rather than a reduction of those on British goods. Thus although this meant a greater liberalization of inter-Empire trade it did lead to an increase in restrictions against the rest of the world. It is debatable how far Imperial preference was responsible for the fact that British exports to Empire countries rose more rapidly than those to the rest of the world after 1933. Britain had always had very strong trade links with Empire countries and, given the difficult trading conditions in many foreign countries, especially in Europe, in the 1930s, it was more or less to be expected that links with the Empire

[1] Though whether the trade improvements were caused by the agreements is debatable. Benham, *op. cit.*, p. 146, felt that British exports would have increased more if they had not been made.
[2] P.E.P., *Report on International Trade* (1937), p. 268.

would become even stronger. However, the Dominions seem to have
been the main beneficiaries from the Ottawa arrangements. Between
1930 and 1938 British exports to Empire countries rose from 43·5
per cent of total British exports to 49·9 per cent, whereas u.k. imports
from the Empire rose from 29·1 to 40·4 per cent of the total over
the same period. Moreover, though the u.k. increased the proportion
of her exports going to the Empire, Dominion importers did not increase their share of imports from Britain. Only Australia registered
an appreciable increase in her share of imports from this country.[1]
Thus while the u.k. was becoming more dependent upon the Empire as
a market, the Dominion countries not only found a relatively secure
outlet for their primary products at a time when market conditions
were difficult, but they also reduced their dependence on Britain as a
source of supply. From the British point of view there was a further
disadvantage from these trading arrangements. As a result of Imperial
preference British imports from non-Empire countries were reduced
thus weakening the ability of foreign countries to purchase goods from
Britain. Furthermore, the increase in sterling made available to Imperial countries through increased British imports was often used to
amortize debts or re-purchase British held investments, whereas if the
currency had been made available to non-Empire countries it might
well have been used to purchase British goods. Finally, the Imperial
preference system hampered Britain in bilateral negotiations with
foreign countries and aroused the anger of both the British farmer
and manufacturer, the one because many Empire primary products
were allowed in duty free, the other because the Dominions continued
to maintain fairly high protection on British goods. It is not surprising,
therefore, that by 1939 the glitter of the Imperial preference system
had become somewhat tarnished.

[1] D. L. Glickmann, 'The British Imperial Preference System', *Quarterly Journal of Economics*, 61 (1947), p. 451.

9 The management of the economy

Introduction

Before 1914 the Government had done very little to develop the art of economic management. In part this no doubt stemmed from the fact that the prevailing *laissez-faire* ideology prevented active intervention in the market. This, of course, did not lead to a policy of complete abdication in economic matters, but it did mean that the State tended to confine its activities to a narrow range of functions which principally included the regulation of economic enterprise (e.g. the Factory Acts and legislation to control the railways) in order to safeguard the consumer and employee, together with the expenditure of relatively small amounts of money on law enforcement, defence of the realm and on certain social services. Consequently the State's instruments of control were both limited and weak. It owned or controlled directly very little and the volume of Government expenditure was generally too small for variations in it to exert a substantial affect on the level of economic activity, even had there been any disposition to use expenditure for this purpose. In fact the prevailing practice of containing the growth of expenditure as far as possible and balancing the budget precluded any real move towards a policy of economic stabilization in the modern sense. A third possible instrument of control, namely monetary policy, was exercised not by the Government but by a private institution, the Bank of England. The main policy weapon was the Bank rate and this was used very vigorously in the late nineteenth and twentieth centuries. By and large variations in the Bank rate were used to regulate the foreign exchanges and preserve the convertibility of sterling and the gold standard rather than to regulate the course of domestic activity, though inevitably the economy was affected by such changes. Indeed, internal adjustments were necessary to achieve external stability. The Government's control over Bank policy was fairly limited and only at times of exceptional crisis did the Government seek to influence the course of monetary policy.

Conditions after the war were potentially much more favourable to State intervention and the development of management techniques. Several reasons were responsible for this change. During the period of hostilities the Government had become a 'giant practitioner' in industry. Eventually most forms of economic activity were controlled in some way or other and by 1918 two-thirds, or possibly more, of all employed workers were engaged in activities subject to government control. Once the emergency had passed these controls were abandoned very rapidly and little attempt was made to retain them for purposes of short-term management as after the Second World War. Nevertheless, the war-time control system provided the Government with considerable experience in economic matters and, although most controls were abandoned soon afterwards, there were a few legacies for the future. Moreover, it could be argued that participation during the war meant that the Government would be less reluctant in peace-time to intervene on the economic front.

The second and perhaps most important effect of the war was the boost it gave to public expenditure. By 1918 total Government expenditure (both central and local) accounted for over one half of G.N.P. compared with only 13 per cent in 1913. The level of expenditure dropped sharply, of course, once military operations ceased, but the proportion of income dispensed by the State never returned to the pre-war level. The war, by raising ideas as to the tolerable level of taxation and by revealing some of the glaring gaps in welfare provisions, caused a permanent displacement effect in total spending. Such forces were in fact already apparent in the decade or so before 1914 as attitudes to social welfare and taxation became more progressive, but there is no doubt that they were greatly strengthened by war-time conditions.[1] As a result the public sector became a much more significant force in the economy. It is true that over the inter-war period there was no very marked tendency for the relative importance of State expenditure to increase, but the level of that expenditure was much higher than pre-war, ranging from between 24 and 30 per cent of G.N.P. Given the importance of the public sector it was

[1] See A. T. Peacock and J. Wiseman, *The Growth of Public Expenditure in the United Kingdom* (1967 ed.), esp. pp. xxxi–xli.

perfectly possible to manipulate expenditure in a way which would help to counter economic fluctuations.

A third important development was in the monetary field. The 'arms-length' approach which characterized the relationships between the Government and the Bank of England with regard to monetary policy before 1914 was gradually abandoned, and the Government began to exert greater influence over the course of monetary policy. The Bank still remained a private institution and theoretically it could operate its policy as it wished. But circumstances dictated that there were advantages to be gained from closer contact between the Bank and the Treasury. In particular, the Government's debt and its borrowing requirements together with the problem of re-establishing the gold standard, maintaining it and then replacing it when abandoned in 1931, virtually ensured that the Bank and the Government had sufficient common interests to make contact and co-operation over monetary policy both worthwhile and profitable.[1] This is not to say that monetary policy was used effectively from a domestic point of view but merely illustrates that the opportunities for using the monetary weapon for management purposes were somewhat greater than before the war, and that any discussion of public policy during this period must give serious consideration to the monetary aspect.

Finally, it should be pointed out that economic conditions were such as to encourage greater Government intervention. Although the secular growth trend was upwards there were black spots in the economy. Certain sectors were stagnating or declining, unemployment was high and fluctuations were somewhat more violent than before the war. Moreover, attitudes were changing as to what constituted a tolerable standard of welfare. Such conditions were virtually bound to dictate a different policy towards economic matters from that which had prevailed before 1914.

[1] The greater degree of co-operation between the Government and the Bank is shown by the fact that in the 1920s it was not uncommon for Chancellors of the Exchequer to give assurances about future movements in the Bank rate. After the abandonment of gold 'the relationship between the Treasury and the Bank of England had to be necessarily closer than ever. Indeed, the whole policy, the whole management of sterling is one which is discussed continuously between the representatives of the Treasury and the representatives of the Bank of England' (Neville Chamberlain in the House of Commons, 21 Dec. 1934). See R. S. Sayers, *Central Banking after Bagehot* (1957,) p. 74; A. Feavearyear, *The Pound Sterling* (rev. ed. by E. V. Morgan, 1963\), p. 356; J. H. Richardson, *British Economic Foreign Policy* (1936), p. 40.

Though there was both scope and grounds for the increasing role of government in the inter-war years this does not mean that the techniques employed were used effectively. In fact from the domestic point of view in particular it is clear that most policies, whether fiscal, monetary, regional, social or specific acts of intervention, were insufficient to meet the needs of the time. From the more enlightened post-1945 standpoint it is evident, as Lundberg has pointed out, that 'the measures taken were more inappropriate, more badly timed, or more obviously wrong than most of the measures of similar importance adopted in the postwar period'.[1] The fact that they were relatively ineffective does not mean that we cannot speak about policy and management. There was certainly much policy action in the inter-war years both at the macro and micro levels and it is perfectly legitimate to refer to economic management. The main difference between the inter-war and post-war years lies not in the range of policies adopted but in the way in which they were applied and in the aims they were designed to achieve. The reasons for the failure of policy will become apparent during the course of this chapter.

The main concern in this chapter is with those instruments of control, namely fiscal and monetary, which affect the economy as a whole, though the final section discusses some of the more specific measures taken to deal with particular problems relating to industry and unemployment. Regional policy has already been covered in Chapter 3 while social policy is more conveniently treated under living conditions and general welfare. Commercial policy, including tariffs and the gold standard, are discussed in the previous chapter. This means that a good part of the policy discussion is relegated to other chapters. This is inevitable for two reasons: first, this chapter would have been extraordinarily long had all policy aspects been covered; second, it was found more convenient and appropriate to discuss certain policy matters alongside the relevant subject material.

Fiscal policy

(a) *The scope of fiscal policy.* It is now generally accepted that fiscal policy can play an important part both in promoting long-term growth and in stabilizing the level of economic activity over the short-term. In order to raise the rate of growth fiscal policy should be directed towards encouraging changes in the level of investment; this can

[1] E. Lundberg, *Instability and Economic Growth* (1968), p. 42.

be done either by raising the level of public investment or by giving incentives to private enterprise, in the form of investment allowances, tax rebates etc. But for the purpose of regulating short-term swings in the level of activity fiscal policy offers somewhat greater scope for action. In general it is likely to be more effective than monetary policy in containing fluctuations in income, especially at the bottom of a slump, though in any event there is bound to be a time lag before changes in policy begin to take effect. Ideally fiscal policy should follow a counter-cyclical course; at or near the top of a boom spending should be curtailed or dampened, while during a downswing or at the bottom of a depression measures should be taken to stimulate expenditure. This can be done by affecting changes in all three components of the national income, consumption, investment and Government spending, though the severity of the fiscal measures, that is whether they are designed to offset changes in all three components or each one individually, will depend upon the magnitude of the swings in income. A mild recession, for example, may call for nothing more than a shift in the distribution of taxation so that income is transferred to those people with a relatively high marginal propensity to consume. A severe slump, however, may necessitate taking action on a wider front.

It follows, therefore, that the Government can affect changes in the national income in several ways. At a time of heavy unemployment and low aggregate demand activity can be stimulated by (a) an increase in Government purchases of goods and services, (b) an increase in Government transfer payments, (c) a reduction in, or a redistribution of, taxes, or (d) a combination of any of these methods. Conversely, during an upswing it would be appropriate to reverse the direction of these regulators. Their effect on consumption and investment will vary according to the nature of the changes made. Tax incentives to business firms will tend to stimulate investment, while a general lowering of taxation or an increase in transfer payments will boost consumption. To a certain extent taxes and transfer payments act as built-in stabilizers. During boom periods tax yields will tend to increase and transfer payments decline thereby moderating the growth in demand, while when income is falling they will work in the opposite direction. But this automatic stabilizing function will not usually be sufficient to counteract sharp fluctuations in activity. For one thing a large part of expenditure is fixed and does not therefore vary automatically with the business cycle. Second, the multiplier effects of tax adjustments and transfer payments tend to be subject to leakages which moderate their impact. For example, part of an increase in transfer payments may leak into savings or alternatively, an increase in taxation to soak up spending in the boom may be offset by dissaving on the part of consumers affected.

A really active fiscal policy will more likely than not necessitate shifts in the level of Government expenditure on goods and services and on investment. Direct government spending will impart a greater boost to the economy in depression than will reductions in taxes or increased transfer payments since in the first round of spending there will be no leakages. In other words, the government expenditure multiplier is larger than either the tax or transfer multipliers. But a policy of spending in a recession will probably lead to deficit financing and this conflicts with the canons of sound finance which prescribe that budgets should be balanced. If therefore priority is given to the latter taxes will be raised to meet expenditure. Does this then mean that a balanced budget exerts no effect on the economy? The answer is no, because of the operation of the balanced budget multiplier. Consumption will not be reduced by the amount of the tax since part of it will be paid out of saving. Second, the tax may be drawn from high income groups with a relatively low marginal propensity to consume and redistributed, through transfers, to people with low incomes and a high marginal propensity to consume. Alternatively, the Government may spend the tax revenue on goods and services or investment with no leakages in the first round, whereas had the money remained in private hands the proportion spent would have been less than one.

The balanced budget device is a relatively inefficient way of expanding income in a depression however. Very large increases in Government spending (and taxes) would be required to impart the desired effect and this would involve a sizeable shift in the allocation of resources from private to public use. However, it is important to bear these points in mind since for most of the inter-war period budgets remained balanced. The extent to which the budget could act as a stabilizing force depended, therefore, on the absolute level of Government expenditure and its relative importance in the national income.

The inter-war years presented an ideal opportunity for experimenting with fiscal policy. High and fluctuating levels of unemployment provided the need for a new approach, while the Government's large claim over resources provided the means to manipulate aggregate demand. Total government expenditure (central and local combined) never fell below 24 per cent of G.N.P. and in some years it was closer to 30 per cent. Taking the period as a whole, Government expenditure in monetary terms showed no tendency to rise though in real terms there was a substantial increase. Local government spending tended to rise slightly faster than central expenditure and on average it accounted for over one third of total public expenditure, though this was a lower proportion than before the war. On the other hand, local authorities accounted for the bulk of the capital expenditure since the central government had few powers to raise finance for investment purposes. Although only forming a small proportion of total government spending, investment by public authorities accounted for a significant share of total domestic investment. For the period as a whole public and semi-public investment formed about 40 per cent of the total, and if housing is excluded the share is somewhat higher, reaching a peak of 50 per cent in the early 1930s.[1] Clearly a claim on investment resources of this magnitude was a potentially powerful weapon in pursuing a counter-cyclical fiscal policy.

To complete the background picture a few words might be added regarding the changes in the structure of Government spending and taxation. Before the war the bulk of Government expenditure went on the purchase of goods and services and 20 per cent or less was paid out in transfers and subsidies. By 1920 the latter accounted for 38 per cent of total spending and with the heavy increase in transfer payments as a result of unemployment this proportion rose to 50 per cent and remained at this level until the later 1930s. The relative importance of different categories of expenditure also changed quite markedly. In 1913 military defence, social services and economic services accounted for 29·9, 33·0 and 12·9 per cent respectively of total expenditure. During the war the budget was dominated by military spending so that by 1918 this item absorbed four fifths of the total and even in 1920 it still accounted for nearly one third. The proportion going to social services had dropped to 25·9 per cent while servicing the national debt, which had been very small in 1913, took 20·4 per cent of all spending. After reaching a peak of 29·7 per cent in 1924 the share taken by the national debt declined steadily to 13·4 per cent in 1938. The importance of military expenditure

[1] Using Feinstein's definition which covers railways, electricity undertakings and other public utilities as well as direct investment by central and local authorities. C. H. Feinstein, *Domestic Capital Formation in the United Kingdom, 1920–1938* (1965), pp. 47–8.

declined until the middle thirties while social expenditure increased so that in 1934 they accounted for 11·2 and 47·0 per cent respectively. Thereafter the trends were reversed as military expenditure rose, and by 1938 the corresponding shares were 29·8 and 37·6 per cent. Perhaps the most important changes were the declines in expenditures on debt servicing and military defence since this released resources for more profitable and socially acceptable uses. Moreover, since debt servicing represented a transfer of income to bondholders whose propensity to consume was relatively low it was a particularly inappropriate way of spending government resources given the high level of unemployment.[1]

Changes in the tax structure were not as great as one might have expected. In 1913–14 five sources contributed 85 per cent of the Central Government's revenue; they were income and surtax (27 per cent), estate duties (16), alcohol (25), tobacco (11) and tea and sugar (6). By the middle of the 1920s these five items still produced 80 per cent of the revenue though there had been a significant shift in the relative importance of each one. Income and surtax now provided 43 per cent of the total while the shares of the other four categories had fallen. Yet despite the continuing importance of direct taxes as a source of revenue in this period the tax base remained surprisingly narrow. Even by 1938 there were less than four million income tax payers and less than one million of these could be classed as wage earners.[2] There were few changes in the sources of local authority revenue most of it being derived from the rates and direct government grants.

(b) *The fiscal record.* Throughout the inter-war period there was no conscious attempt to pursue a policy of deficit financing. In fact budgets of both central and local authorities were balanced or in surplus in every year. A few modifications are required to this general statement. Occasionally budget deficits were recorded notably in the immediate post-war years and again in 1932–3. There was also an

---

[1] These changes were mainly due to the shifting pattern of central government spending since the functional distribution of local authority spending remained fairly stable. In 1938 social services, housing and economic services accounted for 80·2 per cent of all local authority expenditure compared with 78·7 per cent in 1920. All figures are drawn from Peacock and Wiseman, *op. cit.* Appendix Tables.
[2] E. V. Morgan, *Studies in British Financial Policy 1914–1925* (1952), pp. 98–9; and U. K. Hicks, *British Public Finances: Their Structure and Development 1880–1952* (1954), pp. 75–7.

increasing tendency to 'go soft' in depressed years and to avoid covering temporary deficits by raising taxes, though the deficits were not openly revealed. Winston Churchill in the later 1920s displayed 'an unequalled ingenuity . . . in producing a balanced budget out of what was on any reasonable reckoning a deficit.'[1] Finally, local authorities did finance part of their capital expenditure out of loans. But such departures from strict orthodoxy did not constitute an experiment in pump-priming. It would be equally wrong, however, to say that fiscal policy was permanently deflationary or destabilizing.

In the immediate post-war years fiscal policy tended to aggravate the inflationary conditions. War-time fiscal policy had been highly inflationary and by 1917–18 the internal deficit of the Central Government amounted to about 40 per cent of the net national income. Government spending was at an all time high and the budget deficit for 1918–19 amounted to £1,690 million. Partly as a result of the method of financing the banks were in a highly liquid state and there was a large backlog of purchasing power in the hands of the public since spending had been curtailed during the war because of shortages of goods and controls. By the spring of 1919 conditions were such as to call for a policy of fiscal retrenchment. Yet little was done to check the boom. Central Government expenditure, though lower than the year before, continued at a high level in 1919–20 and a budget deficit of £326·2 million was recorded for that year. Local government spending actually increased and the combined budgets of the local authorities ran into deficit, about the only time this happened in the period. An increase in taxation would have eased the inflationary process but this was not forthcoming. Indeed there was some relief, the Excess Profits Duty being halved in the budget of 1919. Apart from this the boom was also aggravated by the large floating debt, a continuance of war-time methods of finance, a lax monetary policy[2] and the abolition of controls.

It was not until the boom was just about to break that the Government decided to deflate. The Budget of 1920 raised taxes and this resulted in a substantial budget surplus for the year. Deflationary budgetary policies were pursued in the next two or three years in an effort to achieve a surplus to pay off the national debt and to pave the way for the return of gold. Though certain taxes were reduced – E.P.D. was abolished and the standard rate of income tax reduced

[1] Hicks, *op. cit.*, p. 151.
[2] Debt financing and monetary policy are discussed below.

from 6*s* to 4*s* 6*d* in the £ between 1921–3 – these measures were too late, and in any case Government expenditure was sharply reduced, most categories, including social services and education, being affected. There is little doubt, therefore, that budgetary policy intensified the downswing of 1921 and delayed the subsequent recovery. However, there were some compensations. Local authority spending rose steadily in 1921 and 1922, partly through a fortuitous delay in the start of housing schemes, and part of this increase was financed out of loans. Thus total government expenditure (in real terms) only fell very slightly in 1921 and 1922 and as a proportion of G.N.P. it was higher than in 1920 (see Table 34). In other words, the high level of local authority spending helped to take some of the bite out of the Government's deflationary policy, at least until 1923.

In 1924 an attempt was made by Snowden to reverse the deflationary policy and this was continued for much of the 1920s by his successors, Chamberlain and Churchill. Some indirect taxes were reduced, the income tax was cut by 6*d* in the pound in 1925, most enterprises secured rate relief in 1929, while there was a substantial increase in social welfare expenditure. Most of these items were covered by increasing tax yields or by revenue from new imposts, e.g. excise duties and a tax on betting, so that with the help of Churchill's window-dressing devices the budget remained more or less balanced. Fiscal policy was not entirely neutral however. Expenditure of both central and local authorities rose in the later 1920s though as a proportion of G.N.P. it remained fairly stable. Moreover, there was some redistribution of income in favour of the lower classes. On balance therefore, budgetary policy was probably mildly inflationary rather than neutral, though with unemployment at around 10 per cent a sharper boost to expenditure would have done no harm.

Fiscal policy was not adapted to meet the needs of the 1929–32 slump; in fact rather the reverse. Fearful that falling tax yields and increasing social expenditure (because of unemployment) would unbalance the budget and undermine confidence in Britain's financial soundness, restrictive measures were adopted. In 1930 income tax and the duties on beer and petrol were raised. But the worst was yet to come in the notorious economy campaign of 1931. The pessimistic report of the May Committee, which forecast an impending budget deficit of up to £120 million unless retrenchment were adopted, led to a series of drastic economies in Snowden's autumn budget. Both indirect and direct taxes were raised and so were unemployment contributions. To contain expenditure the salaries of public employees, including teachers and civil servants, were cut, transfer benefits were reduced and reductions were made in appropriations to the sinking fund. At the same time an economy campaign was launched on the local authorities to cut back on capital spending.

TABLE 34 *Expenditure of central and local government at constant (1900) prices, 1920–39*

	Central government	Local government	Total all government	Per head	As per centage of G.N.P.	Percentage unemployed
	£mn	£mn	£mn	£		
1920	457·6	107·7	565·3	12·9	26·1	2·55
1921	403·1	149·1	552·2	12·5	29·5	15·6
1922	373·1	171·4	544·5	12·3	28·4	13·6
1923	343·1	159·9	503·0	11·3	24·3	11·5
1924	338·2	166·6	504·8	11·2	23·7	9·7
1925	344·0	181·4	525·4	11·7	24·2	11·2
1926	354·5	187·2	541·7	12·0	25·7	14·4
1927	349·5	208·1	557·6	12·3	24·1	9·2
1928	351·2	203·6	554·8	12·2	24·2	11·8
1929	358·2	209·1	567·3	12·4	24·0	9·7
1930	379·7	222·1	601·8	13·1	26·2	16·2
1931	411·5	238·8	650·3	14·1	29·0	22·0
1932	413·7	228·5	642·2	13·9	28·8	22·8
1933	388·8	227·1	615·9	13·2	25·9	19·5
1934	380·3	231·7	612·0	13·1	24·6	16·7
1935	396·3	246·9	643·2	13·7	24·4	14·4
1936	411·9	260·5	672·4	14·3	24·7	11·7
1937	443·5	270·2	713·7	15·1	25·8	9·5
1938	567·8	283·4	851·2	17·9	30·1	12·1
1939					34·9	7·9

SOURCE A. T. Peacock and J. Wiseman, *The Growth of Public Expenditure in the United Kingdom* (2nd ed. 1967), pp. 159, 164–5, 202.

Despite the severity of the measures most of them did not really take full effect until 1932–3 so that total Government spending in real terms continued to rise throughout the depression, and as a proportion of G.N.P. it rose from 24 per cent in 1929 to a peak of 29 per cent in 1931 and then fell back slightly in the following year (see Table

34). Thus Government expenditure exerted a stabilizing effect, albeit a very mild one, during the depression. Moreover, although the budget was safely balanced (except for a small deficit in 1932–3) at a time when conditions dictated a course in deficit financing, the psychological benefits of this should not be ignored. The restoration of financial soundness help to inspire confidence both at home and abroad.[1]

Though perhaps somewhat belated it should have been possible to start an active spending policy in 1932 or 1933 to boost the pace of recovery. For one thing the budgetary problem was much easier after 1932, as a result of rising tax yields, new revenue from the tariff and the reduction in unemployment relief. Secondly, a number of former constraints were removed or modified. By the 1930s the deflationary pressure imparted by debt reduction and funding had been considerably eased and the conversion of a large block of War Loan to a low rate of interest in 1932 saved up to £31 million on annual debt servicing and thus released resources for use elsewhere.[2] After the abandonment of the gold standard and the establishment of the Exchange Equalization Account domestic policy was much less constrained by pressures from the external side than in the 1920s. Moreover, policies abroad, especially in America and Sweden, demonstrated that unbalanced budgets did not lead to financial disaster. Thus once confidence in the pound had been restored there was no obvious reason why a pump-priming recovery programme should not have been put into operation.

The Government failed to grasp the opportunity, however. For nearly two years little was done to relax the economy measures of the depression, and between 1932–4 spending by all public authorities fell quite sharply. The brake was finally relaxed in the budget of 1934. The standard rate of income tax was reduced by 6d (to 4s 6d), the unemployment rates were restored and half the cuts in Government salaries, the other half being made good in the following year. Expenditure therefore began to rise in 1935 though by this time recovery was well under way. Under the influence of military preparations expenditure rose very rapidly in the later 1930s; between 1935 and 1938 total government expenditure rose by over £200 million in real terms over half the increase occurring in 1938. At that date defence

[1] See H. W. Richardson, *Economic Recovery in Britain 1932–9* (1967), pp. 218–9, who perhaps rather overstresses the confidence factor.
[2] Later conversions and the associated fall in short-term rates eventually resulted in savings approaching £100 million in debt servicing. See below.

expenditure accounted for 30 per cent of the total compared with 11 per cent in 1935. Because of rearmament Government expenditure reached a peak in the recession of 1938 and 'there can be little doubt that defence expenditure was one of the major factors which put the brake on the beginning of a cumulative downward process and helped to stabilize activity at a level only moderately below that of the previous peak'.[1] It should be noted, however, that the multiplier effects of increased public outlays were substantially offset by increases in taxation, especially on income. Moreover, the high level of spending in the previous year could be regarded as destabilizing, though given the fact that unemployment was still at 10 per cent the inflationary boost was probably not inappropriate.

Turning to the main individual items of expenditure we find that the stabilizing or destabilizing effects of each one varied somewhat over different phases of the cycle. During the post-war boom military spending fell sharply and hence acted as a stabilizer, but this was offset by increases in most other categories and by the large budget deficit. Most items of expenditure were destabilizing in the subsequent depression the major exception being expenditure on social and economic services which rose sharply in 1921 and then fell. Most items of expenditure, except defence, rose slowly from 1924 but only social services registered an appreciable increase through to the end of the decade. During the depression there were some marked variations. Expenditure on the national debt began to fall in 1929, accelerated in 1932–3 with the War Loan Conversion, and continued on the downward trend for most of the decade. Military spending also fell though not by a very significant amount. On the other hand, between 1929–31 spending on social and economic services rose rapidly and so acted as a stabilizing influence. Thereafter these two items declined until 1934 so that Government expenditure as a whole acted as a drag in the early years of recovery. After 1934 all items except debt service increased and continued to do so down to the end of the 1930s. In the later 1930s, as we have seen, by far the most important item was military spending.[2]

Not all items of expenditure affected the cycle in the same way of course. Debt servicing, for instance, tended to be deflationary since

[1] R. F. Bretherton, F. A. Burchardt and R. S. G. Rutherford, *Public Investment and the Trade Cycle in Great Britain* (1941), p. 92.
[2] This brief summary is based on Table A-15, pp. 184–5, of Peacock and Wiseman, *op. cit.*

it transferred resources to those people with a relatively low propensity to consume. Thus to act as a stabilizing force this form of expenditure should rise in the boom and contract in the slump. The large upswing in debt payments in the post-war boom therefore had a stabilizing influence while the more gentle contractions in the recessions of 1921–2 and 1929–32 also had the same effect. Most other forms of expenditure worked in the reverse direction however. A distinction needs to be made between transfer payments and direct spending. Insofar as the former were financed out of increased taxes and contributions they could only exert a limited influence on the course of the cycle because of leakages in the first round of spending. On this basis a very large increase in social service payments would have been required in the 1929–32 slump to have had any appreciable effect. On the other hand, direct government spending on goods and services and on investment could exert a greater effect even within the constraint of a balanced budget since there were no leakages in the first round of spending. Since direct spending accounted for between 50 and 60 per cent of all government spending and some 40 per cent of all investment was made by public authorities it might be worthwhile to glance briefly at the movements in these two items.

(c) Direct spending and public investment. As one might expect direct government expenditure on goods and services was running at a very high level at the end of the war, accounting for something like 45 per cent of G.N.P. and 62 per cent of all public spending. Once the war had ended this expenditure fell sharply, especially between 1919–20, so that it helped to moderate the boom. Unfortunately, it continued to fall steadily through to 1923; thereafter it rose slowly and levelled out in the later 1920s when on average it was slightly lower than in the two years 1921–2 (see Table 35). In the subsequent slump it followed a counter-cyclical course down to 1931 but then fell back in the last year of recession. During the next two years it remained on a plateau and hence did little to assist initial recovery. After 1934 it rose steadily and accelerated rapidly in the later 1930s when it came to be dominated by armament expenditure.

Public investment followed a more clearly defined counter-cyclical course, particularly in recessions. In 1921, for example, public and semi-public investment rose very sharply at a time when private investment was beginning to tail off (see Table 36). During the next two years it declined largely because of a contraction in local authority

TABLE 35 *Government expenditure on goods and services at constant (1900) prices 1920–38*

	£mn	As a percentage of G.N.P.
1920	384·6	16
1921	301·1	16
1922	281·2	15
1923	250·7	12
1924	256·5	12
1925	270·3	12
1926	279·8	13
1927	291·1	13
1928	285·1	12
1929	291·1	12
1930	303·9	13
1931	322·6	14
1932	307·8	14
1933	306·4	13
1934	313·6	13
1935	342·3	13
1936	380·0	14
1937	428·6	15
1938	556·3	20

SOURCE A. J. Peacock and J. Wiseman, *The Growth of Public Expenditure in the United Kingdom* (2nd ed. 1967), pp. 176–7.

housebuilding.[1] After 1923 public investment rose steadily but levelled out at the top of the boom in the later 1920s. It then rose again in the depression years 1930 and 1931, when private investment was tending downward, so that public investment as a proportion of the total rose from 38·6 per cent in 1929 to 46·4 per cent in 1931. This increase was entirely attributable to non-residential investment. Unfortunately, in the two most critical years, 1932 and 1933, public investment was cut back, though in 1933 this was compensated by a large upswing in private investment. Thereafter both public and pri-

[1] The high level of housebuilding in 1921 was partly due to the belated start after the war and the timing of the subsidy programme. However, this was fortunate since it helped to moderate the slump, while the low level of building in 1919 and 1920 did little aggravate the boom.

vate investment increased through to 1938 though private investment experienced a modest downturn in that year (see Table 36).

TABLE 36   *Gross fixed capital formation in the private and public and semi-public sectors at constant (1930) prices, 1920–38*

	Public and semi-public		Private		All investment	Public as % of all investment
	£mn Total	Dwellings	£mn Total	Dwellings	£mn	
1920	77	19	190	17	267	28·8
1921	124	49	182	25	308	40·5
1922	115	37	167	29	282	40·8
1923	107	13	182	47	289	37·0
1924	125	18	212	67	337	37·1
1925	149	32	236	75	385	38·7
1926	165	49	208	85	373	44·2
1927	185	56	230	91	415	44·6
1928	165	41	246	74	411	40·2
1929	167	35	266	95	433	38·6
1930	184	33	251	89	435	42·3
1931	198	35	229	92	427	46·4
1932	170	31	202	97	372	45·7
1933	145	29	239	139	384	37·8
1934	152	28	315	160	467	32·6
1935	175	31	311	148	486	36·0
1936	202	38	328	140	530	38·1
1937	220	46	328	121	548	40·1
1938	241	52	315	113	556	43·4

SOURCE   C. H. Feinstein, *Domestic Capital Formation in the United Kingdom, 1920–1938* (1965), p. 47.

There were, however, considerable cross-currents in the various categories of public investment. The main items of expenditure were those on dwellings, electricity supply, highways and bridges, social and public services, railways and postal and telecommunications. In the recession of 1921 nearly all of them increased, though in the following year before recovery was properly under way, expenditure in most cases fell, the main exception being expenditure on roads which rose steadily down to 1925. On the other hand, in the early 1930s there were much wider variations. The impact of residential investment was relatively neutral since it remained fairly stable to 1931 and then declined. Capital expenditure by the G.P.O. followed a similar course, while railway investment was well maintained until a year later and then fell sharply in 1933. In the case of road works and social and public services, expenditure rose in the first two years of depression but then both became destabilizing, especially the former, which fell from a peak of £22·9 million in 1931 to £9·8 million in 1933 (1930 prices). The only form of investment to remain unscathed was that in electricity supply which rose steadily throughout the depression largely because of the phasing of the Grid construction programme.[1] From the mid 1930s most forms of public investment were rising and continued to do so until the end of the decade. Several new capital projects were launched at the peak of the cycle in 1937 which coincided with the boom in defence spending, but in view of the downturn of 1938 and the continuing heavy unemployment this apparent cyclical mistiming might be regarded as a blessing.[2]

Local authorities accounted for a fairly large proportion of public investment, more particularly in dwellings, roads, and social and public services. Their investment tended to follow a counter-cyclical pattern though there was never any conscious policy designed to achieve this purpose. Thus in all the main downswings, 1921, 1929–32, 1938, capital spending of local authorities tended to rise and therefore exerted a stabilizing influence. But there were offsetting factors to be taken into account. In general, the expansionary influence of municipal spending was fairly slight partly because expenditure out of borrowed money was largely offset by simultaneous repayments and accumulations out of revenue. For example, between 1930–31 stock exchange share issues by local authorities fell from £41·7 to £8·0 million, a decline greater than in non-public borrowing, and it is clear that they were not prepared to boost expenditure through deficit financing which would have been the most appropriate course to follow in the circumstances.[3] Second, local authorities did not maintain their

[1] Though even this tailed off in the first year of recovery.

[2] *Cf* Richardson, *op. cit.*, p. 224, who seems to feel that conditions called for a dampening of investment in 1937. From a strictly cyclical viewpoint this may be correct though given the patchy nature of recovery a strong investment boom would not appear to have been wholly inappropriate. In any case, an attempt to cut back in 1937 would almost certainly have spilled over into 1938 and thereby aggravated the recession.

[3] U. K. Hicks, *The Finance of British Government 1920–1936*, (1938), p. 126.

spending in the early phase of recovery; as a result of the Government's economy campaign investment was cut back sharply between 1932 and 1935 and it was not until 1936–7 that it regained the previous peak of 1931–2. During the recession of 1938 local authority capital spending continued to rise though again it was financed mainly out of current revenue rather than borrowing. Third, there was very little attempt to concentrate expenditure on those areas with the worst unemployment. In fact expenditure tended to be lowest in those regions where unemployment was severe.[1]

Though local authority expenditure could have been used more effectively as a counter-cyclical weapon, this was hardly to be expected given the Government's appeal for economies in depression, especially in 1921–2 and 1931–2; and their general aversion to raising expenditure out of loans in times of crisis left the local authorities no alternative but to cut back their plans at the most inopportune time. Under these circumstances it is surprising that public investment held up so well during the downswings, though no doubt this resulted from the long gestation period involved in completing projects started at the peak of the boom. But even had there been a conscious attempt to follow a counter-cyclical policy it would not have been easy to carry it out. Given the large number of local authorities considerable planning would have been required to coordinate all the individual investment schemes, a task made non-the-easier by the irregular and unsystematic control exercised by the Central Government over local authority finance. As one contemporary study remarked: 'the task of weaving the constructional activities of so many independent and overlapping authorities into a single plan, and making that plan quickly responsive to a necessary change of economic policy, is bound to be very complicated'.[2]

Of course what was really needed in this period was a long-term unemployment programme, one in particular which would boost expansion in the severely depressed regions and which could be adapted to cyclical changes. The Government's record on this score was equally disappointing. The largest identifiable public works expenditure was the series of grants made by the Unemployment Grants Committee, a body established in December 1920 to assist local authorities with works schemes designed to relieve unemployment. Altogether, by June

[1] Bretherton *et al.*, *op. cit.*, p. 168.
[2] *ibid.*, p. 123.

1932, just over £191 million had been allocated for such purposes, a large part of which (£77 million) was approved between September 1929 and December 1931. Unfortunately, only about £70 million of the total allocated was actually spent compared with some £600 million paid out in benefits and relief in the same period. On the assumption that £1 million expenditure on public works created primary employment of roughly 4,000 (2,500 directly and 1,500 in the production and transport of materials)[1] then the total employment created would be around 280,000 man years. This however does not take into account the full employment multiplier effects. Using a multiplier of two the total employment created from the expenditure of £70 million would have been in the region of 560,000, while had all the £191 million been spent the total man-years created would have been 1,528,000.[2] But even this was small in relation to the 20 million or so man-years which would have been worked had all the unemployed been found jobs. To have created work for all the unemployed in this period would have involved spending something like £2,500 million, that is more than four times the amount paid out in relief and benefits up to 1932.

In view of the high cost of creating employment and the seemingly limited effect of the expenditure actually made, it is not surprising that the Committee's work was brought to a complete halt in 1931–2. At the same time most local authorities, which had carried out unassisted relief work, mainly roadbuilding, wound up their programmes. These had never been large and the total amount spent was probably less than that by the U.G.C.[3] Relief works of all kinds never provided direct employment at any one time for more than 130,000, a very small figure relative to the total unemployment.[4] Nevertheless, despite the limited scale of the schemes it was singularly inappropriate to curtail them at the bottom of the depression. Apart from the Special

---

[1] *ibid.*, p. 331.
[2] A multiplier of two has been used here simply for convenience. As Kahn recognized, it is probably somewhat on the high side since it ignores the effects of lags and leakages and productivity changes. A multiplier of $\frac{3}{4}$ would be more appropriate for secondary employment, giving a total multiplier of $1\frac{3}{4}$. R. F. Kahn, 'The Relation of Home Investment to Unemployment', *Economic Journal*, 41 (1931), p. 186.
[3] See Hicks, *The Finance of British Government*, p. 194. For details of other schemes see R. Skidelsky, *Politicians and the Slump: The Labour Government of 1929–1931* (1967), pp. 302–5.
[4] R. C. Davison, *The Unemployed, Old Policies and New* (1929), p. 51.

Areas legislation, which as we have seen was very limited in scope, no further efforts were made to implement public works to relieve unemployment in the inter-war period.

From the above discussion it is apparent that there was never any serious attempt to develop an active counter-cyclical policy or to carry through a large-scale programme of public works, least of all in the early thirties. As Richardson points out 'deficit financing was scorned, and the most reflationary action – increasing expenditure out of loans – was not even considered'.[1] However, although adherence to the doctrine of the balanced budget effectively constrained the use to which fiscal policy could be put, this did not necessarily mean that it was always a destabilizing force. There was room for manoeuvre within the framework of the balanced budget. As we have seen, various categories of expenditure, transfer payments, public investment and Government spending as a whole, tended to rise or increase their relative importance in the depression years of 1921, 1929–32 and 1938. These upward shifts were largely accidental but they were nevertheless in the right direction and therefore exerted a moderating influence on the downswings. Unfortunately, they were far too small to have much effect and were offset to a large extent by the compensatory tax increases as in 1931–2.[2] Worse still the economy axe was wielded at just the wrong moment that is at the bottom of the depression, 1921–2, 1931–2, so that Government spending not only failed to assist recovery but actually became a net drag in the initial stages of revival. There was, moreover, only a very half-hearted attempt to implement a long-term public works programme and again the chopper came down on this at the most inopportune time.

(*d*) *Reasons for fiscal failure*. It is not difficult to explain why the Government failed to adapt its fiscal policy to meet the conditions of the period. The most obvious point is that an active fiscal policy would have involved deficit financing and unbalanced budgets, a course of action few Chancellors were prepared to contemplate let alone follow. The criterion of sound finance was a balanced budget, or better still, one that produced a surplus. But budget balancing was not simply an end in itself. There were sound reasons, so contempor-

---

[1] Richardson, *op. cit.*, p. 230.
[2] According to Hicks, *The Finance of British Government* p. 303, fiscal policy paid too little attention to the sensitivity of tax yields and so changes in rates during the cycle invariably ran counter to those which economic conditions dictated.

aries thought, why the practice should be followed, at least in the 1920s and early thirties. It was generally believed that deficit financing would lead to a loss of confidence in Britain's financial soundness both at home and abroad. The efforts made to balance the national accounts in the early 1930s and the confidence which this appears to have engendered in business and financial circles suggests that this consideration could not be taken lightly. Budget deficits were associated with inflationary conditions and in turn the latter with a deterioration in the balance of payments. Experiments of this sort could not be contemplated in the 1920s when the authorities were preoccupied with re-establishing and then maintaining the gold standard, since this required a deflationary or relatively neutral fiscal policy. There was also the problem of the national debt to be considered. Until part of it was funded at a lower rate of interest the cost of servicing it was extremely heavy, especially with the relatively high interest charges of the 1920s. It was desirable, therefore, to secure budget surpluses so that part of it could be paid off. Thus the debt became something of a millstone round the Government's neck and the heavy costs involved undoubtedly deterred a more liberal programme of expenditure in other directions.[1]

However, even given these considerations, it was still possible for a liberal spending programme to be carried out within the framework of a balanced budget, especially after 1932 when the restraints imposed by the national debt and the external account had been considerably eased. The greater the volume of expenditure the greater would be the balanced budget multiplier effect. But high spending was almost as bad as budget deficits to many Chancellors. 'The function of the Chancellor of the Exchequer', said Snowden in 1924, 'is to resist all demand for expenditure made by his colleagues....'[2] Moreover, there were at least two contemporary criticisms of public works programmes involving large expenditures, both of which were extreme. One argued that such policies would lead to inflation and a weakening of the balance of payments, and eventually result in crisis, a belief which became increasingly untenable in conditions of severe depression. At the other end of the spectrum was the belief that State expenditure on public works would fail to create employ-

[1] H. L. Lutz, 'English Financial Policy and Experience, 1928–1937', *Proceedings of the Academy of Political Science*, 17 (1937–8), p. 412.
[2] K. J. Hancock, 'The Reduction of Unemployment as a Problem of Public Policy, 1920–29', *Economic History Review*, 15 (1962), p. 332.

ment. This idea was based on the assumption that there was a fixed amount of investment and that any increase in public investment would simply lead to a contraction in activity by private enterprise. Apparently it was a doctrine to which the Treasury attached a great deal of importance,[1] though by 1931 Treasury officials appeared anxious to convince the Macmillan committee that they no longer held this view.[2] But it seems fairly certain that this sceptical attitude to the utility of public works or any other public relief expenditure dominated official thinking during the 1920s and for much of the 1930s. The Government admitted that this was the reason why grants for relief works were restricted in 1925 and undoubtedly it had much to do with the fact that elaborate public relief programmes were not inaugurated in the 1929–32 depression. Civil servants advised against relief works and the politicians accepted their advice. In a memorandum to Ramsey Macdonald in July 1930 Sir John Anderson, permanent under-secretary at the Home Office and head of a specialist secretariat to deal with unemployment, felt that 'we are now reaching the limits of works which will conform to any reasonable standard of economic utility or development. ... The abandonment of any criteria of economic development with the consequential expenditure of public money at this juncture would be disastrous in the shock that it would give to the confidence which it is essential to maintain if the country is to get the benefit of world recovery when it comes. [The Government] must sweep away ruthlessly any lingering illusions that a substantial reduction of unemployment figures is to be sought in the artificial provision of employment'.[3] The advice was quite clear and within less than a year the Government's unemployment programme had been put into reverse.

Today it seems difficult to conceive how official thinking and policy could be so misguided. Nowadays one naturally expects that governments will take action to alleviate downturns in economic activity. But one must bear in mind that a generation or more of Keynesian analysis has done much to reorientate official thinking on such matters. Inter-war governments were still conditioned very much by Gladstonian financial concepts and pre-1914 patterns of economic thought. After all, it was not until 1936, when Keynes published his *General Theory*,

---

[1] K. J. Hancock, 'Unemployment and the Economists in the 1920s', *Economica*, 27 (1960), p. 311.
[2] *Report of the Committee on Finance and Industry*, Cmd 3897 (1931), pp. 203–4.
[3] Skidelsky, *op. cit.*, pp. 216–17.

that the prevailing economic orthodoxy was stood on its head and that the role of fiscal policy in the cycle was fully worked out. It could therefore be argued that until the theoretical base had been laid bare it was futile to expect politicians and civil servants to depart from orthodox economic theory which assumed that a recession could only be cured by retrenchment in expenditure, rationalization and the use of monetary policy. In fact, depression and unemployment were seen rather as a necessary part of the cyclical adjustment process. This belief was based largely on the assumption that crises were caused by over-investment in relation to the volume of savings, which forced up costs and prices and affected profit expectations adversely. Thus the subsequent recession provided an automatic method of adjustment. Since the downturn in activity had been caused by too little saving and high costs it could not be overcome by raising consumption or investment. The only way out was to reduce expenditure and investment and thereby bring about a lowering of costs, which, it was hoped, would lead to a revival in business confidence. Hence the rather narrow Treasury view about investment and the general failure to appreciate the multiple effects of increased investment. Worse still, the concentration of attention on business cycle adjustment processes resulted in a failure to recognize that unemployment was more than simply a short-term cyclical phenomenon.

Yet it would be going too far to say that the absence of Keynesian analysis in its final form was the decisive barrier to the adoption of a counter-cyclical fiscal policy or a more active public works policy.[1] This is especially true in the 1930s when circumstances were more favourable to a break with economic orthodoxy. It is worth noting, for instance, that experiments with modern techniques were being made in the United States, Germany and Sweden during these years with some degree of success. Sweden in particular was not slow to adopt Keynesian ideas even before they had been presented in their final form. As early as 1933 the Government abandoned the principle of balanced budgets and declared its intention of adopting a fiscal policy designed to alleviate cyclical fluctuations.[2]

[1] *ibid.*, pp. 387–8.

[2] D. Winch, 'The Keynesian Revolution in Sweden', *Journal of Political Economy*, 74 (1966), and *Economics and Policy: A Historical Survey* (1969), p. 209. The latter book provides a very good discussion in depth of many of the points made in this section. For developments in other countries, see D. H. Aldcroft, 'The Development of the Managed Economy Before 1939', *Journal of Contemporary History*, 4 (1969).

Furthermore, it should be stressed that many of the main developments in the new thinking had either been worked out or anticipated, albeit in a somewhat crude form, by 1931. Public works as a weapon to combat depression were nothing new, though their implications from an employment-generating point of view were never properly appreciated before 1914. After the war the Labour Party and certain sections of the Liberal Party gave more explicit recognition to their usefulness and from their discussions emerged the concept of the multiplier effect and the notion that public works should be deficit financed rather than financed through increased taxation. Much of the limelight in the debate was captured by Lloyd George (and his band of followers) who, from the early 1920s, had advocated large scale programmes of public investment; though in some respects the Labour movement had anticipated many of the ideas embodied in the programme launched by Lloyd George in *The Nation* in 1924.[1] The culmination of Liberal thinking came at the end of the 1920s with the appearance of the Liberal 'Yellow Book' in 1928, *Britain's Industrial Future,* which, in the following year, became the basis of Lloyd George's election manifesto, *We Can Conquer Unemployment.* Its importance lay in the fact that it called for a massive all-out attack on the unemployment problem involving a capital expenditure of £100 million annually for three years which would provide employment for some $1\frac{1}{2}$ million workers. The programme secured added weight from the approval given to it by Henderson and Keynes in *Can Lloyd George Do It?* In both cases the need for deficit financing and the concept of the multiplier were recognized, even if somewhat implicitly, though it was not until two years later that the multiplier was formulated explicitly by Kahn in the *Economic Journal.* In the same year (1931) the report of the Macmillan Committee appeared which contained an important Addendum, signed by Keynes and five other members,[2] outlining a new approach to policy. The authors felt that monetary policy, on which the Committee placed a great deal of emphasis,[3] would not be sufficient to raise employment to a satis-

[1] D. I. Mackay, D. J. C. Forsyth and D. M. Kelly, 'The Discussion of Public Works Programmes, 1917–1935: Some Remarks on the Labour Movement's Contribution', *International Review of Social History,* 11 (1966), p. 15.
[2] Thomas Allen, Ernest Bevin, R. McKenna, J. Frater Taylor and A. A. G. Tulloch.
[3] *Report of the Committee on Finance and Industry,* pp. 118, 136, 153. The Report of the Committee called for a managed monetary system the principal endeavour of which should be to promote the stability of output and employment at a high

factory level and they rejected a policy of forcing down wages. The direct and indirect multiplier effects of a programme of new capital investment would, however, raise the level of employment and the authors dismissed convincingly the traditional objections to this course of action. 'We are impressed for many reasons with what seems to us to be the greater wisdom and prudence of concentrating public attention on constructive schemes for encouraging national development rather than on efforts to drive down the general levels of salaries and wages.[1]

New ideas on economic policy were not readily received in official circles however. There was a built-in bias against increasing expenditure in times of crisis especially if this entailed an unbalanced budget, and in any case the Treasury stance on public works had hardened somewhat during the course of the 1920s. Given that the Government was preoccupied with the external situation in the early 1930s and was anxious not to disturb confidence further by unsound budgetary practices, it was quite happy to accept the advice of majority opinion, namely that the orthodox line should be followed. This negative approach reached its culmination in the Report of the Committee on National Expenditure (the May Committee) in the summer of 1931. At the time the dissenters from the orthodox view appeared like voices crying in the wilderness, while Keynes himself commanded little support among professional colleagues, though it should be noted that relatively few economists directly opposed public works. But, as Skidelsky points out, a more resolute and competent Government, at least in economic matters,[2] could have done more to exploit the differences of opinion between industry and the City for it was the City and the Treasury rather than business who rejected experiments in public spending.[3] The practical difficulties involved in initiating

---

level by influencing the regular flow of savings into investment at home. The Bank rate was to remain the main weapon of control. But since monetary policy tended to have rather indirect effects on long-term investment, it is difficult to see how it could have achieved these objectives successfully. In fact the Committee doubted the efficiency of Bank rate and cheap credit as stimulants but they were uncertain as to what additional measures were required. To some extent the initial preoccupation with, and attachment to, monetary matters made it difficult for the Committee to conceive of other solutions.

[1] *ibid.*, pp. 203, 208.

[2] Skidelsky, *op. cit.*, pp. 388–90. It was particularly unfortunate, for instance, that J. H. Thomas should have been put in charge of the unemployment problem.

[3] Even Norman, the Governor of the Bank of England, maintained a liberal

L

and organizing schemes of expenditure should not, of course, be over-looked. The signatories of the Addendum to the Macmillan Committee recognized this to be one of the biggest obstacles and stressed that investment projects would have to be planned for some years ahead. Projects would take time to get off the ground and would have to be co-ordinated with the investment programmes of local authorities, by no means an easy task given the large number of local government units.

Macdonald's Government however, was in no way geared to a rigorous unemployment policy. It lacked adequate research and planning facilities for a start. Moreover, attempts to initiate action outside the Treasury by the establishment of the Economic Advisory Council and the Unemployment Committee, achieved very little.[1] They lacked the facilities and executive powers necessary to deal with the problem and they were faced by the determined opposition of Snowden and the Treasury.

Thus despite the steps which had been made by 1931 towards new policy concepts the general environment was not conducive to a sudden shift in policy during the depression itself. Old practices died hard, and given the fact that the new train of economic thought was still as yet incomplete, that Keynes himself was still shifting ground on some points,[2] and that he faced a host of professional critics, it is hardly surprising that those in high office failed to respond to the clarion call.

By 1933 however the position had changed somewhat. The crisis of confidence had been surmounted, recovery was under way and the National Government was firmly in the saddle. Most of the basic ingredients of the *General Theory* had been assembled, they had been

attitude towards public works and expansionist policies. See E. E. Jucker-Fleetwood, 'Montagu Norman in the Per Jacobsson Diaries', *National Westminster Bank Quarterly Review*, Nov. 1968, pp. 65–6.

[1] The Economic Advisory Council was created in January 1930. It consisted of politicians and businessmen, with a staff of five including three economists, and met every month under Macdonald's chairmanship. The Unemployment Committee consisted of four Ministers led by J. H. Thomas.

[2] It was not until late on in the 1931 crisis that Keynes agreed to contemplate the abandonment of gold; prior to this he had conceived a revenue tariff as being a viable alternative to devaluation. Moreover, at this stage he was reluctant to advocate openly unbalanced budgets, though as he himself pointed out schemes for increasing employment and schemes for balancing the budget were not necessarily incompatible. See Winch, *op. cit.*, pp. 150, 166.

debated and analysed in many quarters, and Keynes, at least professionally, no longer ploughed a lone furrow. Prior to Chamberlain's budget of that year a vigorous campaign was launched with the aim of prompting the Government to embark on a policy of loan-financed expenditure designed to raise aggregate demand. It was opened by a series of leaders in *The Times* calling for bold policies of reflation and no less than 37 economists came out in support of expansionist finance and dual budgetary accounting. Even the *Daily Mail* and the *Daily Express* and a number of M.P.'s took up the cause, while Keynes once more graced the pages of *The Times* in an attempt to sway the Chancellor. But Chamberlain stood resolute against the outburst. The budget had to be balanced and in Chamberlain's view this precluded any resort to loan-financed public works programmes. His negative budget speech, which echoed closely those of Snowden and many illustrious but misguided predecessors, set the tone for the rest of the decade. Until 1937, when rearmament policies began to upset calculations, pursuit of balanced budgets remained uppermost in the minds of Chancellors.[1]

The fetish of the Treasury and Chancellors for balanced budgets and the general acquiescence in Government circles generally on this issue must rank as one of the main reasons why, once the crisis had passed, no attempt was made to follow a reflationary fiscal policy. But this was not the only explanation. It was in this period that the vogue for planning came to the forefront. The planning movement was based largely on developments in the industrial field and followed on as a logical extension from the rationalization activities of the 1920s. There was a growing concensus of agreement regarding the need for some kind of planning and support for the movement cut across political groupings.[2] In many respects the policies and ideas of the movement were distinct from those of Keynes though at certain points the two were not unrelated. The main objective of both was to aid recovery, but whereas Keynes directed his attention to macro-management tools the planners concentrated on micro-planning and the coordination and rationalization of industrial activities. For the most part the advocates of this particular type of planning, the chief among

[1] Winch, *op. cit.*, pp. 207–8.
[2] A. Marwick, 'Middle Opinion in the Thirties: Planning, Progress and Political Agreement', *English Historical Review*, 79 (1964).

whom was Harold Macmillan,[1] had only a hazy notion as to what modern fiscal policy was all about, and little progress was made towards reconciling the two sets of ideas. As a result the concepts of both tended to remain distinct and largely unrelated, and the Government, having failed to come to grips with unorthodox budgetary policies, felt that planning (of a kind) provided a viable and less unpleasant alternative. Thus the Conservative Administration of the later 1930s concentrated its efforts on industrial and structural reorganization – a somewhat watered down version of what was advocated by the apostles of planning – as a partial substitute for a more active fiscal policy, and this in turn prevented any progress being made towards a Keynesian position.[2]

Finally it might be argued that once the immediate crisis had passed and recovery was under way the urgency of the problem seemed somewhat less and the need for drastic action correspondingly less imperative. One can almost visualize the sigh of relief from those steeped in the orthodox approach to economic policy even though it had been necessary to cast adrift some of the elements of that policy in the process. Henceforward, it was believed that cheap money, devaluation and the tariff, coupled with the natural forces of recovery, would be sufficient to carry the economy forward. The Special Areas legislation and *ad hoc* planning could take care of the regional and industrial problems. In some respects this diagnosis was not entirely unsound. As it happened natural forces were sufficient to ensure *cyclical* recovery, though no doubt it could have been accelerated had there been a more enlightened budgetary policy. In the final analysis the main defect turned out to be not the absence of an active macro-management policy but the failure to devise a strong regional policy designed to alleviate the long-term structural problems of the depressed regions.[3]

[1] As early as 1928 Macmillan, together with a number of other young Conservatives, had been questioning the adequacy of pre-war economic theory. Subsequently, much of Macmillan's energies went into developing his own brand of industrial planning and there is little evidence that he really appreciated the implications of Keynesian analysis. For the development of his views see *Reconstruction: A Plea for National Policy* (1933), *Planning for Employment* (1935) and *The Middle Way* (1938).
[2] Winch, *op. cit.*, pp. 214–18. See also A. Marwick, *Britain in the Century of Total War* (1968), pp. 241–3.
[3] This point has been stressed earlier and may appear obvious. But it is surprising how easy it is to forget the regional context of the problem when discussing

Monetary policy

(a) *The role of monetary policy*. Nowadays fiscal policy is generally regarded as a more effective instrument of control than monetary policy even though the techniques of the latter are somewhat more sophisticated than those used in the inter-war years.[1] This does not mean, however, that monetary policy is an ineffective instrument of stabilization. Through their control of the money supply and the structure of credit the monetary authorities can exert some influence on the demand for goods and services and on the level of investment. There are a number of ways in which this can be done. The two main traditional techniques are the Bank rate and open market operations. The first of these can be used to influence the general level of interest rates. Bank rate is the price charged by the Bank of England on loans to the discount houses or to other dealers in Treasury and commercial bills. Since most other rates of interest, e.g. on loans, overdrafts and deposits of the commercial banks, are linked to the Bank's penal rate a shift in the latter will effect the whole structure of interest rates in an upward or downward direction as the case may be. Thus by bringing about a change in interest rates the monetary authorities can induce changes in the pattern of spending and the level of investment.[2]

Similarly by the use of open market operations the Bank can regulate the supply of money or volume of purchasing power in the country. If the Bank buys Government securities in the open market this eventually leads to an increase in the balances of the joint stock banks at the Bank of England and since these deposits are the equivalent of cash the commercial banks are in a position to grant further loans and advances and thereby enlarge the credit base. By the reverse process, that is a sale of securities by the Bank, the cash basis of the commerical

Keynesian prescriptions. Certainly macro-policies were highly relevant to the theme of cyclical recovery but they became less relevant once that recovery was complete. It is perhaps unfortunate that Donald Winch in his excellent book *Economics and Policy* pays little attention to the regional problem when discussing theory and policy in the inter-war years. This omission cannot be excused solely on the basis of the state of poverty in regional economics at that time.

[1] Though in the light of recent research in the monetary field this statement probably requires some modification. For a review of monetary policy in this period see D. H. Aldcroft, 'The Impact of British Monetary Policy, 1919–1939', *Revue Internationale D'Histoire de la Banque*, 3 (1970).

[2] Though, as we shall see, interest rates were not an important factor in influencing industrialists' investment decisions.

banks will be reduced and this will lead to credit contraction. Apart from these two measures of control, the monetary authorities have developed (primarily since the war) other techniques of regulating the supply of credit and the terms on which it is made available. These include requests to financial institutions to limit the volume of lending, changes in the banks' cash ratios by the introduction of special deposits, and selective credit controls on consumers. Such techniques were rarely used in the inter-war years though the Bank of England did try from time to time to intimidate the banks into following a particular course of action.

The type of monetary policy to be pursued will depend of course upon prevailing economic conditions. When unemployment is rising, prices falling and development is generally lagging one would expect to see an easy monetary policy. This can be achieved by a reduction in Bank rate, the purchase of securities in the market, by the relaxation of selective controls or by a combination of any of these weapons. Alternatively, if boom conditions require a policy of restraint the direction of the instruments should be reversed in order to reduce the credit base and limit the volume of purchasing power.

This somewhat idyllic account of the way in which monetary policy works needs to be modified in several respects, especially in the context of inter-war conditions. Monetary policy was generally held in high esteem by contemporaries, though this was partly because few other instruments of economic control were available or practised at the time. But even the most ardent monetary enthusiasts recognized its limitations. The Macmillan Committee in particular was forced to admit somewhat reluctantly that the Bank rate was not such a 'beautiful and delicate' instrument after all.[1]

In practice monetary policy is probably more effective in controlling a boom than in stimulating recovery from a slump. Providing they are sufficiently severe, monetary measures will usually check expansionary conditions, assuming of course that fiscal policy is not working in the opposite direction. The big danger here is that to be effective such measures may have to be implemented quickly and with rigour and this in turn may create an emergency and precipitate a slump. On the other hand, it is much more difficult to induce changes at the lower turning point. For one thing there is an effective floor to interest rates and so they cannot be forced down indefinitely – as they can in an upward direction – until something happens. Cheap money and

[1] *Report of the Committee on Finance and Industry*, pp. 97–8.

abundant credit may have little effect in inducing revival from a recession if banks refuse to use their resources to grant new loans or if
businessmen's profit expectations remain depressed. This is not to say
that an easy policy will have no effect at all but rather that it will be
insufficient by itself to halt a downswing or induce a recovery unless
supported by other measures. Second, monetary measures are likely
to be of limited use in correcting a fundamental disequilibrium in an
economy caused by structural maladjustments, a distorted pattern
of costs or by regional imbalance. These kinds of problems require
selective treatment whereas monetary policy tends to be global in its
influence and best suited to bringing about temporary adjustments in
the overall level of economic activity. Third, frequent changes in Bank
rate and credit conditions designed to correct short-term fluctuations
in activity may have an adverse effect on long-term investment because
of the feeling of uncertainty among businessmen caused by rapid
changes in policy. Finally, and most important from our point of
view, monetary policy may not be determined solely by domestic considerations. Monetary measures may have to be used to protect the
balance of payments – e.g. an adverse balance coupled with an outflow of exchange reserves calling for high rates of interest and credit
restriction – and these may well conflict with the needs of the domestic economy. During the inter-war years, or rather more correctly
in the 1920s, the dominating force behind monetary policy was the
need to protect the currency. Essentially Bank rate policy was governed
by changes in the gold and currency reserves and it was used as a
means of maintaining the stability of the exchanges rather than the
stability of business conditions. It was virtually impossible to ride two
horses at once for, as the Macmillan Committee observed, 'so far from
preserving a stability of prices, profit and employment, the maintenance of stable exchanges has the effect of transmitting to our credit
system any serious disturbances, of a cyclical character or otherwise,
which may be affecting the rest of the world'.[1]

The monetary history of the inter-war years can be conveniently
divided into two parts: (a) the years up to 1931 culminating in the
end of the gold standard and (b) the period of cheap money from
1932 onwards. The first is by far the more complex and can in fact
be divided into several phases. But for the most part it was a period
when monetary policy was dominated by external events. The cheap
money phase is more straightforward and has been covered by a

[1] *ibid.*, para. 220.

number of writers. Here therefore we can confine ourselves to a summary of the way in which easy monetary conditions affected recovery
from the slump.

(*b*) *Monetary policy to 1931.* During the 1920s and through to the
financial crisis of 1931 monetary policy was very much influenced
by the problem of the gold standard, first the question of restoring it
and then the struggle to maintain it. But in the early 1920s in particular
there was another equally important problem, namely that of creating
suitable money market conditions to deal with Government borrowing.
Both these factors tended to make for relatively high interest rates
for much of the time. The main point is to establish how deflationary
or restrictive this policy was from the business point of view. First,
however, we must comment briefly on the course of monetary history
through to 1931.

The only time a really deflationary policy was required was in the
boom of 1919–20. This was one of the few instances when internal
and external needs coincided, for the removal of the official 'peg' from
the sterling-dollar exchange in March 1919 was followed by a sharp
fall in the exchange rate.[1] But the Bank of England was extremely
slow to deal with the situation. The Bank rate was not raised to 6
per cent until November 1919 (it had been at five per cent since
April 1919), while a really penal rate of seven per cent, along with
a token form of credit rationing, did not materialize until the early
months of 1920 when the boom was just about to break. Clearly this
action came too late though it should be noted that the Bank was in a
very difficult position at the time. The highly liquid state of the commercial banks and business firms and the existence of a large floating
debt (mainly in the form of Treasury bills) left the Bank with little
effective control over the market. In fact, as Morgan points out,[2] in
the first half of 1919 the Treasury not the Bank was the real arbiter
of market conditions. Moreover, raising the Bank rate tended to in-
convenience the Government's borrowing operations. Not only did it
increase the cost of the debt operations, but if the rate differential between commercial bills and Treasury bills was widened there was the

[1] The removal of the 'peg' marked the official abandonment of the gold standard.
By November 1919 the sterling-dollar exchange rate had fallen to $4·02 and by
February 1920 to $3·40, compared with the previous artificially pegged rate of
$4·76 and the pre-war parity rate of $4·86.
  Morgan, *op. cit.*, pp. 143, 203.

danger that the banks, which were lending liberally in this period, would not take up the Treasury bills coming up for renewal. If this happened the Government would be forced to borrow on Ways and Means from the Bank which would place additional funds in the market and thereby offset the credit contraction brought about by the initial rise in interest rates.

The unfortunate timing of the Bank's policy undoubtedly served to accentuate, if not precipitate, the subsequent downswing, though there were other factors which aggravated the situation; in particular the contraction in Government spending, the deflationary budget of 1920 and the Treasury's decision to limit the note issue. This restrictive policy was maintained until well into 1922. It was not until April 1921 that the Bank rate was lowered to $6\frac{1}{2}$ per cent and even by the end of the year it was still at the relatively high rate of five per cent. The Bank did, however, refrain from reinforcing the deflationary policy by open market operations designed to reduce the assets of the market. Even so, given the domestic situation the Bank's policy was hardly appropriate. In part it can be explained by the weakness of the foreign exchanges. In addition, the adherence to relatively high interest rates reflected the Bank's desire to prevent losing control over the market as it had done in 1919, and at the same time ensure that the market would absorb the large volume of Treasury bills and relieve the Government as much as possible from resorting to Ways and Means Advances.

That the floating debt prevented the Bank from following an independent line of action had been recognized in the boom of 1919–20 and at the time the Government had decided to take steps to reduce it. It was also anxious to lower the rate paid on bills and to avoid borrowing on Ways and Means. But it was not until well into 1921 that the policy really got under way. Between April 1921 and April 1925 the floating debt was reduced by £530 million and that of short-term bonds by £440 million by a policy of funding.[1] This meant, of course, an increase in long-term issues of nearly £1,000 million, the effect of which was to depress security prices and raise long-term rates of interest thus discouraging investment.[2] In the cir-

---

[1] A. E. Feavearyear, *The Pound Sterling* (1963 ed. rev. by E. V. Morgan), p. 356.
[2] Though by the middle of the 1920s the debt problem had been considerably eased there still remained much to be done. In contrast to pre-war most of the debt (84 per cent) remained unfunded at relatively high rates of interest, while a considerable portion of it was of a highly liquid nature such as to attract unstable

cumstances it might have been wiser to retain the large floating debt which could have served as a basis for credit expansion by the banks. Thus the Government's debt operations did exert a deflationary impact on the economy in these years though this was somewhat less severe than often supposed.[1] On the other hand, the policy of funding did reduce the Government's dependence on the Bank and allowed the latter room for manoeuvre, though initially it was the slackening in competing demands for funds in the market as a result of depression that permitted a lowering of interest rates. By the middle of 1922 Bank rate was down to three per cent (July 1922) and a year of easy money followed. Moreover, to offset the deflationary effects of Treasury policy (through a reduction in expenditure and the debt operations) the Bank deliberately pursued a policy of open market operations designed to expand the country's credit base.

The Bank's position had also been considerably eased by the strengthening of the exchanges in 1922–3. The sterling-dollar exchange rate rose to a peak of $4·72 in February 1923 though it began to weaken again after the middle of the year. It was about this time that the question of returning to the gold standard came to exercise a greater influence over the Bank's policy. Ever since the report of the Cunliffe Committee in 1918 the Government had been determined to get back to the standard at the pre-war parity of $4·86 regardless of whether this was the correct one or not. In fact, given the level of costs and prices in Britain compared with those abroad, the former parity rate was too high though the degree to which it was out of line is still the matter of some dispute. It is clear, however, that under the floating exchange system of the early 1920s the sterling-dollar rate remained below the pre-war level, so that in order to achieve the former rate it had to be forced up artificially. Nevertheless, the strength of the exchanges was sufficiently high to allow a four-per-cent Bank rate to be maintained throughout 1924 and it was not until March 1925 that it was raised to five per cent in order to ensure that sufficient funds flowed in from abroad to get the rate back to parity. At no time,

foreign funds thereby increasing the short-term liabilities of London. It was not until the low interest rates of the 1930s that a large scale policy of funding was adopted and by 1936 the structure of the national debt had been placed on a much sounder basis. Funded debt then constituted 52 per cent of the total compared with 16 per cent in 1926, while floating and short-term unfunded debt accounted for only 16 per cent as against 36 per cent in 1926. A. T. K. Grant, *A Study of the Capital Market in Britain from 1919–1936* (1967 ed.), pp. 86–7, 91, 98.

[1] See Hicks, *The Finance of British Government*, pp. 340–2.

however, was it necessary to pursue a hard deflationary policy in order to prepare the way for the return of the gold standard.[1]

It was undoubtedly a mistake to re-establish the gold standard at the pre-war parity though the economic effects of this action can easily be exaggerated.[2] Nevertheless, the overvaluation of the pound in relation to other currencies and the inherent weakness of the post-war gold standard as a whole made the Bank's task of defending it more difficult. Periodic pressures on the balance of payments and short-term reserves made it necessary to adopt a protective policy. The position was eased somewhat in the first two years or so by an out-flow of capital from the United States and by close co-operation between the Bank of England and the New York Federal Reserve Bank. Yet, apart from a short period at the end of 1925, Bank rate remained in the region of $4\frac{1}{2}$ to five per cent down to the beginning of 1929. This was partly because the coal strike of 1926 put pressure on the balance of payments and also partly because lower interest rates at home would have resulted in an outflow of funds attracted by the relatively higher interest rates abroad. As far as possible the Bank tried to avoid disturbances to domestic conditions by offsetting open market operations, with the result that the cash base of the commercial banks remained remarkably stable. Late in 1928 and 1929 the Bank's position became more difficult. The Wall Street boom led to a rise in Federal Reserve discount rates and interest rates generally abroad tended to harden. This put pressure on the British exchanges and resulted in a loss of gold and reserves. By February 1929 the Bank of England's gold stock, which had reached a peak of £173,1 million in September 1928, had been reduced to £150 million. The Bank rate was raised to $5\frac{1}{2}$ per cent but this failed to check the drain of reserves. By September the gold reserves were down to £131 million, the lowest level since the return to gold, and a further one-per-cent rise in Bank rate had to be made at the end of the month.[3] The domestic situation certainly did not warrant such a high rate but there was little else the Bank could do. The immediate cause of the problem was the withdrawal of short-term funds as a result of higher rates abroad and there was little prospect of this being plugged had action not been taken. The loss of gold certainly led to some contraction

[1] Grant, *op. cit.*, pp. 102–3.
[2] A more detailed discussion of the gold standard and its consequences is given in Chapter 8.
[3] Feavearyear, *op. cit.*, p. 364.

in the credit basis though the Bank did everything in its power to offset this by open market operations and the rise in the Bank rate was delayed for as long as possible.[1]

The high rates of interest eventually checked the outflow and by the end of the year the gold reserves had been restored to £150 million allowing a progressive relaxation of Bank rate to five per cent. Meanwhile the Wall Street Crash and the onset of depression had brought interest rates down in New York. Bank rate was reduced in stages to three per cent in the first half of 1930 and again in May 1931 to $2\frac{1}{2}$ per cent. Open market operations were employed to make the rate effective. Although Britain's balance of payments deteriorated during the slump the Bank's gold reserves remained fairly strong until well into 1931. It was not until the financial crisis in the summer of 1931, when institutions all over Europe began to call in their liquid resources, that London's position really became vulnerable. This led to a severe loss of reserves, Bank rate was pushed up sharply, though belatedly, to six per cent and sterling was forced off the gold standard in September of that year.[2]

(c) Extent of deflation. It is clear that for most of the period under review the Bank's policy was determined primarily by non-domestic considerations. Norman, the Governor of the Bank of England, regarded monetary policy as a short-term measure operating in response to changes in the gold reserve and the foreign exchanges.[3] Owing to the weakness of sterling this generally meant a somewhat restrictive monetary policy. Given the weak external position the monetary policy pursued in the 1920s was generally correct; the only snag was that it tended to conflict with internal needs which demanded easier money conditions. But it is by no means certain that monetary policy was as detrimental to industry and trade as contemporaries often supposed, and it is not at all clear whether a cheap money policy would have made that much difference to domestic activity.

The Macmillan Committee appreciated that monetary policy was not altogether appropriate from the domestic point of view and suggested that the business world found it difficult to interpret the meaning of a change in Bank rate in any particular instance. 'They (the

---

[1] *ibid.*, p. 365 and *Report of the Committee on Finance and Industry*, p. 77.
[2] The financial crisis is discussed fully in Chapter 8.
[3] D. Williams, 'Montagu Norman and Banking Policy in the Nineteen-Twenties', *Yorkshire Bulletin of Economic and Social Research*, 11 (1959), p. 39.

business men) may be uncertain whether it merely represents an effort to correct a temporary maladjustment in the international short-term loan position or whether it is the beginning of a contraction which will produce a curtailment of enterprise and business losses until the necessary adjustments have been effected.'[1] This was nothing new however. In fact the Bank had used the rate weapon much more vigorously before 1914 to protect the gold reserve; between 1900 and 1914 it was changed nearly 70 times.[2] In the post-war period, on the other hand, Bank rate was much more stable; the average frequency of change was about half that of the pre-war period and the rate often remained stable for quite lengthy periods of time. Moreover, although Norman did not consider monetary policy as being an instrument for achieving domestic stability the Bank did take more account of internal considerations than it had done before 1914. Rates of interest were raised to a level no higher than was necessary to protect the reserves, and to offset the deflationary effects open market operations were often employed. In fact policy was aimed at producing a minimum of disturbance to the cash basis of the Banking system and as a result the supply of bank money was kept fairly stable, especially in the later 1920s.[3] It was this increasing concern as to the dual task of trying to maintain both external and internal stability simultaneously that helped to bring about the collapse of the gold standard.[4]

On the other hand, if as some recent monetary theorists suggest, the stock of money has a significant influence on the level of economic activity[5] then it could be argued that domestic conditions in the 1920s called for something more than a stable money supply. The opposing view holds that the quantity of money is relatively unimportant. What matters is the overall structure of liquidity and credit conditions and bank lending. These matter because they influence the level of spending, which can be controlled more efficiently by fiscal and budgetary policy. Fiscal policy was fairly neutral in the 1920s while monetary policy did little to reduce the overall liquidity of financial institutions as a whole. No specific measures were invoked

[1] *Report*, para. 218.
[2] R. S. Sayers, *Central Banking after Bagehot* (1957), p. 51.
[3] *ibid.*, p. 52.
[4] E. Nevin, *The Mechanism of Cheap Money: A Study of British Monetary Policy, 1931–1939* (1955), pp. 29–30.
[5] See P. Cagan, *Determinants and Effects of Changes in the Stock of Money 1875–1960* (1965); and A. A. Walters, *Money in Boom and Slump* (1969, Hobart Paper 44).

to restrict the basis of credit or the banks' lending policies.[1] In fact, when the Bank rate was raised to protect the currency the Bank usually implemented offsetting open market operations. The proposition that monetary policy was restrictive depends, therefore, on whether it can be shown that trade and industry experienced difficulties in acquiring finance.

Since Bank rate affects all other rates of interest a high rate will raise the cost of borrowing, particularly on loans, overdrafts and fixed interest securities such as debentures and preference shares. Moreover, high interest rates will mean better returns from non-industrial investments such as gilt-edged securities and make these a more attractive proposition from the investors' point of view. During the 1920s gilt-edged securities, with an average yield of 4.5 per cent, competed strongly for investors' funds and no doubt made it more difficult for industrialists to secure finance in the open market. But without a detailed survey into the methods of industrial financing it is difficult to say how serious this problem was. Much depended upon the individual firms' capacity for self-financing and its future prospects, and these of course varied a great deal. In cases where expectations were good, for example the newer industries, there was probably little difficulty in acquiring finance irrespective of yields on other forms of investment. Stabilization of the currency if anything made things easier for industrialists financing through the capital market. It made prospects appear more favourable and 'probably stimulated activity far more than hindering it through rates being kept somewhat higher on account of the restored international standard.' The trend of new industrial issues was upward, culminating in the boom of 1928–9, and there is no evidence that new developments were hindered by lack of finance through the stock market.[2]

As far as bank advances and overdrafts are concerned it is possible to be a little more specific. It is generally considered that changes in interest rates within a certain range have a limited effect on the businessman's ability and willingness to borrow on overdraft or loan, that is providing no form of credit rationing is imposed. Norman held the view that the rate had little effect on the supply of credit to industry and trade unless it was raised above $4\frac{1}{2}$ to five per cent and held there for any length of time. This view was based on the fact

---

[1] See W. F. Stolper, 'Purchasing Power Parity and the Pound Sterling from 1919 to 1925', *Kyklos*, 2 (1948), p. 258.
[2] Grant, *op. cit.*, p. 108.

that overdrafts and loans were made by the commercial banks at a charge of between $\frac{1}{2}$ and one per cent above the Bank rate but with a minimum floor of about $4\frac{1}{2}$ or five per cent.[1] Thus a $4\frac{1}{2}$ per cent Bank rate was the effective cut-off point up to which the charges of the banks would not vary very much except perhaps at times of extremely low Bank rate, say of 2 per cent. Now after 1921 Bank rate remained at or below the critical rate for much of the 1920s the major exceptions being 1925–6, 1929 and 1931–2, when it hovered around five or six per cent. In other words it can hardly be maintained that businessmen were hindered by steep charges as a result of Bank rate policy during this period.[2] Moreover, the figures for bank advances lend support to this conclusion. Although after the early 1920s the money supply remained fairly stable bankers' advances rose steadily from 1922 onwards (there was a sharp contraction after the post-war boom) and by the later 1920s the volume of lending was substantially higher than it had been in 1919–20. The banks were able to do this by re-arranging their assets. As advances rose investments were reduced so that advances as a proportion of total deposits rose from 45·1 per cent in 1921 to a peak of 55·5 per cent in 1929.

On balance, therefore, it would be difficult to argue that monetary policy exerted a really restrictive effect on the economy in this period. Certainly the Bank did not pursue a severely deflationary policy and it does not appear likely that industrial progress was seriously hindered by the high cost or lack of finance. Moreover, if, as many studies suggest,[3] business firms were affected more by the availability of finance and the psychological effects of frequent changes in interest rates than by the actual cost of finance, then it would be difficult to argue that the monetary policy of the 1920s was particularly harmful. It could even be claimed that the greater stability of interest rates compared with before 1914 provided compensation for the higher cost of borrowing. No doubt had external conditions allowed an easier

[1] T. Balogh, *Studies in Financial Organization* (1947), p. 75; Sayers *op. cit.*, p. 78.

[2] It is interesting to note that if we exclude the immediate post-war years the mean Bank rate was not all that much higher than before 1914. Between 1922–32 the mean annual rate works out at around 4·15 per cent compared with 3·75 per cent, 1904–13.

[3] A series of studies made in the 1930s revealed that in general interest rates had comparatively little influence on businessmen's investment decisions. See J. F. Ebersole, 'The Influence of Interest Rates upon Entrepreneurial Decisions in Business: A Case Study', *Harvard Business Review*, 17 (1938–9), and the papers by Henderson, Andrews and Meade in *Oxford Economic Papers*, 1 (1938), 3 (1940).

monetary policy it would have been more appropriate from the domestic point of view, though it is doubtful whether this would have solved the problems of the 1920s. It was not so much a question, as in the early 1930s, of reviving confidence after a slump. The main problem was the rather patchy nature of development and monetary policy was neither the cause of, nor the cure for, this problem.[1] The high level of unemployment resulted largely from the contraction of the staple export industries and cheap money could not really have alleviated these difficulties. Basically it was a long-term structural problem which required selective fiscal measures and a strong regional industrial policy neither of which were forthcoming in this period.

(*d*) *Emergence of cheap money.* The effect of the financial crisis of the summer of 1931 was to force up interest rates as funds left London. Bank rate jumped from $2\frac{1}{2}$ to $4\frac{1}{2}$ per cent between May and July 1931 and by a further $1\frac{1}{2}$ per cent in September when Britain left the gold standard. The desire to end the strain on the internal economy by abandoning gold paved the way for lower interest rates. Once confidence in the pound had been re-established Bank rate was lowered progressively and by June 1932 it had been brought down to two per cent at which it remained for the rest of the decade.

Although initially the authorities were reluctant to introduce cheap money they were soon convinced that it was the correct line of action to take. During the previous decade considerable criticism had been made about the restrictive effects of high interest rates and the subsequent downswing reinforced these criticisms. The absence of a proper fiscal policy added weight to the view that monetary policy would be the main instrument for stimulating revival from the recession. In order to restore confidence fiscal policy had been deflationary in 1931–2 and it was vital to provide some compensating stimulus to the economy. In 1931 the Macmillan Committee urged that cheap money was essential to recovery[2] and soon afterwards this became the officially accepted policy. There was, however, a more immediate objective. Cheap money was one way of reducing Government expenditure since it lowered the cost of servicing the national debt. The almost indecent haste with which the Government launched the Con-

[1] 'Discount policy was never designed to bring about the readjustment of great industries and their fixed plants, to rectify maladjustments in world trade, or to compel a nation to adapt itself to vast changes in the world's industrial and commercial structure'. W. A. Morton, *British Finance, 1930–1940* (1943), p. 112.
[2] *Report*, p. 136.

version Issue is indicative of their eagerness to reduce the burden. At the end of June 1932 the Chancellor announced the conversion of £2,085 million of five-per-cent War Loan, representing some 27 per cent of the National Debt, to a 3½-per-cent loan. It proved an immediate success, all but eight per cent of it being taken up. Further funding operations at even lower rates of interest were carried out in 1934, 1935 and 1936 and altogether something like £100 million was lopped off the cost of debt servicing.[1] Finally, it should be noted that the high interest rates of 1931 and early 1932 attracted an inflow of short-term funds into London. It was necessary to check these partly because some of them represented hot money flows which were likely to be withdrawn again, and partly because they were forcing up the value of sterling and thereby offsetting the benefits of the original devaluation of the pound when gold was abandoned.

Cheap money could neither have been introduced nor maintained in the 1930s had the domestic economy not been insulated from external factors. Thus in April 1932 the Exchange Equalization Account was established, the primary aim of which was to reduce or eliminate temporary fluctuations in the sterling exchange rate and to insulate the internal economy from the effects of capital and gold flows. As far as the domestic credit structure was concerned the E.E.A. had the opposite effect from that of the gold standard. Under the latter system credit conditions were adjusted or determined by the movement of funds into and out of Britain. The E.E.A., on the other hand, operated so as to prevent foreign capital movements from influencing the domestic credit structure. For this purpose it was given a supply of Treasury bills (£175 million initially, later enlarged by two additions of £200 million in 1933 and 1937) and by suitable purchases and sales of these assets it had to adjust the internal supply of various types of assets to offset the purchases and sales of sterling assets by owners of funds moving into and out of London. This was a complex task which was only accomplished with some difficulty. Although the Fund managed to stabilize the rate of exchange quite successfully, in the process of checking the fluctuations in sterling it acquired a large holding of gold which was effectively sterilized as far as the expansion of the internal credit supply was concerned.[2]

[1] Nevin, *op. cit.*, p. 92–6; and Lutz, *loc. cit.*, p. 412.
[2] For a useful brief review of the working of the Account see 'The Exchange Equalisation Account: its Origins and Development', *Bank of England Quarterly Bulletin*, 8 (1968).

The second line of protection took the form of an embargo on new capital issues. Originally a blanket prohibition of all capital issues, both home and overseas, had been imposed in the summer of 1932 in order to facilitate the War Loan conversion. After September 1932 home issues were freed but a ban on foreign lending (i.e. non-Empire) was maintained so as to prevent a weakening of the sterling exchange and to provide more funds for investment at home. The ban on foreign issues was not watertight and a number of exceptions were granted later in the decade, but it did have the effect of reducing the amount of capital raised on the London market. In the seven years 1931–8 new overseas issues averaged £31 million a year, or 21 per cent of the total new issues in London, compared with an average of £105 million (43 per cent of the total) in the period 1925–31. It is probable, however, that foreign lending would have declined despite the embargo since there were a number of adverse factors operating against foreign loans during the 1930s.[1]

External insulation did not, of course, guarantee the success of the cheap money policy but simply made it possible for the authorities to implement easier credit conditions. The maintenance of this policy also entailed considerable intervention in the market and on at least two occasions, 1933–4, and 1938–9, official policy resulted in a contraction of liquid assets. The detailed steps taken to manage the currency so as to maintain cheap money cannot be entered into here since our primary concern is to determine the impact of cheap money. All that need be said is that the monetary authorities were reasonably successful in keeping rates down, though in the later thirties there was a slight upward pressure on long-term rates, and that for most of the period an expansionary credit policy was being pursued by the banks and other financial institutions.

(e) Cheap money and recovery. Contemporaries probably emphasized unduly the role of cheap money in the recovery of the 1930s. There was in fact a whole host of favourable factors, e.g. devaluation, tariff protection, a shift in the terms of trade, improved confidence as well as natural forces, which make difficult to isolate the causal influence of one single factor. Recent research has done much to add to our knowledge of this period and in general the conclusion seems to be that cheap money was a useful, but not necessarily a vital, element in recovery. However, considerable detailed work is required before a

[1] Nevin, *op. cit.*, pp. 168–9.

final analysis can be made and the following comments are concerned mainly with the way in which cheap money affected bank lending, the new issue market as a source of funds and the building industry.[1]

Both from a quantitative and qualitative point of view it might be expected that the banks would play a significant role in assisting industry and trade in this period. The banks, with rising deposits for most of the period, were in a relatively strong position to grant advances, while cheap money made possible a fall in the cost of borrowing. Yet though the banks pursued an easy credit policy throughout the period there is little sign that they directly expanded the credit base in general. In fact, total bank advances continued to fall even after 1933, when the Bank of England's open market operations had considerably enlarged the cash base of the banking system, and it was not until 1936 that there was a marked upward movement. By 1939 total advances had only just about regained their previous peak of 1929. Over the period the ratio of advances to deposits fell significantly, from 55·5 per cent in 1929 to 39·0 per cent in 1936, and then rose to 44·1 per cent in 1939.

In many categories the contraction in advances outstanding was quite sharp, especially between 1930 and 1936, amounting to 50 per cent in the case of textiles, leather, rubber, chemicals and miscellaneous and retail trades, by about 40 per cent in the heavy industries and mining and by 25 per cent in the case of financial institutions including building societies. The only marked increases in accommodation were those on behalf of the building trades and in 'other advances' (mainly professional and private loans and overdrafts). By 1938 total bank advances had barely reached their previous peak and apart from construction, the entertainment trades and 'other advances', most branches of economic activity registered a contraction in advances compared with 1929.[2]

There are several possible explanations for this rather unexpected trend in advances especially in the industrial sector. Some of the older industries were liquidating previous advances or alternatively, because of their limited scope for expansion or even contraction in some cases, they required less in the way of financial accommodation.

[1] The following account relies heavily on Nevin, *op. cit.*, Richardson, *op. cit.*, ch. 8, and H. W. Richardson and D. H. Aldcroft, *Building in the British Economy Between the Wars* (1968), ch. 9.
[2] Morton, *op. cit.*, p. 261; P. Goetschin, *L'Evolution du Marché Monétaire de Londres (1931–1952)* (Paris 1963), p. 260.

The fact that the banks became more selective in their lending policies, that is discriminating particularly against doubtful debtors as a result of past experience, no doubt reinforced this trend. Second, some borrowers were finding it possible to secure accommodation outside the banking system, that is from insurance companies and other financial institutions. Third, many firms were in a better position, especially when recovery got under way, to finance expansion from internal resources, and this point seems to be substantiated by the trend in new capital issues.[1] Here an important consideration was of course the cost of bank credit in relation to the cost of finance from other sources. Bank charges fell only slowly and the banks' floor to overdraft and loan rates prevented them falling much below $4\frac{1}{2}$ per cent.[2] In other words, the cost of borrowing was only marginally lower than it had been in the previous decade except for the short periods when Bank rate was above about 5 per cent. Of course it has been argued that, within certain limits, borrowers are relatively impervious to the cost of accommodation and that what matters is its availability. On this basis one would have expected advances to the industrial sector to have risen. On the other hand, the cost of bank services must be set against that of other sources of finance. Given the relatively high floor to loan and overdraft rates it was generally cheaper in this period for firms to reduce their bank debt and seek accommodation elsewhere either by using undistributed profits, replacing bank debt by issued capital or by selling their own securities, normally of the gilt-edged type. This last solution was particularly important.[3] With gilt-edged prices high and yields low (around three per cent) it was obviously more expedient for firms to sell their securities at a capital gain to provide working capital, rather than to use them as collateral against bank advances carrying a charge of around $4\frac{1}{2}$ per cent. It appears that industry released a considerable volume of gilt-edged securities in the 1930s, a large part of which was taken up by the banks whose investments more than doubled over the period 1931–6. Thus the banks became an indirect source of finance. It is somewhat surprising, however, to find the banks absorbing gilts when yields were low since one would expect the banks would have been anxious to release their own holdings to provide a

---

[1] See below and *Midland Bank Monthly Review*, Jan.-Feb. 1935, p. 3.
[2] Though by 1935 rate differentiation had become common, with larger and safer borrowers securing rates as low as $3\frac{1}{2}$ per cent.
[3] Goetschin, *op. cit.*, pp. 259–60.

basis for expanding advances. Probably because of the unusual circumstances the banks were forced into this position as a result of the ease and cheapness with which finance could be obtained from other sources. Banks faced competition from other financial institutions such as insurance companies, while industry found it cheaper to reduce their bank debt by selling securities or by placing new issues on the market.

The corollary of this is that the capital market played a significant role in financing the recovery. Cheap money would, other things being equal, tend to facilitate capital financing through the market. First it would push up share prices thus enhancing profit expectations. Second, the fall in interest rates would lower the cost of borrowing on debenture loans and preference shares. And third, the rise in gilt-

TABLE 37 *Security yields and the cost of bank accommodation, 1931–36*

	2½% Consols	Industrial securities Debentures	Preference	Ordinary	Rate of interest on bank accommodation
1931	4·4	6·2	6·8	8·03	5–6
1936	2·9	4·0	4·0	4·50	4–5
Percentage fall	34·1	35·5	41·2	44·0	10–25

NOTE The figures for industrial securities include returns on both old and new issues.

SOURCES Nevin, *op. cit.*, pp. 206, 215; and *Key Statistics, 1900–1966*, p. 16.

edged prices would induce investors to move out of these securities and into industrial shareholdings which offered a higher rate of return. This is more or less what happened. Share prices rose sharply in 1932 and 1933 and by 1936 the index of ordinary industrial shares was nearly twice the level of 1932; the price of Consols rose by about 29 per cent. At the same time the yields on various classes of securities fell substantially as Table 37 shows. The effect of these changes was twofold. On the one hand, the low gilt-edged yields made industrial securities more attractive and investors tended to switch to the latter. Thus insurance companies and investment trusts increased their holdings of industrials at the expense of gilt-edged securities.[1] On the other hand, the release of investment funds and the fall in the cost of borrowing, especially compared with bank overdrafts, made it

[1] See Nevin, *op. cit.*, pp. 264, 267.

easier and cheaper for firms to acquire finance through the capital market.

Given these considerations one would expect to see a rising volume of new issues through the market. Yet the aggregate issues of new capital (excluding those on behalf of the British Government) never regained the 1929 level. Moreover, when interest rates were at their lowest, 1933–6, the average annual amount raised was £171 million compared with £236 million in 1930, while for the years 1927–9 the annual average was as high as £311 million, that is over 80 per cent greater than in the period 1933–6. It would be wrong, however, to conclude from these figures that cheap money had no effect on industrial financing. For one thing they include capital raised by public and semi-public authorities the investment activity of which was not particularly sensitive to changes in the cost of borrowing. The most notable examples here were electricity undertakings and the railways. Second, the total includes overseas borrowing by foreign governments and institutions which was at a low level in these years due to increasing uncertainty abroad, exchange controls, currency depreciations, and, of course, the embargo on foreign lending. Third, there is a certain element of double counting because of the inclusion of issues by financial and investment trusts the money from which was partly used to purchase industrial securities. Finally, some account needs to be taken of changes in the price of capital goods.

A more useful series of figures is that provided by the Midland Bank for home production, trade and industry, but which excludes issues by public boards, overseas borrowers and financial institutions. This series is by no means perfect but when deflated it does provide a better indication of industrial activity on the stock exchange. In real terms new industrial issues rose steadily from the trough of 1931–2 and by 1935–6 they had surpassed the previous peak of the late 1920s, though in the later 1930s they fell back sharply.[1]

It would be difficult however to argue that firms were bursting

[1] The figures from Nevin (p. 222) are as follows:

	£mn.	Index in real terms
1927–28	240·4	100
1929–30	176·3	76
1931–32	70·9	32
1933–34	117·7	57
1935–36	244·1	111
1937–38	146·8	61

to take advantage of the lower costs of borrowing by placing new issues. Only between 1935–6 were they higher than the peak of the late 1920s. Moreover, the sharp contraction in new issues in 1937–8 cannot be explained by the marginal increase in the cost of borrowing. But since investment generally was running at a higher level than compared with the previous decade – for example, annual investment in manufacturing averaged £86 million between 1933–8 as against £68 million in 1924–9 (at constant 1930 prices) – it suggests that an increasing proportion was being financed internally. Presumably, therefore, an increasing proportion of industrial investment was being made out of undistributed or accumulated profits though information on this point is somewhat conflicting.[1] Balogh, for example, concluded that undistributed profits were more important than public issues in financing enterprise and that the expansion of some of the big companies in the newer industries was based largely on internal sources.[2] However, if as seems likely internal sources rather than public issues or bank accommodation were more important in financing recovery, this does not mean that cheaper and easier monetary conditions had no effect at all. Had interest rates been higher the more marginal investment projects might have been choked off either because of the difficulty or high cost of raising new money to finance them or because industrialists found it more profitable to use their cash reserves for investment in gilt-edged securities rather than to finance their own expansion. The fact that industrial concerns were releasing their gilt-edged holdings to the banks to provide ready cash suggests that cheap money was having a favourable effect. Moreover, low interest rates enabled companies not only to raise new funds on more favourable terms but it also allowed them to redeem some existing debt contracted at higher rates of interest. This they apparently did on a considerable scale; between 1933–6 industrial borrowers converted £183.5 million into securities bearing a lower rate of interest, yielding an annual saving of over £2 million.[3]

Finally something must be said about the role of cheap money in the building boom of the 1930s. Considerable emphasis has been placed on the importance of building in the recovery process and in turn to the part played by cheap money in stimulating the boom in the first place.

[1] Richardson, *op. cit.*, pp. 201–2.
[2] Balogh, *op. cit.*, p. 278; *cf* Nevin, *op. cit.*, p. 248.
[3] Nevin, *op. cit.*, pp. 227–8.

For the most part cheap money affected only one segment of building work, namely houses built by private enterprise. It had little impact on the volume of local authority house building since this was determined primarily by the subsidy and slum clearance policies. Similarly, investment in industrial and commercial buildings, which did not rise significantly until the middle of the 1930s, was motivated by economic considerations and profit expectations. Nevertheless, private enterprise housing formed a very important part of building activity in these years. Of the 2·5 million unsubsidized houses built privately in Britain in the inter-war period about 1·8 million, or 72 per cent, were completed between 1932–9. Over the same period investment in private house construction accounted for 54 per cent of all building investment and 27·5 of total gross domestic capital formation.

As far as this sector was concerned lower interest rates had two main effects. First, they made it generally cheaper to build and purchase houses and second, investment in building became a relatively more attractive proposition. Building firms, which relied heavily on short-term credit to carry out their projects, found it easier and cheaper to secure accommodation from the banks. On the demand side, house purchase was facilitated by lower carrying charges on new mortgages and a liberalization of the building societies borrowing terms. Between 1932–6 the interest charges on new mortgages fell from six to 4½ per cent while the length of the repayment period was raised and the initial downpayment lowered. For the average house purchaser these changes meant a substantial reduction in the cost of weekly repayments.[1] Building societies were able to satisfy the demand for new mortgages since they were literally flooded with funds in the 1930s. The shift in relative interest rates made them an attractive and safe investment proposition. The yield on building society shares, which had been indentical to that of Consols in the 1920s, fell much less rapidly than the latter after 1931, with the result that from 1932–37 there was an average yield differential of 0·5 per cent in favour of the building societies. Finally, investment in rented accommodation became more attractive in the 1930s as rents rose and gilt-edged yields fell.

Cheap money probably had a greater impact on the private housing market than on any other form of economic activity. But it is easy to exaggerate its importance. Undoubtedly cheap money facilitated

[1] See Richardson, *op. cit.*, for examples.

house purchase but the timing of the changes in the volume of house building, especially the initial upswing, do not coincide very closely with movements in the interest rate. The upswing in private unsubsidized house building began in the late 1920s and between the year ending March 1929 and March 1931 the number built rose from 66,000 to 131,000. There was a temporary plateau in 1931–2 but by the following year, that is before the easier credit conditions had really begun to bite, output had risen to 149,000. The biggest increase came in the next two years and in 1934–5 some 292,000 houses were constructed by private enterprise. This steep rise was clearly facilitated by falling mortgage rates and easier borrowing terms. On the other hand, the improvement in building society borrowing terms was only effected slowly and it was not until the middle of the 1930s that they were at their best. By that time private housing output had begun to flatten out and in the later 1930s it actually fell.

A second point to bear in mind is that cheap money was not the only factor favouring a growth in house construction. Lower interest rates were associated with, or preceded by, a decline in building costs, rising real incomes, a reduction in Treasury subsidies and a shift in consumer tastes, all of which tended to boost the private sector of the market. The first of these factors is particularly important in connection with the initial upturn in building. According to Bowley's calculations the carrying charges on house purchase began to decline in the late 1920s and between 1930–2 there was a fall of 11·9 per cent.[1] This was largely occasioned by a reduction in the capital costs of construction due to a fall in labour and materials costs. These had been declining since the late 1920s and between 1930 and 1933 the overall index of building costs dropped by 10 per cent. This was sufficient to reduce the weekly costs of house purchase by rather more than a one per cent fall in mortgage rates. Furthermore, the reduction in the capital cost of houses had the additional advantage in that it reduced the initial deposit required on a building society loan. Since these changes took place before lending conditions had been materially eased it suggests that the lower building costs were principally responsible for the inception of the housing boom. And when lower interest rates and more liberal terms became effective after the middle of 1933 their impact was undoubtedly strengthened by the earlier fall in building costs.

In other respects the impact of cheap money was less marked. It

[1] M. Bowley, *Housing and the State, 1914–44* (1945), p. 278.

is unlikely, for instance, that easier credit conditions played a significant part in inducing builders to construct houses though there was a greater degree of speculative building than in the previous decade when interest rates were higher. Credit was not a very significant item in the total costs of construction and changes in the cost of finance had relatively little effect on the volume of work done. The more favourable returns on rented accommodation compared with security yields did stimulate the investment demand for housing to some extent, though the response was not specially strong. Less than one third of the houses built between 1933–9 were for letting.

On balance cheap money cannot be regarded as the crucial element in the recovery of the 1930s. It was perhaps least effective in terms of bank lending and most influential in the housing market, while in the case of the capital market its role was fairly neutral. Yet qualifications need to be made to these conclusions. Indirectly the banks assisted industry by taking up their gilt-edged holdings, while in the housing market cheap money was only one of a number of factors responsible for the boom. But it is difficult to give any precise estimates of the impact of cheap money since there are still many points on which further research is required. It is easy to say, of course, that recovery would have been less vigorous or less smooth had cheaper credit not been available. But from the commercial point of view what probably mattered most was not so much the fall in the cost of finance but the ease with which it could be secured. Nor should the contrast with the previous decade be stressed too sharply, for although interest rates were higher in the 1920s it would be difficult to argue that monetary policy was severely deflationary or that development was held up through lack of finance. The biggest difference between the two decades was that in the 1930s there was general certainty that favourable credit conditions would be maintained,[1] whereas in the 1920s the condition of the internal credit structure was balanced somewhat precariously on the pendulum of the gold standard. Yet of the policy factors favourable to recovery cheap money was probably the most influential. Not that this is saying very much since other factors, such as fiscal policy, depreciation and tariffs etc, hardly had more than a marginal effect on the pace of recovery.

---

[1] '... throughout the period 1932–39 the expectations of investors were continually conditioned by the published beliefs of government and monetary authorities that cheap money would continue. Thus the belief in cheap money helped to make it effective.' Morton, *op. cit.*, p. 248.

Industrial policy

In terms of relieving the unemployment problem the Government's
fiscal and monetary policies failed dismally in the inter-war period.
However, owing to the nature of the unemployment problem it is
doubtful whether such policies could have provided an effective solution. Strong regional and industrial policies were required neither
of which were forthcoming. As we have seen, the Government's regional
policy had a very marginal effect on unemployment. The Government's industrial policy, if one can call it that, was no better. Although
expenditure on economic services was fairly high in this period, accounting for possibly 15 per cent or more of public outlay in the later
1930s,[1] it was not designed specifically to relieve unemployment in
the worst-hit areas. A substantial part of it consisted of capital expenditure on highways, electricity, by the Post Office, on trading
services of local authorities and on public relief works. The remainder
was current expenditure largely in aid of industry and agriculture.
In 1935 this accounted for about £28·8 million over two thirds of
which went on agriculture.[2] This figure does not include expenditure
on interest and loan guarantees or on housing subsidies.

There was no particular pattern about the aid given to industry
and agriculture. It tended to fluctuate more violently than public
expenditure as a whole and was often cut back sharply in times of
depressions as in 1931–2. There was no planned programme of assistance, only 'a multiplicity of measures which were small in scale and
unco-ordinated'.[3] The principles on which aid was dispensed were
never clearly defined though in many cases assistance was given
to declining industries or to promote new industries. The overall effects
were limited and for this reason the details can be dealt with briefly.

The chief forms of assistance were subsidies and interest or loan
guarantees. The largest subsidies were given to housing and agriculture.
The housing shortage after the war and the need to do something
about slum clearance and overcrowding in the 1930s forced the
Government to pass a series of Acts providing Treasury subsidies to
both private and local authority builders. Altogether over 1·8 million
houses, or 42 per cent of the total built between March 1920 and

[1] Peacock and Wiseman, *op. cit.*, p. 178. But compare the differently based
estimates in Hicks, *The Finance of British Government*, p. 63.
[2] *ibid.*, pp. 66, 90.
[3] W. Ashworth, *An Economic History of England 1870–1939* (1960), p. 405.

March 1939, were assisted in this way. Agriculture received a considerable amount of aid in one form or another. Some of the expenditure was designed to promote development of certain aspects such as afforestation, land settlement, drainage, small-holding cultivation and research. Most of the direct subsidy payments, apart from those under the Corn Production Act of 1920, were made in the 1930s and were confined largely to wheat, milk and cattle. They took the form of deficiency or price support payments and formed part of a major programme of agriculture assistance which included protection and organized marketing. The major exception was the beet sugar industry which was subsidized almost continuously in this period. An Act of 1925 granted a 10 year subsidy on a sliding scale to promote the growth of sugar beet in Britain. By the end of 1934 something like £30 million had been paid out in order to achieve a cultivated area of 350,000 acres. Because of the high cost of the experiment the Government only granted a renewal of the subsidy on condition that the extracting factories amalgamated into one large group which became known as the British Sugar Corporation Ltd.

Most of the remaining subsidies went to coal, shipping and civil aviation. In the case of the coal industry large payments (around £40 million) were made in the 1920s, principally 1921 and 1925–6, to stave off strike action as a result of coal owners cutting wages in the face of falling profits. The shipping industry had long benefited from concealed subsidies for carrying the mail but in the depressed conditions of the 1930s more direct aid was doled out to the industry. Under the British Shipping (Assistance) Act of 1935 tramp owners could receive up to £2 million a year to compensate for low freights, while the Treasury advanced money on favourable terms to encourage owners to renovate their fleets. In addition, the Cunard Company received a low interest loan of £8 million towards the cost of building two crack liners for the transatlantic service.[1] Aviation, however, was the only industry to receive subsidies throughout the period. These were designed to assist the growth of a new industry which could not, as Winston Churchill imagined, 'fly by itself'. The failure of the early independent operators in 1921 forced the Government to grant a small amount of aid to the industry on condition that competition was kept to a minimum. In 1923 the system of subsidies was reviewed and as a result the four small companies operating services to the Continent were merged into Imperial Airways which received a large

[1] See S. G. Sturmey, *British Shipping and World Competition* (1962), pp. 107–10.

subsidy for a period of ten years. The company was quite successful in developing Empire routes but tended to neglect its European services. The Company remained heavily dependent on Government assistance however, and in 1935 the subsidy limit was increased and a new company, British Airways, was formed to develop the continental services. But for these subsidies it is doubtful whether aviation would have got very far since no operator made a clear profit at any time during these years.[1]

The second major form of industrial assistance consisted of guarantees on new borrowing. Under the Trade Facilities Acts of 1921–6 the Treasury could guarantee the principal and interest on loans raised by business undertakings for approved purposes. These measures were designed primarily to assist the staple export industries at a time of relatively high interest rates. Altogether, up to March 1927, £74·3 million was guaranteed in this way, mainly in the form of small loans to a large number of firms. The results of the exercise were not very spectacular. The subsequent financial history of many of the assisted firms was not very healthy. One of the chief beneficiaries was shipbuilding which received guarantees for £35 million. This certainly helped the industry through a particularly difficult period and led to the building of a considerable amount of motor tonnage, though at a time when there was much surplus tonnage about it simply aggravated the shipowners' position. During the 1930s this type of assistance was used again – this time for the railways. Between 1935–7 substantial loans were raised by two Treasury companies, the London Electric Finance Corporation and the Railway Finance Corporation, and then relent to the railways mainly for electrification purposes.

The remaining forms of assistance were less direct and their total impact small. One of these was tax concessions. The derating provisions of the 1929 Local Government Act relieved industry and agriculture of some £29 million in tax distributed as follows: industry, £21 million, railways, £4 million and agriculture, £4·5 million. The main idea was to relieve the heavy industries but the subsidy was too widespread and too arbitrarily distributed to make any noticeable difference to industrial costs in any particular industry or region. From time to time other tax concessions were made such as the abatement of the excise duties on beet sugar amounting to £10 million. The Government also sponsored research work much of which was concentrated in the De-

[1] See H. J. Dyos and D. H. Aldcroft, *British Transport: An Economic Survey from the Seventeenth Century to the Twentieth* (1969), ch. 13.

partment of Scientific and Industrial Research set up in 1916. By the 1930s the Department was spending about £0·5 million, in addition to which other Departments, especially the Ministry of Agriculture, made grants in aid of research.

Given the difficulties of the exporting industries it is not surprising that attempts were made to encourage trade, though to some extent these efforts were offset by increasing trade restrictions both in this country and abroad, especially in the 1930s. Shortly after the war a scheme for ensuring exporters' credit risks was started by the Board of Trade. It was conceived as a temporary expedient for dealing with trade difficulties after the war, but in fact the scheme was continued throughout the period though it was not until late in the 1930s that it was made permanent. Between 1930 and 1939 total guarantees were well over £200 million compared with £19 million in the previous decade. Nevertheless, in relation to the total export trade of the U.K. the annual volume of transactions was very small and it is doubtful whether the scheme did much to promote exports of the basic industries.[1] Apart from this not a great deal was done to promote exports except for the rather half-hearted attempts to encourage colonial development (Colonial Development Fund) and stimulate Empire trade (Empire Marketing Board).

Perhaps the only consistent point about the Government's policy is that it made for reduced competition. Policy was designed with this end very much in mind during the 1930s but it was also noticeable in the previous decade. Industrial concentration was forced on the railways in 1921 and on civil aviation in 1924, while the public corporation, a sort of hybrid compromise between public and private control, was used to monopolize certain activities, as for example electricity and broadcasting in 1926 and London Transport in 1933. During the 1930s a wave of restriction schemes emerged covering cotton, coal, shipbuilding, road transport, steel, agriculture and shipping. In most cases the Government was instrumental in promoting these developments. A compulsory cartel scheme, for example, was forced on the coal industry in 1930, competition in road transport was restricted by the Road and Rail Traffic Acts of 1930 and 1933, and the cotton industry was dealt with by the Acts of 1936 and 1939. Similarly, agriculture was protected and subsidized and a series of producer-dominated marketing organizations was established for hops, potatoes,

[1] D. H. Aldcroft, 'The Early History and Development of Export Credit Insurance in Great Britain, 1919–1939', *The Manchester School*, 30 (1962).

bacon and pigs and milk, while special commissions or boards were set up to organize the wheat (1932), herring (1935), sugar (1936), live-stock (1937) and white fish (1938) industries. Very often Government assistance was made conditional on some form of reorganization. For example, the iron and steel industry only secured stiff tariff protection provided it produced a scheme of reorganization, while the renewal of the sugar beet subsidy was made conditional on the amalgamation of the extracting firms.

On the whole the Government's industrial policy achieved very little. Protection or assistance in one form or another did help to stabilize prices and reduce competition. But it did little to improve the efficiency of the industries concerned and the main problem of excess capacity was hardly tackled at all. Many of the arrangements were designed to protect the producer at the expense of the consumer since they tended to protect both efficient and inefficient producers alike, thus reducing the flexibility of the industrial structure. This was particularly true in the case of agriculture where 'British marketing policy is econo-mically unsound, starting from the basis of securing costs of production plus profit on existing methods of production and covering marginal men'.[1] Somewhat similar criticisms can be levelled at the schemes covering industry.[2] It was perhaps unfortunate that the industries most favoured with protection were the older ones with substantial excess capacity. Had competition been allowed to prevail it might have been eliminated more quickly, though ironically this might also have aggravated the unemployment problem in the depressed regions.

[1] G. Walworth, *Feeding the Nation in Peace and War* (1940), p. 503.
[2] See Chapter 5.

10 Material welfare and income distribution

Introduction

Over the course of the inter-war period aggregate national income rose both in monetary and real terms despite fluctuations in its level over the short-term. Even when allowance is made for population change there was still a significant expansion in per capita income. Between 1913 (or 1920) and 1938 real income per head rose by about one third in round terms.[1] Thus on the basis of simple averaging it can be said that the British population was considerably better off at the end of the period than it had been at the beginning. However, this tells us nothing about the distribution of the advances in income. It may well be, for instance, that the bulk of the gain in income accrued to a minority of the population – say in the form of rent, profits etc. – while the vast majority of wage earners failed to secure any significant improvement in their average income. If this were the case then it would be somewhat misleading to conclude that the standard of living of the population as a whole materially improved.

It is important, therefore, to analyse the way in which the total income gain was distributed. Here we shall be concerned primarily with tracing the changes in income of those in employment that is the wage and salary earners or the returns to labour, rather than with income return to capital and property in the form of profits, rent, etc., or from self-employment. The reasons for concentrating on the former are quite simple. The bulk of the population derived its livelihood

[1] This is based on Feinstein's estimates. Earlier estimates suggest a lower rate of expansion.

from being employed while incomes from wages and salaries accounted for nearly 55 per cent of gross national product.[1] Wage earners were by far the largest group; in 1938 they accounted for 77 per cent of total employment and 65 per cent of the total wage and salary bill.[2] Secondly, though the returns to capital and property declined compared with before the war, there was no marked deterioration during the inter-war period and there is little evidence to suggest that the minority class who received the bulk of the unearned income suffered a drop in living standards.[3] In any case, even if it did it was only a relative one and most people in this class had large accumulated reserves to fall back on. By contrast, many wage earners had little in the form of stand-by reserves and for the most part their living standards depended on their current earning capacity. For this class of people any drop in real income constituted a serious problem.

Unfortunately, defining the area of study in no way eases the task of measuring living standards. The problems involved in this regard are numerous. Some of these will become apparent during the course of this chapter but it is as well to mention briefly the most important difficulties lest the reader infers too readily at any particular point that he has arrived at the final answer regarding changes in living standards. For one thing the national wage indices suffer from the most obvious defects of all indices of this type in that they reflect an average which may well represent no one in particular from the population sample. They conceal significant variations in wages between occupations, industries and regions and they cover a working force which varies in composition as regards skill, age and sex. Secondly, wage indices (or more correctly real wage indices in this context) can never measure fully changes in living standards since they leave far too much out of account. They generally refer to fully employed workers and make no proper allowance, if any, for irregularities of employment and hours of work, welfare benefits and payments in kind, and the social and environmental conditions of work and living, e.g. canteen and recreational facilities and housing conditions. The

---

[1] Excluding Forces' pay and employers' insurance contributions. C. H. Feinstein, 'Changes in the Distribution of the National Income in the United Kingdom Since 1860', ch. 4. in J. Marchal and B. Ducros (eds.), *The Distribution of National Income* (1968), p. 119.

[2] A. L. Chapman and R. Knight, *Wages and Salaries in the United Kingdom 1920–1938* (1953), pp. 18, 23.

[3] See below under income distribution.

M

TABLE 38 *Indices of money wages, employment and retail prices, 1913, 1919–38*

(*1930 = 100*)

	Average annual earnings	Average annual wage earnings	Weekly wage rates	Retail prices (cost of living) index	Total employment	Unemployment percentage
	(*1*)	(*2*)	(*3*)	(*4*)	(*5*)	(*6*)
1913	—	52·4	53·2	63·3	—	2·1
1919	—	—	122·3	136·1	—	2·1
1920	132·5	143·7	146·8	157·6	107·1	2·0
1921	126·6	134·6	145·7	143·0	91·7	17·1
1922	106·0	107·9	111·7	115·8	92·4	13·6
1923	99·5	100·0	100·0	110·1	94·4	11·2
1924	100·5	101·5	102·1	110·8	95·7	10·0
1925	101·1	102·2	102·1	111·4	96·8	11·1
1926	100·1	99·3	102·1	108·9	94·2	12·3
1927	100·8	101·5	102·1	106·0	100·1	9·4
1928	100·0	100·1	102·1	105·1	100·6	10·5
1929	100·2	100·4	101·1	103·8	102·3	10·0
1930	100·0	100·0	100·0	100·0	100·0	16·4
1931	98·6	98·2	98·9	93·4	97·2	21·2
1932	97·0	96·3	97·9	91·1	97·6	21·8
1933	96·4	95·3	95·7	88·6	100·1	19·2
1934	97·4	96·4	95·7	89·2	103·5	16·3
1935	98·8	98·0	96·8	90·5	105·7	15·0
1936	100·7	100·2	98·9	93·0	109·5	12·5
1937	102·6	102·8	103·2	97·5	113·8	10·3
1938	105·7	106·3	106·4	98·7	114·0	12·3

NOTES AND SOURCES

Col. 1 All wage and salary earners. A. L. Chapman and R. Knight, *Wages and Salaries in the United Kingdom, 1920–1938* (1953), p. 30.

Col. 2 Covers mining and quarrying, manufacturing, building, transport and communications, utilities, local government and some other services. E. H. Phelps Brown and Margaret Browne, *A Century of Pay* (1968), p. 399 and Appendix 3, U.K., col. 1.

Col. 3 Covers industries and services and based on a constant pattern of employment. *London and Cambridge Economic Bulletin*, 44 (Dec. 1962), p. xiii.

biggest problem in this period was, of course, the unemployment which was only partly offset by increased welfare payments. Thus at best an index of real wages can only measure changes in the wage earnings of those in continuous employment when expressed in a 'composite unit of consumables'.[1] Finally, changes in wage earnings provide an even less accurate guide to movements in the material welfare of the average family, if there is such a thing. For this purpose we need to know more about the composition of the family as regards size, the number of wage earners and dependents and the age and sex of the members of the household.

Clearly therefore there is no single indicator which measures accurately changes in living standards of the population as a whole. Certainly movements in wage indices will give a broad idea of the dimensions of improvement or deterioration, always bearing in mind the many variations from the average, but an accurate assessment must make some allowance for these variations and also take into account some of the factors not covered in the wage indices. Thus once we have charted the main wage trends we must broaden the picture by examining some of these less tangible elements.

Wages and their determination

Table 38 lists three indices of wages and earnings. These figures are all in money terms and represent earnings or rates per man or man-week employed. Thus no inference about living standards can be made from them. The first column is an index of average annual earnings of all wage and salary earners while the second refers to wage earners only and covers mining, manufacturing, building, transport and some services. The third column contains an index of average wage rates paid to employees mainly in industrial occupations. All three indices

[1] E. H. Phelps Brown and Margaret Browne, *A Century of Pay* (1968), p. 157.

Col. 4 Ministry of Labour cost of living index. B. R. Mitchell and Phyllis Deane, *Abstract of British Historical Statistics* (1962), p. 478.

Col. 5 Employment in man-years. Chapman and Knight, *op. cit.*, pp. 32–3.

Col. 6 1921–38, percentage of insured workers unemployed, average of four quarters (March, June, Sept., Dec.). E. M. Burns, *British Unemployment Programs, 1920–1938* (1941), p. 343. Before 1921 percentage unemployed in certain trade unions. London and Cambridge Economic Service, *The British Economy: Key Statistics, 1900–1966* (1967), Table E, p. 8. *Cf* the slightly different estimates in Table 34.

show a broad degree of similarity in their movements. There was a strong and sustained rise during the war and immediately thereafter; by 1918 wages and earnings were roughly double the pre-war level and in the post-war boom they rose to two and one half to three times above the 1913 base. The somewhat lower peak in total earnings (col. 1) in 1920 can largely be accounted for by the lag in salary earnings behind wages. Then came a dramatic collapse which lasted until well into 1923 by which time wages and earnings had fallen to slightly under twice their 1913 levels. After these violent fluctuations movements in wages were very modest indeed. They remained remarkably stable until 1930 when a downward trend set in. But the decline was very moderate compared with that of post-war and was checked in 1934. Thereafter wages rose slowly until 1938 when they were about five or six per cent higher than in 1930 and just about double the pre-war level.

Though the amplitude of the swings in wages moderated considerably after the post-war boom and collapse there was no marked reduction in the flexibility of wages in this period.[1] Downward pressure on wages was possible both in the 1920s and 1930s and generally speaking earnings and wages moved cyclically though with some lag behind the turning points in business activity.[2] However, cyclical conformity was greater after 1929 than in the 1920s apart from the immediate post-war years. Between 1923 and 1929 wages remained very stable despite the fact that employment and output expanded more or less continuously. This poses the question as to whether wage movements can be explained simply as a response to cyclical forces.

There are many possible determinants of wages: trade union pressure on wage claims, changes in unit wage costs and productivity, the state of the labour market as reflected in employment and unemployment trends, price movements and competition. Not all of these necessarily exhibit strong cyclical characteristics. Trade union bargaining power will depend upon the strength of the unions, and its success on that of the employers, while productivity and price movements may cut across the cycle. But in general most of these factors do react cyclically and in many cases there is a close degree of interaction. For example, in a period of rising employment and activity one would expect greater trade union pressure for increased wages, and

[1] J. T. Dunlop, 'Trends in the Rigidity of English Wage Rates', *Review of Economic Studies*, 6 (1938–9), pp. 189–91.
[2] G. Bry, *Wages in Germany, 1871–1915* (1960), pp. 291–2. Bry found the conformity more marked in the case of earnings.

the rate at which wage claims are granted would depend upon the availability of labour and the scope for offsetting rising unit wage costs, either by increased productivity or by passing the costs on to the consumer in the form of higher market prices.[1] Given the fact that during boom periods the labour market will become increasingly tight while prices and productivity will probably rise, the prospects for conceding wage claims may be expected to be fairly good. Conversely, when trade slackens and unemployment rises the presentation of wage claims will diminish, unit costs and profit margins will deteriorate and the scope for wage advances will decline. Moreover, a hard market environment caused by falling prices may lead to a forcing down of wages.

Several attempts have been made to explain wage movements in terms of particular variables and a considerable degree of association has been found between wages and levels of employment and unemployment and prices.[2] Although high levels of unemployment in the inter-war period acted as a brake on wage claims it would be difficult to ascribe variations in wages solely to changes in the degree of unemployment.[3] Wages did fluctuate with unemployment particularly over the short-term, but the severity of unemployment did not determine the absolute wage level while over relatively long periods the correspondence was sometimes weak. For example, rising business activity and a decline in unemployment between 1921–29 was accompanied by a substantial reduction in wages. Probably of equal importance in determining wages was the downward trend in prices which was almost continuous from 1920 to 1933–4. This created a hard market environment for the acceptance of wage claims and during times of very high unemployment, as in the early 1920s and early 1930s, the imposition of wage cuts was relatively easy. The fact that many wages were linked to the cost of living index on a sliding scale basis lends added support to this theory. At the peak of the post-war boom, for example, the level of costs and prices was regarded

[1] Unless of course employers are prepared to accept a narrowing of profit margins.
[2] See A. W. Phillips, 'The Relation Between Unemployment and the Rate of Change of Money Wage Rates in the United Kingdom, 1861–1957', *Economica*, 25 (1958); R. G. Lipsey, 'The Relation Between Unemployment and the Rate of Change in Money Wage Rates in the United Kingdom, 1862–1957; A. Further analysis', *ibid.*, 27 (1960); also Lipsey and M. D. Steuer, 'The Relation between Profits and Wage Rates', *ibid.*, 28 (1961).
[3] Compare the experience of other countries in Phelps Brown and Browne, *op. cit.*, p. 223.

as abnormal while unit wage costs were high in relation to market prices. Once the price boom broke however it was possible to force down wages under sliding scale arrangements, though not without considerable industrial strife. Thus of the aggregate reductions in rates, 55 per cent in 1921 and 38 per cent in 1922 (measured in £s per week) were made under sliding scale arrangements of this sort.[1] Rising business activity and falling unemployment after 1921/22 was accompanied by relative wage stability. This was probably the product of two factors : the weak bargaining position of the trade unions especially after the final defeat of labour in 1926, and the downward pressure on prices. With sagging prices at a time of relatively high unit costs in British industry the scope for wage advances was very limited indeed and it is perhaps remarkable that they remained stable.

The fall in money wages in the early 1930s was only to be expected given the high level of unemployment, the decline in business activity and the accelerated downward trend in prices. Probably one half or more of the decline in industrial wage rates came about as a result of sliding scale adjustments. The industries worst affected were textiles and building[2] though most industries suffered reductions and losses of earnings through short-time working. But what is most remarkable is how moderate the decline in wages was during these years. Wages and earnings declined very much less than in the United States and Germany and compared with the post-war collapse the decline of 5 per cent between 1929 and 1933 looks very moderate indeed. The relative mildness of the British slump and the greater strength of the trade unions in this country account in part for the less drastic fall in wages.

Despite a high level of unemployment throughout the 1930s – on average higher than in the 1920s but declining between 1932–37 – wages advanced fairly steadily in the later 1930s. Only part of this increase can be attributed to the rising cost of living since the latter was still below the pre-depression level even by 1938 (see Table 38). An additional factor was the sectoral inequality in the labour market. From 1935 onwards there was sufficient excess demand in some areas and trades to force up wages despite large pools of unemployment elsewhere.[3] Phelps Brown also suggests that wages were able to drift upwards because the rise in productivity made for a

[1] G. Routh, *Occupation and Pay in Great Britain 1906–60* (1965), p. 115.
[2] *ibid.*, p. 120.
[3] Lipsey (1960), *loc. cit.*, p. 29.

lowering of unit wage costs. In fact, he suggests that they might have risen faster had it not been for the inhibiting effects of the depression on wage claims and the efforts of industrialists to widen profit margins which had previously been squeezed. 'It seems likely that money wages would have risen more than they did, had not the readiness of trade unions to present claims, and of employers to resist them, both been still affected by the experience of 1931–32.'[1]

In the main cyclical forces were the chief determinant of wage movements though the latter did not react quickly to changes in

TABLE 39 *Income and earnings, 1911/13–1938 (£)*

	Average annual money wage earnings	Average annual salary earnings	Income per capita
1911	—	140	—
1913	62·8		49·6
1924	121·7	245	83·6
1938	127·5	240	101·2
% increase			
1911/13–38	103·0	71·4	104·0
1911/13–24	93·8	75·0	68·5
1924–38	4·8	− 2·0	21·1

SOURCES Col. 1, as for col. 2, Table 38; col. 2, Feinstein in Marchal and Duclos, *op. cit.*, p. 120; col. 3, Feinstein current income estimates divided through by total population—'National Income and Expenditure of the United Kingdom 1870–1963', *London and Cambridge Economic Bulletin*, 50 (1964), p. xi.

business activity. Changes in unemployment and prices, especially the latter in the long-term, were the main factors at work. Insofar as the long-term downward trend in prices was exogeneously determined, it might be possible to claim that for part of the time a non-internal cyclical force was at work. There were, in addition, long-term forces making for an increase in the average level of incomes from employment. The redistribution of income in favour of labour raised the average level of earnings of employed workers. Most of the gain accrued to salary workers. There was a marked increase in the number of salaried workers; between 1911 and 1938 the number increased from 1·67 to 3·84 million and the ratio of wage to salaried

[1] Phelps Brown and Browne, *op. cit.*, p. 239.

workers fell from 9·1 to 3·9.[1] Though many salaried occupations were low paid average incomes were generally higher than those of wage earners so that the average earnings of all employees were raised. Although inter-industry shifts of labour had a negligible effect on wage earnings the latter benefited from the fact that the total wage bill remained fairly constant in terms of national income at a time when the proportion of wage earners to total employment was declining slightly.[2]

The main effect of these income changes are summarized in Table 39. Over the period 1913 and 1938 average annual wage earnings rose by 103 per cent an increase which was very similar to that in income per capita of the whole population. Salary earnings rose somewhat less probably by between 70 and 75 per cent.[3] Most of the rise in employment incomes occurred during the war and post-war boom. Between 1924 and the end of the 1930s wages rose by only about five per cent while salary earnings fell slightly. Income per capita however rose by 21·6 per cent in these years.

Wage differentials

The national wage indices are bound to conceal many differences in both the levels and movements of wages between different industries, occupations, skills and regions. These variations were many and varied and it would be impossible to discuss them all here. In any case many of the absolute differences in wages as between one industry and another were of long-standing origin and can be explained quite easily in terms of the nature of the work, composition of the labour force etc. Here we are mainly interested in new trend developments of major importance.

As one might expect wages were generally lower in the older staple industries and their fluctuations through time sharper than those of the newer industries. It can be seen from Table 40 that in the early 1930s the median average weekly earnings in the staple industries of coal, cotton, wool, general engineering and shipbuilding were some 10*s* or more below those of the newer industries. Short-time working was certainly more prevalent in the older sectors and may have affected the average earnings, though it is noticeable that wages rates fell sharply

[1] Feinstein in Marchal and Duclos, *op. cit.*, p. 120.
[2] Income distribution is discussed more fully in the last section of this chapter.
[3] This is only an approximate figure since the salary estimates for pre-war are very tentative.

in these industries during recession.[1] Moreover, the extremes in average earnings were very wide indeed. For example, in the last week in October 1938 the average earnings of adult male workers in jute, wool, cotton and textile finishing ranged between 50s 9d and 57s 6d, whereas in the motor vehicle and aircraft industries they were 83s 3d, in general engineering 73s 7d and in hosiery 75s 1d[2]. Some of the differences may have been due to variations in short-time and overtime working.

TABLE 40 *Median of the distribution of average weekly earnings for male workers (in shillings)*

	Staple industries	New industries	Other industries
1924	52–3	58–2	58–2
1931	45–3	57–4	58–3
1935	47–7	61–5	61–5
1938	57–9	61–3	63–2

Staple industries—coal, wool, cotton, general engineering, shipbuilding.
New industries—chemicals, vehicles, non-ferrous metals, electrical engineering and building.
Other industries—a less homogeneous group mainly consumer goods industries and public utilities.
SOURCE G. Rottier, 'The Evolution of Wage Differentials: a Study of British Data', ch. 15, in J. T. Dunlop (ed.), *The Theory of Wage Determination* (1957), p. 241.

In some of the fast-growing industries overtime was quite extensive despite the high level of unemployment. In building and contracting for instance, over 50 per cent of the workers were employed in excess of the normal working week, while something like two fifths of the male workers covered by the Ministry of Labour's survey in October 1938 were working in excess of normal.[3] On the other hand, it is doubtful whether the low level of earnings in some of the old industries can be attributed primarily to excessive short-time working. Short-time working in the cotton industry, for example, only reduced average earnings by about 3 per cent in October 1938.[4]

[1] See Rottier (cited as source to Table 40), p. 240.
[2] M. P. Fogarty, *Prospects of the Industrial Areas of Great Britain* (1945), p. 11.
[3] R. B. Ainsworth, 'Earnings and Hours of Manual Wage-Earners in the United Kingdom in October 1938', *Journal of the Royal Statistical Society*, A112 (1949), pp. 38, 52.
[4] Fogarty, *op. cit.*, p. 12.

One can generalize too readily however about the level and trend of wages as between old and new industries. By no means all the older industries had low wages. Some occupations had been traditionally low paid, notably textiles where the proportion of women workers was high, but in mining, shipbuilding and engineering earnings were generally high. The main difference was that earnings tended to fluctuate more violently in the staple trades but what they lost in recession they regained in recovery and it seems probable that earnings in these sectors improved relative to those in the new industries taking the period as a whole (see Table 40). Between 1924 and 1938 the largest gains were recorded in iron and steel, shipbuilding, engineering, agriculture and distribution, and the lowest in textiles (a slight fall), building, electricity, mining and many service trades.[1] Nevertheless, in general it would be true to say that earnings and wage rates were lower on average in the old staple industries, either as a result of the incidence of low paid occupations or short-time working, than they were in the expanding industries.[2] From this it follows that average earnings in the depressed areas were lower than in the South and Midlands. Moreover, even within the same industry regional differences in earnings were quite marked. In engineering Knowles and Robertson found significant regional differences in the level of earnings both for skilled and unskilled workers. The highest earnings were in London, the South and the Midlands and as one moved northwards and westwards they tended to decline, the worst areas being Scotland, Wales, Northern Ireland, Yorkshire and Lancashire and Cheshire. The difference between average earnings in the lowest and highest areas was of the order of 30 per cent and there was little narrowing of the differential during the inter-war period.[3] Similarly, the average earnings of Durham coal miners were consistently below those for the industry as a whole throughout the period.[4] Nor were such regional differences confined to the older sectors. They showed up also in the new industries. In rayon, for example, Courtaulds paid higher wages than their competitors but the rates varied geographically between

[1] B. R. Mitchell and Phyllis Deane, *Abstract of British Historical Statistics* (1962), pp. 352–3.
[2] The data are too great to summarize here but interested readers might like to refer to Routh, *op. cit.*, pp. 88, 92, 98, and Chapman and Knight, *op. cit.*, pp. 27, 104, 105, 106.
[3] K. G. J. C. Knowles and D. J. Robertson, 'Earnings in Engineering, 1926–1948', *Bulletin of the Oxford University Institute of Statistics*, 13 (1951), pp. 190, 195.
[4] I am grateful to Dr W. R. Garside for information on this point.

the company's plants.[1] It should be noted however that such differences were more marked in earnings than in wage rates. Due to the increasing extension of nationally negotiated rates of pay discrepancies in wage rates between regions and towns were less significant and in some cases non-existent at all.[2]

Occupational and skill differences were very much larger than differences between industries or regions. This of course was only to be expected. Managers obviously earned more than their junior clerks while skilled operatives in all trades were paid more than labourers or semi-skilled workers. These sort of differences are well known and do not require documentation.[3] What is important is that over the long-term the tendency was for the lower paid workers to improve their relative position vis-à-vis other employees. Thus if we take the broad division between wages and salaries we find that the ratio of average annual wage earnings to those of salaries rose from 0·36 in 1911 to 0·51 in 1924 and 0·54 in 1938.[4] Most of the improvement in the relative status of wage earners occurred during the war and post-war boom when the high demand for labour pushed up the money earnings of manual workers while non-manual earnings or salaries lagged behind. However, since wages were more sensitive to cyclical fluctuations than salaries some of the relative improvement was lost in the early 1920s and again in the early 1930s. But in the recovery of the 1930s there was a further narrowing of the differential between wage and salary earnings, especially in the later part of the decade when annual earnings rose rapidly.[5] On balance between 1924 and 1938 there was a slight improvement in the wage earners' position. Wage rates and earnings rose by about five per cent while salaries fell slightly.[6]

---

[1] See D. C. Coleman, *Courtalds: An Economic and Social History*, vol. 2 (1969), p. 432.
[2] See the figures in *Twenty-Second Abstract of Labour Statistics of the United Kingdom* (1922–1936), Cmd 556, (1937), pp. 72–6.
[3] See Routh, *op. cit.*, p. 104, for examples.
[4] Feinstein in Marchal and Duclos, *op. cit.*, p. 120. The ratio for 1911 is possibly somewhat on the low side since Feinstein's estimate for average annual wage earnings for 1911 (£50) appears to be rather low.
[5] Routh, *op. cit.*, p. 124.
[6] A. L. Bowley (ed.), *Studies in the National Income, 1924–1938* (1942), pp. 92–3; and J. G. Marley and H. Campion 'Changes in Salaries in Great Britain, 1924–1939', *Journal of the Royal Statistical Society*, 103 (1940), p. 552; also G. Routh, 'Civil Service Pay, 1875 to 1950', *Economica*, 21 (1954), p. 216.

Skill differentials among manual workers also narrowed during periods of rising prices and increasing demand for labour. The practice of granting flat rate increases or bonuses was mainly responsible for the reduction in differentials. Again the main change occurred between 1914 and the peak of the post-war boom. Thus the time rates of unskilled as a percentage of those of skilled workers rose from 66·5 to 83·1 per cent in building, from 55·2 to 77·2 per cent in shipbuilding, and from 58·6 to 78·9 per cent in engineering. During the early 1920s the differentials widened though they never returned to pre-war dimensions. From 1924 through to the depression of the early 1930s there was little change in the ratios of unskilled to skilled rates, though in the later 1930s they narrowed once again. By 1939 the proportions for building, shipbuilding and engineering were 76·3, 73·4 and 75·6 per cent respectively.[1] It is perhaps surprising to find that unskilled workers were able to advance their position at a time of heavy unemployment especially since the incidence of unemployment was higher among this class of workers. It would seem to indicate that the normal demand and supply relationships in the labour market did not always operate in the way one might expect. As Routh has observed 'In general, the labour market does not operate in the way conceived by the theory of demand and supply; the price of labour may rise in the face of high unemployment; it may rise at similar pace for occupations showing contrasting demand-supply relationships, or at different rates for occupations showing similar demand-supply relationships.'[2]

Trends in real income

Fortunately the trend of prices was downward in the inter-war years; if this had not been the case the British worker would have enjoyed little improvement in his standard of living. From the post-war peak in 1920 retail prices (cost of living index) fell almost continuously down to 1933–4, after which they rose slowly. The most dramatic declines occurred in the early 1920s and the early 1930s. This fall was sufficient, when set against the movement in wages, to generate a fairly marked

[1] K. G. J. C. Knowles and D. J. Robertson, 'Differences Between the Wages of Skilled and Unskilled Workers, 1880–1950', *Bulletin of the Oxford University Institute of Statistics* 13 (1951), pp. 111–14.
[2] Routh, *op. cit.*, p. 147.

rise in real earnings.[1] In Table 41 the money earnings of all employees and of wage earners (from cols. 1 and 2 of Table 38) have been converted into real terms by deflating with the Ministry of Labour's cost of living index. This latter index has frequently been criticized on the grounds that it is weighted heavily in favour of pre-war working class consumption patterns. However, attempts to revise the index to make it more representative do not appear to make a great deal of difference. The Ministry's index is not very accurate for the early post-war years but thereafter it differs only by a point or two from the new estimates. In fact, for most of the period the movements in the official index and the most recently revised estimates by Stone and Rowe are almost identical.[2]

From Table 41 it can be seen that the real earnings of wage earners rose quite significantly between 1913 and 1920/21 after which they fell slightly and then remained stable until the late 1920s. They then rose almost continuously through to 1935 after which they declined very slightly. The upward movement was somewhat erratic, most of the gains occurring between 1926–27 and 1929–31. By 1938 average real wage earnings were some 30 per cent higher than they had been in 1913 while real income per capita rose by about 31 per cent. The gains were very unevenly distributed over time however. A considerable increase in real wages took place between 1913 and the early 1920s, whereas per capita real income actually declined slightly up to 1924.[3] Thereafter real income per capita rose by nearly 36 per cent through to 1938, whereas real wage earnings increased by less than half this amount.

These of course are only approximate estimates of the advances in real incomes. The nature of the data allows no more than this. We should also point out that these figures may underestimate the increase in real wage earnings. If, as Feinstein suggests, the average money wage was as low as £50 in 1911 then the increase in real wages

---

[1] J. Burnett, *A History of the Cost of Living* (1969), pp. 307–12.
[2] R. Stone and D. A. Rowe, *The Measurement of Consumers' Expenditure and Behaviour in the United Kingdom 1920–1938*, vol. 2 (1966), p. 114; see also Chapman and Knight, *op. cit.*, pp. 28–9.
[3] The national income estimates may understate the growth (or lack of) of income per capita between these two dates. There is no doubt however that wage earners improved their position relative to non-wage earners. The war time and post war inflation hit severely those living on salaries and fixed incomes, while the heavy increase in income tax, profits tax and controls (e.g. on rents) reduced net incomes in the higher brackets and incomes from profits and rents.

TABLE 41 *Indices of real earnings, 1913, 1920–38 (1930 = 100)*

	Average annual real earnings	Average annual real wage earnings
1913		82·8
1920	84·1	91·2
1921	88·5	94·1
1922	91·5	93·2
1923	90·4	90·8
1924	90·7	91·6
1925	90·8	91·7
1926	91·9	91·2
1927	95·1	95·8
1928	95·1	95·2
1929	96·5	96·7
1930	100·0	100·0
1931	105·6	105·1
1932	106·5	105·7
1933	108·8	107·6
1934	109·2	108·1
1935	109·2	108·3
1936	108·3	107·7
1937	105·2	105·4
1938	107·1	107·7

SOURCE Cols. 1 and 2 of Table 38 converted into real terms using cost of living index (col. 4) as deflator.

through to 1938 would be very much greater. But an upper limit of 40 per cent increase between 1913 and 1938 would seem to be generous. However, whatever the exact amount there is little doubt that real wages and incomes rose very much faster than they had done in the couple of decades before 1914.

Most of the increase in real wages has been attributed to productivity advances. Phelps Brown and Margaret Browne have formulated the following identity expressed in average annual percentage rates of change:

$$W_r = P + W_i + B$$

where W_r is the real wage, P the advance in productivity, W_1 the wage/income ratio, that is the share of industry's product going to labour, and B the barter terms on which the units of the wage earner's own product can be exchanged for units of his own consumption. Substituting the relevant values for these terms gives us

$$1·68 = 1·79 + (-0·63) + 0·49$$

for the period 1924–38.[1] Thus the improvement in barter terms due largely to the improvement in the terms of trade between 1929–31, was more than offset by the deterioration in the wage/income ratio so that the actual advance in real wages was dependent entirely on the current increase in productivity. The results of course depend upon the terminal years chosen and it is possible that they rather underestimate the contribution of improving barter terms. Nevertheless, it does appear that the improvement in real wage earnings was very much dependent on productivity growth the absence of which before 1914 was one of the main reasons for the stability of real wages.

An increase in real earnings was not the only gain secured by workers in this period. Hours of work were reduced substantially shortly after the first world war as a result of the eight hour day movement. This reached its culmination in 1919–20. In 1919, 6½ million workers obtained reductions averaging 6½ hours a week without loss of pay, while in the following year a further half million or so were similarly affected. This reduced the average working week to around 48 hours or less compared with 53–54 hours before the war. By contrast the period between 1921 and 1938 was rather lean in terms of reduced working hours. The total number of workers affected by reductions was only a fraction of that of 1919–20 and was more or less offset by increases elsewhere, mainly the miners in 1926.[2] Nevertheless, for most workers there had been an 11-per-cent reduction in nominal working hours, or one hour a day less, compared with pre-war. The total gain to workers can be estimated by converting that part taken out in the form of shorter hours into real terms and adding it to the increase in real earnings. Given that real wage earnings rose by 30 per cent between 1913 and 1938 and assuming a reduction of six hours in the working week giving a total of 48 in 1938, then the overall gain by that date would by $30 + (6/48 × 130)$, that

[1] Phelps Brown and Browne, *op. cit.*, pp. 167, 263.
[2] B. McCormick, 'Hours of Work in British Industry', *Industrial and Labour Relations Review*, 12 (1959), pp. 426–8, 431.

is an increase of 46·3 on the base year. Of this gain 30 percentage points was in the form of increased real earnings and the remainder represented a bonus in the form of leisure.[1]

Paid holidays represented a similar kind of gain. Before the war very few manual workers enjoyed paid holiday leave (excepting Bank Holidays) though salaried workers usually had some provision in this respect. There was a burst of holiday with pay agreements shortly after the war but the movement soon fizzled out in the subsequent slump. By the end of 1929 probably not more than three million employees in all (manual and non-manual) were covered by such agreements. It was not until the late 1930s, partly as a result of legislation in 1938 (Holidays with Pay Act), that the practice of granting paid holidays became at all widespread. Between early 1937 and June 1939 the number embraced under such arrangements jumped from about four to 11 million and by the latter date probably some 50 per cent of all manual workers received a week's paid leave.[2] For those fortunate enough to enjoy this benefit it meant an additional two or three percentage points in real terms. Converting as before the total gain, assuming one week's holiday as being roughly equivalent to one hour reduction in the working week, would be $30 + (7/48 \times 130)$, or almost 49 per cent above the base year.

An increase of around 50 per cent seems a reasonable estimate of the total real gain secured by wage earners (somewhat less for salaried employees) between 1913 and the end of the 1930s. This is probably as far as one can go in quantifying the gains. Most workers also enjoyed other benefits, e.g. unemployment insurance facilities, better canteen and social and recreational amenities. Such improvements are difficult to quantify but it is unlikely that they added a great deal to the total gain given above. In addition, of course, there was a vast extension in public welfare and social services but these were not derived specifically from employment (except unemployment insurance) and can be more conveniently dealt with later.

It should be stressed that the gains so far considered refer mainly

[1] Phelps Brown and Browne, *op. cit.*, p. 209. Insofar as some of the increased leisure was reworked in the form of overtime then the calculation overstates the total gain because of double counting. The effect of this is, however, small.
[2] G. C. Cameron, 'The Growth of Holidays with Pay in Britain', ch. 10, in G. L. Reid and D. J. Robertson (eds.), *Fringe Benefits, Labour Costs and Social Security* (1965), pp. 274–81; L. J. Lickorish and A. G. Kershaw, *The Travel Trade* (1958), p. 44.

to the average industrial worker in full time employment. There were many variations between industries, occupations and regions, but since these have already been discussed in monetary terms there is no need to repeat the exercise once again as they are all to be set against the same cost of living index. More important however is the fact that they relate to individual workers in continuous employment and as such tell us little about the condition of those out of work for lengthy periods of time or the experiences of the individual family. Nor do they provide any guide as to the level of poverty or wealth existing in Britain during this period. It is to a discussion of these aspects that we must now turn.

The family unit

The average family is probably a more misleading and abused concept than the average worker. But short of analysing a whole range of family experiences, the data for which is not available anyhow, there is no alternative but to take a 'typical' family which is to some extent representative of a relatively large sample. Fortunately at this juncture we are interested in a family unit which will tie in with the income data considered above, namely one in which there was at least one adult wage earner in continuous employment.

Expenditure patterns and budgetary surveys suggest that many families enjoyed a considerable improvement in their standard of living during this period. This was certainly true of most middle class households but many working class families also shared in the improvement.[1] The Ministry of Labour's budgetary inquiries (for purposes of its cost of living index) give a rather idyllic picture of the 'average' family experience. The average family depicted was one in which the head of the household had a steady job, drew a regular wage packet and supported one or two children with perhaps a third of income earning age. In 1937–8 the income of this average family was more than double that of 1913–14 and it was spread over 20 per cent less persons due to a decline in the size of the family. Thus in real terms income per capita may have risen by about 60–70 per cent.[2]

[1] Working class being defined as where the main income earner received less than £250 per annum. In 1937, 86 per cent of the population had incomes below this limit. T. Barna, *The Redistribution of Incomes Through Public Finance in 1937* (1945), p. 225.
[2] M. Abrams, *The Condition of the British People, 1911–1945* (1946), pp. 83–4.

A good part of the increase in income, possibly one quarter, went on more food with the result that per capita food consumption rose by some 30–35 per cent. But within the total expenditure on food there had been a significant shift away from the cheap and starchy foods of the filler type towards those with a more nutritious value. Food expenditure patterns for the nation as a whole show that per capita consumption of wheat (and therefore presumably bread), other cereals and potatoes fell steadily over the period – potato consumption per head declined by no less than 22 per cent between 1909/14 and 1934/38 – while there was a significant increase in the intake of dairy products, including butter, cheese, and eggs, fats, sugar, fresh fruit and vegetables. Rather surprisingly, however, the consumption of meat and fish per head declined and this was one respect in which dietary standards were deficient.[1] Thus, by the 1930s the average diet was considerably better than that of pre-war both in calorific and nutritional value.[2]

The bulk of the increase in income went on non-food products however. Increased expenditure on rent, fuel and light, clothing, household equipment, tobacco, newspapers and transport accounted for another 45 per cent of the rise in family income. The remaining 30 per cent went on what might be regarded as luxury products which had scarcely featured in the family's budget before the war, either because they were not available or because they were beyond the range of this class of incomes. Thus expenditure on entertainment and holidays, on services like laundry and hairdressing, and on consumer durable goods such as radios, electrical appliances etc, increased steadily throughout the period. The working classes were even buying their own homes and running their own cars. Luxuries were no longer the sole prerogative of the middle and upper classes. All this could be achieved on a working week of six hours less than pre-war and in many cases a week's paid holiday a year.

The figures for consumer expenditure per head in real terms show a marked increase in this period, from an average of £75·38 in 1910–14 to £92·76 in 1935–8 (1938 prices), that is an increase of approximately 23 per cent.[3] The most dramatic increases occurred

---

[1] J. C. McKenzie, 'Past Dietary Trends as an Aid to Prediction', in T. C. Barker, J. C. McKenzie and T. Yudkin (eds.), *Our Changing Fare*(1966), p. 136; J. C. Drummond and A. Wilbraham, *The Englishman's Food*, (1958 ed.), p. 430.

[2] J. Burnett, *Plenty and Want* (1968 ed.), pp. 298–9.

[3] Stone and Rowe, *op. cit.*, vol. 2, p. 126.

in housing, transport and durable household goods, all of which were income elastic goods and services. But statistics themselves do not always convey a complete picture of the improvements and social changes wrought by improved accommodation, the greater opportunities for entertainment and recreation (e.g. the cinema, radio and the dance halls), the increased possibilities for travel, more leisure time to pursue hobbies, and the reduced drudgery of household chores as a result of better cooking facilities and other household gadgets. Nor do they express the opportunities and greater security provided by the extensive spread of public welfare services such as education and insurance against unemployment, sickness and old age.

If the Ministry's index family was better paid, better fed, better clothed and housed and healthier than its counterpart in 1913, there were at the same time many families for whom grinding poverty was very close at hand. Even after allowing for the effects of unemployment the extent of poverty at the end of the period was surprisingly high and somewhat tempers the average gains secured in these years. A balanced picture of the material welfare of the population must of course take into account the other side of the coin. But before discussing this aspect in more detail a digression will be made into the extent and scope of the social services, their contribution to income distribution and the shortcomings of these services in the light of the then current needs.

The contribution of the social services

It might appear ironic to speak of the greater security provided by the social services at a time when the unemployment insurance system was creaking under the weight of mass unemployment. In fact it was often unable to provide sufficient assistance especially for those whose contributions had run out, so that many were forced back on to the old poor relief or public assistance. Nevertheless, despite certain failings in the system there can be no doubt that the vast extension of public services between 1913 and 1938 provided a greater measure of security and did something to ease, and even raise in some cases, the standard of life in Britain.[1]

The modern welfare system was started in the early twentieth century by the Liberals, but the services which they began were very patchy and up to the first world war the level of social expenditure

[1] P.E.P., *Report on the British Social Services* (1937), p. 161.

per head was very small.[1] In no sense were the services comprehensive and the poor relief remained the great standby for most people. After the war there were considerable pressures to extend the new State services, not the least of which was the persistent unemployment. It was recognized also that the extension of centralized social services would ease the burden on local relief authorities. The approach therefore was to expand the services started before the war and even to introduce new ones. Thus unemployment insurance, which covered a rather limited number of occupations before the war, was greatly extended in 1920 to include 11 million people. Further trades were brought in during the course of the inter-war years so that by 1938 it embraced 15·4 million people, though even then its coverage was not fully comprehensive.[2] The scale of benefits varied a great deal partly because the scheme ran into difficulties as a result of the sheer magnitude of the problem with which it was faced. Similarly, the scope of the health service was extended, though originally its coverage had been wider than the other schemes; by 1939 it included some 20 million people or nearly half the population above the age of 14, compared with 15 million in 1921. Yet this still left nearly as many dependents outside the scheme unprotected against distress and sickness.[3] The third pre-war scheme, that of old age pensions, was not changed in principle but payments were raised to 10s per week and the income limits, above which payments were not made, were increased. In addition, a new contributory pension scheme, together with allowances for widows and orphans, was inaugurated in 1925. By 1937 some 20 million people were covered under the legislation of 1925 and over three million were already receiving benefits.[4] Apart from the insurance schemes there were of course other public services the

---

[1] It is intended here to give only the very briefest outline of the growth and development of the social services. The literature is extensive for those interested. See, for example, W. H. Wickwar, *The Social Services: An Historical Survey* (1936, 1949); J. S. Ross, *The National Health Service in Great Britain* (1952); P.E.P., *Report on the British Social Services* (1937) and *The British Health Services* (1937); S. J. Curtis, *History of Education in Great Britain* (7th ed. 1967). There is also a contemporary statistical analysis by Sir Gwilym Gibbon, 'The Public Social Services', *Journal of the Royal Statistical Society*, 100 (1937). The best short general survey is to be found in S. Pollard, *The Development of the British Economy, 1914–1950* (1962), ch. v, esp. section 2. Also M. Bruce, *The Coming of the Welfare State* (1961), ch. vi.

[2] Pollard, *op. cit.*, p. 249.

[3] Bruce, *op. cit.*, p. 213.

[4] *ibid.*, pp. 218–19.

most important of which were education, child care and housing. All of these were extended or improved in the course of the period though educational policy still left much to be desired. Though a more effective pattern of education was emerging[1] and facilities in schools were improved – for example by the widening of curricula and the reduction in the number of oversize classes – there still remained much scope for further progress. Fisher's Education Act of 1918 was a step in the right direction but even this forward looking legislation fell foul of economy cuts. It proved impossible to push the school leaving age beyond 14, while higher education still remained very much the preserve of the rich. But perhaps the most promising area of success was in housing where intervention occurred on a grand scale. The local authorities built over one million houses which were mostly for letting to low income families, while in the 1920s private builders received Treasury subsidies.

The upshot of all this activity was that expenditure on social services rose rapidly and absorbed an increasing share of the national product. Total government expenditure on all services in monetary terms rose from £101 million in 1913 to £438 million in 1929 and to £596 million in 1938, equivalent respectively to 4·1, 9·5 and 11·3 per cent of the gross national product. In per capita terms the expenditure amounted to £12·5 in 1938 compared with £9·6 in 1929 and £2·2 in 1913. After allowing for price changes this represented a more than threefold increase between 1913 and 1938.[2]

This expenditure did not represent solely a shift of income from rich to poor. The redistributive effect was modified in several ways. For one thing both rich and poor alike stood to gain from the social services. In fact in some cases, notably education and housing, it was the better off manual workers and the middle classes who gained most. Secondly, some of the welfare schemes were financed in part by the workers themselves. It has been estimated that employees' weekly insurance contributions rose from 1·9 per cent of average industrial

[1] By the end of the 1930s the pattern of secondary education, consisting of grammar and modern schools, had taken shape with division between primary and secondary education taking place at the age of 11.
[2] Social services covered are education and child care, health services, national insurance—unemployment, sickness benefits and pensions—national assistance, housing (subsidies and capital expenditure) and food subsidies. A. T. Peacock and J. Wiseman, *The Growth of Public Expenditure in the United Kingdom* (2nd ed. 1967), Tables A-15 to A-17, pp. 184–91.

earnings in 1912 to 2.3 per cent in 1938.[1] Thirdly, compared with before the war the burden of taxation on the lower income groups (under £250 a year) had increased considerably despite the move towards a more progressive income tax. This was largely because of the increasing incidence of indirect taxes which were very regressive at the lower end of the income scale. In fact, no less than two thirds of all indirect taxes were paid by those earning less than £250 per annum. Thus a married man with three children under 16 earning £100 a year paid 10·4 per cent of his income in tax (all indirect) in 1937–8 as against only 5·4 per cent in 1913–14.[2] Altogether persons with incomes below £250 a year paid £14 million in direct taxes, £407 million in indirect taxes and £57 million in social insurance contributions.[3]

Notwithstanding these qualifications there was some redistribution of income through progressive direct taxation and social service expenditure. It is difficult to give very precise estimates of the amount since much depends on the assumptions made and the allocation of indivisible benefits. A thorough study made by Barna for 1937 concluded that, whatever assumptions were made regarding the distribution of indivisible expenditure, the direction of the redistribution of income was definitely from the rich to the poor, and that the amount was best put at £200–250 million a year. This was equivalent to about five or six per cent of the national income with outside limits ranging from two to 14 per cent according to differing assumptions. The bulk of the gain went to those with incomes under £125 a year, while those in the £125–250 income bracket benefited only to a small extent. The total effect was to raise the incomes of the working classes by 8 – 14 per cent and reduce those of the upper and middle classes by 10–18 per cent according to the assumptions adopted.[4] Most other

---

[1] Pollard, *op. cit.*, p. 207.

[2] In fact this estimate understates the burden of taxation in 1937–8 since to secure comparability with pre-war certain indirect taxes (e.g. petrol and protective duties) have been excluded from the calculation. If all taxes are taken into account then a married man (with two dependent children) earning £100 a year paid 18 per cent of his income in tax. See G. F. Shirras and L. Rostas, *The Burden of British Taxation* (1942), pp. 55–8.

[3] Figures are for 1937, Barna, *op. cit.*, p. 214.

[4] *ibid.*, pp. 232–3; *cf* U. K. Hicks, *Public Finance* (1947), p. 299, who reckoned that redistribution levelled up incomes in the two lowest incomes brackets (under £125 and £125–250) by converting per capita production incomes of £54 and £69 respectively into consumption incomes of £59 and £64.

estimates were less elaborate than those of Barna and in general suggested a lower rate of redistribution. Colin Clark calculated that before the war the working classes contributed in taxation more than the cost of the social services from which they benefited, whereas by 1935 they contributed only 79 per cent of the cost and stood to gain up to £91 million.[1]

Though by the end of the period the redistribution of income was at a higher level than in any previous year, and probably more extensive than in any other country, the total effect was relatively small. If, for instance, the level of unemployment in 1937 (1·5 million) had been reduced by about one half this would have raised the national income by the same order of magnitude as the amount redistributed.[2] There were in any case limits to the extent to which redistribution could be carried and to the effects it would have. Hicks reckoned that working class standards of living were more likely to be raised by increases in production than by changes in income distribution.[3] Moreover, in relation to the level of working class incomes and the degree of poverty prevailing in Britain in 1937, the amount redistributed was pitifully inadequate. The unemployed man and his family might possibly have been better off in the 1930s than the unskilled labourer in work before the war, but this was very much a relative judgement and, as we shall see, the spectre of poverty had by no means been banished from British society.

Thus, remarkable though the extension of social services was in this period it was by no means fully adequate to meet the needs of the time. Benefits, especially for the unemployed, often fell short of human needs, while many of those who had exhausted their insurance claims were forced on to means test assistance and poor relief. As late as 1936 some 330,000 persons were on poor relief and another

[1] C. Clark, *National Income and Outlay* (1937), pp. 146–8. See also U. K. Hicks, *The Finance of British Government, 1920–1936* (1938), pp. 56, 59, and G. D. H. Cole and M. I. Cole, *The Condition of Britain* (1937), p. 335. A more recent estimate by an American scholar gives a net transfer as high as £386 million or 8·8 per cent of the national income. Of this total, £274 million went to those with incomes under £125 a year, £101·4 million to those earning between £125–250 and £10·7 million to those between £250–500. The main loss (£294·4 million) was suffered by those with incomes over £2,000 per annum. These estimates exclude local government expenditure. A. M. Cartter, *The Redistribution of Incomes in Postwar Britain* (1955), p. 66.
[2] Barna, *op. cit.*, p. 233.
[3] J. R. Hicks, *The Social Framework* (1942), p. 190; see below.

600,000 on means test assistance, while throughout the 1920s between 350–450,000 were in receipt of outdoor relief. There were too,
as is so often the case with public welfare schemes, many people
drawing benefits of one kind or another who could well afford to do
without them. By end of the 1930s the whole system of social security
was badly in need of reorganization. Each service had been developed
separately and in a piecemeal fashion to meet specific needs. There
was no comprehensive programme of insurance and the great projects
of 1911 and 1925 fell far short of Chamberlain's 'circle of security'.[1]
Certain groups of people were excluded from the system altogether
while inadequate provision was made for those who had exhausted
claims to benefit. The administration of the schemes was often exceed-
ingly complex, the unemployment and poor relief schemes in particular,
and this must have caused confusion in the minds of both administ-
rators and applicants alike. There was a considerable degree of overlap
between the various facilities and much still lay outside the system.[2]
Thus for example, although a large proportion of the population was
covered by national health insurance, the provision of hospital services
was divided among voluntary organizations, poor law authorities,
public health authorities and private bodies. The unnecessary overlap
and lack of co-ordination were perhaps not surprising in view of the
fragmented way in which they had developed. But in view of this
Topsy-like growth it is even more surprising that no comprehensive
review was undertaken into the principles on which the services were
based, the results achieved and the interrelations between the different
services. Given the absence of review and restructuring, the social
services remained in many respects less comprehensive than the much
abused Poor Law which, for all its deficiencies, 'did provide a comprehensive service and it did take into account the many closely related
social needs of those who applied to it for help. Moreover, they (the
new social services) have left wide gaps which have had to be filled
by the Poor Law after all'.[3] In other words, notwithstanding the
growth of public welfare services of one sort or another, the Poor Law
remained as a residual service to meet the needs of those not entitled,
or not qualified to receive benefits under the existing schemes.[4]

---

[1] Bruce, *op. cit.*, p. 220.
[2] P.E.P., *Britain's Health* (1939), p. 195.
[3] P.E.P., *Report on the British Social Services* (1937), pp. 43–4, 177–8.
[4] D. C. Marsh, *National Insurance and Assistance in Great Britain* (1950), p. 25.

The spectre of poverty

Most of the evidence points to a considerable improvement in the standard of living and welfare of the British people during the period under review. Not only was there a significant increase in real incomes and real wages but, partly as a result of this improvement and together with the extension of community services, the nation generally was better fed and clothed and was housed in better conditions than those prevailing before the war. The statistics again point to an improvement in the national health and physical well-being of the population. Death rates declined, children were on average taller and healthier than their parents had been, and the worst forms of malnutritional diseases, such as rickets and scurvy, had all but disappeared by the second world war. Tuberculosis, measles, diarrhoea and bronchitis accounted for far fewer children's deaths than in 1911, and influenza was the only disease which caused more.[1] The standardized death rate per 1,000 persons in England and Wales, for example, fell from 13·5 in 1911–14 to 9·3 in 1937, while infantile mortality declined by over 58 per cent between 1900 and 1939.[2] The expectation of life was very much higher than it had been at the end of the nineteenth century. The vast improvement in the quality of men examined for military service in the second world war compared with those examined in the 1914–18 war, suggests that the standard of health was very much better than it had been twenty years earlier.[3]

But progress and poverty still marched together if not hand in hand. The average statistics conceal a great deal of suffering and distress. 'No matter how much the statistics pointed to a general increase in real income there was no doubt, as the uneasy social conscience discovered, that very many families were still, in the thirties, ill fed, ill housed, ill cared for when illness struck'.[4] Material progress by-passed a large section of the community leaving many families close to the poverty line. Disraeli's *Two Nations* took on a new form and poignancy as a gulf emerged between the haves and the have nots among the working classes.[5] Unemployment was an important factor in this distress but it was not the only one.

[1] P.E.P., *Britain's Health* (1939), p. 187.
[2] Sir John Boyd Orr, *Food and the People* (1943), pp. 17, 43.
[3] C. L. Mowat, *Britain Between the Wars, 1918–1940* (1955), p. 513. Mowat's ch. 9 on social conditions in the 1930s is by far the best written to date.
[4] *ibid.*, p. 502.
[5] And given popular vent in John Hilton's, *Rich Man, Poor Man* (1944).

It is difficult to make an exact assessment of the degree and extent of poverty in the inter-war years. This is not for the want of evidence but rather because of the profusion of reports and surveys of social conditions, all of which used different standards to define poverty or minimum human needs, and which were carried out in different towns and regions at various dates in the period. However, since the standards set were generally very low such differences need not worry us unduly here.

By far the most useful survey was the one made for York in 1936 by Seebohm Rowntree.[1] It was not only a very thorough and scholarly survey but it had the advantage of being a repetition of a similar study of the same town in 1899, and therefore made available some comparative data to work on. The worst type of poverty, 'primary poverty', was found to be very much less than it had been in 1899, accounting for 6·8 per cent of the population as against 15·5 per cent in the earlier year. These must be considered minimum figures however, for the standard set was so low as to be unrealistic short of some superhuman housekeeping feat, and even then the resources allowed would not have sufficed to prevent some impairment of bodily health. Consequently, in his later survey Rowntree was forced to revise his standard upwards. He postulated a minimum income for a family of five (two adults and three children) of 53s a week, or 43s 6d excluding rent. Even this standard, as Rowntree himself admitted, was desperately low, for even if the income was guaranteed for 52 weeks of the year it would require constant skill on the part of the housewife to ensure no waste, and practically all of it would be absorbed in providing the absolute necessities for physical health.[2] On this revised basis he found that 31·1 per cent of the working class population of York, or nearly 18 per cent of the total population of the town, had insufficient income to meet the new poverty line. Furthermore, some 14·2 per cent of the working population lived in abject poverty since their incomes were less that 33s 6d a week, while only 36·1 per cent had incomes of 20s or more above the poverty line.[3] Over 75 per cent of the poverty in York could be attributed to three causes: (1) 28·6 per cent on account of the head of the family being out of work; (2) 14·7 per cent because of old age, which was probably the worst kind of poverty; and (3) 32·8 per cent to the fact that the

[1] B. S. Rowntree, *Poverty and Progress* (1941).
[2] B. S. Rowntree, *The Human Needs of Labour* (1937), p. 125.
[3] Rowntree, *Poverty and Progress, op. cit.*, pp. 456–7.

chief income earner, though in regular work, did not earn enough to support his family. The greater part of the income of the first two classes came from the social welfare payments, 80 per cent in the case of the unemployed and 66 per cent for those in old age. On the other hand, families whose poverty was due primarily to inadequate earnings derived only 1·7 per cent of their income from this source.[1]

Several other social surveys were carried out for different areas or towns in the late 1920s and early 1930s, and, though the standards varied somewhat, all came to fairly similar conclusions. The Bristol survey of 1937 reported that about 10·7 per cent of the working class families were poverty stricken and, as in the case of York, the primary causes were unemployment, inadequate wages, old age and, to a lesser extent, sickness. Family size also determined in part the degree of poverty since over 50 per cent of the families with four or more children were in poverty, as were one quarter of those with three children.[2] A new survey of London, using a lower standard than that later employed in the surveys of York and Bristol, found nearly 10 per cent of working-class families in poverty in 1928.[3] Surveys using similar standards were carried out for Merseyside, Liverpool and Southampton in the years 1929 and 1931, and these revealed proportions of 17·3, 16·1 and 20 per cent respectively.[4] Other surveys were also produced for Tyneside, Sheffield, Birmingham and a number of smaller towns.

Certain general conclusions can be drawn about poverty from these social surveys. In most large towns and urban areas in the decade or so before 1939, some 15–20 per cent, sometimes less sometimes more, of the working class population were unable, in spite of assistance from welfare services, to afford a diet that would prevent ill health. This figure is only feasible, moreover, if we assume extreme abstention on the part of the working classes concerned from the simple pleasures and comforts of life. The income available to these families allowed nothing for what we would regard as necessities today. If we relax this assumption then the degree of poverty would certainly be higher. Secondly, unemployment was by no means the only cause of poverty. About one third could be attributed to unemployment

[1] *ibid.*, p. 457.

[2] H. Tout, *The Standard of Living in Bristol* (1938).

[3] H. Llewellyn Smith, *The New Survey of London Life and Labour* (1930–5, 9 vols.).

[4] D. C. Jones, *Social Survey of Merseyside* (1934, 3 vols.); P. Ford, *Work and Wealth in a Modern Port: An Economic Survey of Southampton* (1934).

and inadequate benefits,[1] perhaps another third to inadequate earnings even though employment was regular, while a further 16 per cent was caused by the problem of old age. Most of the remaining poverty could be ascribed to sickness and minor causes. Finally, probably some 25 per cent of working class children were born into families who could not afford a proper minimum diet. In many of these poverty-stricken families the head of the household and his wife might, if they were lucky, enjoy an interlude of relative prosperity between the time the children became wage earners and the approach of old age when once again poverty returned.[2]

TABLE 42 *Weekly per capita income and expenditure on food*

Group	Income per head per week (sh.)	Est. exp. on food (sh.)	Number in group (mn.)	% population
1	up to 10	4	4·5	10
2	10–15	6	9·0	20
3	15–20	8	9·0	20
4	20–30	10	9·0	20
5	30–45	12	9·0	20
6	above 45	14	4·5	10

Even more startling were the revelations made by Sir John Boyd Orr in 1936 in his book, *Food, Health and Income.* In brief, Orr claimed that one half or more of the British population was undernourished. Orr divided the population into six groups according to per capita income and weekly expenditure on food. These are produced above. Only the last two groups could afford really adequate diets, while only group 6 had a surplus of all dietary constituents considered. The diets of all other groups were deficient in some respect especially in calcium, though the first group was by far the worst, being seriously short of all ingredients for a balanced diet, fats, proteins, vitamins. Thus about one tenth of the nation (including perhaps 20 per cent of the country's children) was badly fed, while another 10 per cent were very well fed; probably a further 30 per cent of the population were reasonably well-fed leaving half the population who, though by no means starving, were undernourished in some respect.[3]

[1] The majority of unemployed men with families were in poverty.
[2] Abrams, *op. cit.,* p. 106.
[3] Sir John Boyd Orr, *Food, Health and Income* (1936); see also Drummond and Wilbraham, *op. cit.,* p. 446.

Orr's findings caused a stir and came in for much criticism. The study was based on a very small sample of family budgets and made no proper allowance for regional variations. Altogether some 1200 budgets were examined, a large proportion of which was taken from the north of England and from families of low earnings. His basic standard involved a higher expenditure on food than most others simply because it aimed at providing a balanced diet as well as one which was adequate in calorific value 'such that no improvement can be affected by a change in the diet'. Even so, it was generous in relation to the British Medical Association's diet of 1933, which provided 3,400 calories a day for the average man at an estimated cost of about 6s. Applied to Orr's findings this would probably leave about 30 per cent of the population (groups 1 and 2) with insufficient diet.[1] Orr himself admitted that there had been a considerable increase in per capita food consumption compared with pre-war,[2] and by the end of the 1930s average calorie intake was more or less equal to the standard set by the B.M.A. In a later work he suggested that perhaps one third of the population had diets insufficient to maintain good health.[3] His original findings may have exaggerated the extent of undernourishment simply by underestimating the proportion of income spent on food. Even Kuczynski, who was by no means an unbiased observer, concluded that no more than 10 million people, or just over 20 per cent of the population, were underfed, underclothed and badly housed in 1937.[4]

Even allowing for variations in the standards adopted and the assumptions made by the various writers, it is clear that a substantial proportion of the population was living in some state of poverty. At a

[1] After allowing for some price increase in food after 1933 and a deficiency in the B.M.A. diet. The standards set by the social surveys and the B.M.A. were said to be too low thereby underestimating the extent of poverty. See R. F. George, 'A New Calculation of the Poverty Line', *Journal of the Royal Statistical Society*, 100 (1937), p. 92.

[2] Per capita expenditure on food at constant 1938 prices rose from £21·59 in 1910–14 to £27·25 in 1935–8. Stone and Rowe, *op. cit.*, vol. 2, p. 126.

[3] Sir John Boyd Orr and David Lubbock, *Feeding the People in War-time* (1940), p. 1. Though it should be noted that Orr's original findings were largely confirmed by the more extensive dietary survey undertaken by Sir William Crawford in 1936–7. This covered all social classes and was based on 5,000 family budgets drawn from seven main cities. Sir William Crawford and H. Broadley, *The People's Food* (1938).

[4] J. Kuczynski, *A Short History of Labour Conditions under Industrial Capitalism*, vol. 1, *Great Britain and the Empire 1750 to the Present Day* (1942), pp. 88–9.

guess the proportion might be put at between 20 and 30 per cent, while up to one half was deficient in vitamins. Families living below the poverty line might have been able to afford an adequate diet but only at the expense of other necessities such as clothing and shelter. Their incomes were so low that only careful spending enabled them to eke out a bare existence. For some however the problem was an educational rather than a financial one. A nutritionally adequate diet might have been possible for many distressed families had not ignorance, prejudice, lack of time or lack of facilities prevented them from attaining it.[1] Moreover, many families with incomes which allowed a level of subsistence above the poverty line had little to spare for luxuries and next to nothing to fall back on in times of need or unexpected crisis. Despite an increase in small savings, including those of the working classes, the majority of families had very little saving or wealth on which they could draw in times of emergency. Hilton estimated that about one third of Britain's families owned no savings or wealth worth speaking of, while another third had a minute amount, less than £100, and most of this was in the form of property, furnishings and clothing.[2]

These estimates are only approximate but it seems unlikely that they are very far out. It is true that small savings (in Post Office accounts, trustee savings bank accounts, etc.) grew rapidly in the interwar period and by 1934 amounted to £1,307 million excluding deposits in building societies.[3] Unfortunately, no breakdown is available of savings over different income ranges though it is unlikely that they were all made by the middle and upper income groups (incomes over £250 a year) since the average propensity to save of the working classes (incomes below £250) was not negative, but ranged between 0·075 and 0·1.[4] However, the growth of small savings was not necessarily incompatible with the absence of any savings among a significant sector of the working class community since only the better paid working class families were in a position to save. Campion suggested that the ownership of savings and wealth, that is savings bank deposits, Government securities and houses, was widespread among different

[1] Burnett, *op. cit.*, p. 317.
[2] Hilton, *op. cit.*, p. 33.
[3] G. D. H. and M. I. Cole, *op. cit.*, p. 77; E. Nevin, *The Mechanism of Cheap Money* (1955), p. 256.
[4] The average propensity to save of persons with incomes over £250 a year was between 0·3 and 0·36 (including business savings). E. A. Radice, *Savings in Great Britain 1922–1935* (1939), p. 72.

classes. In 1936 over eight million persons over the age of 25 possessed more than £100 each. But this still left about two thirds of the adult population with less than £100 a piece and presumably there were some who had no savings at all.[1] A sample survey for 1948 revealed that, though National Savings (that is trustee savings bank deposits, saving certificates, Post Office bank deposits and Government securities on the Post Office Register) were spread over 59 per cent of the adult population (15 and over), nearly 41 per cent of that population had no savings at all, while nearly one quarter had less than £50 a piece.[2] Of course there were other channels through which the working classes saved such as friendly societies, co-operative societies and industrial provident associations, though it seems unlikely that the 41 per cent with no balance in the National Savings Movement had very much more in these other institutions. It seems fairly safe to conclude therefore, that about one third at least of Britain's families had nothing between them and destitution apart from their weekly wages, welfare benefits or old age pensions. If these failed to materialize then circumstances could be very difficult indeed.

As one might expect the problem of poverty and distress was greater in the northern half of the country including Scotland and in Wales than it was in the South. Here unemployment was higher and more prolonged, incomes were lower and living conditions less congenial than in London and the South. We have already discussed the marked variations in unemployment and how these affected incomes.[3] Unfortunately regional incomes indices are not available but a rough estimate of regional income distribution has been made for 1934 by Harrison and Mitchell.[4] This was based on the earnings of the chief income earner of the family and the results are produced in Table 43. It can be seen that the proportion of low incomes (below £4 per week) was higher, and the proportion of high incomes (£10 or more a week) lower, in nearly all the northern areas compared with those in London and the South. In South Wales and Northumberland and Durham, for example, nearly 80 per cent of incomes fell in the lowest category as against 68 per cent for London and the South, while the

[1] H. Campion, *Public and Private Property in Great Britain* (1939), p. 120.
[2] Esme Preston, 'Personal Savings Through Institutional Channels, 1937–1949', *Bulletin of the Oxford Institute of Statistics*, 12 (1950), p. 246.
[3] See above, Chapter 3.
[4] G. Harrison and F. C. Mitchell, *The Home Market: A Handbook of Statistics* (1936), p. 64.

proportions in the high income category were correspondingly low. Rather surprisingly, the Midland regions also showed a rather high proportion of low income families, while North and Central Wales had a distribution slightly more favourable than that of the South.[1]

Lower average earnings and the high incidence of unemployment were largely responsible for the unfavourable income distribution in the North compared with elsewhere. The position was particularly serious for those unemployed for any length of time and with large families since welfare payments were hardly commensurate with past

TABLE 43   *Regional distribution of income classes in 1934*

	A	B	C
Great Britain	5·3	21·3	73·4
North and Central Wales	7·3	25·9	66·8
London and S.E.	6·4	25·4	68·2
South-west	7·6	24·1	68·3
Eastern	5·7	21·4	72·9
Scotland	3·4	21·8	74·8
Northern Rural Belt	6·3	17·8	75·9
Lancashire and Cheshire	5·0	18·8	76·2
West Midlands	5·3	17·7	77·0
West Riding	3·5	19·4	77·1
East Midlands	4·2	17·3	78·5
Northumberland and Durham	2·9	18·3	78·8
South Wales	4·8	15·3	79·9

A = chief income earner received £10 a week or more
B = chief income earner received £4 10s a week or more
C = chief income earner received below £4 a week.

earnings. A sample survey carried out by the Ministry of Labour in August 1937 into the wages previously earned by applicants for benefit revealed that benefit rates fell short of earnings by a large margin. The average weekly benefit, including dependents' allowances, paid to adult men was around 24s 6d a week as against a median earning rate of 55s 6d.[2] What this kind of situation meant in terms of human exper-

[1] This area was something of an exception due to the high proportion of retired persons and rentiers resident there.
[2] R. M. Titmuss, *Poverty and Population* (1938), pp. 240–1. Though there were some who were better off on unemployment relief than when working. P.E.P., *The Social Services* (1937), p. 163.

ience was described graphically by a miner from Crook who had been unemployed since 1927:

'It's just over seven years since I was stood off and we've lived on about thirty-six bob during that time, that's me and the wife and the six kids. The rent's not bad, eight and six, but it's replacing breakages, clothing, extra nourishment for the kids and furniture that we find difficult to get. I've a bit of an allotment that brings us potatoes and cabbages but we don't often get meat and as for fruit you just can't buy it. At first I used to feel bitter and want to do something violent . . . I suppose if conditions worsened we might risk it . . . but as long as you've got the dole regular, well, you think twice before doing anything militant.'[1]

And this was by no means the worst case. Some families in Hammersmith, affected by unemployment in the early 1930s, were living on as little as 1s 7d per head for food (per week), while even some of those in work were restricted to sums below 4s a week.[2] Such desperate conditions resulted in the moral degradation of workers, and in some cases the break up of the family.[3]

Living and environmental conditions were generally poorer in the North than in the South. The worst aspect was housing. Despite the rapid rate of housebuilding in the inter-war years the extent of overcrowding and slum conditions remained serious even by the end of the period. In many of the large towns and urban areas of the North the slum and overcrowding conditions assumed gigantic proportions. Easily the worst area was Scotland. The *Overcrowding Survey* of working-class dwellings (1935–6) revealed that 22·6 per cent of all Scotland's working class houses were overcrowded, compared with 3·8 per cent of those in England and Wales. In some parts around Glasgow, notably Motherwell, Clydebank and Coatbridge, the proportions were as high as 40 per cent or more. The standard set moreover was by no means a generous one. There were no areas which quite matched the Scottish position in England and Wales; though most large towns suffered badly from overcrowded dwellings the proportions were very much less than in Scotland. The two worst counties were Northumberland and Durham with 12·0 and 11·2

[1] J. Newsom, *Out of the Pit* (1936), p. 20. I am grateful to Dr Garside for this reference.
[2] Drummond and Wilbraham, *op. cit.*, p. 446.
[3] See J. Laver, *Between the Wars* (1961), pp. 138–9, for the tragedy of a skilled engineer's family.

N

per cent of their families living in overcrowded dwellings in 1936, while in the towns of Sunderland and Hebburn the proportions were as high as one fifth to one quarter. The position was much better further South though one or two towns, notably London and its suburbs, had a serious problem. Likewise with slums, the problem was generally a great deal worse in the North.

Such conditions coupled with low incomes and all that this meant in terms of dietary standards etc, were bound to affect the health and well-being of the inhabitants of these areas. Richard Titmuss has brought out clearly the difference between North and South in this respect.[1] Generally speaking, the population of the former was less healthy and more subject to disease and mortality than that of the latter. The expectation of life at birth and at all ages, for example, was considerably lower in the North and in Wales than elsewhere. Infantile mortality in the South-east was 47 per 1,000 live births in 1935 compared with 63 in Wales, 77 in Scotland and 76 in Northumberland and Durham. The rate of maternal mortality was twice as high in these areas compared with London and the South-east. By the end of the 1930s overall death rates in the South-east and Eastern counties were only 89 per cent of the general rate for England and Wales, whereas those in Northumberland, Durham, Lancashire, Cheshire and South Wales ranged between 115–17 per cent of the national rate.[2] Similarly, the incidence of disease and illness was also greater. Northumberland and Durham, for example, had an excessive incidence of tuberculosis compared with the rest of the country.

The analysis of inter-war living conditions illustrates only too clearly the paradox of progress and poverty. On the one hand, a substantial proportion of the population enjoyed higher real earnings, more leisure, improved living conditions and better social amenities, while at the same time a submerged fraction of the population lived in poverty and distress caused by low earnings, unemployment, old age and other factors. But despite the severity of the latter it would probably be inaccurate to conclude that the one offset the other. Poverty is very much a relative concept and its measurement is determined by the generally accepted standard of comfort at any point in time. As average living standards rose the poverty line inevitably shifted upwards but this did not necessarily preclude a reduction in the extent of poverty

[1] See *Poverty and Population*, esp. pp. 87, 102–3, 173, 221.
[2] See Eva M. Hubback, *The Population of Britain* (1947), pp. 31–2.

compared with what had gone before. Judgement on the period has been clouded by the depression and mass unemployment and also by the fact that the problem of poverty was investigated much more thoroughly and systematically than ever before. This has tended to throw in to sharp focus the worst aspects of the period. But the facts show that improvement in material welfare was not incompatible with poverty. Perhaps the fairest assessment of the period is that of Burnett.[1] 'Hunger-marches and the dole seem inconsistent with a rising standard of living, yet probably the truth is that the proportion of very poor fell between the wars and that of the moderately prosperous increased. It is also true that the problem of poverty had changed – that although the numbers of the 'old poor', of miserably paid unskilled and casual workers, had diminished, there had arisen a 'new poor', of skilled workers whose skill had been made useless by the process of industrial change. Unemployment and underemployed miners, shipyard workers and cotton weavers made up the new 'submerged tenth', and their plight was all the more pitiful because it contrasted with the relative prosperity they had once known. That in 1939 there should still have been a submerged fraction of any size was bad enough, but in 1914 the existence of a submerged third had scarcely been revealed. No one could seriously doubt that the working classes on the eve of the Second World War were better fed, better clothed and better housed than their parents had been a generation earlier.'

The distribution of income and capital

We have already had occasion to refer to the question of income distribution and its redistribution through welfare payments. It is now time to examine the subject in a little more detail and to draw the main threads together. Perhaps of greatest interest to the economic historian is the fact that the early twentieth century saw the beginning of a long-term trend towards a lessening of income inequality[2] and a simultaneous shift of factor shares in the national income.

---

[1] Burnett, *op. cit.*, p. 319.
[2] Though recently Soltow has suggested that income inequality has been decreasing for several centuries and that the trend was simply accelerated in the twentieth century. Actually, before the twentieth century the main changes took place within the upper income brackets rather than a redistributive shift between rich and poor. Lee Soltow, 'Long-run Changes in British Income Inequality', *Economic History Review*, 21 (1968), p. 29.

As regards the shares of income going to labour and capital the position is fairly straightforward. In the half century or so before 1914 employment incomes (wages and salaries) as a proportion of gross national product remained remarkably stable. On average they accounted for a little less than half the total income, the remainder going to rent, interest, profits and income from self-employment. By the end of the 1930s (1935–8) the share of wages and salaries had risen to just about 59 per cent as against 47·3 per cent in 1910–14.[1] There were several reasons for labour's increased share in total income. The quality of labour improved and the number of employees increased more rapidly than the total population. Employees as a proportion of the gainfully occupied population rose from 87 per cent in 1911 to 90 per cent in 1921 and 93 per cent by 1951. At the same time there was a concomitant decrease in the numbers self employed.[2] Thus income from self-employment (including farmers' income) fell from 16·2 per cent in 1910–14 to 13·2 per cent (of total income) by the end of the 1930s. Profits and mixed incomes were also squeezed during this period. The most significant losses were in rent and net property income from abroad, the reasons for which are fairly obvious. The share of rent in total income declined from 11·0 to 8·8 per cent and that of income from abroad from 8·4 to 4·1 per cent.[3]

One or two points should be noted regarding this redistribution of factor shares. First, most of it occurred during and early after the war. By the early 1920s employment incomes already accounted for 58·5 per cent of total income and this proportion remained more or less stable until the second world war. Non-employment incomes, though lower in relative terms compared with pre-war, held up remarkably well after the early 1920s. This is particularly true of profits, interest and rent, which tended to maintain or even increase their shares over the period.[4] The share of income from self-employment

---

[1] These proportions include Forces' pay and employers' contributions. Excluding these the proportions were 45·3 for 1910–14 and 54·9 for 1935–8. Feinstein in Marchal and Duclos, *op. cit.*, pp. 116–7, 119.

[2] Feinstein has attempted to allocate the income from self-employment between labour and capital. The effect of this is to raise throughout the proportion of income going to labour though it does not materially affect the nature of the long-term distributive shift. See Feinstein in Marchal and Duclos, *op. cit.*, pp. 125–6.

[3] *ibid.*, pp. 116–7; Phyllis Deane and W. A. Cole, *British Economic Growth, 1688–1959* (1962), pp. 246–7.

[4] Returns on equities and Consols, for instance, though lower than before 1913,

declined steadily after its initial post-war peak. Secondly, most of the gain in employment incomes accrued to salary earners. The long-term share of wages remained remarkably steady within one or two percentage points of 38 (except 1910–14 when it fell to 34·5), whereas the share of salaries rose from 10·8 per cent just prior to the war to 17·9 per cent by 1935–8. This in turn was due to the rapid growth in the numbers in salaried occupations rather than to an above average increase in salaried earnings.[1] The number of salary earners rose from 1·67 million in 1911 to 3·84 million in 1938 while the number of wage earners remained almost constant.[2] It should be noted that the stability of the wage share depends in part on the classification adopted. The large body of administrative, technical and clerical labour has been defined as salaried, while income from self-employment has been allocated entirely to the side of capital. Nevertheless, even though the division between salary and wage earners may be somewhat arbitrary, in practice there can be no doubt about the significant upward shift in the share of income going to labour (wages and salaries together) during the period.

The fact that more than half the total income went to labour by the end of the period does not of course mean that there had been a significant levelling of incomes between different income bands. Almost certainly the inequality of income distribution was less than it had been pre-war, but the movement towards a more even distribution was very moderate with the result that the income pyramid (to use Hilton's phrase)[3], still had a very broad base and a sharp point. In 1938, 55·5 per cent of distributed personal income before tax was shared among 87·2 per cent of the income receivers all earning less than £250 a year (that is the working classes), while the remaining 44·5 per cent went to a mere 12·8 per cent of the income recipients with earnings over £250 a year. Furthermore, the top one per cent of the income receivers (over £500 a year) absorbed about 29 per cent of the total

held up remarkably well and in real terms were very much higher than after the second world war. See A. J. Merrett and A. Sykes, 'Return on Equities and Fixed Interest Securities, 1919–1966', *District Bank Review*, 158 (June 1966), pp. 31, 36, 40, 41. For rates of profit, see Phelps Brown and Browne, *op. cit.*, p. 414.

[1] In fact, as pointed out earlier, average salary incomes lagged behind wages between 1913 and 1938 with the result that the temporary loss of share suffered by wages in the decade or so before the war was soon recovered.

[2] Feinstein in Marchal and Duclos, *op. cit.*, p. 120; *cf* Chapman and Knight, *op. cit.*, p. 19.

[3] Hilton, *op. cit.*, p. 39.

distributed.[1] Unfortunately, comparable breakdowns are not available for earlier years, but a partial analysis by Stamp for 1914 appears to indicate that the distribution was more uneven before the war. At that date some 45 per cent of personal income went to only $5\frac{1}{2}$ per cent of the people with separate incomes, leaving 55 per cent for distribution among nearly 95 per cent of the income recipients. The top one per cent accounted for about 30 per cent of total income.[2]

Clearly the levelling up process was not very marked though it is nevertheless apparent. It appears to have been confined largely to the middle and lower income bands since the top income bracket maintained its share fairly well. Moreover, as with the shift in factor shares, most of the redistribution probably took place during and early after the war when the higher income brackets failed to keep pace with the rise in prices.[3]

These figures take no account of taxation and transfers the overall effect of which was to reduce the inequality further. Before 1914 direct taxation of income had been proportional rather than progressive, so much so that even the highest incomes were taxed at a rate of less than 10 per cent. During the war income tax rose sharply and, though reduced afterwards, it was kept at a much higher level than before the war. At the same time it was made much more progressive so that the main burden fell on higher incomes, £1,000 and over, whereas on low incomes (under £250) it was negligible. Thus on an income of £1,000 the proportion taken in direct tax in 1937–8 was more than double what it had been in 1913–14, 8·7 as against 4·0, on incomes of £2,000 nearly four times larger, 15·6 compared with 4·0, while for incomes above this range the rise was even steeper. On an income of £20,000 the percentage tax rate was 47·5 per cent in 1937–8 compared with only 8·1 per cent before the war. Conversely, on incomes of £500 and below direct taxes

---

[1] Based on D. Seers, *The Levelling of Incomes Since 1938* (1951), p. 34; *cf* Barna, *op. cit.*, pp. 74–5. If undistributed profits and undistributed personal incomes are included the income distribution pattern is slightly more uneven since the bulk of this income accrued to the higher income brackets.

[2] Sir Josiah Stamp, *Wealth and Taxable Capacity* (1922), p. 87; *cf* A. L. Bowley, *The Change in the Distribution of the National Income, 1880–1913* (1920), p. 22.

[3] L. R. Connor, 'On Certain Aspects of the Distribution of Income in the United Kingdom in the Years 1913 and 1924', *Journal of the Royal Statistical Society*, 91 (1928), p. 64.

were either eliminated or reduced to very small proportions.[1] It should be noted, however, that most of the restructuring of the tax burden took place during and early after the war; the changes thereafter were fairly small.

The overall impact of these changes in direct taxation was somewhat less than one might imagine though at least it was in the right direction. In 1938 the lower income groups (under £250 a year) absorbed 59·6 per cent of the post-tax distributed personal incomes as against 55·5 per cent before tax, while those with incomes above this limit now retained only just over 40 per cent. The share of the top one per cent of the income recipients was reduced from 29 to about 24·4 per cent. The share absorbed by intermediate range incomes, that is between £250–500, remained practically stable at 16 per cent both before and after tax.[2]

The levelling up of incomes through progressive direct taxation was offset in part by the regressive nature of indirect taxation. The latter fell heavily on the lower income groups and with the increase in the range and size of indirect taxes during the period the burden of indirect taxation on the lower income brackets was greater than before the war, though somewhat less than in the immediate postwar years. Thus although the lower income ranges escaped most direct taxation, a married man with three children and an income of £200 or less contributed between 8–10 per cent of his income to indirect taxes in 1937-8.[3] This was roughly double the pre-war proportion. As incomes rose the proportionate burden of indirect taxation fell though it was generally greater than before the war. Thus on an income of £500 it was 4·9; on £1,000, 3·1; on £2,000, 2·4; while on incomes of £10,000 and above it was well below one per cent.[4] On the other hand, the lower income groups were the main beneficiaries of social transfer payments. The net effect, as observed earlier, was that the incomes of the working classes (under £250 a year) were raised by between 8–10 per cent through redistribution, the bulk of the gain going to those with incomes of less than £125 per annum. In

[1] These calculations are for a married man with three children under the age of 16. Shirras and Rostas, *op. cit.*, p. 58.

[2] Seers, *op. cit.*, p. 34.

[3] Because of the exclusion of certain indirect taxes from these calculations the burden of indirect taxation on the lower income brackets is somewhat understated. See note 2 to page 372.

[4] As before these calculations are all based on a married man with three children under 16. Shirras and Rostas, *op. cit.*, p. 58.

turn, the incomes of the middle and upper classes were reduced by between 10–18 per cent.[1]

Despite the approximate nature of the calculations, it is evident that the trend was towards a greater equality of incomes. Even so, the distribution of income was still very uneven by the end of the period. There was clearly further scope for levelling up through taxation and transfer, though there was a limit to which the process could be carried or to the effect it could have on lower incomes. Hicks calculated that by cutting out surplus consumption above £500 free of taxes would leave a maximum of £365 million or $8\frac{1}{2}$ per cent of the national income for redistribution. If this had been transferred to the working classes the effect would have been to raise their incomes by a further 15 per cent, or by considerably less than the real gain in income of these classes between 1913 and 1937.[2]

If incomes were still unevenly distributed by the end of the 1930s private wealth or capital was even more so. In 1936–8, 10 per cent of the total number of persons over the age of 25 owned 85 per cent of the private capital, while 74 per cent was owned by five per cent and the top one per cent held over one half (55 per cent). Yet even this was an improvement on what had gone before. Just before the first world war (1911–13) one per cent of the population owned 70 per cent of the total capital, while the top 10 per cent held around 90 per cent. The spread of wealth was most noticeable among small capital holders, that is those with over £100 but less than £1,000. The number in this category increased rapidly and the capital held nearly tripled between 1911–13 and 1936–8, thereby raising the share of this group from 10 to 12 per cent. The main losers appear to have been the very large property owners with holdings of over £100,000.[3]

[1] See above, p. 372.
[2] The estimate is based on 1937 data. J. R. Hicks, *The Social Framework* (1942), pp. 189–90; *cf* Stamp, *op. cit.*, p. 100, who came to a somewhat similar conclusion in 1922.
[3] Kathleen M. Langley, 'The Distribution of Capital in Private Hands in 1936–1938 and 1946–1947', *Bulletin of the Oxford Institute of Statistics*, 12 (1950), pp. 349, 355, and 13 (1951), pp. 44–7. See also H. F. Lydall and D. G. Tipping, 'The Distribution of Personal Wealth in Britain', *Economica*, 23 (1961).

Bibliography

The bibliography has been arranged on a chapter basis so as to enable readers to select literature on those themes or subjects which they wish to pursue in greater depth. Several of the bibliographical references are of course relevant to more than one chapter or section but as a rule each reference is only listed once. The bibliography is by no means exhaustive but it does include most modern works and a fairly extensive selection of earlier works which are still of some relevance. A separate list of statistical sources has not been included, nor has any attempt been made to comment on the key items since fairly comprehensive statistical and bibliographical guides have already been published in D. H. Aldcroft and H. W. Richardson, *The British Economy, 1870–1939* (1969).

General Texts

D. H. Aldcroft and H. W. Richardson, *The British Economy 1870–1939* (1969)
H. W. Arndt, *The Economic Lessons of the Nineteen-Thirties* (1944)
W. Ashworth, *An Economic History of England 1870–1939* (1960)
A. L. Bowley, *Some Economic Conesquences of the Great War* (1930)
British Association, *Britain in Depression* (1935)
                      Britain in Recovery (1938)
G. D. H. Cole, *British Trade and Industry* (1932)
E. V. Francis, *Britain's Economic Strategy* (1939)

H. D. Henderson, *The Inter-war Years and Other Papers* (1965)
A. E. Kahn, *Great Britain in the World Economy* (1946)
W. A. Lewis, *Economic Survey 1919–1939* (1949)
W. Meakin, *The New Industrial Revolution* (1928)
A. S. Milward, *The Economic Effects of the Two World Wars on Britain* (1970)
C. L. Mowat, *Britain Between the Wars, 1918–1940* (1955)
S. Pollard, *The Development of the British Economy, 1914–1950* (1962)
A. W. Rather, *Is Britain Decadent* (1928)
R. S. Sayers, *A History of Economic Change in England, 1880–1939* (1967)
A. Siegfried, *Post-War Britain* (1924)
I. Svennilson, *Growth and Stagnation in the European Economy* (1954)
A. J. Youngson, *Britain's Economic Growth, 1920–1966* (1967)

1   *The Growth of the Economy in Perspective*

D. H. Aldcroft, 'Economic Progress in Britain in the 1920s', *Scottish Journal of Political Economy*, 13 (1966)
D. H. Aldcroft, 'Economic Growth in Britain in the Inter-War Years: A Reassessment', *Economic History Review*, 20 (1967)
D. H. Aldcroft and P. Fearon (eds.), *Economic Growth in Twentieth Century Britain* (1969)
A. L. Bowley (ed.), *Studies in the National Income, 1924–1938* (1942)
C. Clark, *The National Income, 1924–31* (1932)
C. Clark, *National Income and Outlay* (1937)
C. Clark, *The Conditions of Economic Progress* (1957 ed.)
Phyllis Deane and W. A. Cole, *British Economic Growth, 1688–1959* (2nd ed. 1967)
J. A. Dowie, 'Growth in the Inter-War Period: Some More Arithmetic', *Economic History Review*, 21 (1968)
C. H. Feinstein, 'Production and Productivity, 1920–1963', *London and Cambridge Economic Bulletin*, 48 (1963)
C. H. Feinstein, 'National Income and Expenditure of the United Kingdom, 1870–1963', *London and Cambridge Economic Bulletin*, 50 (1964)
W. G. Hoffmann, *British Industry, 1700–1950* (1955 ed.)

J. B. Jefferys and D. Walters, 'National Income and Expenditure of the United Kingdom, 1870–1952', *Income and Wealth*, 5 (1955)

J. Knapp and K. S. Lomax, 'Britain's Growth Performance: The Enigma of the 1950s', *Lloyds Bank Review*, 74 (1964)

League of Nations, *Industrialisation and Foreign Trade* (1945)

K. S. Lomax, 'Production and Productivity Movements in the United Kingdom since 1900', *Journal of the Royal Statistical Society*, A122 (1959)

K. S. Lomax, 'Growth and Productivity in the United Kingdom,' *Productivity Measurement Review*, 38 (1964)

London and Cambridge Economic Service, *The British Economy: Key Statistics, 1900–1966* (1967)

A. Maddison, 'Output, Employment and Productivity in British Manufacturing in the Last Half Century', *Bulletin of the Oxford University Institute of Statistics*, 17 (1955)

A. Maddison, 'Economic Growth in Western Europe, 1870–1957', *Banca Nazionale del Lavoro Quarterly Review*, 12 (1959)

A. Maddison, 'Growth and Fluctuation in the World Economy, 1870–1960', *Banca Nazionale del Lavoro Quarterly Review*, 15 (1962)

A. Maddison, *Economic Growth in the West* (1964)

B. R. Mitchell and Phyllis Deane, *Abstract of British Historical Statistics* (1962)

O.E.E.C., *Industrial Statistics, 1900–1959* (1960)

D. C. Paige, F. T. Blackaby and S. Freund, 'Economic Growth: the Last Hundred Years', *National Institute Economic Review*, 16 (1961)

V. Paretti and G. G. Bloch, 'Industrial Production in Western Europe and the United States, 1900–1955', *Banca Nazionale del Lavoro Quarterly Review*, 9 (1956)

E. H. Phelps Brown and B. Weber, 'Accumulation, Productivity and Distribution in the British Economy, 1870–1938', *Economic Journal*, 63 (1953)

A. R. Prest, 'National Income of the United Kingdom, 1870–1946', *Economic Journal*, 58 (1948)

T. M. Ridley, 'Industrial Production in the United Kingdom, 1900–1953', *Economica*, 22 (1955)

L. Rostas, 'Industrial Production, Productivity and Distribution in Britain, Germany and the United States, 1935–37', *Economic Journal*, 53 (1943)

G. L. Schwartz and E. C. Rhodes, 'Output, Employment and Wages in the United Kingdom, 1924, 1930, 1935', memorandum no. 75 of the Royal Economic Society (1938)

2   *Fluctuations in Economic Activity*

G. B. Braae, 'Investment in Housing in the United Kingdom, 1924–38', *The Manchester School*, 32 (1964)

W. H. Beveridge, 'Unemployment in the Trade Cycle', *Economic Journal*, 49 (1939)

I. Bowen, 'Building Output and the Trade Cycle (U.K. 1924–38)', *Oxford Economic Papers*, 3 (1940)

M. Bowley, 'Fluctuations in House-building and the Trade Cycle', *Review of Economic Studies*, 4 (1936–7)

R. F. Bretherton, F. A. Burchardt and R. S. G. Rutherford, *Public Investment and the Trade Cycle in Great Britain* (1941)

D. J. Coppock, 'The Causes of Business Fluctuation', *Transactions of the Manchester Statistical Society* (1959)

D. C. Corner, 'Exports and the British Trade Cycle: 1929', *The Manchester School*, 24 (1956)

C. H. Feinstein, *Domestic Capital Formation in the United Kingdom, 1920–1938* (1965)

H. Feis, 'The Industrial Situation in Great Britain from the Armistice to the Beginning of 1921', *American Economic Review*, 11 (1921)

R. M. Goodwin, 'The Problem of Trend and Cycle', *Yorkshire Bulletin of Economic and Social Research*, 5 (1953)

R. A. Gordon, *Business Fluctuations* (2nd ed. 1961)

P. E. Hart, 'Profits in Non-manufacturing Industries in the United Kingdom, 1920–1938', *Scottish Journal of Political Economy*, 10 (1963)

P. E. Hart, *Studies in Profit, Business Saving and Investment in the United Kingdom, 1920–1962*, Vol. I (1965), Vol. II (1968)

H. V. Hodson, *Slump and Recovery, 1929–1937* (1938)

International Labour Office, *Public Investment and Full Employment* (1946 Montreal)

R. F. Kahn, 'The Relation of Home Investment to Unemployment', *Economic Journal*, 41 (1931)

P. J. Lund and K. Holden, 'An Econometric Study of Private Sector Gross Fixed Capital Formation in the United Kingdom, 1923–1938', *Oxford Economic Papers*, 20 (1969)

E. Lundberg, *Instability and Economic Growth* (1968)

H. W. Macrosty, 'Inflation and Deflation in the United States and the United Kingdom, 1919–23', *Journal of the Royal Statistical Society,* 90 (1927)

A. Maddison, 'The Post-War Business Cycle in Western Europe and the Role of Government Policy', *Banca Nazionale del Lavoro Quarterly Review,* 13 (1960)

R. C. O. Matthews, *The Trade Cycle* (1959)

A. J. Merrett and A. Sykes, 'Return on Equities and Fixed Interest Securities, 1919–1966', *District Bank Review,* 158 (1966)

F. V. Meyer and W. A. Lewis, 'The Effects of an Overseas Slump on the British Economy', *The Manchester School,* 17 (1949)

O. Morgenstern, *International Financial Transactions and Business Cycles* (1959)

E. H. Phelps Brown and G. S. Shackle, 'British Economic Fluctuations, 1924–1938', *Oxford Economic Papers,* 2 (1939)

A. C. Pigou, *Aspects of British Economic History, 1918–1925* (1948 ed.)

H. W. Richardson, *Economic Recovery in Britain, 1932–9* (1967)

H. W. Richardson, 'The Economic Significance of the Depression in Britain' *Journal of Contemporary History,* 4 (1969)

L. Robbins, *The Great Depression* (1934)

I. M. Sahni, 'A Study of Share Prices, 1918–1947', *Yorkshire Bulletin of Economic and Social Research,* 3 (1951)

A. Salter, *Recovery* (1932)

J. A. Schumpeter, *Business Cycles,* Vol. 2 (1939)

3   Regional Patterns of Development

G. R. Allen, 'The Growth of Industry on Trading Estates, 1920–39, with Special Reference to Slough Trading Estate', *Oxford Economic Papers,* 3 (1951)

R. G. D. Allen and B. Thomas, 'The Supply of Engineering Labour under Boom Conditions', *Economic Journal,* 49 (1939)

W. Ashworth, *The Genesis of Modern British Town Planning* (1954)

Barlow Commission, *Report of the Royal Commission on the Distribution of Industrial Population,* Cmd. 6153 (1939–40)

W. H. Beveridge, *Unemployment – A Problem of Industry* (1930)

W. H. Beveridge, 'An Analysis of Unemployment', I, II, III, *Economica,* 3 (1936), 4 (1937)

W. H. Beveridge, *Full Employment in a Free Society,* (1944)

M. Bowley, 'Some Regional Aspects of the Building Boom, 1924–36', *Review of Economic Studies,* 5 (1937–8)

A. K. Cairncross (ed.), *The Scottish Economy* (1954)

A. D. Campbell, 'Changes in Scottish Incomes, 1924–49', *Economic Journal,* 65 (1955)

N. H. Carrier and J. R. Jeffrey, 'External Migration, 1815–1950: A Study of the Available Statistics', *Studies on Medical and Population Subjects,* 6 (1953)

W. A. Carrothers, *Emigration from the British Isles* (1929)

D. G. Champernowne, 'The Uneven Distribution of Unemployment in the United Kingdom, 1929–36', *Review of Economic Studies,* 5 (1937–8), 6 (1938–9)

H. Clay, *The Post-War Unemployment Problem* (1929)

G. H. Daniel, 'Some Factors Affecting the Movement of Labour', *Oxford Economic Papers,* 3 (1940)

R. C. Davison, *The Unemployed, Old Policies and New* (1929)

R. C. Davison, *British Unemployment Policy since 1930* (1938)

S. R. Dennison, *The Location of Industry and the Depressed Areas* (1939)

M. P. Fogarty, *Prospects of the Industrial Areas of Great Britain* (1945)

D. L. Foley, *Controlling London's Growth* (1963)

H. Frankel, 'The Industrial Distribution of the Population of Great Britain in July 1939', *Journal of the Royal Statistical Society,* 108 (1945)

D. Friedlander and R. J. Roshier, 'A Study of Internal Migration in England and Wales: Part 1', *Population Studies,* 19 (1965–6)

T. E. Gregory, 'Rationalisation and Technological Unemployment', *Economic Journal,* 40 (1930)

W. Hannington, *The Problem of the Distressed Areas* (1937)

C. E. V. Leser and Anne H. Silvey, 'Scottish Industries during the Inter-War Period', *The Manchester School,* 18 (1950)

H. Makower, J. Marschak and H. W. Robinson, 'Studies in Mobility of Labour: A Tentative Statistical Analysis', *Oxford Economic Papers,* 1 (1938)

H. Makower, J. Marschak and H. W. Robinson, 'Studies in Mobility of Labour: Analysis for Great Britain, Part I', *Oxford Economic Papers,* 2 (1939)

H. Makower, J. Marschak and H. W. Robinson, 'Studies in Mobility

of Labour: Analysis for Great Britain, Part II', *Oxford Economic Papers,* 4 (1940)
Minister of Labour Gazette
Political and Economic Planning, *Report on the Location of Industry* (1939)
Report of the Royal Commission on Population, Cmd. 7695 (1949)
H. W. Singer, 'The Process of Unemployment in the Depressed Areas (1935–38)', *Review of Economic Studies,* 6 (1938–9)
H. W. Singer, 'Regional Labour Markets and the Process of Unemployment', *Review of Economic Studies,* 7 (1939–40)
H. W. Singer, *Unemployment and the Unemployed* (1940)
H. W. Singer and C. E. V. Leser, 'Industrial Productivity in England and Scotland', *Journal of the Royal Statistical Society,* 111 (1948)
J. Sykes, 'The Development Areas', *The Manchester School,* 17 (1949)
J. Sykes, 'Remedies for Localised Unemployment', *The Manchester School,* 19 (1951)
B. Thomas, 'The Influx of Labour into London and the South-East, 1920–1936', *Economica,* 4 (1937)
B. Thomas, (ed.), *The Welsh Economy* (1962)
R. C. Tress, 'Unemployment and the Diversification of Industry', *The Manchester School,* 9 (1938)
Ellen Wilkinson, *The Town That was Murdered* (1939)

4   *Sources of Growth*

T. Barna, 'The Interdependence of the British Economy', *Journal of the Royal Statistical Society,* A115 (1952)
W. Bowden, 'The Productivity of Labour in Great Britain', *Journal of Political Economy,* 45 (1937)
J. G. Crowther, *Discoveries and Inventions of the 20th Century* (1955)
E. F. Denison, *Why Growth Rates Differ* (1968)
E. Devons, 'Output per head in Great Britain, 1924–33', *Economic Journal,* 45 (1935)
W. A. Eltis, *Economic Growth: Analysis and Policy* (1966)
A. W. Flux, 'Industrial Productivity in Great Britain and the United States' *Quarterly Journal of Economics,* 48 (1933–4)
R. Fry, 'The British Business Man, 1900–1949', *Explorations in Entrepreneurial History,* 2 (1949–50)

J. Jewkes, D. Sawers and R. Stillerman, *The Sources of Invention* (1958)

N. Kaldor, 'A Model of Economic Growth', *Economic Journal,* 67 (1957)

C. P. Kindleberger, 'Obsolescence and Technical Change', *Bulletin of the Oxford University Institute of Statistics,* 23 (1961)

C. P. Kindleberger, *Economic Growth in France and Britain, 1851–1950* (1964)

S. Kuznets, 'Retardation of Industrial Growth', *Journal of Economic and Business History,* 1 (1929)

D. S. Landes, *The Unbound Prometheus: Technological Change and Industrial Development in Western Europe from 1750 to the Present* (1969)

R. C. O. Matthews, 'Some Aspects of Post-War Growth in the British Economy in Relation to Historical Experience', *Transactions of the Manchester Statistical Society* (1964)

R. K. Merton, 'Fluctuations in the Rate of Industrial Innovation', *Quarterly Journal of Economics,* 49 (1935)

H. W. Richardson, 'The Basis of Economic Recovery in the 1930s: A Review and a New Interpretation', *Economic History Review,* 15 (1962)

H. W. Richardson, 'Over-commitment in Britain before 1930', *Oxford Economic Papers,* 17 (1965)

H. W. Richardson and D. H. Aldcroft, *Building in the British Economy Between the Wars* (1968)

E. Rothbarth, 'Causes of the Superior Efficiency of U.S.A. Industry as Compared with British Industry', *Economic Journal,* 56 (1946)

W. E. G. Salter, *Productivity and Technical Change* (1960)

R. S. Sayers, 'The Springs of Technical Progress in Britain, 1919–39', *Economic Journal,* 60 (1950)

J. Schmookler, *Invention and Economic Growth* (1966)

R. M. Solow, 'Technical Change and the Aggregate Production Function', *Review of Economics and Statistics,* 39 (1957)

5   *The Basic Industries*

Lord Aberconway, *The Basic Industries of Great Britain* (1927)

D. H. Aldcroft, 'The Performance of the British Machine Tool Industry in the Inter-war Years', *Business History Review,* 40 (1966)

G. C. Allen, *British Industries and their Organisation* (1951 ed.)

G. C. Allen, *The Structure of Industry in Britain* (1961)

P. W. S. Andrews and E. Brunner, *Capital Development in Steel* (1951)

Balfour Committee, *Reports of the Committee on Industry and Trade* (1926–30, H.M.S.O.)

A. Beacham, 'Efficiency and Organisation of the British Coal Industry', *Economic Journal,* 55 (1945)

D. L. Burn, *The Economic History of Steelmaking, 1867–1939* (1940)

D. L. Burn, (ed.) *The Structure of British Industry* (1958, 2 vols)

T. H. Burnham and G. O. Hoskins, *Iron and Steel in Britain, 1870–1930* (1943)

N. K. Buxton, 'The Scottish Shipbuilding Industry Between the Wars: A Comparative Study', *Business History,* 10 (1968)

N. K. Buxton, 'Entrepreneurial Efficiency in the British Coal Industry Between the Wars', *Economic History Review,* 23 (1970)

J. C. Carr and W. A. Taplin, *History of the British Steel Industry* (1962)

C. F. Carter and B. R. Williams, *Industry and Technical Progress* (1957)

H. Clay, 'The Financing of Industrial Enterprise', *Transactions of the Manchester Statistical Society* (1932)

H. J. D. Cole, 'Machinery Prices Between the Wars', *Bulletin of the Oxford University Institute of Statistics,* 13 (1951)

M. Compton and E. H. Bott, *British Industry* (1940)

P. L. Cook and R. Cohen, *Effects of Mergers* (1958)

W. H. B. Court, 'Problems of the British Coal Industry Between the Wars', *Economic History Review,* 15 (1945)

G. W. Daniels and J. Jewkes, 'The Post-war Depression in the Lancashire Cotton Industry', *Journal of the Royal Statistical Society,* 91 (1928)

E. Davies, *National Capitalism: the Government's Record as Protector of Private Monopoly* (1939)

E. Davies, *National Enterprise: The Development of the Public Corporation* (1946)

M. E. Dimock, *British Public Utilities and National Development* (1933)

J. H. Dunning and W. A. Thomas, *British Industry* (1961)

P. Fitzgerald, *Industrial Combination in England* (1927)

P. S. Florence, 'The Statistical Analysis of Joint-Stock Company Control', *Journal of the Royal Statistical Society,* 110 (1947)

P. S. Florence, *The Logic of British and American Industry* (1953)

W. R. Garside, 'The North-Eastern Coalfield and the Export Trade, 1919–39', *The Durham University Journal*, 62 (1969)

L. Gordon, *The Public Corporation in Britain* (1938)

P. E. Hart and S. J. Prais, 'The Analysis of Business Conuntration: A Statistical Approach', *Journal of the Royal Statistical Society*, 119 (1956)

H. F. Heath and A. L. Hetherington, *Industrial Research and Development in the United Kingdom* (1946)

J. Hurstfield, 'The Control of Raw Material Supplies, 1919–1939', *Economic History Review*, 14 (1944)

L. Jones, *Shipbuilding in Britain* (1957)

J. H. Jones et alia, *The Coal-Mining Industry* (1939)

H. Leak and A. Maizels, 'The Structure of British Industry', *Journal of the Royal Statistical Society*, 108 (1945)

H. Levy, *The New Industrial System* (1936)

Liberal Industrial Inquiry, *Britain's Industrial Future*, (1928)

A. F. Lucas, *Industrial Reconstruction and the Control of Competition* (1937)

D. N. McCloskey, 'Productivity Change in British Pig Iron, 1870–1939', *Quarterly Journal of Economics*, 82 (1968)

D. H. MacGregor et al., 'Problems of Rationalisation: A Discussion', *Economic Journal*, 40 (1930)

A. M. Neuman, *Economic Organisation of the British Coal Industry* (1934)

Political and Economic Planning, *Report on the British Coal Industry* (1936)

Political and Economic Planning, *Industrial Trade Associations* (1957)

T. H. O'Brien, *British Experiments in Public Ownership and Control* (1937)

E. C. Rhodes, 'Output, Labour and Machines in the Coal Mining Industry of Great Britain', *Economica*, 12 (1945)

R. Robson, *The Cotton Industry in Britain* (1957)

W. A. Robson (ed.), *Public Enterprise* (1937)

L. Rostas, 'Productivity of Labour in the Cotton Industry', *Economic Journal*, 55 (1945)

L. Rostas, *Comparative Productivity in British and American Industry* (1948)

L. Rostas, *Productivity, Prices and Distribution in Selected British Industries* (1948)

H. A. Silverman, *Studies in Industrial Organisation* (1946)

J. F. Sleeman, *British Public Utilities* (1953)

W. Smith, 'Trends in the Geographical Distribution of the Lancashire Cotton Industry', *Geography*, 26 (1941)

F. W. Taussig, 'Labour Costs in the United States Compared with Costs Elsewhere', *Quarterly Journal of Economics,* 39 (1924)

F. Uttley, *Lancashire and the Far East* (1931)

6 *New Industries and the Building Trades*

P. W. S. Andrews and Elizabeth Brunner, *The Life of Lord Nuffield* (1955)

H. H. Ballin, *The Organisation of Electricity Supply in Great Britain* (1946)

A. P. Becker, 'Housing in England and Wales during the Business Depression of the 1930s', *Economic History Review,* 3 (1950–1)

M. Bowley, 'Local Authorities and Housing Subsidies since 1919', *The Manchester School,* 12 (1942)

M. Bowley, *Housing and the State, 1919–44* (1945)

M. Bowley, *Innovations in Building Materials* (1960)

E. J. Cleary, *The Building Society Movement* (1965)

R. H. Coase, *British Broadcasting: a Study in Monopoly* (1950)

D. C. Coleman, *Courtaulds: An Economic and Social History,* Vol. 2 (1969)

T. A. B. Corley, *Domestic Electrical Appliances* (1966)

G. Donnithorne, *British Rubber Manufacturing* (1958)

P. Fearon, 'The Formative Years of the British Aircraft Industry, 1913–24', *Business History Review,* 43 (1969)

D. C. Hague, *The Economics of Man-Made Fibres* (1957)

D. W. F. Hardie and J. D. Pratt, *A History of the Modern British Chemical Industry* (1966)

J. Harrop, 'The Growth of the Rayon Industry in the Inter-War Years', *Yorkshire Bulletin of Economic and Social Research,* 20 (1968)

E. Jones, 'Price Leadership in the Rayon Industry', *The Manchester School,* 12 (1941)

G. Maxcy and A. Silberston, *The Motor Industry* (1959)

K. Maywald, 'An Index of Building Costs in the United Kingdom, 1945–1938', *Economic History Review,* 7 (1954–5)

S. Miall, *History of the British Chemical Industry* (1931)

A. Plummer, *New British Industries in the Twentieth Century* (1937)

Political and Economic Planning, *Report on the Supply of Electricity in Great Britain* (1936)

Political and Economic Planning, *The Market for Household Appliances* (1945)

R. L. Reiss, 'Municipal and Private Enterprise Housing', *Building and Society* (1945)

H. W. Richardson, 'The New Industries Between the Wars', *Oxford Economic Papers,* 13 (1961)

H. W. Richardson, 'The Development of the British Dyestuffs Industry Before 1939', *Scottish Journal of Political Economy,* 9 (1962)

R. Robson, *The Man-Made Fibres Industry* (1954)

S. Rowson, 'A Statistical Survey of the Cinema Industry in Great Britain in 1934', *Journal of the Royal Statistical Society,* 99 (1936)

M. Sanderson, 'The Universities and Industry in England, 1919–1939', *Yorkshire Bulletin of Economic and Social Research,* 21 (1969)

Sir Henry Self and Elizabeth M. Watson, *Electricity Supply in Great Britain* (1952)

Society of Motor Manufacturers and Traders, *The Motor Industry of Great Britain, 1939* (1940)

S. G. Sturmey, *The Economic Development of Radio* (1958)

B. Weber, 'A New Index of Residential Construction, 1838–1950', *Scottish Journal of Political Economy,* 2 (1955)

B. Weber and J. Parry Lewis, 'New Industrial Building in Great Britain, 1923–38: A Problem of Measurement', *Scottish Journal of Political Economy,* 8 (1961)

T. I. Williams, *The Chemical Industry* (1953)

C. Wilson, *The History of Unilever,* Vol. 2 (1954)

7   *Transport and the Service Sectors*

D. H. Aldcroft, *British Railways in Transition: The Economic Problems of Britain's Railways since 1914* (1968)

D. H. Aldcroft, 'The Decontrol of British Shipping and Railways after the First World War', *Journal of Transport History,* 5 (1961)

D. H. Aldcroft, 'Britain's Internal Airways: The Pioneer Stage of the 1930s', *Business History,* 6 (1964)

D. H. Aldcroft, 'The Railways and Air Transport in Great Britain, 1933–1939', *Scottish Journal of Political Economy,* 12 (1966)

D. H. Aldcroft, 'Innovation on the Railways: The Lag in Diesel and Electric Traction', *Journal of Transport Economics and Policy,* 3 (1969)

T. Balogh, *Studies in Financial Organisation* (1947)

E. Birkhead, 'The Financial Failure of British Air Transport Companies 1919–24', *Journal of Transport History,* 4 (1960)

Dorothea Braithwaite and S. P. Dobbs, *The Distribution of Consumable Goods: An Economic Study* (1932)

E. Brunner, *Holiday Making and Holiday Trades* (1945)

K. Burley, *British Shipping and Australia, 1920–1939* (1968)

D. N. Chester, *Public Control of Road Passenger Transport* (1936)

H. J. Dyos and D. H. Aldcroft, *British Transport: An Economic Survey From the Seventeenth Century to the Twentieth* (1969)

P. Ford, 'Competition and the Number of Retail Shops, 1901–31', *Economic Journal,* 45 (1935)

'Decentralisation and Changes in the Number of Shops, 1901–1931', *Economic Journal,* 46 (1936)

R. Higham, *Britain's Imperial Air Routes, 1918 to 1939* (1960)

R. Higham, 'Quantity vs. Quality: The Impact of Changing Demand on the British Aircraft Industry, 1900–1960', *Business History Review,* 42 (1968)

J. A. Hough, *Co-operative Retailing, 1914–1945* (1949)

L. Isserlis, 'Tramp Shipping Cargoes and Freights', *Journal of the Royal Statistical Society,* 101 (1938)

J. R. Jefferys, *Retail Trading in Britain, 1850–1950* (1954)

H. Levy, *The Shops of Britain: A Study of Retail Distribution* (1947)

L. J. Lickorish, and A. G. Kershaw, *The Travel Trade* (1958)

C. W. McMahon and G. D. N. Worswick, 'The Growth of Services in the Economy, I. Their Stabilising Influence', *District Bank Review,* 136 (1960)

F. G. Pennance and B. S. Yamey, 'Competition in the Retail Grocery Trade, 1850–1939', *Economica,* 22 (1955)

J. A. R. Pimlott, *The Englishman's Holiday* (1947)

Political and Economic Planning, *The British Film Industry,* (1952)

H. Robinson, *The British Post Office, A History* (1948, New Jersey)

H. Smith, *Retail Distribution* (2nd ed., 1948)

W. Smith, *An Economic Geography of Great Britain* (2nd ed., 1953)
S. G. Sturmey, *British Shipping and World Competition* (1962)
G. Walker, *Road and Rail* (2nd ed., 1947)
W. L. Waters, 'Rationalisation of British Railways', paper to the American Society of Mechanical Engineers, New York, May 1938

8   *The External Account*

D. Abel, *A History of British Tariffs, 1923–1942* (1945)
D. H. Aldcroft, 'The Early History and Development of Export Credit Insurance in Great Britain, 1919–1939', *The Manchester School,* 30 (1962)
R. E. Baldwin, 'The Commodity Composition of Trade: Selected Industrial Countries, 1900–1954', *Review of Economics and Statistics* 40 (1958)
F. Benham, *Great Britain under Protection* (1941)
A. I. Bloomfield, *Monetary Policy under the International Gold Standard* (1959)
H. S. Booker, *The Problem of Britain's Overseas Trade* (1948)
W. A. Brown, Jnr., *The International Gold Standard Re-interpreted, 1914–34* (1940, 2 vols., New York)
G. N. Butterworth and H. Campion, 'Changes in British Import Trade, 1924–36' *The Manchester School,* 8 (1937)
T. C. Chang, 'The British Balance of Payments, 1924–1938', *Economic Journal* 57 (1947)
T. C. Chang, *Cyclical Movements in the Balance of Payments* (1951)
S. V. O. Clarke, *Central Bank Co-operation, 1924–31* (1967, New York)
J. B. Condliffe, *The Reconstruction of World Trade* (1941)
H. F. Fraser, *Great Britain and the Gold Standard* (1933)
A. L. Ginsberg and R. M. Stern, 'The Determination of the Factors Affecting American and British Exports in the Inter-War and Post-War Periods', *Oxford Economic Papers,* 17 (1965)
D. L. Glickman, 'The British Imperial Preference System', *Quarterly Journal of Economics,* 61 (1947)
T. E. Gregory, *The First Year of the Gold Standard* (1926)
T. E. Gregory, *The Gold Standard and its Future* (3rd ed., 1934)
N. F. Hall, *The Exchange Equalisation Account* (1935)
S. E. Harris, *Exchange Depreciation* (1936)

R. G. Hawtrey, *The Gold Standard in Theory and Practice* (5th ed., 1947)

Sir Herbert Hutchinson, *Tariff-Making and Industrial Reconstruction* (1965)

S. V. Kaliski, 'Some Recent Estimates of "the" Elasticity of Demand for British Exports – An Appraisal and Reconciliation', *The Manchester School*, 29 (1961)

R. Kindersley, Articles on Overseas Investment in *Economic Journal*, 40–49 (1930–9)

C. P. Kindleberger, *International Short-term Capital Movements* (1937)

C. P. Kindleberger, 'Industrial Europe's Terms of Trade on Current Account, 1870–1958', *Economic Journal*, 65 (1955)

C. P. Kindleberger, *The Terms of Trade: A European Case Study* (1956)

C. P. Kindleberger, 'Foreign Trade and Growth: Lessons from British Experience since 1913', *Lloyds Bank Review*, 65 (1962)

W. A. Lewis, 'World Production, Prices and Trade, 1870–1960', *The Manchester School*, 20 (1952)

A. Loveday, *Britain and World Trade* (1931)

G. D. A. MacDougall, 'British and American Exports: A Study Suggested by the Theory of Comparative Costs. Part I', *Economic Journal*, 61 (1951)

E. B. McGuire, *The British Tariff System* (1939)

H. W. Macrosty, 'The Overseas Trade of the U.K., 1924–31', *Journal of the Royal Statistical Society*, 95 (1932)
'The Overseas Trade of the U.K., 1930–39', *Journal of the Royal Statistical Society*, 103 (1940)

A. Maizels, *Industrial Growth and World Trade* (1963)

K. Martin and F. G. Thackeray, 'The Terms of Trade of Selected Countries, 1870–1938', *Bulletin of the Oxford University Institute of Statistics*, 10 (1948)

I. Mintz, *Trade Balances during Business Cycles: U.S., and Britain since 1880* (1959, New York)

D. E. Moggridge, *The Return to Gold, 1925: The Formulation of Economic Policy and its Critics*, (1969)

Political and Economic Planning, *Report on International Trade* (1937)

Political and Economic Planning, *Britain and World Trade* (1947)

J. H. Richardson, *British Economic Foreign Policy* (1936)

E. A. G. Robinson, 'The Changing Structure of the British Economy', *Economic Journal*, 64 (1954)

Royal Institute of International Affairs, *Monetary Policy and the Depression* (1933)

Royal Institute of International Affairs, *The Future of Monetary Policy* (1935)

Royal Institute of International Affairs, *The Problem of International Investment* (1937)

R. S. Sayers, 'The Return to Gold, 1925', ch. XII in L. S. Pressnell (ed.), *Studies in the Industrial Revolution* (1960)

W. M. Scammell, *International Monetary Policy* (1957)

W. M. Scammell, 'The Working of the Gold Standard', *Yorkshire Bulletin of Economic and Social Research*, 17 (1965)

M. Fg. Scott, *A Study of United Kingdom Imports* (1963)

E. M. Shenkman, *Insurance Against Credit Risks in International Trade* (1935)

R. C. Snyder, 'Commercial Policy as Reflected in Treaties from 1931 to 1939', *American Economic Review*, 30 (1940)

R. B. Stewart, 'Great Britain's Foreign Loan Policy', *Economica*, 5 (1938)

H. Tyszynski, 'World Trade in Manufactured Commodities, 1899–1950', *The Manchester School*, 19 (1951)

L. Waight, *The History and Mechanism of the Exchange Equalisation Account 1932–39* (1939)

D. Williams, 'London and the 1931 Financial Crisis', *Economic History Review*, 15 (1962–3)

D. Williams, 'The 1931 Financial Crisis', *Yorkshire Bulletin of Economic and Social Research*, 15 (1963)

D. Williams, 'The Evolution of the Sterling System', in C. R. Whittlesey and J. S. G. Wilson (eds.), *Essays in Money and Banking in Honour of R. S. Sayers*, (1968)

R. E. Zelder, 'Estimates of Elasticities of Demand for Exports of the U.K. and the U.S., 1921–1938', *The Manchester School*, 26 (1958)

E. Zupnick, *Britain's Post-war Dollar Problem* (1957)

9   *The Management of the Economy*

D. H. Aldcroft, 'The Development of the Managed Economy Before 1939', *Journal of Contemporary History*, 4 (1969)

D. H. Aldcroft, 'The Impact of British Monetary Policy, 1919–1939', *Revue Internationale d'Histoire de la Banque,* (1970)

P. W. S. Andrews, 'A Further Inquiry into the Effects of Rates of Interest', *Oxford Economic Papers,* 3 (1940)

R. J. Ball, 'Some Econometric Analysis of the Long-Term Rate of Interest in the United Kingdom, 1921–61', *The Manchester School,* 33 (1965)

T. Balogh, 'Economic Policy and Rearmament in Britain' *The Manchester School,* 7 (1936)

R. Bassett, *Nineteen Thirty-One Political Crisis* (1958)

F. Benham, 'The Muddle of the Thirties', *Economica,* 12 (1945)

A. Boyle, *Montagu Norman* (1967)

H. Clay, *Lord Norman* (1957)

V. F. Eliasberg, *The Growth of Public Employment in Great Britain* (1957)

A. E. Feavearyear, *The Pound Sterling* (rev. ed. 1963)

R. Frost, 'The Macmillan Gap, 1931–53', *Oxford Economic Papers,* 6 (1954)

P. Goetschin, *L'Évolution du Marché Monétaire de Londres* (1931–1952), (1963 Paris)

R. M. Goodwin, 'The Supply of Bank Money in England and Wales, 1920–38' *Oxford Economic Papers,* 3 (1941)

A. T. K. Grant, *A Study of the Capital Market in Britain from 1919 to 1936* (1967)

T. E. Gregory, 'Lord Norman: A New Interpretation', *Lloyds Bank Review,* 88 (1968)

K. J. Hancock, 'Unemployment and the Economists in the 1920's', *Economica,* 27 (1960)

K. J. Hancock, 'The Reduction of Unemployment as a Problem of Public Policy, 1920–29', *Economic History Review,* 15 (1962–3)

A. Harrison, *The Framework of Economic Activity* (1967)

R. F. Harrod, *The Life of John Maynard Keynes* (1951)

H. D. Henderson, 'The Significance of the Rate of Interest', *Oxford Economic Papers,* 1 (1938)

R. F. Henderson, *The New Issue Market and the Finance of Industry* (1951)

U. K. Hicks, *The Finance of British Government, 1920–1936* (1938)

U. K. Hicks, *Public Finance* (1947)

U. K. Hicks, *British Public Finances: Their Structure and Development, 1880–1952* (1954)

J. K. Horsefield, 'Currency Devaluation and Public Finance, 1929–37', *Economica*, 6 (1939)

L. J. Hume, 'The Gold Standard and Deflation: Issues and Attitudes in the Nineteen-Twenties', *Economica*, 30 (1963)

T. W. Hutchison, *A Review of Economic Doctrines, 1870–1929* (1953)

P. B. Johnson, *Land Fit for Heroes: The Planning of Reconstruction, 1916–1919*, (1969, Chicago).

E. E. Jucker-Fleetwood, 'Montagu Norman in the Per Jacobsson Diaries', *National Westminster Bank Quarterly Review*, Nov. 1968

J. M. Keynes, *General Theory of Employment, Interest and Money* (1936)

W. T. C. King, *History of the London Discount Market* (1936)

A. W. Kirkaldy (ed.,) *British Finance during and after the War, 1914–21* (1921)

F. Lavington, *The English Capital Market* (1921)

D. S. Lees, 'Public Departments and Cheap Money, 1932–38', *Economica*, 22 (1955)

D. S. Lees, 'The Technique of Monetary Insulation, December 1932 to December 1937', *Economica*, 20 (1953)

R. Lekachman, *The Age of Keynes*, (1967)

H. L. Lutz, 'English Financial Policy and Experience, 1928–37', *Proceedings of the Academy of Political Science*, 17 (1937)

R. M. MacIntosh, 'A Note on Cheap Money and the British Housing Boom, 1932–37', *Economic Journal*, 61 (1951)

D. I. Mackay, D. J. C. Forsyth and D. M. Kelly, 'The Discussion of Public Works Programmes, 1917–1935: Some Remarks on the Labour Movement's Contribution', *International Review of Social History*, 11 (1966), Part I.

Macmillan Committee, *Report of the Committee on Finance and Industry*, Cmd. 3897 (1931)

H. Macmillan, *The Middle Way* (1938)

B. Mallet and C. O. George, *British Budgets, Third Series, 1921–22 to 1932–33* (1933)

A. Marwick, 'Middle Opinion in the Thirties: Planning, Progress and Political "Agreement" ', *English Historical Review*, 79 (1964)

J. E. Meade and P. W. S. Andrews, 'Summary of Replies to Questions on Effects of Interest Rates', *Oxford Economic Papers*, 1 (1938)

E. V. Morgan, *Studies in British Financial Policy, 1914–25* (1952)

E. V. Morgan and W. A. Thomas, *The Stock Exchange* (1962)

W. A. Morton, *British Finance, 1930–1940* (1943)

E. Nevin, 'The Origin of Cheap Money, 1931–1932', *Economica*, 20 (1953)

E. Nevin, *The Mechanism of Cheap Money: A Study of British Monetary Policy, 1931–1939* (1955)

A. T. Peacock and J. Wiseman, *The Growth of Public Expenditure in the United Kingdom* (2nd ed. 1947)

E. H. Phelps Brown and G. L. S. Shackle, *Statistics of Monetary Circulation in England and Wales, 1919–37*, Memorandum no. 74, 1938, of the Royal Economic Society

R. S. Sayers, *Central Banking After Bagehot* (1957)

R. S. Sayers, 'Monetary Thought and Monetary Policy in England', *Economic Journal*, 70 (1960)

G. L. S. Shackle, *The Years of High Theory: Invention and Tradition in Economic Thought, 1926–1929* (1967)

R. Skidelsky, *Politicians and the Slump: The Labour Government of 1929–1931* (1967)

M. Stewart, *Keynes and After* (1967)

W. F. Stolper, 'British Monetary Policy and the Housing Boom', *Quarterly Journal of Economics*, Supplement, 56 (1942)

W. F. Stolper, 'Purchasing Power Parity and the Pound Sterling, 1919–1925', *Kyklos*, 2 (1948)

J. Sykes, *A Study of English Local Authority Finance* (1939)

R. H. Tawney, 'Abolition of Economic Controls, 1918–21', *Economic History Review*, 13 (1943)

S. E. Thomas, *British Banks and the Finance of Industry* (1931)

R. J. Truptil, *British Banks and the London Money Market* (1936)

A. A. Walters, 'Monetary Multipliers in the U.K., 1880–1962', *Oxford Economic Papers*, 18 (1966)

A. A. Walters, *Money in Boom and Slump* (1969)

G. Walworth, *Feeding the Nation in Peace and War* (1940)

L. L. Watkins, 'The Expansion Power of the English Banking System', *Quarterly Journal of Economics*, 53 (1938)

D. Williams, 'Montagu Norman and Banking Policy in the 1920's', *Yorkshire Bulletin of Economic and Social Research*, 11 (1959)

D. Winch, *Economics and Policy: An Historical Study* (1970)

10   *Material Welfare and Income Distribution*

M. Abrams, *The Condition of the British People, 1911–1945* (1946)

[*Twenty-Second*] *Abstract of Labour Statistics of the United King-dom* (1922–1936), Cmd. 5556 (1937)

P. Abrams, 'The Failure of Social Reform, 1918–1920', *Past and Present* (1963)

R. B. Ainsworth, 'Earnings and Hours of Manual Wage-Earners in the United Kingdom in October 1938', *Journal of the Royal Statistical Society,* A122 (1949)

T. Barna, *The Redistribution of Incomes Through Public Finance in 1937* (1945)

H. L. Beales and R. S. Lambert (eds.), *Memoirs of the Unemployed* (1934)

G. Bernbaum, *Social Change and the Schools, 1918–1944* (1967)

D. Black, *The Incidence of Income Taxes* (1939)

A. L. Bowley, *Wages and Income in the United Kingdom since 1860* (1937)

A. L. Bowley, *Prices and Wages in the United Kingdom, 1914–20* (1921)

A. L. Bowley and M. H. Hogg, *Has Poverty Diminished?* (1925)

Sir John Boyd Orr, *Food, Health and Income* (1936)

Sir John Boyd Orr, *Food and the People* (1943)

Sir John Boyd Orr and D. Lubbock, *Feeding the People in War-time* (1940)

A. Briggs, 'The Welfare State in Historical Perspective', *Archives Européennes de Sociologie* (1961)

M. Bruce, *The Coming of the Welfare State* (1961)

G. Bry, *Wages in Germany, 1871–1945* (1960)

J. Burnett, *Plenty and Want* (1968 ed.)

J. Burnett, *A History of the Cost of Living* (1969)

E. M. Burns, *British Unemployment Programs, 1920–1938* (1941)

G. C. Cameron, 'The Growth of Holidays with Pay in Britain', ch.10, in G. L. Reid and D. J. Robertson (eds.), *Fringe Benefits, Labour Costs and Social Security* (1965)

H. Campion, *Public and Private Property in Great Britain* (1939)

A. M. Carr-Saunders and D. C. Jones, *A Survey of the Social Structure of England and Wales* (1937, 2nd ed.)

A. M. Carr-Saunders, D. C. Jones and C. A. Moser, *A Survey of Social Conditions in England and Wales* (1958)

A. M. Cartter, *The Redistribution of Incomes in Postwar Britain* (1955)

A. L. Chapman and R. Knight, *Wages and Salaries in the United Kingdom, 1920–1938* (1953)

E. W. Cohen, *English Social Services* (1949)

G. D. H. Cole and M. I. Cole, *The Condition of Britain* (1937)

L. R. Connor, 'On Certain Aspects of the Distribution of Income in the United Kingdom in the Years 1913 and 1924', *Journal of the Royal Statistical Society*, 91 (1928)

Sir William Crawford and H. Broadley, *The People's Food* (1938)

S. J. Curtis, *Education in Britain Since 1900* (1952)
   History of Education in Great Britain (7th ed. 1967)

Sir Noel Curtis-Bennett, *The Food of the People, being a History of Industrial Feeding* (1949)

G. W. Daniels and H. Campion, *The Distribution of the National Capital* (1936)

J. C. Drummond and A. Wilbraham, *The Englishman's Food* (1958 ed.)

J. T. Dunlop 'Trends in the Rigidity of English Wage Rates', *Review of Economic Studies*, 6 (1938–9)

H. Durant and J. Goldman, 'The Distribution of Working-Class Savings', *Bulletin of the Oxford Institute of Statistics*, 7 (1945)

C. H. Feinstein, 'Changes in the Distribution of the National Income in the United Kingdom since 1860', ch. 4 in J. Marchal and B. Ducros (eds.), *The Distribution of National Income* (1968)

W. R. Garside, 'The Durham Miners Between the Wars', *Durham and Its Region* (1970, the British Association)

R. F. George, 'A New Calculation of the Poverty Line', *Journal of the Royal Statistical Society*, 100 (1937)

Sir Gwilym Gibbon, 'The Public Social Services', *Journal of the Royal Statistical Society*, 100 (1937)

R. Graves and A. Hodge, *The Long Weekend: A Social History of Great Britain, 1918–1939* (1940)

W. Greenwood, *Love on the Dole* (1933)

W. Hannington, *Unemployed Struggles, 1919–1936* (1936)

R. W. Harris, *National Health Insurance in Great Britain, 1911–1946* (1946)

G. Harrison and F. C. Mitchell, *The Home Market: A Handbook of Statistics* (1936)

J. R. Hicks, *The Social Framework* (1942)

J. Hilton, *Rich Man, Poor Man* (1944)

A. G. Hines, 'Trade Unions and Wage Inflation in the United Kingdom, 1893–1961', *Review of Economic Studies*, 31 (1964)

Eva M. Hubback, *The Population of Britain* (1947)

A. Hutt, *Condition of the Working Class in Britain* (1933)

D. C. Jones, *Social Survey of Merseyside* (1934, 3 vols.)

K. G. J. C. Knowles, *Strikes – A Study in Industrial Conflict* (1952)

K. G. J. C. Knowles and D. J. Robertson, 'Differences Between the Wages of Skilled and Unskilled Workers, 1880–1950', *Bulletin of of the Oxford University Institute of Statistics*, 13 (1951)

K. G. J. C. Knowles and D. J. Robertson, 'Earnings in Engineering, 1926–1948', *Bulletin of the Oxford University Institute of Statistics*, 13 (1951)

J. Kuczynski, *A Short History of Labour Conditions under Industrial Capitalism, Vol 1., Great Britain and the Empire, 1750 to the Present Day* (1942)

Kathleen M. Langley, 'The Distribution of Capital in Private Hands in 1936–1938 and 1946–1947', *Bulletin of the Oxford University Institute of Statistics*, 12 (1950), 13 (1951)

W. T. Layton and G. Crowther, *An Introduction to the Study of Prices* (1935)

F. Legros Clark (ed.), *National Fitness* (1938)

H. Levy, *National Health Insurance* (1944)

R. G. Lipsey, 'The Relation Between Unemployment and the Rate of Change in Money Wage Rates in the United Kingdom, 1862–1957: A Further Analysis', *Economica*, 27 (1960)

R. Lipsey and M. D. Steuer, 'The Relation Between Profits and Wage Rates', *Economica*, 28 (1961)

H. Llewellyn Smith, *The New Survey of London Life and Labour* (1930–5, 9 vols.)

G. A. N. Lowndes, *The Silent Social Revolution* (1937)

H. F. Lydall and D. G. Tipping, 'The Distribution of Personal Wealth in Britain', *Economica*, 23 (1961)

B. McCormick, 'Hours of Work in British Industry', *Industrial and Labour Relations Review*, 12 (1959)

G. C. M. M'Gonigle and J. Kirby, *Poverty and Public Health* (1936)

J. C. McKenzie, 'Past Dietary Trends as an Aid to Prediction', in T. C. Barker, J. C. McKenzie and T. Yudkin, (eds.), *Our Changing Fare* (1966)

J. G. Marley and H. Campion, 'Changes in Salaries in Great Britain, 1924–1939', *Journal of the Royal Statistical Society*, 103 (1940)

D. C. Marsh, *National Insurance and Assistance in Great Britain* (1950)

D. C. Marsh, *The Changing Social Structure of England and Wales, 1871–1961* (rev. ed. 1965)

A. Marwick, 'The Labour Party and the Welfare State in Britain 1900–1948', *American Historical Review*, 73 (1967)

A. Marwick, *Britain in the Century of Total War: War, Peace and Social Change 1900–1967* (1968)

G. Newman, *The Building of a Nation's Health* (1939)

G. Orwell, *The Road to Wigan Pier* (1937)

E. H. Phelps Brown and Margaret Browne, *A Century of Pay* (1968)

E. H. Phelps Brown and P. E. Hart, 'The Share of Wages in the National Income', *Economic Journal*, 62 (1952)

A. W. Phillips, 'The Relation Between Unemployment and the Rate of Change of Money Wage Rates in the United Kingdom, 1861–1957', *Economica*, 25 (1958)

Pilgrim Trust, *Men Without Work* (1938)

Political and Economic Planning, *The British Health Services* (1937)

Political and Economic Planning, *Report on the British Social Services* (1937)

Political and Economic Planning, *Britain's Health* (1939)

S. Pollard, 'Trade Union Reactions to the Economic Crisis', *Journal of Contemporary History*, 4 (1969)

Esme Preston, 'Personal Savings Through Institutional Channels, 1937–1949', *Bulletin of the Oxford University Institute of Statistics*, 12 (1950)

J. B. Priestley, *English Journey* (1934)

E. A. Radice, *Savings in Great Britain, 1922–1935* (1939)

E. C. Ramsbottom, 'The Course of Wage Rates in the United Kingdom, 1931–1934', *Journal of the Royal Statistical Society*, 98 (1935)
'Wage Rates in the United Kingdom, 1934–1937', *Journal of the Royal Statistical Society*, 101 (1938)
'Wage Rates in the United Kingdom in 1938', *Journal of the Royal Statistical Society*, 102 (1939)

E. C. Ramsbottom, 'Changes in Labour Conditions during the Past Forty Years', *Transactions of the Manchester Statistical Society* (1941–2)

E. C. Rhodes, 'Distribution of Incomes in the United Kingdom in 1938 and 1947', *Economica*, 17 (1950)

E. C. Rhodes, 'Distribution of Earned and Investment Incomes in the United Kingdom in 1937–38', *Economica*, 18 (1951)

E. C. Rhodes, 'The Distribution of Incomes and the Burden of Estate Duties in the United Kingdom', *Economica*, 18 (1951)

J. H. Richardson, *Industrial Relations in Great Britain* (1938)

J. S. Ross, *The National Health Service in Great Britain* (1952)

G. Rottier, 'The Evolution of Wage Differentials: A Study of British Data', ch.15 in J. T. Dunlop (ed.), *The Theory of Wage Determination* (1957)

G. Routh, 'Civil Service Pay, 1875 to 1950', *Economica*, 21 (1954)

G. Routh, *Occupation and Pay in Great Britain, 1906–60* (1965)

B. S. Rowntree, *Poverty and Progress* (1941)

D. Seers, *Changes in the Cost of Living and the Distribution of Income Since 1938* (1949)

D. Seers, *The Levelling of Incomes since 1938* (1951)

G. F. Shirras and L. Rostas, *The Burden of British Taxation* (1942)

Lee Soltow, 'Long-run Changes in British Income Inequality', *Economic History Review*, 21 (1968)

Sir Josiah Stamp, *Wealth and Taxable Capacity* (1922)

J. R. Stone and D. A. Rowe, *The Measurement of Consumers' Expenditure and Behaviour in the United Kingdom, 1920–1938,* Vol. I (1954), Vol. II (1966)

R. M. Titmuss, *Poverty and Population* (1938)

R. M. Titmuss, *Birth, Poverty and Health,* (1943)

H. Tout, *The Standard of Living in Bristol* (1938)

G. Walworth, *Feeding the Nation in Peace and War* (1940)

W. H. Wickwar, *The Social Services: An Historical Survey* (1936, 1949)

A. Wilson and G. S. Mackay, *Old Age Pensions* (1941)

LIST OF TABLES

o

BIBLIOGRAPHICAL NAME INDEX

The entries refer to authors of works cited or listed in the bibliography. A 'b' after the page number refers to the bibliography and an 'n' denotes a footnote reference

SUBJECT INDEX

for, 156; decline in world importance of, 160; disinvestment in, 157; earnings in, 359; employment trends in, 147; excess capacity in, 158–9, cutback in, 158–9; export dependence of, 148, 155; export losses, 156–7; geographical concentration of, 148; home demand for cotton products, 157; inefficiency of, 157; lag in technical innovation in, 157–8; looms in, 158–9; overcapitalization of, 155; post-war speculation in, 35–6, 155; production trends, 155–6; rationalization of, 158; regulation of, 158, 348; short-time working in, 94, 359; spindles in, 158; use of rayon by, 157, 188

Cotton Industry (Reorganization) Act (1936), 159

Courtaulds, 188, 189; dominance of, 189; issued capital, 189; leadership of, 189–90; regional wage differences, 360–1

Credit, 331; bank advances, 332–3, 337; credit policy of banks, 332–3, 337; cheap money and, 337–9; credit conditions generally, 344; credit facilities, 241; cost of, 332–3, 338; rationing of, 326; structure of, 323; see also under Bank advances and Monetary policy

Credit Anstalt, 270

Cricket, 240

Crook, 383

Cumberland, 87, 94, 103, 148

Cunard Company, 226, 346

Cunliffe Committee (1918): report of, 328

Currencies: devaluation, see under that heading; overvaluation of pound sterling, 38, 250–3, 328–9; undervaluation of Belgian and French currencies, 39

Cutlery, 146

Cycles: Juglar cycles, 25, 29, 30, 72, 76; Kitchin cycles, 25, 29; Kondratieff cycles, 25; Kuznets cycles, 25, 66,

70; for cycles generally see under heading of Fluctuations

Cyfarthfa, 103

Czechoslovakia, 281

Daily Express, 321

Daily Mail, 321

Daimler airway, 228

Dairy products: consumption of, 368

Dance halls, 240

Death rates: decline in, 375; regional, 384

Debenhams, 232

Debenture loans, 339

Defence, 306–7, 311; contracts, allocation of (by regions), 103, 105; proportion of public expenditure on, 301–2, 307; as a stabilising influence, 307

Deflation: deflationary policy after 1920, 36, 327; monetary policy and, 330–4; and 1931 crisis, 270

Denmark: growth in, 19–21; shipping of, 226

Department of Scientific and Industrial Research: expenditure of, 348

Departmental stores, 232–3

Depressed areas, see under Special areas

Derating, 347

Derbyshire, 88, 97, 98, 148

Devaluation, 42, 255, 274, 278; and balance of payments, 283–4; check to deflationary tendencies, 285; in countries other than Britain, 281, effects of, on British trade, 282, 285; demand elasticity requirements for a successful devaluation, 279–80; effect on price-cost structure, 285; effects of British devaluation on other countries, 283; gains from British devaluation, 281–5; income effects of, 280–2, 283; magnitude of 1931 devaluation, 279; price effects of, 280, 282, 283, 284; possible effects of a devaluation, 279–81; and trade balance, 283, 284; see also under Balance of

payments and Gold standard

Devon, 83

Diarrhoea, 375

Diet: of average family, 368; deficiencies in, 377, 378, 379; dietary standards of British nation, 378, 379, variations in, 379; and poverty line, 376; see also under Poverty

Disease: incidence of, 375, 384

Distributive trades, 97, 230–6, 290; capital growth in, 118, 236; cyclical behavior of, 34, 42; earnings in, 360; employment growth in, 118, 119, 120, 208, 209, 230; expansion of output, 208, 209, 230; growth analysis of, 118; investment fluctuations, 62–3, 65; merchanting, 231; productivity decline in, 118, 230, reasons for, 235–6; retail distribution, development of, 231–5; size of units in, 231ff; unemployment in, 208; wholesaling, 231; see also under retail distribution and wholesale distribution

Docks, 119, 208; naval dockyards, 139

Doctors, 237

Dole, see under Unemployment assistance

Domestic electrical appliances: expenditure on, 195; manufacturing position, 197–8; mass production of, 198; reasons for growth in use of, 125, 195; tariff protection and, 198

Domestic service, 119, 238

Dominions, see under Empire

Drink: decline in consumption of, 241

Drink industry: 249; cyclical behaviour of, 49, 50, 53; growth analysis of, 120ff

Drugs, 199

Dumping: in British market, 289

Dundee, 92

Durham (county), 83; coal miners, wages of, 360; death rate in, 384; earnings in, 381, 382; expansion of building activity in, 203; expectation of life in, 384; industrial structure of, 88–91, 94; maternal mortality in, 384; overcrowding in, 383; share of net industrial output, 82; tuberculosis in, 384; unemployment in, 94

Dyestuffs, 141; dependence on Germany for supply of, 199–200; exports of synthetic dyes, 200; financial assistance to encourage home production of, 200; imports of, 200; output of, 200

Earnings, 357; of average family, 367–8; average earnings, 352, 357, 358; decline in, 356; inadequate earnings as a cause of poverty, 376, 377, 378; indices of, 352, 364; inter-industry differentials in, 358–60; level of, 359; occupational differences, 361; ratio of wage to salary earnings, 361; real earnings, trends in, 362–4; determinants of, 364–5; regional breakdown of, 382, 383; regional differences, 360, 382, 383; skill differentials, 361–2; total real gains, 366; see also under National income, Poverty, Salaries, Standard of living and Wages

Eastern Europe, 292; exchange control in, 281; financial position of, 40–1

Eastern region: death rates in, 384; earnings in, 382

Economic Advisory Council, 320

Economic crisis: financial crisis of 1931, 369–78; of 1929–32, 17, 40–3; see also under Financial crisis (1931)

Economic growth: assessment of, 12; base year selection, 16, 19; compatible with unemployment, 12, 136; contribution of capital and technical progress to, 130–3; contribution of productivity to, 113, 118ff; factor

inputs and, 118ff; international comparisons of, 18–21; inter-temporal comparisons of, 15, 17–18, difficulties of making, 15; in inter-war years, ch. 1, esp. 13, 17–18, 19–22; neo-classical approach to, 112–3; potential for, 12; rates of growth of selected indicators, 13, 19, 21; relationship between output growth and factor input growth, 119–20; regional variations in, 78–82, statistics on, 88–9; residual and, 118ff; statistical basis of measurement, 13–14, reliability of, 15; sources of, ch. 4; in Western Europe, 19–21

Economic services: expenditure on, 345; proportion of public expenditure on, 301

Economic thought: developments in, 316–21; Gladstonian financial concepts, 316; Keynesian analysis, 316–17, forerunners of, 318–19, Keynesian ideas abroad, 317; slow acceptance of new ideas, 320

Economies of scale, 116, 117, 144, 145; in building materials production, 205

Economist, the, 197n

Edinburgh, 91

Education, 237; improvement in, 371

Education Act (1918), 371

Efficiency: in coal industry, 152–4; in cotton industry, 157; effects of changes in business organization on, 142–5; effects of size of plant and firm on, 144–5; see also under Productivity and separate industries

Eggs: consumption of, 368

Electric cookers, 125, 195

Electric irons, 125, 195

Electric water heaters, 125

Electrical engineering industry, 95, 96, 97, 98, 116, 129, 130, 177; branches of, 191, 197–8; competitive strength of, 196–7; cyclical behaviour of, 39, 42, 47, 49, 52; employment in,

180; exports of, 196, 197; geographical concentration of, 196; growth analysis of, 120ff; imports of electrical products, 196, 197, 198; production trends, 196; productivity performance, 121, 122, 196; unemployment in, 180; weaknesses of, 191, 198, reasons for, 191–2

Electrical machinery, 141, 191, 197

Electrical products, 191, 249; agreements among manufacturers, 140–1; expenditure on, 368

Electrical wires and cables, 141

Electricity (Supply) Act (1919), 192

Electricity Commissioners, 192–3

Electricity supply industry, 97, 116, 129, 130, 139, 171, 177, 179, 340; concentration in, 144; construction of Grid system, 193; consumption of electricity, 191, 194, 195; cyclical behaviour of, 38, 39, 42, 44, 49, 50, 53, 311; demand for coal from, 151; distribution of electricity, 193–4; domestic consumers, 191, 194; earnings in, 360; effects of supply extension on consumer durable sales, 195; employment in, 180; extension of the use of electricity, 194; generation facilities, 192–3; growth analysis of, 118, 119, 120ff; impact of electricity, 194–5; investment cycles in, 61–2, 64, 65, 311; multiplicity of generating units in, 192; price of electricity, 192, 193, 194; rationalization in, 192–3; slow extension of supply facilities, 191–2; as a stabilising force, 61, 311; stimulus to electrical engineering, 196; unemployment in, 181; weaknesses of, 191

Embargo: on new capital issues, 336

in electricity supply, 61–2, 64, 65, 311; foreign investment, see under that heading; in housebuilding, 67–70, 310, 342, 343; in manufacturing, 63–4, 341; opportunities for, 43, 45; in plant and machinery, 64; public investment, 301, 308–14; in railways, 311; share absorbed by construction, 65, 67, 202; in transport and communications, 61–2, 311; volatility of, 26, 45, 58, 59, 64–5; see also under Foreign investment and separate industries

Iron and steel industry, 92, 93, 98, 116, 142, 145, 290; competition in, 169, 170, 171, suppression of, 173; concentration in, 140–1; consumption of coal by, 151; decline in importance of iron, 169–70; developments in East Midlands, 98; earnings in, 360; employment trends in, 147; excess capacity in, 169–70, elimination of, 173; expansion of capacity, 169; export dependence of, 148; export share, 249; exports of iron and steel, 170, 171, composition of, 170; fuel economy in, 172, 173; geographical concentration of, 148; growth analysis of, 120ff; high cost producer, 174; home demand for steel, 170; imports of iron and steel, 170, 172, inefficiency of, 171, 172, 173, 174; integration of, 173, 174; mergers in, 173; new steels, 201; output of blast furnaces, 173; position of, 169; production trends, 169–70, 171; productivity advance in, 172; rationalization of, 173–4, 349; recovery in, 171–2; share of world output, 170, 171; size of firms in, 173; structural weaknesses of, 172; tariff protection for, 172, 173, 292, 349; technical developments in, 171, 172,

173; use of scrap in, 170; world output of steel, 170
Italy, 281; growth in, 19–21; price of electricity in, 192; rayon, 190; shipping in, 225

Japan, 41, 158, 282; as competitor in cotton textiles, 156; as a market for British exports, 248; as a market for British tissues, 161; rayon, 190; share of world exports, 21–2; shipping in, 225
John Lewis Partnership, 232
Joint stock companies, 138; divorce between ownership and control in, 139
Juglar cycles, 25, 29, 30, 72, 76
Jute industry, 121, 146; earnings in, 359

Kahn, R. F.: and the multiplier, 318
Keynes, J. M.: and demand for new economic policy, 318–19, 321; development of Keynesian analysis, 316–20, 321; *General Theory* of, 316, 320; lack of professional support for ideas of, 319; and the planning movement, 321; see also under Economic thought
Kidsgrove, 83
Kitchin cycles, 25, 29
Kondratieff cycles, 25
Kuznets cycles, 25, 66, 70

Labour: as a factor input, 113–14, 115, 118–19, in different industries, 120–6; mobility of, 100–2, assisted, 101, 108, difficulty of inducing, 136; share of national income accruing to, 386, 387, increase in, 386–7; shortages of, 45, 71, 106, 136; as a source of growth, 113–14, 115, 118–19, 120ff
Labour force, 15; rate of growth of, 136; in relation to population growth, 136
Labour market, 355; inter-industry shifts of labour, 358; operation of, in relation to wages, 362; sec-

toral inequality of, 356
Labour Party: and public works, 318
Lace industry, 98
Lancashire, 104, 110; concentration of employment in, 94, 148; cotton industry, 148, 155ff; death rate in, 384; earnings in, 360, 382; geographical diversity of economic experience in, 94–5; growth of industrial development in, 88–91, 106; industrial structure, 88–91, 94–5, adaptation of, 95; share of net industrial output, 94; short-time working in, 94; unemployment in, 87, 94; uneven spread of new developments, 95
Lancashire Cotton Corporation, 159
Larkhall, 103
Latin America, 247, 269
Laundries and dry cleaning, 119; expenditure on, 368; unemployment in, 208
Lawyers, 237, 238
Leather industry, 92, 96, 146, 290; concentration in, 141; cyclical behaviour of, 42, 47, 49, 50, 53; growth analysis of, 120ff
Leeds, 99
Leicestershire, 97
Lever combine, 199
Liberal Party, 318; Liberal 'Yellow Book', *Britain's Industrial Future*, 318
Life expectancy, 375, 384
Lincolnshire, 97; steel output in, 98
Linen industry, 121, 146
Liquidity crisis, see under Financial crisis (1931) and International liquidity
Littlewoods, 233
Liverpool, 99; social survey of, 377
Livestock, 349
Living conditions, see under Standard of living
Llanelly, 83
Lloyd George, D., election manifesto, 318; and public works, 318
Local authorities, 313; economic activities of, 139; expenditure by, 303, 304,